THE LIBERATION OF THE CAMPS

THE
LIBERATION
OF THE CAMPS
THE END OF THE HOLOCAUST AND ITS AFTERMATH

DAN STONE

YALE UNIVERSITY PRESS
NEW HAVEN AND LONDON

For information about this and other Yale University Press publications, please contact:
U.S. Office: sales.press@yale.edu   www.yalebooks.com
Europe Office: sales@yaleup.co.uk   www.yalebooks.co.uk

Typeset in Minion Pro by IDSUK (DataConnection) Ltd
Printed in the United States of America.

Library of Congress Cataloging-in-Publication Data

Stone, Dan, 1971-
    The liberation of the camps: the end of the Holocaust and its aftermath / Dan Stone.
      pages cm
    Includes bibliographical references and index.
    ISBN 978-0-300-20457-5
    1. World War, 1939–1945—Concentration camps—Liberation.   2. Concentration camps—Europe—History—20th century.   3. Holocaust, Jewish (1939–1945)   4. World War, 1939–1945—Refugees.   5. World War, 1939–1945—Jews.   I. Title.
    D805.A2S74 2015
    940.53´185—dc23

                                                                              2015000674

A catalogue record for this book is available from the British Library.

10 9 8 7 6 5 4 3 2 1

Contents

Abbreviations

AACI – Anglo-American Committee of Inquiry on Palestine
DP – Displaced Person
HIAS – Hebrew Immigrant Aid Society
IRO – International Refugee Organization
JAP – Jewish Agency for Palestine
JCRA – Jewish Committee for Relief Abroad
JDC – American Jewish Joint Distribution Committee (the 'Joint')
JRC – Jewish Relief Committee
JRU – Jewish Relief Unit
NATO – North Atlantic Treaty Organization
ORT – Organization for Rehabilitation and Training
POW – prisoner of war
RAMC – Royal Army Medical Corps
RASC – Royal Army Service Corps
SHAEF – Supreme Headquarters, Allied Expeditionary Force
UNHCR – United Nations High Commission for Refugees
UNRRA – United Nations Relief and Rehabilitation Administration
USFET – United States Forces, European Theater
WJC – World Jewish Congress

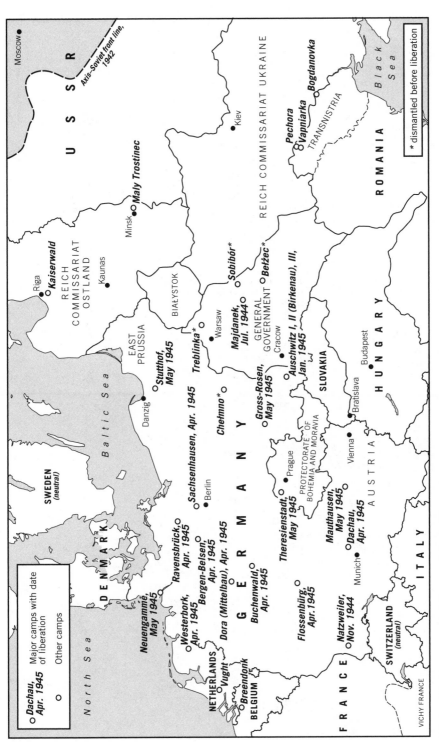

Major Nazi camps and dates of their liberation

(French zone)
Rothschild Hospital
○ **(US zone)**
(Soviet zones)
Vienna
(British zones)

Wittenau (French zone)
○
(British zone)
(Soviet zone)
Dueppel Center
○ **(US zone)**
Berlin

North Sea

D E N M A R K

Baltic Sea

Neustadt ○

NETHERLANDS

(British zone)

Belsen ○
Hohne ○

Berlin ▢

P O L A N D

G E R M A N Y

(Soviet zone)

Lichtenau ○
○ Eschwege Air Base

Bad Salzschlirf ○

Zeilsheim ○ ○ Ziegenhain
(French zone)
Babenhausen ○
Lampertheim ○ ○ Bensheim
○ Bamberg

○ Fuerth

C Z E C H O S L O V A K I A

○ Schwäbisch Hall

Stuttgart ○
○ Heidenheim

F R A N C E

(French zone)
Ulm ○
Biberach ○
○ Leipheim
Landsberg ○ Munich ○
Feldafing ○
Föhrenwald ○
(US zone)
Deggendorf ○
○ St Ottilien
○ Gabersee
Pocking Pine City ○
Wels ○
○ Linz
Vienna ▢
(Soviet zone)
Ainring ○
Bad Reichenhall ○ ○ Salzburg
○ Ebensee
Hallein ○

S W I T Z E R L A N D

Saalfelden ○
(French zone)
○ Admont

A U S T R I A

○ Judenburg
(British zone)

Badgaslein ○

HUNGARY

○ Major camps for displaced
Jewish persons, 1945–46

------ Named Allied zones of
occupation

I T A L Y

Y U G O S L A V I A

Main DP camps

Introduction:
Explaining Liberation

'Who really knows what happened on the day of liberation? Who of us
had the strength at 70 or 80 pounds to know?'
SIGGI WILZIG

'Silence. The morning came to a halt on the stroke of ten:
hovering over the street, peace – and a certain horror.'
MIKLÓS RADNÓTI (1938)[1]

'Oh my Liberation, how brilliant I imagined you!', writes Francine
Christophe, a French Jewish girl in Bergen-Belsen at the end of the war,
in her memoir *From a World Apart*. Then she goes on: 'Several women
are molested, one of our companions is even raped in front of her son!'
'Oh my Liberation, how joyful I imagined you!', Christophe again writes;
then: 'Mother, lying on a stretcher placed on the ground of the little
courtyard, has typhus, and I'm waiting for them to come and get her to take
her to the hospital set up by the Russians. I talk to her, and already she can
no longer hear me, for the typhus has made her deaf. I shuffle from one
foot to the other, standing in front of her, and I listen, my eyes filled with
tears.' By the time, a few sentences later, Christophe gets to wondering
how it is that the deportees' song 'Oh joyful land where we can love, love
forever' has made the rounds of all the concentration camps, the irony
needs no further elucidation: the sweetness of the occasion is filled also
with sorrow.

In the popular imagination, the liberation of the Nazi concentration camps was a joyous affair, bringing an end to the inmates' torments. From the Red Army's films of the liberation of Majdanek and Auschwitz to the final scenes of *Life is Beautiful*, *Schindler's List* and many other films, documentaries, museum displays and books, liberation has been portrayed as a single, rapturous moment in time. And yet, for every camp survivor like Spanish communist intellectual and courier Jorge Semprun who went dancing and womanising in Paris there were thousands of others who physically recovered very slowly indeed, who were mentally scarred for life by their experiences, or who died in the post-liberation period from the wounds inflicted upon them in the camps. Many missed the moment of liberation altogether, being too ill to comprehend what was happening, and only later understood how their situation had changed. 'The British had liberated us, yet nobody cheered,' writes Freddie Knoller of his liberation at Belsen. 'Eerie silence marked the moment of our liberation. We were too weak, and had experienced too much, to feel joy. It was only when the British distributed a bowl of rice and hot milk that we understood that we might one day be human beings again.'[2] Examining the weeks and months after the Allies reached the camps reveals the true complexities of liberation. They might be summed up by the words of survivor Hadassah Rosensaft:

> Soon the euphoria and hysteria were over. There was joy, yes – we were free, the gates were open – but where were we to go? The liberation had come too late, not only for the dead, but for us, the living, as well. We had lost our families, our friends, our homes. We had no place to go, and nobody was waiting for us anywhere. We were alive, yes. We were liberated from death, from the fear of death, but the fear of life started.[3]

Liberation, in other words, was a process, something that happened over time – sometimes a very long time. Not only were many survivors far from feeling joyful, often they were just as far from being healed. Nor were they – especially Jewish camp survivors – able simply to return to their homes.

Studying the liberation of the Nazi camps reminds us first that an important part of the history of the Holocaust has been largely overlooked by scholars.[4] It merits retelling not just because liberation was a more complex process than might be assumed, nor because it was solely a joyful phenomenon which brought the survivors quickly back to normal life. Rather, as I show here, the events surrounding the liberation of the camps have to be understood not just as a long coda to the Holocaust but as fundamental to the unfolding of the postwar years in Europe, to the geopolitics of the Cold War and, thanks to the significance of these events for Palestine, to the future of the British Empire in general and the Middle East specifically. Liberation constitutes a bridge between the war years and the postwar. With respect to Jewish survivors of what later became known as the Holocaust – the Nazis' murder of the European Jews – the fear, anger and hopes of the survivors, especially when they were confronted with Allied policy towards them, drove a large proportion to reject Europe as a home for Jews and to insist that only Palestine could provide a viable Jewish future. Non-Jewish survivors of the Nazi camps found too that they – especially if citizens of the Soviet Union or of lands now claimed by the Soviets – would be used as bargaining chips in the quickly worsening relationship between the Western Allies and the Soviets.

The international politics of dealing with refugees were forged in this period, with DPs, both Jewish and non-Jewish, at the heart of the negotiations. At the same time as the Western Allies embarrassed the Soviets by encouraging anti-communist DPs in their campaign not to be 'repatriated' to the USSR, so the Soviets discomfited the Western Allies by painting British intransigence over Palestine – as the Jewish DPs and the Yishuv (the Jewish community in Palestine) saw it – as a failure of the moral imagination in the face of the victims of the evil Nazi regime. The Soviet position, which provided cynical, short-term support for Israeli independence, contributed to the worsening of US-British relations as the Americans too criticised British policy over Palestine. This they did partly for their own reasons of encouraging Jewish emigration to Palestine so that Jews would not come to the US *en masse*, but with the effect of making the Americans, at least on this issue, uncomfortable bedfellows of the Soviets. From the varying experiences of liberation undergone by inmates in different camps in different locations, to the culture of the Jewish DP camps and the place occupied by DPs in Cold War diplomacy, the importance of liberation extends beyond our understanding of it as 'the end of the Holocaust'. The murder of the Jews and the collapse of the Third Reich helped to shape the pattern of the postwar world.

It hardly needs to be said that in presenting this history of liberation I am not suggesting that the defeat of the Nazi regime was anything other than necessary and good. Nor do I suggest that it might have been accomplished more easily or kindly than was the case, with the exception of some instances of mistreatment of survivors. But as the years pass, and we are less immediately overcome by emotion, our ability to comprehend the full horror of what transpired at the end of the war increases. Just as we now appreciate that the Normandy landings brought harm to the population of northern France at the same time as they fulfilled a vital duty, so we can now see that the liberation of the camps did not immediately bring about an end to the camp inmates' suffering. Certainly there was a reversal in the survivors' fortunes in that they were no longer under the direct whims of Nazi guards and their collaborators; but they remained physically, mentally and emotionally scarred by Nazism long afterwards. Whilst many 'recovered' physically, most would be haunted for the rest of their lives by what they had experienced. One survivor, whose words contradict our desire for liberation to mean 'closure', the end of the ordeal, asked: 'what was the purpose of our having survived? A feeling of deep hopelessness brought cold perspiration to my whole body . . . Suddenly the question of where I was going to live now that I was liberated, became a load bearing down on me like a mountain.'[5] Another simply says of liberation: 'Then I knew my troubles were *really* about to begin.'[6]

And no wonder, when one reads the early postwar accounts given by survivors. In a short, enigmatic document sent to the Jewish Historical Commission in Poland at war's end, one young Polish survivor of Auschwitz and Mauthausen, who refers to cases of cannibalism and eating excrement in the final, desperate weeks of starvation in Gusen (a sub-camp of Mauthausen), offered the following vignette:

> Some 2,000 of our comrades were gassed and burned a week before liberation. I do not know by what miracle I survived. As I write now, I remember a children's game. A small child picks up a handful of sand and says: 'I had this many children.' He throws the sand in the air. Some of it falls on the ground. 'That many died,' cries the child; he catches the rest: 'and this many lived.' In this way, for five years we were thrown in the air and caught or dropped.[7]

Another Polish survivor, interviewed in Italy in 1946, described going back to Poland after being cared for by UNRRA and the Red Cross and recoiling from the experience: 'Any Jew who still owns anything in Poland, then it is better he . . . that he leaves, because if he remains, then death threatens him. And it was too painful for me when I saw strange people who have . . . have my property, live in my flat. But the most terrible was that I found no one any more. From a family which had numbered seven persons, I alone had remained.' The discovery that his family had not survived was worse than the response of the gentile Poles: 'That shook so that I did not want to remain anymore.'[8] He left after two and half weeks for Germany, where he helped to establish a kibbutz in Segersdorf DP camp. At the time of his interview he was equating his treatment at the hands of the British – who captured and held him after he tried to enter Palestine – with that of the Germans. One thirteen-year-old Hungarian Jewish girl, Magda Bloom, who arrived in the UK on the Children from the Concentration Camps scheme in 1945 and settled in Birmingham, was 'liberated' in Bergen-Belsen, but she 'hardly cared. The previous night her mother had died, and as the British tanks rolled down the street she had been taken from the barracks.'[9]

For many survivors, the post-liberation period was characterised above all by loneliness. It is hard to imagine, let alone describe, this pain of one's world having disappeared, but one gets a sense of it at the end of Claude Lanzmann's film *Shoah*, when Simha Rotem, the underground fighter known as 'Kazik', recalls re-entering the Warsaw Ghetto following its liquidation in April 1943 in order to look for survivors:

I was alone all the time. Except for that woman's voice, and a man I met as I came out of the sewers, I was alone throughout my tour of the ghetto. I didn't meet a living soul. At one point I recall feeling a kind of peace, of serenity. I said to myself: 'I'm the last Jew. I'll wait for morning, and for the Germans.'[10]

One survivor of Theresienstadt who later became a rabbi reports the same sensation:

I remember after liberation, I suffered probably more from the loneliness and the isolation, more than during the Holocaust period . . .

Feeling of, yes, I'm alive, but that's it. The rest doesn't matter. No ambition. For what? For who? No initiative. If I am to stand, I'm standing. So I am standing. If you tell me to sit down, I'll sit down. That was real for a long time.[11]

Again and again, survivors, whether interviewed one year or half a century after the event, describe the existential angst of discovering that their families had been killed, that they alone remained. Coupled with the common experience of being made unwelcome in their home towns – where often local gentiles had taken over their apartments and houses, hardly expecting anyone to return to claim them – this discovery made many wonder why they had survived at all. Stories of weeks and months of exploitation and abuse, struggling to travel and find food and shelter, unpaid work, illegally crossing borders and ending up in a new variety of camp – in the land of the perpetrators – are the norm.

The soldiers who first entered the Nazi camps would also be scarred for life by the experience. Leon Bass, a private in the US army, did not know what a concentration camp was when his officer told him that was where they were going: 'but on this day in April I was going to have the shock of my life,' he said. 'Because I was going to walk through the gates of a concentration camp called Buchenwald . . . I could never forget that day because when I walked through that gate I saw in front of me what I call the walking dead.'[12] Or, as the American liberators of Gunskirchen put it, 'As we entered the camp, the living skeletons still able to walk crowded around us and, though we wanted to drive farther into the place, the milling, pressing crowd wouldn't let us. It is not an exaggeration to say that almost every inmate was insane with hunger.'[13] One British medical student in Belsen, John Roger Dixey, described the scene more than three weeks after the camp's liberation: 'I remember when VE Day came and we went into the hut which by now was getting a bit more organised, we said in a multitude of languages, "You'll be glad to hear that the war is over, Germany is defeated, the war is over," there was practically no response at all – no cheering, or waving or "well done-ing". They just looked at us: the war's over, but not for them. I think they knew there was little hope for them.'[14] And Lieutenant Albert A. Hutler, Displaced Persons Officer for the US Seventh Army in Mannheim, wrote to his wife that: 'The war is officially over but there isn't a great deal of excitement around here. It may sound horrible to say this but there isn't as much joy in my heart as I anticipated because I fear for the peace.' Specifically, he feared for the future of the DPs: 'they are free but they are dazed', he wrote. 'They are free but in their hearts they will never be able to cast off the last five years when they were under the protective custody, the benevolent guidance of their German teachers.'[15] Survivors could express concern for the liberators too; one, Vera Karoly, recalled 'looking at the British soldiers who had come to liberate us. That look of utter horror in their eyes I shall never forget. It was obvious to me that they could hardly tell the difference between the piles of corpses lying there in the camp and the emaciated survivors.'[16] Edith Birkin, who subsequently became an artist in England, recalls that 'the British troops were very young – about the same age as me, some of them. They were horrified at the sight of us, and who could blame them?'[17]

Inmates and Allied soldiers were not the only people present when camps were liberated. In some of the camps where they had not had time to flee, there were SS guards and their subordinates, including members of the Wehrmacht and collaborators of various nationalities including Hungarians, Ukrainians, Yugoslavs and Balts. At Belsen, the Catholic chaplain Edmund Swift reported that on their first day of being forced to dispose of corpses, 'a party of Wehrmacht soldiers broke down completely. Having deposited about two dozen bodies in the grave, a corporal ripped off his Iron Cross and stamped it into the ground. The rest of the company followed suit and tore off their badges and decorations in sheer disgust.'[18]

There were also many civilians present, sometimes because they lived in the vicinity but also because in some cases, during the last days of the camps, civilians were made responsible for transferring a camp to Allied authority, as at Ebensee. In other instances they had simply tried to bring supplies to the dying inmates. Many civilians – a majority of them women, as photographs testify, since the men were still at the front or being held as POWs – were taken on 'tours' of the liberated camps as part of the Allies' denazification process. Their views are hard to access but their presence should not be overlooked. Hauptsturmführer Franz Hoessler, 'a notorious figure from the SS Totenkopf underworld', apparently began to cry when he was arrested by the British.[19] He claimed that he had joined the SS in 1933 because he was unemployed but, by his own admission, enjoyed a successful career in the

Nazi camps, holding senior positions at Auschwitz and Dora-Nordhausen. In his affidavit for the Belsen trial, Hoessler claimed that:

> When the English were arriving near Belsen I was told by Oberst Harries that the English would shoot all SS on sight who offered resistance. In spite of this I volunteered to stay behind with five others, who were Wilhelm Dorr, Paul Fritsch, Eugen Hahnert, George Kraft and Franz Stofel, and in addition two cooks whose names I do not know. The camp I was at [Dora] was guarded by Hungarians. Bergen-Belsen camp was being guarded by the Wehrmacht during the truce, having relieved SS About twelve to fifteen SS escaped from the camp and a lot also left from the other camp.

The judges did not believe his claims that he had tried to be kind to the inmates, that he had tried to leave the SS and, most implausibly, that 'It was not nice to be a Nazi nor was it a privilege.'[20] He was sentenced to death and hanged. Other guards, such as Romanian *Volksdeutscher* ('ethnic German') Obersturmführer Fritz Klein, were more contrite. Klein acknowledged in his affidavit: 'I realize that I am as responsible as those from the top downwards for the killing of thousands in these camps, particularly at Auschwitz.'[21] He too was hanged. Belsen's commandant Josef Kramer (still remembered as 'the beast of Belsen') had also awaited the arrival of the British – perhaps, as Derrick Sington, one of the first British officers into Belsen, surmised, not understanding that in doing so he courted death. Instead, he offered the British a 'grotesque attempt at collaboration' which they received with disdain.[22] In a similar display of naivety or perhaps out of a desire to be discovered, Franz Ziereis, the commandant of Mauthausen, remained in the vicinity of the camp after the arrival of the Americans. Most of the SS guards had disappeared shortly before they got there. Ziereis was spotted five days after the liberation of the camp. He opened fire on the soldiers who were sent to arrest him, and was shot. While in the 131st US Evacuation Hospital dying of his injuries he gave an incoherent 'final statement' to his interrogator Charles Hager of the US Intelligence Service, laying the blame for atrocities at the hands of many other senior SS figures except himself, and recounting how he had watched the surrender of SS companies to the Americans through his field glasses. He died a few days later.[23]

Many locals in Mauthausen were rounded up by the Americans and made to dispose of corpses and clean the barracks, perhaps, as one early historian of the camp believed, to prevent the inmates from lynching them.[24] At Ebensee, the notorious sub-camp of Mauthausen, local citizens were intimately involved in the process and aftermath of liberation. A local priest, Franz Loidl, recalled in his 1946 book entering the camp shortly after the Americans:

> In the confusion of questions and stories that now fall upon us my head truly buzzes. I know still that I often shook my head and beat my hands together with the exclamation: 'horrifying!' We listen to most of them sympathetically and shaken, because we see how speaking out does them good. Sometimes in somewhat strong words, I cannot help giving vent to my emotions out of honest indignation over especially striking occurrences.[25]

Yet although one can find similar expressions of horror after the fact, some locals did not want to have to continue thinking about what had taken place under their noses. Many citizens of Ebensee objected to the idea of preserving the camp as a memorial, and in 1949 plans were unveiled to build new apartment blocks on the former camp ground. The plans did not come to fruition, thanks largely to the decision to rebury the bodies of those who had died in public places at the end of the war in a new collective grave in the former Ebensee camp. But such developments reveal, as one historian perceptively notes, that for the locals, 'It was difficult for many of them to see that the region to which their lives were still attached by reason of personal experience and family ties had been transformed by recent events into a landscape scarred with a universal moral significance far transcending the local world of their experience.'[26] So it was for many former concentration camp sites.

* * *

The Nazi camps on the eve of liberation were very different from how they looked just months earlier. In Germany the war could only be fought on the basis of the more than 10 million foreign labourers who took the place of conscripted men, many of whom lived in camps. But one has to distinguish between these labourers, who belonged to the *Ausländereinsatz* (foreign labour) system, and the concentration camps run by the SS – the latter of which will be the focus here. The foreign labourers were more or less well treated; that is to say, at least they were kept alive. Depending on where they happened to end up, they were all required for work and a rational calculation underpinned their positions. By contrast, the inmates of concentration camps were there to be beaten into submission, and if they died it was of no significance, especially if they were Jews, communists or social democrats.

The camps were initially set up on an unorganised basis – the so-called 'wild camps' of the first year or two after the Nazi takeover. The earliest 'proper' camps were Dachau and Oranienburg, later Sachsenhausen, camps which attracted a great deal of attention, including from the foreign press. They were places that served the purpose of ensuring that the Nazi suppression of political opposition was appreciated by the regime's enemies – a process that worked swiftly and brutally. This is why only two of the SS's six original concentration camps, Dachau and Lichtenburg, were in operation at the end of 1937. When Buchenwald was established in that same year, it was not, as is often assumed due to the later predominance of communists among the prisoner functionaries, a camp for political prisoners; these had already been dealt with in the first two years of Nazi rule. Rather it was a camp primarily for 'asocials' and other 'Aryans' who refused to accommodate themselves to Nazism, including Jehovah's Witnesses, the 'work-shy', habitual criminals and homosexuals. Their numbers were small – just 7,750 at the end of 1937[27] – but it was their presence that led to the new camp's bucolic name. Logically it should have been called Ettersberg, since that is where it is located; yet Theodor Eicke, the Inspector of Concentration Camps, wrote to Himmler in July 1937 that it 'cannot be used' because of the Ettersberg's association with Goethe. Eicke's objection was not that the great man should not be sullied by being linked with a concentration camp, but that his revered name should not be associated with the *Volksgemeinschaft*'s rejects.[28]

The point is important because it reminds us that the SS camps were initially used for the purposes of crafting the racial community and eliminating political opponents, real and imagined. The expansion of the camp system in 1938 – by the end of June 1938 there were about 24,000 inmates in the SS's concentration camps, mostly 'asocials' and other outsiders such as homosexuals, Jehovah's Witnesses and Austrian political prisoners – was a result of Himmler's increasing power and his plans to expand the SS empire. The change is signalled in the administration of the camps, which were run at first by the Inspectorate of Concentration Camps (IKL) until 1942 and then by the SS's Business Administration Main Office (WVHA), a name that encapsulates Himmler's aspirations. The camps were changing all the time in terms of their number and prominence and the make-up of the inmates. But they remained constant in their aim of terrorising the people that the Nazis named as their enemies. The murder of the Jews was a later development and one that changed the shape of the camp system altogether. Jews had always numbered among the concentration camp inmates, usually as political prisoners, and, as Jews, were subjected to especially rough treatment. But after Kristallnacht (9–10 November 1938), Jews targeted as such made up a consistently high proportion of the camps' inmates.[29]

Just as this attack on the Jews presaged the large-scale persecution to come, so the camp system began rapidly to expand just before the start of the war. Large numbers of Czechs, veterans of the Spanish Civil War and, especially, Poles boosted the numbers of camp inmates in 1940, which rose to 53,000. New camps began to open, such as Neuengamme and Auschwitz. The latter was neither originally a camp specifically for Jews nor a death camp, but was designed to hold Polish political prisoners. The invasion of the Soviet Union in June 1941 brought about another expansion of the camp system, with notable camps built at Lublin (Majdanek) and Stutthof. Some 38,000 Soviet 'commissars' were murdered in Action 14f14 in 1941–42, and over the course of the war some 3 million Soviet POWs died in SS captivity.[30]

In September 1942 there were about 110,000 camp inmates; this number shot up to 224,000 a year later, 524,286 a year after that, and over 700,000 by the start of 1945, as the SS desperately tried to substitute forced labour for the shortcomings of the Third Reich's war economy.[31] New camps, such as Mittelbau-Dora where V2 rockets were built, suddenly emerged and grew into huge, brutal factories where workers, instead of being productive in any economically meaningful sense, died in large numbers. Such huge numbers meant that far from being hidden from view, 'concentration camps in public spaces' became the norm and 'the camp world invaded everyday life as never before'.[32]

Once again, one needs to distinguish, at least at first, between the SS concentration camps such as Buchenwald, Dachau and Sachsenhausen, and, later, Neuengamme, Ravensbrück, Mauthausen, Stutthof and Gross-Rosen, which were designed to brutalise the inmates – and in which death was common – and the death camps that were pure killing facilities, not administered as part of the regular concentration camp system. The latter are regularly referred to as concentration camps when in fact they were no such thing. No one was 'concentrated' at Chełmno, Bełżec, Sobibór or Treblinka, which together account for a little less than a third of the Holocaust's victims. The exceptions were Majdanek and Auschwitz, which by 1942 combined the functions of concentration and death camps and, especially at Auschwitz, also had massive slave labour operations attached. As well as being the primary site of the genocide of the Roma (Gypsies), about 1 million Jews were murdered in the gas chambers at Auschwitz-Birkenau, including some 437,000 Hungarian Jews deported in spring 1944. Transit camps and labour camps associated with the administration of the Holocaust were also established, such as Herzogenbusch in the Netherlands. The difference between all these sorts of camps was not very widely understood during the war. This lack of clarity, combined with the chaos of war's denouement which brought the different camps crashing together, contributed to the confusion over the geography and operation of the Holocaust for years after the end of the war. With the exception of Auschwitz and Majdanek, it was only late in the war that the systematic murder of Europe's Jews became entangled with the wider history of the concentration camps.

For the inmates, life in the concentration camps was brutal. It is often depicted in crude Darwinian terms as a struggle for survival. Although there are many recorded instances of assistance and mutual aid amongst inmates in the camps, staying alive required more than luck. 'In the camps', wrote Joop Zwart, a prominent Dutch political prisoner in Belsen, later in his 1958 testimony, 'the conditions could not be measured with the moral standards of a free society. Nobody could afford to help first somebody else with a thing he himself needed most.' This individualistic disregard for others might have enabled some to endure, but it also hindered the survival of the many. There are also, contrary to Zwart's claims, many instances of survivors testifying to the importance of being one of a pair or small group.[33] Zwart claims that 'with more solidarity among the prisoners it is my conviction that many more thousands could have been saved. But it seemed as if the people in the camps did their very best to shed their best qualities as quickly as possible for their very worst qualities. So not only envy, but betrayal and worse, reigned.'[34] This harsh judgment certainly tells us something about how the camps functioned, though Zwart omits to mention that these conditions were not those of the inmates' own making. If they did not live up to the standards of decent behaviour, we might remember that this was one of the consequences of the camps the Nazis intended.

One of the main confusions in our understanding of the Holocaust concerns the role played by work. The term 'annihilation through labour' (*Vernichtung durch Arbeit*) is widely understood to refer to a deliberately conceived Nazi policy. In fact, the decision to use concentration camp inmates, as opposed to foreign forced and volunteer labourers, for work only took place in the late stages of the war with the German economy suffering severe shortages in manpower. It was at this point – autumn 1944 – that large numbers of sub-camps appeared. Gross-Rosen, for example, had over a hundred sub-camps by the end of 1944 and, with nearly 77,000 inmates, held some 11 per cent of the total concentration camp population.[35] Where concentration camp inmates (as opposed to forced labourers) were forced to work, this was only ever a temporary measure designed to extract as much of value out of inmates before their deaths. Particularly for Jews, work was only meant as a brief interlude, a necessary evil.[36] It was, as one historian says, 'a measure of last resort for a mercilessly overheated armaments industry and in a system whose downfall was ever more likely in view of the hopeless state of the war.'[37] When some SS managers attempted to 'modernise' their enterprises, they nevertheless took it for granted that the lives of their workers would be short and they rarely made any efforts to increase productivity by improving living conditions or food quantity. Still, memoirs of inmates of the sub-camps of Gross-Rosen or Neuengamme, for example, report that conditions were far preferable to those at Auschwitz, from where many of them had been deported. The collapse of the Third Reich in the spring of 1945 thus meant that Jewish camp inmates who were being used as slave labourers were (on average) actually in somewhat better health than those who were not working. Certainly they would have died if the war had lasted longer, but slave labour prolonged the lives of many to the point at which they outlived the regime. Many of these workers – Jews and non-Jews – were not liberated where they worked, however, for they had been forced to march elsewhere in the Third Reich's dying days.

The last months of the camp system are the most important for understanding liberation. We need to consider why there were so many people incarcerated in the camps just before the end of the war and why that number included a large number of Jews – a fact that seems paradoxical when we think of the Nazi mania for killing Jews. With the Reich collapsing, huge numbers of inmates were forcibly evacuated from the camps that were under imminent threat of discovery by the Allies and sent into the heart of Germany on what the victims named 'death marches'; the name has subsequently become common currency since it so accurately captures the absurd viciousness of the process, and identifies the marches as part of the Holocaust. This meant that the camps still in existence in early 1945 were heavily overburdened with vast numbers of already ill and dying inmates, in chaotic conditions where caring for concentration camp prisoners was low on the Third Reich's administrators' list of priorities. Dachau in April 1945, claims one historian, could no longer be distinguished from the other sites of mass murder.[38] Belsen, a camp that had been opened in 1943 as a holding camp for 'privileged' inmates (ones whom the Reich thought could be useful in negotiating with the Allies), was functioning like a death camp because huge numbers were dying there every day from lack of food and water: in March 1945 alone, 18,000 inmates died.[39] The camp system as such was imploding along with SS bureaucracy in general. The individual camps became true disaster zones in which immense human suffering was the norm. If there was a collapse in the distinction between the murder of the Jews and the function of the concentration camps, the reason for it lay in the fact that the majority of Jews liberated at Dachau, Buchenwald, Sachsenhausen and Bergen-Belsen were survivors of the camps in the east – including many Jewish slave labourers who had been in small sub-camps – who had been marched westwards in the face of the Soviet advance.

These so-called 'death marches' – which one historian calls a continuation of the Final Solution by other means[40] – marked the last phase of the Holocaust. A huge number of camp inmates lost their lives in these cruel marches. The immediate reason for them was the determination that prisoners should not fall into enemy hands, but neither could they be transported via a road and rail system that was facing collapse and in which the movement of troops, German refugees and forced labourers took priority over concentration camp inmates. On 21 July 1944 the commander (*Befehlshaber*) of the Sipo and SD in the General Government of Poland issued a decree ordering that 'The liberation of prisoners or Jews or their falling into the hands of the enemy, whether the western powers or the Red Army, must absolutely be avoided.'[41] Three days later Majdanek was liberated. The SS redoubled its efforts not to let large numbers of inmates be found alive in the camps, and began evacuations before camps fell into enemy hands. What this meant in practice was that tens of thousands of mostly sick, weak, and undernourished camp inmates were forced to take to the roads in the middle of winter en route to unknown destinations. The statistics are obscene: of the 714,000 recorded camp inmates in January 1945, at least one-third died 'on the exhausting evacuation marches, in the transport trains which took weeks to reach their destination, and (particularly) in the hopelessly overcrowded reception camps in the months and weeks immediately before the end of the war'. Probably around half of the victims were Jews.[42] But there were also death marches where the majority of those killed were not Jews, because there had been few Jews in the originating camps. As the leading historian of the death marches notes, the Nazis still hated and feared the Jews, but the victims of the death marches made up a new collective whose 'common denominator was, first and foremost, the demonic and essentially fantastic threat it posed to the murderers'.[43]

The camp inmates were made to walk large distances. Although the geographical destination of the marches may not have been known or decided as the inmates set off, that many were to die en route was clearly foreseeable. The Nazi term 'evacuation' (*Evakuierung*) was a euphemism disguising extermination, an emotional journey that no map can portray.[44] No wonder that the victims were terrified of what was happening; some owed their lives to the marches, as they were able to escape from them, but most must have had little hope that they would survive. They were permanently surrounded by death. André Grevenrath, interned as a communist in Sachsenhausen, wrote about the death marches in the 1960s:

The strange march of thousands, some of whom had been crammed together in the narrowest space for years in the camp, already caused many losses on the second day, indeed for older comrades in a very weak physical state even on the first ... At first we didn't see what happened to comrades who lay exhausted at the roadside ... On the third day of the march we saw the first signs of what had happened where earlier marches had used these streets: we could see the corpses of those left behind, killed with a shot to the neck, lying in graves right next to people's homes on the street and covered only with a few handfuls of earth or else uncovered.[45]

Many testimonies describe the realisation that fellow evacuees were being killed. Moshé Garbarz, marched out of Janischowitz, a sub-camp of Auschwitz, recalls that:

With every rifle shot we think that the Polish Resistance or the Red Army, which is very close by, is attempting to free us. We haven't begun to imagine the truth: the Auschwitz stragglers are being executed. If we have to slow up, it's only to give the SS time to gun these stragglers down and clear the road of their bodies.[46]

Similarly, Erika Kounio Amariglio writes: 'Every so often we heard gunfire and automatically accelerated our pace. The gunfire was meant for those who could not walk fast enough and fell behind, the last in the line. The more time passed, the more often we heard the sharp crack of gunshots.'[47]

The marches themselves are a complex phenomenon, one which historians have struggled to comprehend.[48] A few points can be made, however. First, the death marches took place in public space; they passed through numerous towns, villages and countryside, and brought many civilians into the sphere of the perpetrators. 'The killing', as one historian concisely puts it, 'was now coextensive with the landscape.'[49] Second, they constitute what one historian calls 'a long process of slow and gradual extermination, prolonged over days and weeks, during which the murderer and his victims advance in lockstep'.[50] Yet the Third Reich's leadership, to the extent that it was in control of the process, seems to have wavered between a desire to kill all the camp inmates and a sense that there was merit in keeping some alive. At best, one can say that the life or death of the victims was a matter of the guards' capricious decision-making. Their actions were heavily influenced by their bitter resentment at the downfall of the Reich, their fear for their own lives in the case of Allied victory, and a feeling that, as the Allies advanced deeper into Germany, the regime's claims about the power of 'the Jew' were being proven correct. The conditions were ripe for brutal, large-scale and carnivalesque violence.

The death marches also remind us that not all Holocaust survivors were liberated in a camp, and provide some explanation of the fact that many survivors were simply too weak to live even though they had been liberated. Many experienced their liberation as a sudden, unexpected absence of guards rather than as an arrival of Allied liberators – or sometimes as a combination of both. Death marches sometimes came to a halt when the guards fled and left the struggling survivors to fend for themselves. Ernst Bornstein, for example, recalled that he and hundreds of other Eastern European Jewish inmates of Mühldorf, a sub-camp of Dachau, were transported by train on 26 April. After travelling forty miles in a day and a half, the train stopped east of Munich and sat on a siding:

> Suddenly we realized that the SS who had been guarding our wagon had disappeared. We looked out of the wagon and saw the guards gathered round the camp commandant [*Lagerführer*], who was making a short speech to them. After a few minutes the SS men came back, opened the wagon doors wide and told us we were free.[51]

After plundering the supply trains for food, Bornstein and his comrades were attacked, Gauleiter Paul Giesler having decided to reverse the release order and force them back onto the train. Continuing its journey, at Tutzing near the Starnberger See the train was bombed by American planes; when the Americans later found it they discovered fifty-four dead bodies inside.[52]

The death marches also explain why the camps liberated by the Western Allies were not the main centres of the Holocaust; in fact these camps had little at all to do with the systematic programme to murder the Jews. Most of the Jews killed in what we now call the Holocaust were murdered in face-to-face killings at the edge of death pits in eastern Poland and the western Soviet Union (the Baltic States, Belarus, Ukraine and western Russia), in the ghettos of occupied Poland and in the death camps. Of those camps, the key ones (Chełmno and the 'Operation Reinhard' camps of Bełżec, Sobibór and Treblinka) had been dismantled long before the end of the war, and the other major sites, Majdanek and Auschwitz, were liberated by the Red Army who found them almost empty of people. If the Western Allies had little to say about 'the Holocaust' in the immediate postwar period, that is not only because that term did not yet exist, but also because the camps they liberated were not 'Holocaust' camps and because Jews constituted fewer than one-third of the survivors, who also included very large numbers of non-Jewish Poles and Soviet POWs. Millions of forced labourers were also liberated and for the Allies it was not always easy in the pandemonium of the end of the war to understand the difference between different categories of deportees.

In terms of understanding how the Allies – the soldiers, doctors and nurses, reporters and photographers – responded to what they saw in Dachau, Buchenwald and Belsen, it is important to bear in mind that these were not established as death camps and that Jews were by no means the only people in the camps when they were liberated. At liberation many political prisoners and forced labourers from almost every country in Europe were to be found in the camps. Indeed, it has been suggested that the rowdiness and willingness of liberated camp inmates – Russian forced labourers especially – to engage in violence against the German civilian population was the main reason why the military authorities decided to force them back into the camps.[53] But, as we will see, along with people unwilling to return to Soviet or Soviet-held territory, such as Balts and Ukrainians, the Jewish element among the survivors soon became hard to overlook, for unlike the majority of the liberated who were able to return home quickly, most Jews had nowhere to go.

The picture was further complicated by the fact that the liberation of Eastern Europe led to communist dictatorship. In Western Europe people distrusted sources of information coming from the communist-occupied east, and in Eastern Europe very specific narratives about liberation could not be questioned. Since the end of the Cold War the 'liberation narrative' that underpinned communist rule – that is, that the communists defeated fascism and freed the region – has been discredited. In consequence, the liberation of the camps by the Red Army, an aspect of Soviet propaganda actually rooted in fact, was brushed aside. Since the Red Army really did defeat fascism, it is unfortunate that this fact has been scored out as part of the otherwise legitimate process of condemning communism. It is now necessary to narrate the story of the end of the Holocaust in a way that allows for proper recognition of the role played by the Red Army without, on the one hand, ignoring or dismissing it in the manner of post-communist nationalism or, on the other hand, enlarging the notion of 'liberation' to justify communist rule.

Unsurprisingly, statistics present a serious problem: all figures relating to Holocaust survivors are approximate and historians will never be able to know for sure how many survivors were liberated in 1944–45, how many died in the immediately following days, weeks and months, and how many were subsequently joined in DP camps by Eastern European Jews seeking refuge in Central and Western Europe. But if exact numbers are impossible to obtain, historians reckon that among the survivors of the camps liberated in 1945, there were about 90,000 Jews, less than a third of the total number of prisoners liberated in the Nazi concentration camps in 1945. Of that 90,000, many died in the first weeks, leaving between 60,000 and 70,000 remaining. The same number again survived forced labour camps, either in hiding or with partisan groups. And another 250,000 of the approximately 400,000 Eastern European Jews who had fled into the Soviet Union – mostly ending up in Central Asia – were still alive in 1945. The majority of them returned to Poland when the Soviets allowed them to do so, but remained there only briefly.[54] Between 1945 and 1948, 250,000–330,000 Jews passed through the DP camps in the American and British zones of occupied Germany. After the summer of 1945, then, camp survivors constituted a minority of Jewish DPs, the majority of whom were Jews from Eastern Europe who had not been in German camps in 1945; some were camp survivors returning to Germany after finding that they were unable to return home, but most were Jews who had survived in hiding or with partisans, or returnees from Soviet exile. Yitzchok Perlov, for example, author of a book recounting his time in exile in the Soviet Union, ended his writing with his return to a Poland that was now 'Earth violated, earth tortured, filled with blood . . .'[55] The reasons for such people to move on yet again were obvious. Returnees from Soviet exile, as Atina Grossmann reminds us, 'included virtually the only Eastern European Jews to enter the DP camps in family groups that included young children'.[56]

These figures should be set in context: at the end of the war there were some 20 million people on the move in Europe, including about 12 million ethnic Germans expelled from their homelands east of Germany's 1937 borders, and about 7 million who were classed as 'Displaced Persons' (DPs, i.e. nationals other than German in Germany at the end of the war). On 9 November 1943 the United National Relief and Rehabilitation Administration (UNRRA) was set up with the task to 'plan, co-ordinate, administer or arrange for the administration of measures for the relief of victims of war in any area under the control of any of the United Nations through the provision of food, fuel, clothing, shelter and other basic necessities, medical and other essential services'.[57] Additionally, it was tasked with assisting exiles to return home, assuming that camps set up for that purpose – and many were makeshift in the extreme – would only have a temporary existence. To assist in the process, a basic distinction was drawn by the Allies between displaced persons and refugees. The former were defined as 'civilians outside the national boundaries of their country by reason of the war, who are: 1) desirous but are unable to return home or find homes without assistance; 2) to be returned to enemy or ex-enemy territory.' The latter were defined as individuals 'not outside the national boundaries of their country'.[58] In both cases there was an assumption – soon to be proved wrong – that everyone had a home to go to.

Judgements about UNRRA's accomplishment should bear in mind that repatriating DPs was only part of its work, and the task of providing food and medical relief to people across a war-torn continent was daunting. Impressively, UNRRA and the Allies repatriated 5.8 million DPs by September 1945 in what one commentator called 'a near-miracle in logistics'.[59] Nevertheless, by the start of 1946 about 1 million 'non-repatriables' remained, around half of them non-Jewish Poles, Ukrainians and Balts unwilling to return to Soviet-controlled territory. Indeed, the question of whether or not Soviet citizens should be forcibly repatriated was the sticking point which undid UNRRA and led to its replacement by the American-dominated IRO (International Refugee Organization).[60] Despite having signed an agreement in October 1944 with the USSR to the effect that Soviet citizens would be repatriated, and despite reiterating the agreement at Yalta in February 1945, in the months following the war the Americans and British vacillated in their response to the wishes of the DPs.[61] Thus the 'temporary' camps gradually took on an air of permanence, as they acquired the institutions necessary for a settled life, such as schools, nurseries, medical clinics and vocational training centres. Thus began what Malcolm Proudfoot, who ran refugee relief operations for the US Army, called 'the static phase'.[62] In Germany, where most of the DP camps were located, conditions were appalling: cities had been destroyed and there was little functioning infrastructure; food was scarce and disease rampant; and massive population movements exacerbated the problems. Relief operations at the DP camps have often been criticised for their inadequacy, as we will see. But it should be borne in mind that these camps existed in the context of a devastated country in which Nazi ideology had left the population fearful of the Allied occupiers and where, as one historian notes, 'simply keeping the ex-enemy population alive from day to day was going to be a major task'.[63] Proudfoot was being serious when he wrote that 'Compared with general conditions prevailing throughout the remainder of Germany and in certain countries of Eastern Europe, the lot of the displaced person was an easy one.'[64]

Within a few weeks of the liberations, non-Jewish survivors were free to return to their homes and most did so, as did Jews from Western Europe. Those who were left fell into two main categories. The first group comprised Eastern Europeans who did not want to go back to countries being taken over by communism and Soviet citizens who refused to return to the USSR (Ukrainians especially); as of 1946 this first category of survivors took advantage of the new concept of being 'unwilling' to be repatriated in order to avail themselves of state protection for fear of political persecution.[65] The second category was comprised of Jews who were deemed 'non-repatriable', because they feared anti-Semitic attacks if they were to go back to their countries of origin.

After the first few post-liberation months, Jews made up an increasingly noticeable portion of the DP population. The Jewish population in the DP camps, especially in the American zone, was rapidly swelled by Eastern European Jews fleeing their homelands – primarily Poland; these people were not technically DPs as they were not in Germany at war's end but they were treated as such by the Americans. The British were less flexible but nevertheless did accept Jewish refugees into the DP camps, at Belsen in particular. In fact, less than a tenth of the non-repatriable DPs were Jewish Holocaust survivors and, as we have seen, by the autumn of 1945 only a minority of those who were had been liberated in the Nazi camps.

This book's focus on the Jews reflects the particular experiences that they had undergone during the war and their particular fate after it, a fate which separated them from the other DPs. Writing just before the end of the war in April 1945, political philosopher Hannah Arendt presciently observed that the problem of statelessness would become one of the defining characteristics of the postwar world. 'It would be a good thing', she wrote, 'if it were generally admitted that the end of the war in Europe will not automatically return thirty to forty million exiles to their homes, and that only a relatively small proportion of all the refugees, stateless people and emigrants will automatically lose their status and reassume the normal one of citizens of a state.' Indeed, she went further and predicted that 'A very large proportion, many of them settled abroad for decades, will regard repatriation as deportation and will insist on retaining their statelessness.'[66] With respect to the DPs, it was in fact a minority, but a significant minority, who refused to return 'home'; with the 'last million', the scale of the phenomenon was something that Arendt had accurately foreseen.[67] Among them, the Jews presented special difficulties for the liberators: they were more deeply traumatised, they often had nowhere to return to, no remaining family and no hope. They were regarded suspiciously by the liberators, who often did not understand what they had been through, and who considered them primitive, unhygienic and demanding. The ways in which the DPs and the Allies negotiated with one another and learned to understand each other is a focus of this book.

UNRRA was dissolved in June 1947 to be replaced by the IRO, which was tasked with resettling the non-repatriable refugees in countries other than those of their origin. The IRO was then replaced by the United Nations High Commission for Refugees (UNHCR) in 1951 as the immediate wartime measures merged into the new postwar settlement in which the UN found its operations increasingly hamstrung by the emerging Cold War. By this point, the remaining DPs were those who refused to return to their countries of origin and those, primarily Jews, who were holding out more specifically to be admitted to a country of their choosing. Although UNRRA achieved a great deal, its record with respect to the Jewish survivors is not unblemished. The organisation sorted DPs by nationality and was very resistant to the idea that Jews ought, because of their specific suffering, to be classified separately. Here the organisation was in accord with the occupying Allied forces. UNRRA and the British and American militaries were not in favour of creating Jewish camps and their personnel were frustrated by the Jewish survivors' constant movement from camp to camp in search of relatives and friends. Nor were they initially receptive to the argument being vociferously made by Jewish survivors that housing them alongside collaborators of the same nationality (Hungarian, Ukrainian or whatever the case might be) was an outrage which constituted a continuation of their suffering. That policy did change in the late summer of 1945. Then, between UNRRA's inability to handle a small but problematic population group that could not easily be resettled and the late arrival of Jewish aid organisations into Germany – which, when they came, primarily supplied material aid and food but could do little officially to assist with resettlement – the Jews were condemned to a protracted limbo in DP camps.[68] Some of these camps were on the site of former Nazi camps – Landsberg, for instance – whilst others were in barracks, labour camps, hospitals and other buildings. Sometimes these 'camps' were very small; outside of Belsen in the British zone, for example, DP camps might consist of no more than a few apartment blocks suitably signposted.

These Jewish DP camps were only to emerge in the western occupation zones. Indeed, they emerged and grew largely because of the number of Jews leaving their former homes in Eastern Europe to which they had initially returned after the war from exile in the Soviet Union. In the Soviet-occupied zone (later the GDR), some 7,000 German Jews remained on the territory but they returned to their former hometowns and were not therefore housed in DP camps.[69] Former concentration camps began to be used to house political prisoners and they were designated by the communist authorities as 'special camps'. Following long-term Allied plans as definitively set out in the Potsdam Agreement of 2 August 1945, the Soviets (like the British and Americans) arrested and interned Nazi functionaries in ten 'special camps' at the end of the war. These camps remained in existence until 1950; among them were Sachsenhausen (Special Camp No. 2) and Buchenwald (Special Camp No. 7), the latter of which, though liberated by the Americans, fell into the Soviets' occupation zone and was therefore administered by the Soviets as of August 1945. According to figures released by the Soviets to the GDR's Christian Democrat interior minister, Peter-Michael Diestel, in 1990 there were 122,671 Germans imprisoned in the special camps. Of these, 42,889 died whilst in the camps and a further 756

were sentenced to death and executed. In other words, although the absolute figures for internment were similar to the American and British zones,
the rate of death in the camps (35 per cent) was far higher in the Soviet
camps even though conditions in some of the American- and British-
administered ones were far from adequate.[70] The discovery of mass graves
containing the bodies of somewhere between 6,000 and 13,000 inmates in
Buchenwald in 1984 was not something the communist authorities decided
to mention in the exhibition which opened in the former camp the following
year.[71] In the western zones, former concentration camps such as Dachau,
Neuengamme, Flossenbürg and Esterwege were also used to house German
suspects, including suspected war criminals and camp guards, but
conditions in them, though unpleasant, were never as harsh as in the
Soviet special camps. The reason is that the latter were tools in the social
reorganisation that the communists were engineering in Eastern Europe,
by which 'anti-fascist democracy' would emerge on the basis of the destruction of the bourgeoisie as a class.[72] By early 1950, the special camps' useful
lifespan had ended and, now for the most part empty of DPs and German
suspects, they either fell into disrepair or became museums.[73]

The Allies also sought, in their different ways, to eradicate Nazism. The
extent of the denazification process varied a great deal from zone to zone
and changed over time, but one policy that was crucial in the immediate
aftermath of the war was that of forcing former Nazis and local people to
confront the Third Reich's crimes. Soldiers and civilians alike were obliged
to watch newsreels of the camps and many local dignitaries and functionaries were taken on tours of the camps. It is hard to know what they thought
of the liberation – though journalist I.F. Stone wrote that the Germans,
'obsequious or sullen, gave me little sense of change'[74] – but it is possible to
learn about the interaction of German locals with the liberated camps and
the survivors, especially as the DP camps took on a more permanent feel.

Whatever their views about Nazism – and clearly Nazi attitudes did not
disappear overnight – German civilians were drawn to the camps as places
of trade, employment and sexual possibilities. Anti-Semitic stereotypes
about Jews were important here: the idea that Jews had international
connections and were better fed than Germans, or that they were canny
businessmen, no doubt energised connections between DPs and civilians.
Such ideas also bred resentment and humiliation and allowed complex

feelings of rage and bitterness about the defeat of Germany, complicity with the Nazi regime, and terrible postwar living conditions to be displaced onto supposedly criminal Jewish DPs. This was especially so since many German civilians looked enviously at the support being offered to Jews by foreign charities with the result that 'many began to weigh Auschwitz against Dresden and to compare the forced emigration of Germans from the East with the persecution of the Jews'.[75] The persistence of such views also meant that some Germans could 'salve their consciences with the belief that the Jews had been at least partially responsible for their own persecution' and to focus instead on their own suffering, from the firebombing of Dresden or the mass rapes carried out by advancing Soviet troops, to the expulsion of Germans from the east and the large numbers of POWs still in Soviet captivity.[76] Such interactions were relatively short-lived, however; once the majority of DPs had left Germany by the early 1950s the Jews who remained were a small number of Jewish Germans rebuilding their shattered communities and a very small number of so-called 'hard core' DP cases who could not or would not be moved. Where the rest were concerned, there was a mutual feeling amongst DPs and Germans that the departure of the DPs was best for all concerned.[77]

The policy of forcing Germans to confront the crimes of the Nazis was in some respects counterproductive, but it fulfilled several basic needs: not only a kind of revenge displacement, forcing a sense of shame onto the German people, but also an articulation of or forcible confrontation with the 'open secret' that everyone already knew. The results were mixed: many Germans felt ashamed by what they were seeing but that did not necessarily translate into a miraculous 're-education'.[78] Consider the words of Jürgen Bassfreund who, when asked if he had had contacts with 'real Germans' since the end of the war, replied:

> Yes. I had contacts with Christians and I must tell you that these people have almost no understanding for our situation. When you tell some people that you are coming from a concentration camp they say, 'Well my relatives were killed by bombs and that is just as bad.' And then there are others who say that they didn't know what was going on in the concentration camps and if they would have known they couldn't say anything anyway, because they would have been afraid that they themselves could

be taken to concentration camps. There are quite divergent viewpoints. I must tell you, however, that one hears but very rarely an admission on the part of the Germans that these things were wrong.[79]

Nevertheless, not all the survivors welcomed the confrontations, seeing the 'tours' as intrusions on their privacy and leaving them feeling like exotic objects in an anthropology show. Thomas Geve, still only fourteen years old when he was liberated at Buchenwald, noted that after being rounded up by the Americans, the locals 'followed the loudspeaker van through the camp and trudged past our shabby barracks as if on some pilgrimage or funeral'. Although mildly irritated by a few girls who, 'dressed in short skirts, giggled', he was most offended by policemen and railway officials still wearing their Nazi-era uniforms: 'if their wearers' professional pride had really been exceeded by a dislike of things reminiscent of the Nazis', Geve wrote, 'they would have discarded them. As it was, they had not even bothered to obliterate all the swastika markings.' Geve claims that the tours only ceased when some of the survivors 'threatened to attack them'.[80] The Jewish DP camps, as they had soon become, were then generally free from internal disruption – though Jews were regularly harassed on German streets and there were some notorious police raids inside the camps. But they ended up lasting longer than anyone could have foreseen in 1945.

*   *   *

This book is based largely on survivor testimony, both written and spoken, of which there is now a vast amount. The growth in oral testimony collection projects has also led to considerable research into how memory is affected by traumatic events. Where earlier scholars were suspicious of attempts to describe events that had taken place decades before, now historians, traditionally wary of testimony as an 'intentional' document (i.e. written after the events it describes, not part of them), have demonstrated how vital it really is, confirming the view long held by oral historians that memory is a valuable source. Especially where traumatic or life-changing events are concerned, witnesses can often be shown to be remarkably reliable in their testimony even after many decades.[81] Besides, when writing about the immediate aftermath of the war (the years 1945–48), survivors' words are as much a part of the period as are 'official' documents. The interviews conducted by the innovative David Boder, for example, who was the first to use a wire recorder to capture survivors' testimonies, are increasingly recognised as a remarkable resource. They remind us not only of the value of testimonies *per se*, but of the need to place them (like all sources) in historical context. Boder conducted his interviews at a time when the survivors' words did not make sense; their interlocutors did not have a 'history of the Holocaust' in their heads to help them, and he continually had to push his interviewees to explain seemingly incredible events.[82] I have thus relied on testimony, not uncritically but with a general willingness to accept witness statements since over such huge numbers they tend to agree with one another. But testimonies are accompanied by official reports, journalistic accounts, statements by liberating soldiers and relief workers, and documents from the relief organisations, including the American Jewish Joint Distribution Committee (the JDC or 'Joint'), the Organization for Rehabilitation and Training (ORT) and the Jewish Committee for Relief Abroad (JCRA). Thus although specific details can always be questioned, and although some survivors' accounts have become refined over time,[83] there is little ground for worrying that eyewitness accounts are flawed.

A number of photographs are also included here. Over the decades we have become familiar with 'atrocity photographs' from the liberation period: masses of corpses, naked bodies, the juxtaposition of the living and the dead. I have instead placed more emphasis on photographs from the DP camps, many of them taken by DPs themselves. These are thus not just illustrations; rather they show how the survivors responded to Nazi and Allied images of camp inmates as mere victims by presenting themselves as conscious and active agents. Their photographs simultaneously presented to the world their plight as continued 'prisoners', and advertised the fact that they had goals and aspirations plus the wherewithal to bring them to fruition. They not only mocked the Allied triumphalism that accompanied much of the liberation, but provided evidence of empowerment after years of degradation and suffering.

For all our ability to understand the sorrows as well as the joys of liberation, and for all that we have plentiful sources of all varieties, some aspects of the Holocaust will always remain opaque to our understanding. The ways in which historians have tackled the Third Reich and its crimes have changed considerably since 1945; the Holocaust in particular is the subject of a vast and sophisticated body of historical scholarship.[84] Yet despite the powerful explanations that historians and other scholars have offered, there is a feeling that does not change over time, and that is the sense of mystery that remains at the enormity of what the Nazis and their collaborators did. This was already apparent immediately after the events, not just in famous cases such as Primo Levi's Auschwitz dream of being back at home, telling his family his ordeal and not being believed, but in official publications too. For example, reflecting on the liberation of Gunskirchen very soon after the event, Corporal Jerry Tax wondered at the speed with which the disgusting sites of the camp had been removed, so that the whole thing took on a dreamlike quality:

> That night, as the free men of France, Poland, Russia, Yugoslavia and the Balkans prepared for their first untroubled sleep since a madman with a comic mustache took control of an ambitious Germany, the spirit of a new Europe was being born in their hearts.
> Who knows what the Germans were thinking?[85]

There is no definitive answer to that question, but it is a question that has plagued survivors throughout their lives. Liberation freed them from Nazi rule but not from its effects. As Ernst Israel Bornstein writes, 'While a former inmate of a concentration camp may laugh and be merry with others, he aches and bleeds inside because the old wounds will not heal. Even though he has left the spatially limited concentration camp, the terrible atmosphere of the camp still encompasses him; it is as though the KZ were still inside him.'[86]

CHAPTER ONE

Liberated by the Soviets

'One sees only death and distress, the former is better because we
cannot give people life, even if they remain alive.'
ALISAH SHEK, Theresienstadt, 9 May 1945

'I am a person who was liberated from the Holocaust . . . [who] can't
show the happiness. First of all I thank God that we survived. But from
the other side I don't know how to thank [God] that I lost everybody! . . .
So how happy can I be? . . . So that's, that's, that's the bottom line.'
REBECCA C., interview, 20 January 2000[1]

The Red Army film of the liberation of Auschwitz shows crowds of
inmates in their striped uniforms cheering as the barrier beneath the
infamous 'Arbeit macht frei' gate is raised. Although this sequence was an
outtake only inserted into the film in the 1980s, it is a moment now
inscribed into the world's consciousness. Yet even in its original version the
film was a reconstruction, made several days after Soviet troops first
arrived. The film is still valuable, of course; it depicts the camp and the
state of its inmates merely days after they had been freed from Nazi rule.
It also evidences the Soviets' thinking about the propaganda value of
filming liberation, incensing the Soviet people against the Germans, as
well as aiding the process of punishing the perpetrators: the films soon
found their way into the Nuremberg trials. The Soviets' demand for 'vengeance and justice' was thus facilitated by their liberation films.[2] But what

the Auschwitz film does not show is the true nature of the moment of liberation.

That is because for most of the people who were left in Auschwitz when the Soviets arrived there was no 'moment' of liberation. Those left behind after the SS forced the inmates on death marches westwards were the sick, such as George Kaldore, interviewed in Tradate, Italy, a year later. Kaldore, aged twenty-three at the time of the interview, was from Szombathely and, like many young Hungarian Jews, had been drafted into a Hungarian labour battalion in 1940 before being returned to Hungary. In the spring of 1944, following the German occupation of Hungary, the Hungarian Jews were deported to Auschwitz. They were the last major Jewish population group in Europe to be targeted: 437,000 people deported in full view of the watching world ('800,000 Jews face reign of terror', as the *Daily Mail* put it on 9 May 1944). Kaldore himself was picked up on the streets in June 1944, carrying false papers which identified him as Christian, and was sent on a transport to Birkenau. After working in various labour units, including at the Buna works, Kaldore contracted a fever in December 1944 and was sent to the camp 'hospital' where an operation was carried out on one of his swollen feet. Although Kaldore was nearly healed by the middle of January, he kept reopening the wound on his foot in order to remain in the warmer environment of the hospital. And then one day the doctors in charge left, along with the rest of the camp. Some 400 sick inmates remained. Fearing that the SS would kill them all before they too departed, Kaldore got up, dressed in some civilian clothing he found in the stores and, together with another Hungarian, hid in an air-raid shelter. Here is how Kaldore described the last days:

> We see in the street in front of the lager there go crowds of SS men, soldiers are marching, automobiles, tanks at high speed, and there walk Polish people and Reichs-Germans and Volks-Germans with wagons, and they transport their clothes and move on. We see that something was in the offing. That liberation is coming for us, and we walked away from the bunker. We entered the first village. We went into [the house of] a Polish peasant, and we told the Polish peasant to let us come in. He could see that the Germans are running away and that the Russians are coming. He took us into his house and gave us a bit to eat. He himself did not have much.

For two days we were hiding with this peasant, and at night the Russians arrive. When the Russians arrived we ourselves went back to the lager and in the lager people were rejoicing. But of the four hundred people there remained only about two hundred people. The others had died from starvation, had died from typhus which started to ravage there, and we had nothing on our bodies. We had already long beards, three–four weeks old, and there were these musselmen who had only bones and flesh – flesh, do I say? They had nothing [on their bodies], only bones and bones.[3]

The Soviet soldiers fed the remaining inmates with food taken from the local Poles, then advised them to walk – which Kaldore did, with his pus-ridden foot – to Cracow, from where they could try to get home. Eventually making his way back to Budapest with the aid of the Soviets, Kaldore found none of his relatives left there. He worked for some time for the JDC in Szombathely then travelled illegally to Italy, registered with UNRRA and, like so many others, was at the time of his interview waiting for the chance to immigrate to Palestine. Although he was not in the camp hospital at the moment the Soviets arrived, Kaldore's experience of liberation – just a continuum in a series of travails – is far more indicative of what actually transpired than is the Red Army film.

To understand the camp liberations carried out by the Soviets, we need to rely on the Red Army films of the liberation, some reportage, the Extraordinary State Commission reports, and later testimonies of survivors and some liberating soldiers. There are far fewer available sources like the *Buchenwald Report*, nurses' diaries or other army reports for these camps than there are for those liberated by the Western Allies, and there are no official Soviet documents ordering the liberation of the camps. However, we do know that the Soviets liberated the first of the major camps, Majdanek, in July 1944, and the most famous, Auschwitz, in January 1945, before liberating Sachsenhausen and Ravensbrück in April and Stutthof, Gross-Rosen and the 'ghetto-camp' Theresienstadt in May. Most of the inmates had been evacuated from several of these large camps on forced marches and transports to the west before the Soviets arrived, leaving behind only a small number of mostly very ill prisoners. The Soviets also overran and occupied the territories where the death camps of Bełżec, Sobibór and Treblinka had stood, and discovered many of the grisly details of what had transpired there.

Such differences in sources aside, the Soviet liberators' encounters with the camps were no less shocking for them than they were for the Americans and British, as memoirs and soldiers' letters show. And those few inmates who were in the camps when the Soviets arrived have described the scenes in the same variety of ways as have those who were liberated in the western camps. What is so striking is that although the camps liberated by the Soviets included the main killing sites, very few people remained in them by the end of the war, so that the majority of survivors were in fact liberated by the Western Allies in camps that had not been pure extermination facilities. Thus, the picture of who found whom, what and where was confusing at the outset; and this confusion contributed to the many misunderstandings that arose in the West about the Nazi camps and their victims, which took many years of research to put right.[4]

The misunderstandings were also compounded by the Soviets' manipulation of the reports of what they found. For them the fact that the victims, especially of the Reinhard camps, were predominantly Jews was of little ideological use. The Soviets wanted to portray the defeat of fascism as a victory for international working-class anti-fascism and to represent Nazism's victims as people who had died in the name of the anti-fascist cause – a notion that was incompatible with the fact that the Nazis' primary victim group was targeted on 'racial' grounds. Red Army journalist Vasily Grossman published an insightful and powerful essay on Treblinka in the autumn of 1944 (based on interviews with some of the few survivors), an essay which would later be used at the Nuremberg trials. Yet by the time *The Black Book* – the large-scale account of the murder of the Jews on Soviet territory that Grossman produced with Ilya Ehrenburg – was ready to print in 1948, it was suppressed by the Soviet authorities, the plates of the book destroyed. As one historian says, this was 'a graphic symbol of the Soviet Union's determination to reject a special Jewish claim for suffering in the course of the Great Patriotic War.'[5]

In 1944, however, the fresh discoveries made by the Red Army could still be publicised with relatively little interference. Grossman wrote of Treblinka that 'By the time it had been fully destroyed [on 23 July 1944], the prisoners could already hear the distant rumble of Soviet artillery.'[6] Although there was no liberation at Treblinka (as it had been dismantled by the Germans), the discovery of the camp should be included here, as it was a profound induction for the Soviets into the world of Nazi mass murder, one which informed their response to the still-functioning camps that they encountered later. Or, rather, Grossman's essay provided a powerful induction, with its stirring rhetoric:

> The defenders of Stalingrad have now reached Treblinka; from the Volga to the Vistula turned out to be no distance at all. And now the very earth of Treblinka refuses to be an accomplice to the crimes the monsters committed. It is casting up the bones and belongings of those who were murdered; it is casting up everything that Hitler's people tried to bury within it.[7]

Grossman's descriptions of walking across the site of the former camp must have been almost unbelievable in 1944. As he said, and as the later wave of liberations was to prove, 'There is much now to think about, much that we must try to understand.'[8] Since the Red Army was overrunning eastern Poland and had discovered Majdanek at the same time as the article on Treblinka appeared, Grossman's words were especially potent.

The official Soviet response to the camps was primarily to make use of them, through film and the press, for 'vengeance and justice' – in other words, to promote the communist cause in Europe. Yet the Soviets did not neglect the care of those survivors left in the camps. Film units were sent in to make useful propaganda material and committees of investigation were established to investigate Nazi crimes, but tending to the survivors, at least in the short term, was also a priority. Medical assistance was rendered, and many soldiers and medics went to great lengths to care for survivors. Still, as we will see, in contrast to the camps liberated by the Western Allies, where most of the survivors of the camp system were found, the Soviet aid programmes were wound up relatively quickly. Many of the camps occupied by the Soviets were turned into 'special camps' for POWs and political prisoners, which remained in existence for far longer than the equivalent POW camps administered by the Western Allies' since they proved useful in effecting the social change required for the imposition of communist rule.

*   *   *

Liberation did not always occur at a camp. In March and April 1944, before any of the camps had been uncovered, the Red Army liberated the Jews of

Transnistria, the area of Ukraine between the Dniestr and Bug rivers occupied by Romania. Here, between 380,000 and 400,000 Jews, as well as several thousand Roma, had been killed in appalling conditions. Jews and Roma had been forced into ramshackle camps and ghettos, or left to fend for themselves.[9] But in all the Nazi-occupied territories of the Soviet Union, Transnistria and the city of Czernowitz (Cernăuţi, today Chernivtsi in Ukraine) were the only places where the Red Army liberated towns and ghettos in which Jews were actually alive.[10] As one survivor, Solomon Shapira, remembered, 'On the morning of March 19, 1944, the first Soviet army patrols appeared … The column advancing toward us contained large numbers of Jewish soldiers. These would leave the column and come toward us, hugging and kissing us and telling us that we were the first living Jews they had come across on their way from Stalingrad.'[11]

When the Soviets reached the Dniestr, over 50,000 deported Jews as well as around 10,000 local Jews (6 per cent of the pre-occupation Jewish population) were still living, thanks to the vacillation of the Romanian authorities in the face of impending defeat as well poor organisation in the administration of the area. Additionally, and uniquely among perpetrator regimes, Antonescu's government, seeing the way the war was going and hoping to change its image, had introduced a repatriation scheme: Jews from the Regat (the Old Kingdom that existed before Romania's post-First World War territorial expansion), Dorohoi, and orphans under the age of fifteen would be allowed to return to Romania. After delays and further maltreatment – fuelled by Antonescu's warnings about a postwar Judeo-Bolshevik takeover of Romania – several thousand orphans were sent back to the country. The Soviet arrival in Transnistria ended this scheme, so that, these orphans aside, 43,519 Romanian Jewish citizens from Bessarabia and Bukovina were left in Transnistria, as well as about 10,000 who had not been able to get out of Czernowitz before the Red Army arrived. Since these areas, with the exception of southern Bukovina, were regarded by the Soviets as part of the USSR, these Jews were now considered Soviet citizens and thus were unable to leave.[12] Sometimes this led to families being separated. The ten-year-old daughter of Frieda Weiss, a former deportee by then back in Bucharest, had been sent to an orphanage in Odessa to await transport to Palestine, but since she had been born in Nepolocăuti, near Czernowitz, once the Soviets arrived she could not leave Soviet-occupied territory.[13]

Liberation in Transnistria therefore did not mean a swift end to the survivors' travails. Apart from being unable to leave the area, some were sent to the front or were forced to join work battalions; all faced a long ordeal trying to make the short journey back to Romania.[14] And the Jewish communities were devastated. Yosef Govrin, who survived Transnistrian ghettos and camps as a child and subsequently went on to become the Israeli ambassador to Romania, recalls that after liberation he fell ill for about six weeks. He was well enough to attend VE Day celebrations in Czernowitz, and it was there that the enormity of the disaster struck him: 'The devastation caused by the war and the fact that I was an orphan came home to me very forcefully on Victory Day . . . To this day, Victory Day over Nazi Germany, instead of arousing all that triumph . . . it was then, as a boy, that I grasped the full scale of the destruction . . . and really, Victory Day is engraved in my memory to this day as a day of . . . not as a day of celebration!'[15]

By 1946, and despite these obstacles, many of the survivors had managed to make their way into Romania by posing as being from the Regat. They were joined by thousands of Jewish refugees from elsewhere in Central and Eastern Europe, who headed for Romania in the belief that it would be easier to reach Palestine or other countries from there. Their situation in postwar Romania was, however, desperate, with widespread anti-Semitism compounded by the communist authorities' unwillingness to assist them and the famine of winter 1946–47. As late as summer 1947, a Hashomer Hatza'ir representative could say of the Jews of Iași that:

Visiting these soup kitchens and the poor Jewish neighbourhoods in Iasi can traumatize even a person who has already seen penury and hardship and was prepared for horrible sights. Anyone who saw these living dead, the exhausted old men and women, and people aged 40-something with dimmed eyes, the pale children, with swollen bellies and covered with boils, who walk around almost naked even in the autumn chill, the 'houses' in which these unfortunates live in unimaginable overcrowding – would never be able to forget what he saw.[16]

What happened in Transnistria during and at the end of the Holocaust was unique and is a potent example of how 'liberation' could happen far away from any camp.

The first of the Nazi camps to be discovered by the Red Army was Majdanek (also known as KL Lublin) in July 1944. Majdanek had played a vital role in the Nazis' camp system and took on a high profile in the Soviets' liberation narrative. A large concentration camp, it was situated in the area of central Poland known as the General Government which was occupied but not annexed to the Reich. Thanks to its location in the area under the control of the brutal SS-Brigadeführer Odilo Globocnik, SS and Police Leader for Lublin, Majdanek also became the headquarters of Operation Reinhard, the programme to exterminate the Jews of Poland in the camps of Bełżec, Sobibór and Treblinka, coordinated by Globocnik. Majdanek saw the murder of over 80,000 Jews (40,000 Jews over just two days at the start of November 1943 – a killing spree referred to as 'Operation Harvest Festival'). It was also the base for Globocnik's pet slave-labour project, *Ostindustrie*, which helped to build the SS's economic empire, and was the central store for the belongings of those killed at the Reinhard camps. At the end of the war, vast barracks full of shoes, glasses, suitcases and other belongings were discovered there, and on liberation it provided a wealth of powerful imagery. Indeed, for the British journalist Alexander Werth who had been travelling with the Red Army, the 'Chopin Warehouse' (named after the street on which it stood) in which the belongings of the murdered were stored and sorted, was 'perhaps the most horrifying thing of all':

> The Chopin Warehouse was like a vast, five-storey department store, part of the grandiose Maidanek Murder Factory. Here the possessions of hundreds of thousands of murdered people were sorted and classified and packed for export to Germany. In one big room there were thousands of trunks and suitcases, some still with carefully written-out labels; there was a room marked *Herrenschuhe* and another marked *Damenschuhe*; here were thousands of pairs of shoes, all of much better quality than those seen in the big dump near the camp. Then there was a long corridor with thousands of women's dresses, and another with thousands of overcoats.[17]

Together, the camps in the Lublin region (primarily Majdanek and the Reinhard camps) were responsible for the murder of more of the Nazis' Jewish victims than Auschwitz.[18]

In March 1944, with the Soviets fast approaching, the order had been given to evacuate the camp. From the start of April, Majdanek's inmates began to be transferred to Belsen, Natzweiler, Gross-Rosen, Ravensbrück and Auschwitz. Some 12,000 inmates were transferred, leaving behind, in the words of the communist-period guidebook to the camp, 1,500 'cripples and Soviet POWs' and 180 political prisoners who had been used as prisoner-functionaries.[19] As the Soviets came closer, the order was given first to dismantle the camp barracks and then to destroy evidence of crimes, such as the gas chamber and documents – orders that could not be fully carried out for lack of time. By the time the 8th Guards Army, led by General Chuikov, arrived on 22 July, only 500–1,000 inmates were left in Majdanek. The description of the liberation by a Polish inmate, Klemens Drzewiecki, contrasts markedly with any notion one might have of a climactic moment:

Only in the evening [of 22 July], after we had made sure that no one was guarding us, did we begin to prepare for departure. As it was night, we postponed leaving the camp until the morning, i.e. until Sunday, 23 July 1944. Only then did we leave the camp. We decided to go to the town. The camp was left behind us, but fear made us stay in Lublin cellars until Monday. I remember that when we were leaving the camp there were about a thousand of us. In this way, thanks to the rapid advance of the Red Army, we were freed from the death camp and inferno of Majdanek.[20]

The Russians and others who witnessed the camp were shocked not only by the emaciated state of the few survivors remaining there, but by the scale of the site itself. Alexander Werth was most struck by 'the vast monumental, "industrial" quality of that unbelievable Death Factory two miles from Lublin'.[21]

Konstantin Simonov's 'The Extermination Camp', a piece on Madjanek published in the Red Army newspaper *Kraznaia zvezda* (Red Star) on 10, 11 and 12 August and broadcast on the radio, had a 'devastating' effect in the Soviet Union – much as the research for it had had on Simonov himself. He begins by stating that, despite not being in possession of all the facts, 'I cannot remain silent, I cannot wait. I want to speak at once, today, about the first traces of this crime that have been revealed, about what I have heard during the past few days, and about what I have seen with my own eyes.'[22]

In fact he had been able to establish a considerable amount of reliable information, including Majdanek's use as both concentration camp and death camp: 'This was a veritable slaughter house, the daily number of deaths in which was regulated by two circumstances: first – the number of arrivals in the camp, and secondly, the number of labourers required at the different stages of the indefinitely continuing building operations.'[23] Simonov's article was published in French and English before the end of the war, but was regarded suspiciously in the West and soon fell into obscurity in the Soviet Union too, thanks to the Soviets' tendency to downplay Jewish suffering in favour of working-class anti-fascism. (Although Simonov does not highlight the fact that most of Majdanek's victims were Jews, an attentive reader can work it out.) But the piece is important not only for being the first such account of a camp after liberation, but also for establishing literary norms and imagery that would be used in future depictions of the camps: the gas chambers, the barbed wire, and the mountains of belongings.[24] Indeed, the huge quantities of clothing to be found in the Majdanek stores was Simonov's best evidence for the scale of the murder carried out there, and he employs it as part of the justification for punishment: 'I don't know which of them burnt the bodies, or which of them simply did the killing, which of them tore the footwear from the feet of their victims, or sorted the women's underclothing and the children's frocks. But as I gaze at this vast clothing store I think to myself that a nation which gave birth to those who did this must, and will, bear responsibility for what its representatives have done.'[25]

Another article, by Boris Gorbatov in *Pravda*, was equally powerful. Again the focus is not on the fact that more Jews were killed at Majdanek than any other group, but Gorbatov did offer details of the gas chambers, torture and the piles of clothes, and claimed that Hitler's aim had been to 'exterminate everything humane in occupied Europe'.[26] Alexander Werth also described his amazement at seeing the gas chambers, the mounds of ash at the other end of the camp, the crematorium and the trenches full of corpses, apparently Soviet POWs, by which point he had 'seen enough, and hastened to join Colonel Grosz, who was waiting beside the car on the road. The stench was still pursuing me; it now seemed to permeate everything – the dusty grass beside the barbed wire fence, and the red poppies that were naively growing in the midst of all this.'[27]

Such articles deepened the sense of horror and anger that Red Army soldiers felt upon seeing and reading about Majdanek, and confirmed Soviet propaganda about Nazi bestiality. One soldier responded to a discussion of the Extraordinary State Commission for the Ascertainment and Investigation of Crimes Committed by the German-Fascist Invaders and Their Accomplices with this outburst: 'While hearing the results of the German atrocities investigation in Majdanek, my heart burns with hatred. The Germans took my father, mother, and wife with two children, and they might have been killed in Majdanek. The hour of taking revenge on the German beasts has struck. I swear that I will fight the Nazis mercilessly until I pour out all of my hatred on to the Germans.'[28] Following organised tours of the camp by survivors, the soldiers were even more enraged. One said that 'During the German occupation, I witnessed their crimes, but such horrifying atrocities as I saw with my own eyes at Majdanek I had yet to see. I am a young soldier, and participated in different battles two times only, fought the Nazis ruthlessly, but now I will beat them even more for the honest people's deaths killed at Majdanek.' The officers responded similarly; S. Gryzlov said that his tour of Majdanek 'made a lasting effect on me. Here, the Nazis burned thousands of people like fire logs. The Germans committed atrocities unprecedented in history. When I arrive in my subdivision, I will tell my warriors and we will fight the Nazis with even more hatred.'[29]

As well as being the first camp to be liberated, Majdanek was also the first liberated camp to be filmed. The Red Army was accompanied by two teams of filmmakers recording what the soldiers came across for the purposes of creating future war-related propaganda. Like Simonov's article on Majdanek, the 1944 film *Vernichtungslager Majdanek* (Majdanek Extermination Camp), which also dealt with the work of the Polish-Soviet Extraordinary Commission in documenting Nazi atrocities, is significant in establishing an iconography for the representation of the camps: the gas chambers, barbed wire and mounds of shoes. Its approach was copied in numerous later films, such as the Auschwitz liberation film, the 're-education' film *Todesmühlen* (Mills of Death) and Alain Resnais's *Night and Fog* (1956). But *Vernichtungslager* also established certain norms, especially in the Soviet and Polish contexts, which constitute misrepresentations of the Holocaust. In particular, Jews are mentioned only in passing, with viewers being afforded no sense of the Nazis' specific targeting of Jews at Majdanek or generally during the war.

Instead the emphasis is on the suffering of non-Jewish Poles, with specific mention of the Polish officers killed at Katyn – an especially cynical strategy given that the Soviets and not the Germans were responsible for their deaths. With its stress on Polish suffering, the film places the victims in a Catholic context, with attention paid to Christian symbols and Christian burials. Again, not only does this obscure the fact that most of the Nazis' victims in Majdanek were Jewish, but the Christian imagery was also a transparent attempt by the communist war propagandists to win Polish support. The film itself was not widely seen, however, its influence being felt only indirectly insofar as its approach was adopted by later liberation films and some of the first postwar feature films about Nazism and its crimes, such as Wolfgang Staudte's *Die Mörder sind unter uns* (The Murderers Are Among Us, 1946).[30]

One unusual testimony concerning the liberation of Majdanek comes from Bernhard (Ben) Storch, a Jewish Pole who fought in one of the Polish units attached to the Red Army in order to support his family who were in exile in Siberia, having fled Poland at the start of the war. Storch's division was among those that discovered Sobibór and liberated Majdanek. Later, as an American citizen, Storch recalls discovering Majdanek and being unable at first to understand what it was – the gas chambers were marked 'Bath Disinfection – For Sanitary Reasons' – and he and his colleagues entered innocently into them. Only after walking deeper into the camp and coming across the crematoria and the remains of human bodies, Storch says, did he begin to comprehend what had taken place at Majdanek: 'It was terrible. You had the ovens, you had the bones, and you go over to the side and you have this huge mountain of ash, [but] you don't think that it is ash.' After about 45 minutes in Majdanek Storch's division was moved on to Warsaw and then towards Berlin. On 22 April his unit was involved in the liberation of Sachsenhausen, the first time Storch had freed living human beings. Demobbed in September 1945, Storch and his new wife Ruth realised that there was no future for Jews in postwar Poland. They found themselves in a Munich DP camp until April 1947 when they were able to immigrate to the US. Storch is one of the very few American citizens who was a Jewish member of a Polish unit attached to the Soviet forces involved in the liberation of the eastern camps.[31]

* * *

Majdanek may have seemed like an aberration upon its discovery in July 1944. But in 1945, beginning with Auschwitz, the worst rumours and reports about the Nazi camps would all be confirmed. Auschwitz has become famous as the 'capital of the Holocaust'. It was the zenith of the Nazis' killing operations, with the most technologically sophisticated gas chambers – a fact that should not blind us to the visceral brutality of what went on there, or confuse us into thinking that the process was 'smooth' or free from violence – and the place that saw the largest variety of deportees. The Jews of eastern Poland were mostly shot in pits outside their towns; those from the General Government, if they had not died in the ghettos, were killed in the Reinhard camps, Chełmno or Majdanek. Only a minority of the Polish Jews were killed at Auschwitz. But the Jews from the rest of Europe (again, apart from those killed *in situ* such as in Serbia or Transnistria) were for the most part sent to Auschwitz. Many tens of thousands also passed through Auschwitz, sometimes only for a matter of days, en route to slave labour camps or other camps, and so the number of witnesses to the site is large. Had the war gone on for longer, the Nazis planned to expand Auschwitz even further, as can be seen in plans and on the ground at Birkenau, with the projected new site of 'Mexico' already underway in 1944. Auschwitz was thus already vast, and meant to get larger; as well as still being largely intact at the end of the war, the number of people who had seen it or one of its three main camps (Auschwitz I, the main camp; Auschwitz II Birkenau, the death camp; and Auschwitz III, Buna-Monowitz, the slave labour plant) was substantial.

Many survivor testimonies mention Auschwitz, whether as a place through which they transited, somewhere they stayed for a time, or where they worked on a slave labour detail at the mercy of the control and arbitrary cruelty of the guards and kapos, fearing the regular selections for the gas chambers. Yet only a very small number were there at the camp's liberation on 27 January 1945, for by the time the Red Army approached the SS had forced the inmates who could still walk to leave on death marches. Some 65,000, mostly but not all Jews, were evacuated and forced westwards.

So what we know as the 'liberation' of Auschwitz was a scene quite different from the mental image we have of huge crowds converging on the Allies' jeeps, as at Buchenwald, Dachau, Belsen and Mauthausen. In the vast complex of Auschwitz (including all three main camps), 7,000 sick people were not easy to find. A further 500 or so were left behind in smaller sub-camps such as Blechhammer, Janinagrube and Neu-Dachs. One of them, Anna Chomicz, offered this account, which reads like a stock communist-approved version of events:

> We heard the detonation of a grenade near the entrance to the camp. We quickly looked out and we saw some Soviet scouts who were advancing towards us, their rifles ready to fire. In an instant we attached onto poles sheets of red fabric fragments in the shape of a cross. On seeing us the scouts lowered their arms and a warm and spontaneous welcome took place. Since I know Russian I said to one of the scouts, 'Welcome to you, victors and liberators!' In response we heard: 'You are free at last!'[32]

A ten-year-old child at the liberation, Eva Mozes Kor describes a more spontaneous and emotional reaction:

> We ran up to them and they gave us hugs, cookies and chocolate. Being so alone a hug meant more than anybody could imagine because that replaced the human worth we were starving for. We were not only starved for food but we were starved for human kindness. And the Soviet Army did provide some of that.[33]

It was only later, after she asked someone where she ought to go, that Kor realised liberation in itself did not mean that what followed would be straight-forward: 'I didn't even know where on earth I was, much less where my home was. You had to be a little smarter than I, a ten-year-old girl in a concentration camp, to know what direction to start out in and where to go.'[34]

Gerhard Durlacher, who later became a sociology professor at the University of Amsterdam, describes in his memoir how his liberation barely interrupted his fever:

> Through a veil of tears I see the round faces of soldiers peer around the corner like bashful boys. Events now tumble over one another, like a speeded-up film. The drone of army trucks replaces the clatter of horse-shoes. German men and women wrap us like infants in gray blankets

and lay us down with anxious care in the trucks, with horses snorting in the background. Young Russian soldiers with the friendly and aston-ished eyes of children look on, their rifles against their chests, calling to one another, occasionally helping. Submissively, like a small child, I let things happen and fall asleep in the truck, holding the bread I had been given like a teddy bear in my arms.

Durlacher could hardly have done otherwise – he was too ill to stand. It took several days before he started to 'discover the world around me' and weeks of recovery before he could travel, via Prague and Paris, back to Apeldoorn, where he reports that he received a frosty reception. No one wanted to hear of Durlacher's experiences, for they 'would spoil the glow of liberation and expose the self-deceit of many'. The new inhabitants of his parents' house would not allow him in and when he did find some relatives and friends, they subjected him to tales of 'the hardships of the occupation which made me choke back the unspeakable'.[35]

Of the inmates who were in Auschwitz's hospital at the moment of liber-ation, none came to be more celebrated than Primo Levi. It is impossible to do justice to the complexity of ideas and simplicity of prose with which Levi describes his liberation (as with everything he writes about). It is thus worth citing a long passage, which follows the arrival of four Soviet horsemen riding along the road outside the barbed-wire perimeter of the camp:

> They did not greet us, nor did they smile; they seemed oppressed not only by compassion but by a confused restraint, which sealed their lips and bound their eyes to the funereal scene. It was that shame we knew so well, the shame that drowned us after the selections, and every time we had to watch, or submit to, some outrage: the shame the Germans did not know, that the just man experiences at another man's crime; the feeling of guilt that such a crime should exist, that it should have been introduced irrevocably into the world of things that exist, and that his will for good should have proved too weak or null, and should not have availed in defence.

More than any other author of a Holocaust testimony, Levi captures the swirling, mixed emotions to which liberation gave rise:

So for us even the hour of liberty rang out grave and muffled, and filled our souls with joy and yet with a painful sense of pudency, so that we should have liked to wash our consciences and our memories clean from the foulness that lay upon them; and also with anguish, because we felt that this should never happen, that now nothing could ever happen good and pure enough to rub out our past, and that the scars of the outrage would remain within us for ever, and in the memories of those who saw it, and in the places where it occurred and in the stories that we should tell of it.

This confusion, this simultaneous 'attack of mortal fatigue' that accompanied 'the joy of liberation' accounts for 'why few among us ran to greet our saviours, few fell in prayer'.[36]

*   *   *

From the other side of the fence, it is harder to know what the Red Army soldiers who overran Auschwitz thought as they were not encouraged to speak openly about their experiences. We know that 231 soldiers were killed in the fighting to take over the three main camps of Auschwitz, Birkenau and Monowitz, including two who died in front of the gates of Auschwitz I.[37] What the liberators felt upon entering the camp is more difficult to glean. Certainly the Red Army's attitudes were coloured by the instructions and slogans put out by the Sovinformbiuro which encouraged them to hate the enemy: 'It is impossible to defeat an enemy without learning how to hate him with all the soul's powers'; 'We will not forget, we will not forgive'.[38] Such official slogans had a long-lasting effect, as did the re-imposition of control over what soldiers and journalists could say after the war. At a 1981 conference – during a moment of rising Cold War tensions – Soviet General Vassily Petrenko gave little sense of his own reaction to the camp beyond saying that it 'was not very pleasant'. Instead he offered a standard list of the gruesome activities carried out by the Nazis at Auschwitz which gave away nothing of his own emotions or thoughts at the time.

When the 60th Army of the 1st Ukrainian Front liberated Auschwitz they had already passed corpses on all the roads around – bodies of those who had fallen and been shot on the evacuation marches. They discovered a further 600 dead among the few living survivors left behind inside the camp, as well as vast quantities of human remains and possessions. Alongside suitcases, spectacles, spoons, bowls, toys, some 837,000 women's coats and dresses, 370,000 men's suits, 44,000 pairs of shoes and other belongings, the Soviet troops found piles of prosthetic limbs and 305 sacks of human hair weighing a total of 7.7 tons – estimated to be the hair from about 140,000 victims.[39] The Nazis had destroyed much but had not had time to get rid of everything. As one of the few historians to have investigated how soldiers responded to the liberation of the Nazi camps has justly written, 'neither the Sovinformbiuro nor the army's political departments could invent a better piece of propaganda than what the Nazis had left behind in Poland – the extermination camps'.[40]

To the extent that we can access the Red Army's views, it is through memoirs and letters. Vasily Gromadsky, an officer of the 60th Army, offered this description:

> I realized that they were prisoners and not workers so I called out, 'You are free, come out!' ... They began rushing towards us, in a big crowd. They were weeping, embracing us, and kissing us. I felt a grievance on behalf of mankind that these fascists had made such a mockery of us. It roused me and all the soldiers to go and quickly destroy them and send them to hell.[41]

Georgii Elisavetskii, another of the first Soviet soldiers to enter the camp, admitted in 1980 that 'My blood runs cold when I mention Auschwitz even now.' He described the liberation in dramatic detail:

> When I entered the barrack, I saw living skeletons lying on the three tiered bunks. As in fog, I hear my soldiers saying: 'You are free, comrades!' I sense that they do not understand [us] and begin speaking to them in Russian, Polish, German, Ukrainian dialects; unbuttoning my leather jacket, I show them my medals ... Then I use Yiddish. Their reaction is unpredictable. They think that I am provoking them. They begin to hide. And only when I said to them: 'Do not be afraid, I am a colonel of Soviet Army and a Jew. We have come to liberate you' ... Finally, as if the barrier collapsed ... they rushed towards us shouting, fell on their knees, kissed the flaps of our overcoats, and threw their arms around our legs. And we could not move, stood motionless while unexpected tears ran down our cheeks.[42]

It was following the collapse of the Soviet Union that General Vassily Petrenko himself wrote about Auschwitz in terms that seem far less constrained by ideological concerns:

> I who saw people dying every day was shocked by the Nazis' indescribable hatred toward the inmates who had turned into living skeletons. I read about the Nazis' treatment of Jews in various leaflets, but there was nothing about the Nazis' treatment of women, children, and old men. It was at Auschwitz that I found out about the fate of the Jews.[43]

At the time, however, Soviet reports, including a key article by Boris Polevoi in *Pravda* on 2 February 1945, failed to mention Jews, as did the reports on the work of the official investigation of May 1945.[44] Besides, the liberation of the camp was not a key strategic aim of the Red Army, which was simply attempting to advance westwards as swiftly as possible and whose liberation of Auschwitz was 'an incidental by-product of the Russian winter offensive'.[45] At the same time as Auschwitz was being liberated, some 1.2 million Soviet soldiers were breaking through the German blockade east of Leningrad and on the evening of the 27th there was a 324-gun salute on the River Neva.[46] Yet the Red Army cared for survivors all the same, and if ordinary soldiers echoed the vocabulary of the official propaganda in their letters home they were no less heartfelt for that. One such is a letter written by twenty-six-year-old Pyotr Nikitin to his parents in which he tried to describe what he had witnessed at Auschwitz:

> My dear ones, I have no words to relate to you what we had seen on our difficult soldiers' path. How to settle accounts with these bloody, damned fascist-degenerates for all their evil deeds? There is no punishment horrible enough, and no one could ever come up with an appropriate retribution. Please know, my dear parents, that we will take revenge on the enemy for everything. We will forget nothing, and we will never forgive.[47]

*   *   *

The Soviets, assisted by the Polish Red Cross and local inhabitants, immediately set about organising aid and food for the Auschwitz survivors, as well as documenting the camp. Red Army field hospitals and a Red Cross hospital were established and between them they cared for more than 4,500 patients, mostly Jews but also a large number of Polish Gentiles, including a group of 160–170 women deported to the camp from Warsaw during the 1944 uprising. They were suffering from many maladies, but especially tuberculosis. Most of those left behind were older prisoners (aged forty-five and over) and children under the age of fifteen. The medical relief work was hard, hampered by the lack of supplies and the filthy conditions in the barracks, though it improved as survivors were gradually transferred to brick barracks in Auschwitz I.[48] The survivors were terrified of showers, associating the name 'Sauna' (the camp term for the shower block where registered inmates were shaven and disinfected before entering the camp) with selections prior to gassing; they feared injections, which had been used by the SS to kill with phenol; and they frequently 'stole' bread which the nurses would then discover under their mattresses. One Polish Red Cross nurse, Maria Rogoż, described her first nightshift in February 1945:

Eleven women died during the first night duty. I had to personally remove their bodies from the bunks and haul them out to the corridor. The stretcher-bearers took them away early the following morning. Throughout the night women from every corner of the ward would call out to me 'Schwester! Schieber!' (Sister, the bedpan). They were suffering from Durchfall – a kind of dysentery. So I was constantly carrying bedpans to and from the patients. There was no one else to help me.[49]

Only in April and May did the medical situation become more regular, and by then many of the survivors had already returned home. But it would be a long road to recovery, as Tadeusz Chowaniec, a Polish doctor who arrived in the camp three days after liberation, noted, with just a hint of exasperation:

In a brick barracks we found several female prisoners, two or more to a bunk. Was it really the third day after the liberation? Had time stopped for these women – had nothing changed for them? Only the wild shooting of the SS men could no longer be heard, and the dogs did not yelp anymore, but the women still wore their striped garb. They had difficulty moving; it seemed as though every movement was carefully thought out and assessed. Their expressionless, mostly cold eyes aroused shame in us. Had they used up all their joy and enthusiasm on the first day, when all the prisoners rushed into the arms of the Soviet soldiers? They had the same bunks, but now they were free and knew that food was no longer a problem. I was sure that their apathy would fade and they would enjoy their freedom when their aching bones, slack muscles, and emaciated bodies had returned to their normal condition, when they had really and truly been restored to life.[50]

As late as June 1945 there were still, according to the author of a report for the Jewish Relief Unit in London, 300 Jews too weak to leave Auschwitz. But it was reported that 'the Russians are caring for them well, providing white bread, wurst and sugar.'[51]

The best-known action performed by the Soviet liberators was to produce what is today the most famous film of the camps' liberations. Cameraman Aleksandr Vorontsov recalls that he filmed Auschwitz at about 3pm on the day of the liberation and then again a few days later, when the film crew asked some of the surviving women to return to their barracks so that their living conditions could be recreated. But once the camp had been cleaned up and the survivors restored to health, Auschwitz disappeared from the Soviet press and official reports and the genocide of the Jews became a subject best avoided.[52] For the survivors, the future was open but not necessarily something to look forward to. One relief worker told Auschwitz survivor and doctor Lucie Adelsberger how distraught so many surviving Polish Jewish women were at being the sole members of their families still to be alive. 'It would have been better', she said, 'had they not survived'. Adelsberger adds that she was 'not entirely wrong, at least as far as outlook and the joy of being alive are concerned', though it is quite clear that most survivors would not have preferred to be dead.[53] Given what we know about Auschwitz, which now does duty as the world's shorthand for evil, the sad reality of the survivors' post-liberation prognosis should hardly surprise us, though it injects a degree of sobriety into what we still like to think of as the 'happier', postwar half of the twentieth century.

*   *   *

Until mid-1944 the inmates of Stutthof camp, on the Baltic Sea near Danzig, were mostly Poles and Russians. After some 49,000 Jews were sent there, the composition and nature of the camp changed radically. Women inmates were now clearly in the majority, and they also made up the majority of those killed.

Of the 49,000 Jews who arrived in mid-1944 some 11,000 were transferred elsewhere, but nearly 27,000 died in the camp or during the process of evacuation in 1945.[54] What the Germans called 'evacuation marches' were chaotic; one survivor, Gertrude Schneider, recounts how with her mother and sister she was sent from Stutthof to a sub-camp at Sophienwalde, and thence on a march west. Resting in a barn full of dead and dying horses and other forced marchers near the small town of Chinov, the Russians suddenly appeared and shot the SS guards. 'For us', writes Schneider, 'freedom had come, with all its glories, with all its disappointments and the pain of finding out the extent of the Jewish people's destruction, with all its responsibilities, and with all of life's uncertainties.'[55] In the camp itself, conditions were appalling, as in this description of December 1944:

A typhoid epidemic spread among us. The girls fell ill and lay in their filth, no longer able to get up. We relieved ourselves in the bowls from which we ate, and we threw the excrement out of the window. When a hand trembled and the girl did not have the strength to turn the bowl outside, the excrement spilled onto the heads of others. First Gutka fell ill. After her, Lonia, Lolka, Marilka, Bella, and Leah. The disease spared no one. The girls lay shivering on the floor, their eyes glistening with fever. I stood over them helplessly, only able to get a little water. I moved from one to the other, moistening their lips. I was the last to get sick.[56]

The Jewish camp was burned down by the Nazis in March 1945, just days before most of Stutthof's remaining inmates were deported by boat across the Baltic Sea, in what would prove just as catastrophic a manoeuvre as the death marches. The inmates did not know where they were going. They drank sea water, and were thrown overboard. Large numbers were murdered.[57] When Stutthof was liberated by the 48th Army of the 3rd Belorussian Front on 9 May 1945, no more than 2,000 of the camp's original inmates were there.

Shortly before the Soviets discovered Stutthof, a huge forced march cleared out most of the inmates of Sachsenhausen outside Berlin. Of 50,000 or so prisoners in Sachsenhausen (a camp intended to hold 10,000), most of whom were recent arrivals from camps further east, over 30,000 were marched north-west. Some 16,000 ended up in the Below Forest near Wittstock, where they were forced to camp in the open for six nights (23–29 April) before the Red Cross was permitted to distribute food.[58] Those who were not shot or did not die en route were 'liberated' on the road in the area around Schwerin after noticing that the SS had deserted them. Those who were 'liberated' on the marches often found the process disorienting, since they only discovered they were free upon realising that their guards had disappeared; contact with Allied soldiers usually came somewhat later.[59] In any case, the first liberating soldiers were unable to stay for long. For the newly-freed Sachsenhausen survivors, the military situation – the final stage of the capture of Berlin – was too pressing. Thus they were forced to stay put and make the best of the situation; they shared a common fate, in that although they had been freed from SS terror, they had not yet truly received their freedom.[60]

The 3,000 or so inmates left in Sachsenhausen found that although they were free of the SS, the camp hierarchy system – with political prisoners at the top, criminals and 'asocial elements' in the middle, and homosexuals, Roma and Jews at the bottom – remained in force until the Red Army took full control of the camp after the capture of Berlin on 2 May.[61] Earlier in the camp's life the criminals had ruled; with the 'politicals' now in charge, crucially the Jews and other 'weak elements' faced a less uncertain fate.[62] Most camp inmates did not see their liberators until a day after the first Soviet and Polish soldiers appeared on 22 April, since they were too weak to move. Günther Lues, who stayed behind to care for the sick and evaded the death march, wrote in January 1946 to a friend who had been transported: 'It happened quickly and painlessly . . . Exactly 20 hours after your march out, more precisely 17 hours after the disappearance of the last SS troops and the prisoners being dragged along by them, we who had remained behind in uncertainty were free.' He went on to describe how he had helped to clean up the sick and then fallen into a deep sleep – 'No wonder, after all the confusion and being swamped with work', he added. 'On awaking the next morning you first had to get used to the fact no roll-call bell would sound, that you didn't need to worry about an inspection by either the "Blockobi" [block elder] or the SS. It truly seemed a miracle that the whole camp business to which we'd become accustomed over years was suddenly over.'[63]

The Red Army soldiers and the Polish medics who accompanied them were as shocked by the condition of the inmates here as at the other camps: 'They look terrifying. Pale, anaemic, with see-through faces, emaciated to the bones, with thin arms and legs and hands, only skeletons. Hundreds lie on their bunks and do not even have the strength to raise their heads.'[64] Michal Chilczuk, a member of the communist Polish People's Army (*Armia Ludowa*), speaking directly to survivors at a later conference, said: 'You, sir, saw soldiers with nice uniforms, in good physical health. But what I saw were people I call humans, but it was difficult to tell they were humans.'[65]

Still, with Soviet support, the remaining former inmates were able to commandeer food from the population of nearby Oranienburg and to begin the process of 're-educating' the Germans. 'It has come to light', reads one report of the days after the liberation from the 1970s (and the GDR context should be borne in mind), 'that despite the proximity of the camp they knew little of the terrible occurrences, of the liquidation of 18,000 Soviet Prisoners of War in autumn 1941 by a shot to the neck, of the liquidations of tens of thousands over the years up to the great liquidations of thousands of TB cases, Jews, "high traitors", Soviet Prisoners of War and others by gas in early 1945. They knew nothing of the liquidation of 4 million Jews in Auschwitz. Therefore it is reasonable and important to open the population's eyes.'[66]

*   *   *

Ravensbrück, the SS's concentration camp for women, was liberated on 29–30 April 1945. Although many women had passed through the camp, by the time of its liberation it was more or less empty, as was its sub-camp Malchow. Many of its inmates were liberated whilst on death marches, or after arriving at Belsen or Theresienstadt, or were rescued by the Swedish Red Cross in a scheme led by Count Folke Bernadotte who negotiated with the SS for the release of approximately 7,500 Ravensbrück inmates, about 1,000 of whom were Jewish. In other words, most did not experience 'liberation' in the sense of being in a camp when the Red Army arrived, but rather through events triggered by their anticipated arrival. We need, therefore, to redefine 'liberation', in this case as something that could happen before the official German surrender of the camp. One survivor, Rebecca C., explains her rescue from Ravensbrück at the end of the war by the Red Cross as if it were a dream:

We stood at the *Appell* [roll call] and they announced that tomorrow we have to be ready to . . . to be liberated. In the meantime they put us into a room, a big room, for fifty people; they pushed in 125 people . . . and then they opened the doors and they let us out. But how many had fit in . . . Don't ask. When we came out . . . believe me, just talking about it, I can't believe it myself! What I went through! And I went through and I survived! I can't believe it . . . So we came, I came out. Count Bernadotte stood by one of the buses . . . I wasn't able to lift myself up. I just stood. So he held out his hand to help me get on the bus. And when I was in the bus, I hope that it's over. And it was over.[67]

A similar account is given by one of Ravensbrück's many French inmates, Marthe Masson. After being showered and given clothes, she and some others who had been chosen were led to the Appellplatz:

A pair of women who are better informed tell us that the Red Cross is coming to pick us up. Something must really have been going on, for we go to the door and are handed a whole loaf of bread and a piece of sausage. We pass through the door without realizing that we are now free, since we can still hear the SS shouting. They are still standing there with their weapons. We carry on the same way until we are out of the camp. Then we walk along a large, straight road on which we finally see ten trucks with a large red cross covering them. Only at this point do we realize that this means freedom. Our hearts are heavy as we climb on to the trucks because we are leaving behind comrades who are very sick, many of whom will not make it home.[68]

Indeed, many women who were liberated on death marches from Ravensbrück immediately made their way back to the camp in order to try and help those who had been left behind.

Another survivor, Erna M., was deported from Auschwitz to Ravensbrück on a death march in January 1945, and from there to Malchow. At the end of April, she was sent from Malchow on another death march but, after two days on the road, the group discovered that the war had ended. Like Rebecca C. she was taken by surprise:

Suddenly the SS vanished . . . We just couldn't believe it; we stood there and we were free. Then, of course we hid in the forest until the soldiers said, 'Come out, you are free, the war is over.' But we could not believe it. If someone tells me today they did believe it, well I guess that's their nature! But I was not able to comprehend it. Because if you are imprisoned for such a long time – three and half years – and suddenly someone tells you, you are free as a bird, that is . . . and most of all, the gassing that I saw in Auschwitz. What were the chances that I would survive it all, I got through selection three times![69]

Likewise, Micheline Maurel, author of a prize-winning 1950s memoir of Ravensbrück, recounted the story of the end of the war in a way that almost eludes the idea of 'liberation' altogether. After being marched out of the camp at war's end, the forced marchers were suddenly abandoned; their overseers panicked after the group was passed by retreating German soldiers. Maurel and three comrades slept in a field for a night. After two nights in a barn, the four women entered a house in the village of Waren, where they found food. They were interrupted by a *Feldgendarme* and four soldiers who lined them up against the wall to shoot them. Just then a shout from outside about the Russians changed the soldiers' minds and they ran. Finding a barn to sleep in, the women were disturbed this time by gunfire, which continued until they could hear the sound of Russian voices and they knew they were safe. 'And so the first hours of my freedom were spent sleeping – the best and the deepest sleep I have ever enjoyed.'[70] By the next morning, though, one of her friends had already been raped by a Russian soldier and the two of them were too ill to go anywhere. Reports of rape were not uncommon, though camp survivors suffered less in this regard than German women civilians. The Red Army soldiers 'raped any female they came across – even old women were not spared, one of our comrades told us', wrote Erika Amariglio, a Greek survivor of Auschwitz and Malchow. After the initial wave of fury and violence in the first twenty-four hours, though, the regular occupation army arrived, which Amariglio described as 'trying to impose some order on this chaos, to feed the hungry people, to arrange shelter for them'.[71] Still, camp survivors' experience of rape was no doubt one of the reasons that the liberated inmates preferred not to remain under Soviet jurisdiction any longer than they had to.

The experience of being suddenly abandoned seems to have left the survivors in limbo, terrified of doing anything for fear of attracting attention to themselves and, in any case, hardly knowing which way to turn: 'They just left us standing and vanished', says one survivor of Ravensbrück of her 'liberation' on the way to Theresienstadt from Malchow.[72] Amid the confusion, survivors faced the basic problem of immediate isolation and loneliness and, at least at first, an inability to translate their freedom into happiness. For the Jewish survivors, whose families and whole communities had been destroyed, this loneliness was especially acute:

> I took liberation for granted. I expected it, I didn't celebrate. There were dances, there was a dance going on, I remember one night. The Russians, Russian women prisoners and the Polish women prisoners and whoever was there – there was a castle and you had to go up the hill to get to it. And they were dancing. And we couldn't dance. We knew what had happened and we knew that there was no home to go back to. And to us it was, yes, we were free, we were alive, but there was no way to throw us into a celebration of any kind.[73]

Unlike most non-Jewish survivors, such as forced labourers, the Jewish survivors had nowhere to go and little hope of finding anyone left alive in their former homes. Hence after recuperating under Soviet medical care, which at Ravensbrück lasted until June, many made their way to the DP camps in the western zones of occupied Germany. Micheline Maurel knew that 'liberation' did not mean the end of the horror; her memoir ends with an 'invocation' that she wrote in 1948 on coming across a set of documents on the war:

> My poor, my dear companions, all alike, all wretched, you the survivors and you the dead, I know it well: the camps have not been liberated. Each survivor has brought his camp back with him; he tries to obliterate it; he tries to stifle in the barbed wire and under the straw mattresses all those despairing *schmustics* [*Musselmänner*, or inmates on the verge of death], but suddenly a date or a photograph brings back the entire camp around him. He would like to run away, shielding his eyes with his arm in order not to see, howling in order not to hear. But the entire camp

rises again slowly, for it has not been destroyed and nothing has made up for a single day of suffering.[74]

There were some 3,000 women, most of them very ill, still in Ravensbrück main camp when advance units of the 49th Army of the 2nd Belorussian Front, led by Captain Boris Makarov, arrived there on 30 April. The Soviets were especially intrigued by Ravensbrück once they learned that among the inmates was Rosa Thälmann, the wife of German communist leader Ernst Thälmann. One former soldier, Sergei Garbusik, recalls the women shouting 'Russians, Russians!' and hearing many different languages. The women carried the 'emaciated, ragged, and sick' among their comrades out of the barracks so that they could witness and take part in the liberation. 'It was painful', recalled Garbusik, 'to see these women and girls crying with joy.'[75] For many, however, as Marie-Claude Vaillant-Couturier wrote in her diary, the help came too late – women were still dying as the trucks came to take the last sick survivors away.[76]

Captain Makarov recalled seeing women who were 'skeletons covered with skin who at first could not believe that a Russian officer was really there.'[77] Guided around the camp by Antonina Nikiforova, a Russian prisoner doctor, Makarov had the unpleasant duty of telling Rosa Thälmann, who was in the same weakened condition as the other women, that her husband had been killed – something that he knew thanks to reports in the Soviet press.[78] Many of the survivors must have felt the same way as Alina Bacall-Zwirn, who was liberated in the sub-camp of Neustadt-Glewe. After breaking into a store and taking sugar, flour and cigarettes, she tried to contemplate what was happening: 'I went on top of the garbage dump, and I looked out, and I thought I'm going crazy. I couldn't talk, I couldn't smile, I couldn't do nothing.'[79]

*　*　*

Gross-Rosen was originally established as a sub-camp of Sachsenhausen in 1940 but a year later became an autonomous concentration camp. After the camp was expanded in summer 1944 it had over a hundred smaller sub-camps attached to it, including many attached to the SS's DEST (German Earth and Stone Works) enterprise. Others included a complex of twelve camps for men known as Riese, which was set aside for the building of Hitler's secret underground headquarters in the nearby Eulen mountains, an I.G. Farben factory at Dyhernfurth where poison gas was produced, and the former textile factory at Brünnlitz, where the Jews, including 1,100 who came from Płaszów, were protected by Oskar Schindler. By autumn 1944, Jews were the largest group of inmates, most of them coming from Poland and Hungary, but smaller numbers also from Belgium, France, Greece, Yugoslavia, Slovakia and Italy. They were deported to Gross-Rosen and its sub-camps, forty of which were only established in 1944, throughout the war years to work as slave labourers. With 78,000 inmates, a third of them women, Gross-Rosen held 11 per cent of the total concentration camp population in late 1944. As with most of the camps situated in Upper Silesia and occupied Poland, Gross-Rosen and its sub-camps were partly evacuated in early 1945, beginning with the sub-camps furthest to the east, on or just over the right bank of the Oder. About 44,000 were deported, almost half of them Jews (about 35 per cent of the total number of Jewish inmates), and sent on forced marches into the Reich. Despite orders to transport the sick and immobile in wagons, many were shot by the guards.[80] The inmates of the main camp were evacuated by train, in open goods wagons without food or adequate clothing, so many died on the journey. One deportee recalled shortly afterwards that 'the snow and rain poured down from heaven as if without mercy and we were not getting anymore any food at all. And every morning when we, so to speak, got up, when we opened our eyes with daybreak, we had to throw out of the car two, three people because they had died overnight.'[81] Another account presents a similar, though in crucial details different, picture:

> We prisoners [were] driven into the wagons like cattle for slaughter . . . In the harsh winter, we stood in the roofless wagons so tightly hemmed in that we could hardly move. Over the course of the journey from Gross-Rosen to Mauthausen, which lasted several days and nights, numerous prisoners died of exhaustion. Since the corpses were not taken out of the wagons during the journey, we were practically standing among the dead. I can still remember how during the night many prisoners jumped from the wagons in order to flee. The guards, who were equipped with spotlights, shot the escapees with machine pistols. You could hear non-stop shooting virtually throughout the night over the whole goods train.[82]

The deportees were sent to Bergen-Belsen, Dachau, Buchenwald, Flossenbürg, Mauthausen, Dora-Mittelbau and, in a few cases, to Neuengamme, Ravensbrück and Sachsenhausen. It is not clear what happened to the rest, although many were liberated by the Soviets between February and May, and some went on to create Jewish committees which helped to return inmates to their home countries and to represent Polish Jews in the immediate postwar period. One such was Tadeusz Cytron, a surgeon who had been interned in the Wüstergiersdorf sub-camp; he remained there after liberation to treat the sick and kept careful records of them. The inmates of thirty-five sub-camps, including Görlitz, whose inmates had been sent on an evacuation march and then marched back to the camp several weeks later because the proximity of the frontline prevented their further passage, were liberated by the Soviets on 8 or 9 May. These inmates – the very last to be liberated – were desperate to get out:

> Before dawn there's no one at the gate, no Germans. We see no one anywhere around. I told them, 'Don't go out, it's a provocation. You go out – they'll start shooting.' It was the morning of May 9. Suddenly, we heard banging on the gate. We saw the Russians' wagons. So we knew by then. They said, 'You're liberated.' First we ran away. Just to get away, first of all to get out of the camp. We were hungry. We had this hunger.[83]

We are told that in another camp, unaware of what was happening but conscious of a silence that suddenly descended, the inmates used wooden poles to break out of the fences and 'dozens, hundreds of people raced into the fields frantically', thinking that a trap had been set for them by the guards.[84]

* * *

Finally, on 9 May the Soviets liberated the ghetto-camp Theresienstadt (Terezín), a few days after the SS had handed it over to Paul Dunant, the representative of the International Red Cross. Czech health workers began the process of fighting the typhus epidemic and on 14 May the Soviets declared the camp a quarantine zone for two weeks. The nearly 30,000 inmates there knew that they were among the last to be freed. Yet in a sense they were fortunate to have remained in Theresienstadt; some 87,000 others had been deported to Riga, Maly Trostinec, Sobibór, Treblinka, Auschwitz and elsewhere and, of these, only 3,600 survived. Most famously, Theresienstadt deportees became the inmates of the so-called 'family camp', section BIIb of Auschwitz-Birkenau, in which the inmates were kept alive – to the bewilderment of the other Auschwitz inmates – from September 1943 to March 1944 so that a Red Cross delegation could, as it requested, visit a Jewish 'labour camp' to see how the Nazis were treating the Jews. Once the Red Cross had visited Theresienstadt and declared itself happy that the Jews there were being satisfactorily cared for – thanks to the Nazi programme of beautifying the camp and giving it the air of a self-regulating town in the weeks before the inspection – the Auschwitz 'family camp', created in the event of the Red Cross requesting a follow-up visit, was surplus to requirements. The 3,792 people who had been transported in September were gassed on 8 March 1944 – the single biggest mass murder of Czech civilians during the Second World War. With the liquidation of the family camp, some 3,500 men were sent off to work as slave labourers; the 6,500 men, women and children who still remained were gassed between 8 and 10 July.[85]

In Theresienstadt itself, conditions were worsening at the end of the war but, as a 'ghetto-camp' – an old walled fortress town in which the Jews were confined, rather than a purpose-built concentration camp – they did not reach the devastating levels found at Belsen or Mauthausen.[86] On 29 January, seventeen-year-old diarist Alisah Shek noted that a rumour had been going round that an open cattle truck carrying people from Auschwitz had passed through Bauschowitz, and that the camp had apparently been 'occupied' a week earlier. 'And today it's –13 degrees. That's enough, one doesn't need to say any more.' Shek's worry? 'Perhaps my father was there, perhaps he went past. Perhaps he knew. Perhaps ... Don't think about it.'[87] But at Theresienstadt they still had more than three more months to wait, and many more evacuees to see. On 20 April Shek recorded that 1,800 'people from the camps' arrived in twenty-five wagons: 'stinking, infested cattle wagons, inside stinking, infested people, half alive, half dead or corpses'. This was just the start: between 20 and 30 April there were 12,555 new registrations in Theresienstadt and the camp's population rose from 17,515 to 29,227.[88] On 8 May, VE Day, Shek witnessed the return of forced evacuation marches which had left the camp in December 1943 and May 1944, heading first to Auschwitz and then the Sachsenhausen sub-camp of Schwarzheide: '3 weeks on the road, arrived on foot. From 1,000, 250 left.' Hardly surprising that the night before, on hearing of the German surrender, Shek could only write: 'Surrender signed, no one rejoices. There is still a silence in me . . . I am tired, the world has made me tired, forever?'[89] Two days later the Russians arrived, but before that the inmates hardly knew what was happening:

> One thinks that nothing had happened. That all is as it had been. One ventures forward. Looking toward all sides one goes a few steps. And looks and is astonished and understands it not: nowhere can a German uniform be seen. No guards; no watchers . . . The Germans have fled. Unobserved. The Germans have gone! They have fled![90]

Or, as another survivor, Käthe Stark, put it, 'our prison guards left us without a stir, of which we were completely unaware'. Only a few days later when the Russians arrived did Stark feel that 'Now it's finally happened, we are liberated.'[91]

For those who had been transported to Theresienstadt from a succession of other camps, the fact of liberation was almost too much to bear. Nechama Epstein-Kozlowski, for example, a Polish-Jewish woman who had been in the Warsaw ghetto, Majdanek, Auschwitz, Belsen and a small camp in Aschersleben near Magdeburg, was forced to walk for two weeks to reach the 'ghetto-camp'. In her postwar interview with David Boder, Epstein-Kozlowski wanted to indicate her joy, not to mention amazement, at surviving, but her words led back in a more sombre direction. 'We heard the Russian tanks were here. And we didn't believe [it] ourselves', she begins. 'We went out, whoever was able. There were a lot of sick who couldn't go. We went out with great joy, with much crying. We had lived to see the moment of liberation. And that is how our grief had ended.' But her grief had not ended, or at least a different grief was now taking hold. Just a few sentences later, after discussing the post-liberation deaths of many survivors from overeating and typhus, Epstein-Kozlowski adds:

> Later on it was cleaned up. But I had also gone through the typhus. I didn't have anybody, all alone. All night I lay and cried, 'What will I do now? I have remained alone, without a home, without a father and without a mother. And now freedom. What did I survive for?' I was alive crying, but my fate had not been completely lost . . .

What she meant was that she was able to cling on to some hope and managed to get to Warsaw, where she joined Kibbutz Ichud and met her husband. Like many others, they smuggled themselves across borders into Italy, from where they were waiting for the chance to get to Palestine.[92]

Shmuel Krakowski was among 500 survivors of an original 4,000 who were sent to Theresienstadt on a death march from Rehmsdorf, a sub-camp of Buchenwald. Like many of his friends, Krakowski was 'in agony' and the Russians arrived just in time to save his life. Unlike many of his friends, Krakowski was strong enough to run out to greet the liberators, who saved his life by giving him some sugar. The joy of Krakowski's liberation was tempered not only by the fact that many of the weakest did not survive, but also by the stories that the Jewish soldiers of the Red Army told the survivors. One, from Vilna (Vilnius), who had fought in Stalingrad, informed them that on their advance westwards, 'To their great sorrow, in all the liberated places they found no Jews.' Theresienstadt was the first place they had liberated where they found substantial numbers of Jewish survivors. Krakowski notes how the mood darkened as they heard this news:

> Thus, we learned that our fate was much worse than we had expected. Although we had seen a lot and experienced the worst, we still had hoped, still had dreamed. All those days we had struggled to survive, hour after hour, day after day, there had been no time to grasp the enormity of our tragedy. Now everything became clear. No longer were our families waiting for us; no homes to go back to. For us, the victory had come too late, much too late.[93]

Gradually, those who could do so returned to their homes. For the German Jews, buses were sent from the various cities to collect them. Gerty Spies, originally from Munich, was one of the last to be collected. As she got on to the bus back to Munich, she was unsure how she felt: 'To leave Theresienstadt – my dream for three years, a dream of an eternity! How did it happen that a dream stopped being a dream? But in reality, we left ourselves behind, in an almost inconceivable hurry we distanced ourselves from the world into which fate had thrust us, a world to whose terrors and sufferings habit shackled us.'[94] As another survivor, Eva Roubíčková, who spent six weeks in the ghetto hospital recovering from typhoid, writes in the afterword to her diary:

Leaving Theresienstadt meant freedom for the first time in four years. I should have been elated. I was not. I was deeply unhappy, emotionally numb. Life seemed to have lost its meaning. I could not understand why I had survived. At first I hoped to find someone else from my family, but after meeting people coming from Poland and learning for the first time of the gas chambers and extermination camps, I realized I was alone and would never see my family again.[95]

But Roubíčková was lucky: she was reunited with her former boyfriend, who had been in England with the Czech army, and they married in August 1945. At the moment of liberation, however, she like many others faced an uncertain future.

*   *   *

Uncertainty was the norm for all survivors, for those liberated in a camp as well as those who were informed of their freedom on the open road or, very commonly, who were 'liberated' not by Allied soldiers but merely by the fact of war's end, in what we might call an 'ordinary liberation'. Pinkhus Rosenfeld, for example, was sent from the Łódź ghetto with his two sons to Auschwitz; there they were fortunate enough to be sent to work in a factory near Chemnitz, where the conditions, by comparison with Łódź or Auschwitz, were 'not so bad'. The factory was evacuated on 13 April and the workers were marched to Czechoslovakia, in a walk that lasted until 7 May and during which 150 of the 450 who set out died of exhaustion and starvation or were killed. When they arrived in the vicinity of Marienbad, the SS guards – the same ones who oversaw them at Chemnitz – simply announced that the end had come: 'And there we already saw that there is no more . . . we are already surrounded from all sides, so while walking . . . somehow we . . . we could feel that the skin is already burning on the SS men, so we sat down and we said we are not going any further. And he said too, "Well, I am setting you free".' After this the SS men 'scattered and left us'. Rosenfeld and his fellow workers begged for food from the local Czech people, who 'treated us very decently' – and that was the end. Rosenfeld's sons subsequently fell ill and spent three months in hospital in Prague before being transferred to Landsberg DP Camp, where Rosenfeld tried to find out how he could claim the property rights to a house he claimed to own in Tel Aviv. At the time of his interview with David Boder he was in Paris and working at 'Kibbutz Hénonville' (Hénonville DP camp), hoping to get to Palestine and, like many other interviewees, claiming that conditions in the DP camps were barely better than under the Germans. For Rosenfeld the moment of liberation constituted a relatively minor detail in his story, certainly not one that merited much discussion.[96]

A similar tale is told by those liberated at lesser-known camps. Bela Braver was born in Poland in 1913 and after being deported to Auschwitz was sent to Lichtewerden in Czechoslovakia, where he was freed by the Red Army:

> The camp guard who came to open the gate said: 'You are free and you can leave.' All the guards with the dogs that used to stand in every corner had disappeared. It was all gone, as though it had never been. It was one of the miracles! The Russians entered, and we were in such a condition that no one moved, no one went out. We did not laugh, we were not happy, we were apathetic – and the Russians came. A general came in, he was Jewish. He told us that he was delighted, as this was the first camp in which he had found people still alive. He started to cry; but we didn't. He wept and we didn't.[97]

The Soviets also liberated many survivors who had escaped from smaller camps and were wandering the countryside, or people who had been in hiding. These encounters were also often characterised by confusion and bewilderment as much as joy and relief. Sally Alebarda, for example, describes simply encountering the Russians who were surprised to see prisoners in marked clothing, but does not offer any views on whether this was a joyous occasion or not.[98] Eva Tichauer was a German-Jewish refugee in Paris when she became a victim of the infamous Vel d'Hiv round-ups in July 1942, and found herself in Auschwitz. In January 1945 she was sent on a death march to Ravensbrück, Malchow, Leipzig and finally inexplicably marched eastwards, to the banks of the Elbe where, on hearing that the Russians were coming, the guards abandoned her and the other women on the march. Her awareness of being 'liberated' consisted of seeing, as dawn broke on 23 April, 'a superb-looking Ivan, a Soviet soldier, perched on an abandoned baker's cart, his legs stretched apart, who in a gesture of triumph throws us the first loaf of freedom'.[99]

Naomi Samson hid as a child with her mother for nearly two years in the floor space under a barn until the Soviets arrived. During that time, she later reflected, she had envied the cows she could see through the cracks, dreamed that she was in fact an animal, and witnessed torturous exchanges between her mother and the people who were hiding them. After the liberation, Samson and her mother were shocked to discover that the few surviving Jews in the area needed to be guarded by Soviet soldiers for fear of local gentile Poles attacking them.[100] And Samson could hardly take in that Goraj, her home town, was so changed: 'I opened my eyes, and all I saw was this strange place. A strange world all around me. A world I didn't like.' Samson was eager to leave: 'As we rode out of Goray, I turned to my mother and said, "Mama, I never want to see this town again!" Mama put her arm around me and squeezed me tight and close to her.'[101]

Olga Lengyel fled a death march from Auschwitz and survived several spells of hiding and passing as Aryan in the chaotic last days of the war until, taking courage from the sight of the retreating Wehrmacht, she found herself in a small Polish village when the Russians arrived.[102]

After a spell in the Janowska concentration camp in Lwów, Leon Wells was in hiding in the town when the Russians came. Yet the final arrival of the day he had dreamed of was far more difficult than he had expected: the first Soviet soldier he talked to told him that since only Jewish collaborators had survived, he must be one of them. Local people, too, regarded him suspiciously, although Lwów was his home town. It was, he writes, hard to describe his feelings: 'When, until yesterday, the problem had been to escape being killed, survival dominated one's every thought; today this was not a problem anymore. Today the anguish for those who had been killed flooded over me . . . I was guilty in the eyes of the people and of the Russian officer for being alive. The only question anyone asked me was, why was I alive?'[103] Wells arrived at his parents' former apartment to discover that a shoemaker and his family from across the street now lived there. They were quick to assert their ownership, but Wells told them he simply wanted somewhere to stay until he was able to walk properly again, so they made up what used to be his father's bed for him. 'So passed the first day of liberation – the day that so many had waited for', writes Wells. 'I had lived to see it.' A unique case is that of Frida Michelson, one of very few survivors of the massacres at Rumbuli, who was hidden with anti-Nazi partisans and a family in Riga. When the Red Army arrived and Michelson presented herself, the soldiers' instinct was to suspect her of having been a Nazi collaborator since all they knew of the Jews was that they had been exterminated. It was only by telling her story in Yiddish to a Jewish sergeant that Michelson and her ethnic German rescuer were saved.[104] Sometimes, indeed, Jewish women who emerged from hiding or passing as Aryan were interned by the Soviets, especially if they were German speakers.[105]

Examples of these 'ordinary liberations' can be multiplied many times over, especially of those who survived the death marches from Auschwitz. One such was M. Lichtenstein, who gave his testimony to the Wiener Library in 1962, initiating a series entitled *Documents of Nazi Guilt*. Lichtenstein escaped from a death march when the officer in charge stopped to relieve himself, but was lucky to survive after being found by a German soldier a few days later with a comrade sleeping in a barn. Having asked what should be done with the two escapees, the soldier's commanding officer, conscious of the imminent end of the war, replied, 'Well, let them go.'[106] Such stories are both common and extraordinary, illustrating perfectly what Primo Levi called the 'moments of reprieve', those unaccountable split-second decisions which meant the difference between life and death. Not all were as fortunate as Lichtenstein – or Kitty Hart, or Trude Levi, or the other survivors who have given testimonies that tell of heart-stopping moments of luck – and many Holocaust victims did indeed lose their lives in similar circumstances at the end of the war, when 'liberation' was imminent.

Stories such as those above remind us that sometimes ghetto and camp inmates were liberated in unexpected ways. In our minds we carry a template, a standard narrative of the 'Holocaust experience', which ends with the camp survivors being liberated amid joyous scenes at a camp. But there are many exceptions, reflecting the variety of experiences which made up the Holocaust. For those in hiding, in forced labour camps outside of the SS's camp system and others attached to sub-camps, the Holocaust often ended in strangely 'ordinary' or non-dramatic ways. And whether it was dramatic or not, for all, liberation was a moment of confusion and mixed emotions rather than of unalloyed joy: 'Free, I don't know what it means, I forgot. I'll need some time to get used to it again. First of all, I have to sleep. I doze off despite the noise. I close my eyes. I slumber like someone who's been liberated, and I don't feel it.'[107]

CHAPTER TWO

The Western Allies

'Buchenwald was a fact that will stink through the years of history, and if we ever forget it then God help mankind because we shall then have sunk to a level as low as that of the men who made this camp – which is lower than mankind should be and stay alive.'

PERCY KNAUTH

'I was in Dachau when the German armies surrendered unconditionally to the Allies. It was a suitable place to be. For surely this war was made to abolish Dachau and all the other places like Dachau and everything that Dachau stands for. To abolish it forever. That these cemetery prisons existed is the crime and shame of the German people.'

MARTHA GELLHORN[1]

On 23 November 1944, French troops entered the Natzweiler-Struthof camp in Alsace. High up in the Vosges mountains, the beauty of its setting contrasts with what transpired there. Evidence of torture and murder was clear, and the French also found a small gas chamber, where eighty-six Jews from Auschwitz had been sent to be killed, in order that their bodies could be used for anatomical research by Professor August Hirt at the 'Reich University' in occupied Strasbourg.[2] Yet perhaps because it was the only such site of horror that the Western Allies had uncovered at that point, even many of those who actually saw the camp, such as American reporters and soldiers, were unable to make sense of what they had seen; some even dismissed it as aberrant or unimportant within the larger context of winning the war. Unlike the Soviet photographers who had been documenting atrocities in the Soviet Union for three years by the time they reached Majdanek, American and British photographers 'had little professional or personal experience with Nazi atrocities'.[3] Although the persecution of German political enemies, Jews and the citizens of occupied nations, especially Slavs, had been well documented since the inception of the Nazi regime, and even though Allied governments had been issuing statements condemning the murder of the Jews from 1942, there seems to have been a widespread inability to transform such knowledge into belief or a conscious acceptance of what such knowledge really meant.[4] Only once it became clear, in April 1945, that Natzweiler was neither an aberration nor even the most awful of the camps, did the people of Western Europe and the US start to get to grips with what the Nazis had done. As the celebrated photographer Margaret Bourke-White said, 'If we had encountered just one camp run by a maniac, we would have considered it merely the work of madness. But at a certain stage in the advance of our armies we began meeting these camps everywhere.'[5]

The change in perception began on 4 April 1945 when US troops arrived at Ohrdruf, a sub-camp of Buchenwald, not far from Weimar. There was no one alive there. The SS guards had marched 9,000 of its inmates to Buchenwald; the other 4,000, too ill to walk, they had killed or left for dead. When the American soldiers arrived they were confronted by bodies 'piled everywhere, making passage impossible'. For the first time, American liberating soldiers had some sense of what a Nazi camp was like:

> I was totally unprepared for what we found in Ohrdruf. I had heard of concentration camps, of course, but until the moment when we entered Ohrdruf and found the bodies strewn all about, I imagined them to be giant work camps employing slave labour – three meals a day and a bed at night in exchange for unpaid labour.[6]

The fact that General Eisenhower, the Supreme Commander of Allied Forces in Europe, visited the camp on 12 April, and testified to what his troops had uncovered there, undoubtedly helped to overcome the widespread sense of suspicion about 'atrocity stories', a suspicion that was a legacy of the First World War.[7] Eisenhower instructed American troops in the area to visit Ohrdruf with the words, 'We are told that the American soldier does not know what he is fighting for. Now, at least, he will know what he is fighting *against*.' And he cabled London and Washington, imploring politicians and journalists to take seriously the reports from Germany: 'We are constantly finding German camps in which they have placed political prisoners where unspeakable conditions exist. From my own personal observation, I can state unequivocally that all written statements up to now do not paint the full horrors.'[8]

The day after they entered Ohrdruf, the Americans arrived at Dora-Nordhausen in the Harz mountains, where slave labourers worked on the production of V2 rockets in underground factories. About fifteen miles before the camp, one of the Americans later recalled, 'it hung in the air. I cannot describe it. It was just a penetrating odour ... we later found out this was the odour from the camp itself.'[9] As well as another 2,700 unburied corpses, at Nordhausen the Americans also found some 3,000 survivors. And so began the process of initial shock followed by the herculean effort to care for the living, often, at least at first, with absurdly inadequate supplies. Within days Western Allied troops had liberated Buchenwald, Flossenbürg, Dachau and Bergen-Belsen, and, in May, Mauthausen and its sub-camps, including Ebensee and Gusen, and Neuengamme and its sub-camps. Canadian troops later liberated transit camp Westerbork in the Netherlands. These are just some of the best-known camps, of which (when one includes sub-camps) there were hundreds.

The camps liberated by the Western Allies are far better documented than those liberated by the Soviets in terms of official documents, reports and survivor testimonies – largely a result of the vastly greater numbers of people involved. One sees the sense of bewilderment and shock, and not only joy, that prevailed at the moment of liberation just as clearly in these cases as in those of the liberation of Majdanek or Auschwitz. One man, Baruch Gewürtz, who claimed to have been forced to gas people at a death camp near Riga, exclaimed to Percy Knauth in Buchenwald: 'They have cursed me with the memory of all those dead, and even if I get out of Buchenwald now, I'll never feel free!'[10] Zalman Grinberg, a doctor and former inhabitant of the Kovno ghetto, appointed by the Americans to run a hospital for Jewish survivors at St Ottilien, could say in a speech marking a month since the liberation of Kaufering (a large network of sub-camps of Dachau): 'We have met here today to celebrate our liberation, but it is a day of mourning as well. We are free, but we do not understand our freedom, probably because we are still in the shadow of the dead.'[11]

When dealing with the camps liberated by the Western Allies (what I call here for convenience 'western camps') it is crucial to remember that the chaos in them as the Americans, Canadians or British arrived was in no small measure a result of the death marches that had brought inmates of eastern camps to the western half of the Reich. The distinction between 'eastern' and 'western' camps is thus something of a false one since, particularly amongst the Jewish survivors of Buchenwald, Dachau and Belsen, most had been in the 'eastern' camps until the months and weeks before the liberating troops arrived. Nevertheless, from the point of view of survivors' post-liberation treatment, being liberated by the Red Army or by the Western Allies did make a difference, as we will see.

One of the first crucial points of distinction was the Western Allies' initial inability to understand the difference between the camps they had liberated and those freed by the Soviets. First, the Western Allies distrusted the reports in *Pravda* and other Soviet outlets. With the exception of the *Illustrated London News*, which reported on Majdanek on 14 October 1944 with the expressed aim of proving that reports of Nazi crimes were not exaggerated, the British press only mentioned Soviet reports of Auschwitz or Majdanek with a tone of disbelief.[12] When the *Daily Mail* reported on Majdanek on 4 September 1944, it did so in a short piece which reported how Lieutenant-General Milmar Moser, commander of German forces in Lublin, had written to the Red Army (by whom he was being held captive) to announce: 'I consider it my duty to tell the whole truth about the extermination camp built by the Nazis near Lublin.' But the paper placed 'extermination camp' in inverted commas, thus implicitly questioning the term, and the whole article played into a popular distinction between the 'clean' Wehrmacht and the evil SS.[13] The BBC refused to use a report sent to them from Majdanek by journalist Alexander Werth, thinking it was 'a Russian propaganda stunt' and, as Werth rightly says, 'it was not till the discovery in the west of Buchenwald, Dachau and Belsen that they were convinced that Maidanek and Auschwitz were also genuine'.[14]

By contrast, Belsen, Dachau and Buchenwald were all described in the Western press as the worst of the Nazi camps, although none were extermination centres. In Britain, Belsen came to emblematise the Nazi camps as a whole, just as Buchenwald did in the US.[15] CBS reporter Edward R. Murrow's famous report from Buchenwald was entitled 'They died 900 a Day in "the Best" Nazi Death Camp'.[16] Furthermore, just as until the end of the war there was a reluctance among the politicians and populations of the UK and the US to believe 'atrocity stories', so now press reports wrote of victims in terms of national groups, people who had suffered as the Nazis had invaded their countries; as a consequence, the specific nature of the catastrophe that had befallen the Jews disappeared.[17] These responses were neither entirely surprising nor, when seen in historical context, especially reprehensible. All those involved in the liberation of the camps, whether soldiers, relief workers, military chaplains or journalists, testified to the incomprehensibility of what they were seeing, and so if they at first failed to grasp that many of the people they encountered were Jews who had been transferred from the east that was an understandable mistake. It was a miscomprehension that would have important ramifications, however, as the liberated camps became DP communities and as the Allies had to develop policies for dealing with survivors who, in due course, would be termed 'non-repatriable'. Besides, before the war there had been many attempts to alert the British and American public to the particular animosity held by the Nazis towards the Jews, and afterwards it was known that Jews were among the victims.[18]

Sometimes the same people who had reported during the war on rumours that the Nazis were murdering the Jews, such as the *New York Times'* Milton Bracker, were unable to connect those reports with what they now saw at the war's end – in Bracker's case, at Natzweiler, which he dubbed 'the Lublin of Alsace'.[19] The problem was that in the immediate aftermath of the war, with millions of people on the march across Europe, it seemed invidious (and, for the British, somehow distasteful, as if one were perpetuating a 'Nazi way of thinking') to point to the Jews specifically as a victim group, especially as the absolute numbers of surviving Jews were small by comparison with the millions of forced labourers and refugees on the march across Europe. Occasionally the attempt was made, as with Chief Rabbi J.H. Hertz's letter of 28 May 1945 to *The Times*:

His Grace the Archbishop of Canterbury in his stirring letter to his diocese, as well as the writer of the obituary notice on Himmler, both in *The Times* of to-day, refer to the horrors of the concentration camps. But there are Nazi horrors far vaster and more unspeakably foul, and these have not been effectively brought home to the larger British public. It is therefore not generally known that the Nazis have exterminated 5,000,000 Jews – and millions of non-Jews in monster crematory and asphyxiation halls, by machine-gunning, clubbing to death, and mass drownings. On one single day, November 3, 1943, at Maidanek, the central human slaughter-house in Poland, 18,000 Jews were done to death, accompanied by the music of bands playing tango-marches in mockery of the agony of the victims.[20]

Indeed, even the liberators did their best to make this point clear, as Derrick Sington explained:

By the end of our second day in Belsen we had been able to find out the nationality groups in the camp. About 25,000 out of the 40,000 inmates were women, and of these some 18,000 were Hungarian, Polish, Rumanian, Czech and German Jewesses. They were a large part of the survivors of European Jewry, hastily piled into Belsen as the advance of the Allied armies from East and West forced the Germans to evacuate the extermination camp of Auschwitz-Birkenau in Poland and the scores of slave-labour camps in Silesia and North East Germany. The greater part of these Jewish women were sole survivors of families who had perished in the gas chambers of Birkenau and Treblinka.[21]

But for the most part, the genocide of the Jews was subsumed into larger, familiar and more palatable narratives of national suffering during warfare. One consequence of this way of thinking was that those found at camps were segregated and housed along national lines, with the result that Jewish survivors of the Holocaust were sometimes housed together with former Nazis and anti-Semitic collaborators. The liberators and the liberated therefore often had very different understandings of what was going on, if they could conceptualise it at all.

The Liberators

The first liberated camp still to contain a sizeable number of inmates was Buchenwald, near Weimar. Established in 1937 as a concentration camp for political prisoners, by early 1945 it was massively overcrowded with survivors of the Holocaust and other prisoners who had arrived on forced marches. A week before the Americans arrived there were about 44,000 inmates in the camp, but the Nazis transferred 23,000 of them by train to Theresienstadt, Flossenbürg and Dachau. Of the trains sent to Dachau, several were liberated en route and one only arrived at the camp near Munich after a tortuous three-week journey. That meant there were still over 20,000 inmates in the camp on 11 April.

Many of the US infantrymen were there for just a brief length of time, but it was long enough to sear itself into their minds forever. Louis Blatz, an eighteen-year-old in the 80th Infantry Division, said that on seeing Buchenwald's inmates on 12 April it occurred to him that the Nazis 'didn't care one way or another. They treated them as animals. It was just horrible. Because it was hard to breathe. The odor, the smell, the air. The crematoriums, some of them still had bodies burning in 'em, so you could still smell it. And it was a relief on our part to get away from it, but you couldn't forget, you couldn't forget.'[22] On the same day, Ventura De La Torre, a twenty-year-old Californian, was amazed by the people he saw in the camp: 'Some just had a piece of blanket covering them. And their knees were nothing but skin and bone. Their ribs . . . a terrible sight to see them. When we went in, some of those guards, they had changed into inmates' [uniforms] – but some of the people recognized them. I heard that [the prisoners] killed some of them. And then they had the ovens there. Oh, it was the smell – when I think about it, I can almost smell that.'[23] Harry Herder, echoing so many testimonies from the Holocaust which note how the Nazis sought to deprive the Jews of their human status, said:

> None of us, no one in our company, even amongst those who had been the originals, was prepared for what we were now surrounded by. It was not 'human.' It did not seem real. But it was all too real, it was the only life that some of the prisoners had known for years. Maybe it was all too human. Maybe this is what we are.[24]

Guy Stern, a German who came to the US in 1938 and was working as a US intelligence officer interrogating prisoners at the end of the war – and whose parents were last heard of in the Warsaw ghetto (presumed murdered at Treblinka) – recounts how even the toughest soldiers broke down when they encountered the camp. Seeking some sign of normality, Stern saw the usually unflappable Sergeant Hadley with his arm across his face, 'bawling like a child'.[25] There were about 21,000 living inmates when the Americans arrived, of whom some 4,000 were Jews and about 850 were children. Within days a thousand had died and many others were close to death. As Edward Murrow wrote: 'There surged around me an evil-smelling stink, men and boys reached out to touch me. They were in rags and the remnants of uniforms. Death already had marked many of them, but they were smiling with their eyes.'[26]

The exact chronology of the liberation of Buchenwald is, unsurprisingly, confused – and made more so thanks to the quasi-myth of the communist inmates' 'self-liberation', a feat which in the GDR expanded into one of the founding moments of the anti-fascist pantheon – to the extent that American involvement was almost entirely ignored.[27] After 1938 the leading role of the 'greens' (criminals) among the inmates was broken and, despite an attempt to reassert themselves in 1942, the 'reds' (political prisoners) took charge and formed an anti-fascist Camp Committee. Contrary to the myth, the communist-led Camp Committee had taken up arms against the guards at the moment – the morning of 11 April – when the SS withdrew, leaving Camp Elder Hans Eiden in charge, only hours before the first US troops arrived. It does not diminish their bravery or audacity in establishing an underground organisation or in collecting and hiding weapons to point out that the inmates knew the Americans were coming. Stefan Heymann, one of the inmates, wrote that 'We prisoners had found out from the press and radio that the American army had reached the area around Eisenach' on Sunday 1 April. 'That', he wrote, 'was our Easter present, and we fervently hoped that the liberators would soon appear in Buchenwald.'[28] A jointly-written report on the day of liberation concluded, in a way that would soon become inadvisable in the eastern zone of occupied Germany, that the 21,000 liberated prisoners of numerous different nationalities 'owed it to the US Third Army and their own international collaboration that on 11 April, 1945, fascist slavery had ended for them and a new life in freedom had begun.'[29]

Among those American soldiers who entered Buchenwald on 11 April, Egon Fleck and Edward Tenenbaum were the first to produce a detailed report on what they saw. In their eighteen-page account, they described how they encountered the self-styled Camp Committee which they praised for the fact that 'Instead of a heap of corpses, or a disorderly mob of starving, leaderless men, the Americans found a disciplined and efficient organization in Buchenwald.'[30] Without shying away from describing the power-games that maintained the communists' control over the other inmates, including having objectors placed on transport lists and controlling the distribution of food parcels, Fleck and Tenenbaum appraise the communists' ends as justifying their means. Asserting that they were 'sustained by the sacred egoism of their mission', Fleck and Tenenbaum conclude in social-Darwinist terms that the communists 'became hard, surviving not for themselves but in the name of the proletarian future of Germany . . . They consider themselves almost the sole valuable residue of the great process of selection which was the concentration camp system.'[31]

The next morning, Fleck and Tenenbaum witnessed the *Freiheitsappelle* or 'freedom roll call', organised by the Committee, which they celebrated as 'an incredible experience, as hard to forget as the sight of the camp's crematorium, the fresh corpses, and the living dead of the so-called "small camp"'.[32] Heymann describes the scene: 'On the morning of April 12, a festive roll call took place in Buchenwald, at which the comrades of the individual nations marched by together, singing their national anthems. After addresses by the representatives of the great nations, an American lieutenant greeted the liberated comrades.'[33] 'It was', said Fleck and Tenenbaum, 'the rebirth of humanity in a bestial surrounding.'[34] Startlingly, to our ears, they did not flinch from describing the inmates of the 'Little Camp', who were regarded by the communist-dominated 'aristocracy' of the Upper Camp as 'bandits', in decidedly distasteful terms: 'They are brutalized, unpleasant to look on. It is easy to adopt the Nazi theory that they are subhuman, for many have in fact been deprived of their humanity.'[35] Others were equally shocked, such as Captain Melvin Rappaport. Discovering the children's block, which he described as 'a little concentration camp within a concentration camp', Rappaport was sickened by what he saw. The inmates (who, he later discovered, included Elie Wiesel and the future Chief Rabbi of Jerusalem, Israel Lau) 'were starving and hungry and cold and miserable. It was like a pack of wild beasts, just running around this enclave in there. They looked at me, and I was looking at them. I didn't know what to say. It was unbelievable.'[36]

A week after the liberation, and following an invitation from Eisenhower on the 19th, a British parliamentary delegation visited Buchenwald. In its report to the Prime Minister the delegation was quite clear about the fact that despite the commonly-used term 'prisoners', the inmates 'should not be confused with military Prisoners of War'; they comprised mainly political internees and Jews from Germany, Austria, Czechoslovakia, Poland and other occupied countries, and forced labourers from across Europe. Behind the delegation's official mandarin presentation one gets a strong sense of their shock: 'Although the work of cleaning the camp had gone on busily for over a week before our visit, and conditions must have been improved considerably, our immediate and continuing impression was of intense general squalor; the odour of dissolution and disease still pervaded the entire place.'[37] After briefly summarising the inmates' huts, the 'hospital' and the mortuary block, and hearing of torture, cremation and medical experiments (and being assured that conditions in other camps further east 'were far worse than at Buchenwald'), the delegation, though cheered by the visible signs of medical treatment and recovery and activity among the survivors, concluded with a final, moving paragraph:

> In preparing this report, we have endeavoured to write with restraint and objectivity, and to avoid obtruding personal reactions or emotional comments. We would conclude, however, by stating that it is our considered and unanimous opinion, on the evidence available to us, that a policy of steady starvation and inhuman brutality was carried out at Buchenwald for a long period of time; and that such camps as this mark the lowest point of degradation to which humanity has yet descended. The memory of what we saw and heard at Buchenwald will haunt us ineffaceably for many years.[38]

Perhaps the most moving of all the descriptions of Buchenwald was penned by American journalist Percy Knauth. Until 1941, when he feared for his safety and for that of his French wife whose journalist's exit visa was not in order, Knauth had been Berlin correspondent for the *New*

York Times. Now he was returning as a correspondent for *Time* and *Life* magazines, having spent the previous four years reporting from the Middle East and the Balkans. Nine days after the camp was liberated, Knauth arrived, 'and the sight of Buchenwald burst on our eyes'.[39] Knauth's prose, which beautifully describes atrocity, replicates the barbaric juxtaposition by which Nazis taunted their captives: a vicious place with a bucolic name (Buchenwald means 'beech forest' in German, just as Birkenau means 'birch meadow'). Here Knauth describes his arrival at the camp as a convoy of former prisoners were marching to bury two newly dead French inmates:

> In all my life I never dreamed of such a sight. The last light of the setting sun was red behind the marching men, and as they came, a dead hush fell on everything around. We stood in the command car, full lives behind us and the full life of victory close ahead, and watched the depths of human misery parade before us. I had never seen death before – I had been close to it, but somehow its stunning fact had always passed me by. Numbly, I saw death now, and before I left the camp that evening I saw it reduced to such ordinariness that it left me feeling nothing, not even sickness at my stomach.[40]

As in Fleck and Tenenbaum's report, Knauth was most shocked and upset by the 'Little Camp', around which a Czech surgeon guided him. Here he discovered the camp's real, hidden horror: there were no people on the streets as in the main camp, because here they were too weak to walk; the people lying on the embankments by the huts 'looked like dead men, except that now and then some of them moved'.[41] The men in the barracks 'were emaciated beyond all imagination or description' and 'many just lay in their bunks as if dead'. Here is how Knauth summarised the camp:

> What it all boiled down to was that here in Buchenwald human life was as nothing. Nobody gave a damn about it except the individual whose life it was, and he could be taken past the point where he cared. Buchenwald was not an extermination camp like Maidanek or Auschwitz, where prisoners were systematically killed by the thousands. In Buchenwald nobody gave a damn whether a prisoner lived or died. The SS men who guarded the camp would, if they felt like it, kill a man

more casually than they would kill an animal – snuff out his life as they might that of an insect that they happened to see before them on the road. It is difficult to conceive this, but it was so.[42]

Knauth's measured description – his first report in *Time* was more raw – is among the most polished and insightful of the immediate post-liberation descriptions, but already a few days after the initial opening of the camps we see how the visceral emotions of the first encounters were being replaced by analysis. The journalist's powers of description were supplanting the soldiers' shock. Remarkable statements – 'It was not the fact of death that was so awful – it was the fact of death-in-life'; 'Until the day when I saw Buchenwald I respected men'[43] – were taking over from simple statements of astonishment. Later the popular memory of the camps liberated by the Western Allies would lose Knauth's subtleties, and his correct distinction between Buchenwald and the extermination centres in occupied Poland would be forgotten for the best part of five decades.

After Buchenwald, the next major camp to be liberated by the Americans was Dachau, on 29 April, just days after some 7,000 inmates, most of them Jews, had been sent on a forced march to Tegernsee further to the south. In the main camp the Americans found more than 30,000 prisoners; including Dachau's more than thirty sub-camps, some of them very large, the total rose to 67,665 registered prisoners. Of this number, some 22,000 were Jews and most of the rest were political prisoners. The bare numbers conceal a concatenation of appalling stories; they also tell us nothing about the state of the camps' inmates when the soldiers arrived. For that we need to listen to the liberators themselves. For as American nurse Ann Franklin wrote shortly after working at Dachau, the survivors 'couldn't be liberated. What they needed was medical care, lots of it and as soon as possible.'[44]

Sergeant Scott Corbett was a reporter for the *Rainbow Reveille*, the division's newspaper. In his first report he stated that what the Americans found at Dachau 'bears out every atrocity told about the first great concentration camp in the twelve years of its existence'.[45] The numerous reports filed by the liberating soldiers and the reporters accompanying them all confirm Corbett's words. Indeed, as Corbett's colleague James Creasman, another army reporter, wrote of those who went first into the camp:

Seasoned as they were to stark reality, these trained observers gazed at the freight cars full of piled cadavers, no more than bones and skin, and they could not believe what they saw ... Riflemen, accustomed to witnessing death, had no stomach for rooms stacked almost ceiling-high with tangled human bodies adjoining the cremation furnaces, looking like some maniac's woodpile.[46]

Each of these first correspondents, like the soldiers they were with, struggled to find the words; unsurprisingly, similar formulations occur again and again throughout their writings (especially bodies stacked 'like cord-wood'), as they grappled for a vocabulary adequate to the task.

The emotions of those Allied personnel involved in liberating the Nazi camps were still raw many years after the events. Douglas Kelling, division psychiatrist of the US 45th Infantry Division who entered Dachau on the day of its liberation, recalled at a 1981 conference that the 'prisoners' in the camp 'were starving, a forced starvation; many were sick. Their faces were depressed in a fixed stare; their appearance was one of resigned hopelessness. Their gait was listless, slow, and', Kelling said, 'I am sure many at times wished that they were dead instead of being confined in such a cruel, unbelievable place.'[47] Felix L. Sparks, another member of the 45th Infantry Division (at twenty-nine years old, one of the US Army's youngest battalion commanders) recalled in 1995 that the troops' first encounter with Dachau was a 'traumatic shock' and that the scene that he witnessed on entering the camp 'numbed my senses': 'The men of the 45th Infantry Division were hardened combat veterans. We had been in combat almost two years at that point. While we were accustomed to death, we were not able to comprehend the type of death that we encountered at Dachau.'[48]

William Quinn, intelligence officer for the US Seventh Army, said at the 1981 conference that on entering Dachau, 'the impact was so great on me that I didn't really understand what I was looking at. I couldn't believe what I had seen.'[49] He decided there and then, so he later said, to document these terrible aspects of the camp; the result was the booklet *SS Dachau*, one of the first postwar publications on the Nazi camps. It comprised three discrete reports undertaken by different sections of the Seventh Army (with a foreword by Quinn) and combined careful observation with a burning anger, the latter justified by the photographs of famous scenes such as the corpses lying next to cattle trucks on the rail track just outside the camp. 'In spite', the second section begins, 'of the fact that one had known of its existence for years, has even spoken to people who had spent some time there, the first impression comes as a complete, a stunning shock.'[50] Below the statement is a large photograph of corpses at the side of the railway, bodies that still lay there as the report was being written. First Lieutenant William Cowling also recalled the corpses on the railway track as his initiation into the horrors of Dachau, and reports how he and two journalists were mobbed by inmates as they entered the camp: 'The people were thin, dirty, and half starved. They rushed to the American officer and the two newspaper reporters and attempted to shake their hands, kiss their hands or face, or just to touch their clothing. They even grabbed them and threw them up into the air, shouting in many different languages the whole time. Many of the men were crying and a good percentage of them were half-crazed with excitement and the brutal treatment which they had received while in the camp.'[51] The scene is perhaps best summed up by Marcus Smith, a doctor with a US Army Displaced Persons team who arrived at Dachau on 30 April 1945 and stayed for several weeks to help with the process of medical relief:

> An incredible sight, a stench that is beyond experience. Horror-stricken, outraged, we react with disbelief. 'Oh God!' says Rosenbloom. Ferris silent, and so is Howcroft, his vocabulary inadequate to describe this circle of evil. I hear Hollis, our car-counting driver, say that even primitive, savage people give a decent burial to their own dead and the dead of their enemies. I shut my eyes. This cannot be the twentieth century, I think. I try to remember the redeeming attributes of man. None comes to mind.[52]

Buchenwald and Dachau were the largest of the camps liberated by the US, but many other camps made an equally terrible impression on those who first saw them. Wöbbelin, a sub-camp of Neuengamme situated near Schwerin, was 'a sight that you never forgot and a smell that you never get out of your nose.'[53] Landsberg, twenty miles from Munich, made a similar impression: 'What we saw at the camp our minds could not comprehend. Even after months of combat we could not accept the gruesome sight and stench of the bodies. I regarded the inmates with pity, anger, repulsion and awe, since they were human beings who were defenceless.'[54] A young soldier

involved in the liberation of Gunskirchen, a sub-camp of Mauthausen near
Lambach in Austria, could hardly find the words to describe the survivors:
'I often didn't think they would survive any journey to anywhere. I had
never seen anybody so emaciated, just literally skeletons, you know,
breathing skeletons. I used to ask myself, "Is this a man or a woman I'm
speaking to?" A few of them knew English and were able to converse, and
as I said, mentally they weren't rational either. How they survived, how they
spoke afterwards if they survived I wouldn't know.'[55]

At Dora, the first soldiers into the camp also found the living and the
dead mixed together and sometimes hard to tell apart:

> The camp was literally a charnel house, with the distinction that a small
> proportion of the bodies therein were not quite dead. As the camp was
> cleaned out the living and the dead were found intermingled indiscrim-
> inately, and in some cases bodies had to be carefully examined by
> medical personnel to ascertain whether they contained life or not. Those
> that were living were in such advanced stages of starvation, and
> frequently tuberculosis, that there was little hope for them.[56]

Elsewhere, in slave labour camps, liberating soldiers such as the Jewish
Sidney Aronson were surprised when the women liberated in Salzwedel (a
sub-camp of Neuengamme which provided women workers for a munitions
firm) turned out not to be as emaciated as those found in the more famous
camps.[57] Nevertheless, the women in Salzwedel were suffering from malnutrition and dreadful sanitary conditions, and one former inmate remembers
the liberators for 'how wonderfully kind they were to us. How remarkable it
was that under the dirt, disease, rags and lice, these soldiers could see human
beings, young girls.'[58] Slowly the Allies worked out the difference between
slave labour camps and concentration camps, where conditions had plum-
meted following the arrival of large numbers of death-march survivors.

The last camps the Americans reached were among the most terrible. At
Mauthausen in Austria, troops of the 11th Armored Division of the US 3rd
Army arrived on 5 May. Former Staff Sergeant Albert J. Kosiek recalls that:

> Behind that fence were hundreds of people who went wild with joy
> when they first sighted us. It's a sight I'll never forget. Some had just

blankets covering them and others were completely nude, men and women combined, making the most emaciated looking mob I have ever had the displeasure to look upon. I still shake my head in disbelief when that picture comes before me, for they hardly resembled human beings. Some couldn't have weighed over forty pounds. The place turned into an uproar and it was evident that if these people weren't stopped shortly bloodshed would be impossible to avoid.

Kosiek was overwhelmed by the cheering which made him feel like a celebrity, but also by the appalling conditions he found at Mauthausen and at its sub-camp of Gusen. After seeing bodies piled up – 'you wouldn't think they were human beings if you did not recognize certain features. They were being chewed up by rats and no one seemed to care' – and viewing the gas chambers, Kosiek wrote: 'I never saw so many dead people lying around in all my life. I saw things that I would never have believed if I hadn't seen them with my own eyes. I never thought that human beings could treat other human beings in this manner. The people that were alive made me wonder what kept them alive. They were only skin and bones.'[59]

Other liberating soldiers felt the same way. George Sherman, a nineteen-year-old from Brooklyn, was on patrol near Linz, assigned to look out for the Russians approaching from the east. When his patrol smelt a bad odour on the wind they went to investigate and discovered Mauthausen. When they entered:

> We didn't know what the hell to think. We had heard through Stars and Stripes about a couple of the other camps that were [liberated] early on, the main one [Auschwitz] being found by the Russians, so we surmised what it was. We were dumbfounded. The people – the prisoners coming up to us and not knowing what to say. But it's just – you have no words. You're looking at this, and it's kind of hard to believe.[60]

Another soldier, Duane Mahlen, remembers that 'the survivors looked like they were dead'. Yet another, LeRoy Petersohn, a medic with the 11th Armored Division, threw himself into what was a terrible task: 'I had seen a lot before we ever got to that camp, but I was more affected by seeing the people that were starved and just skin and bone. And all the things they did to those people affected me far more than having to be out in the field, patching some of our men up.'[61]

The reports from Buchenwald, Dachau, Mauthausen and the smaller camps liberated by the Americans are now iconic in the ways they fuel our 'collective memories' of the Holocaust. Such reports tend to suggest that the camps were 'another world', a notion that is only half true and which, if taken too far, can have the opposite effect to that intended. The idea that the camps were separated from the rest of humanity is meant to indict the evil of their creators and operators; in fact the camps were tied deeply into local, national and international economies and, all protestations to the contrary notwithstanding, few historians believe any more that local German and Austrian civilians had no idea what these places were or what went on inside them. The reports also serve the purpose of providing a retrospective justification for the war, something that was noted at the time, as it seemed to justify propaganda that the Germans were evil; as time has passed, however, we tend to see the reports less as explanations for going to war and more as descriptions and evidence of the Holocaust. But Jews, though making up a substantial proportion of the survivors, were not the majority by any means, and only in retrospect does it seem odd that their specific experiences were not focused on in the way that subsequently became the case. The camps that the Western Allies liberated, as already noted, were not major killing centres of the Holocaust until the very last stages of the camp system's existence. In fact, as we shall see in Chapter 3, it is striking how rapidly the military, chaplains, relief workers, politicians and others did actually realise that more needed to be done for Jews in particular, especially in the American zone.

Nevertheless, the revisions of the past that accompanied the end of the Cold War, and the downplaying of anything that smacks of 'sympathy' for communism, mean that it is all too easy to overlook the roles played by the international committees formed by inmates towards the end of the war. Spaniards in Mauthausen and German, Polish and Czech communists in Buchenwald and Sachsenhausen all played an important part in transferring command of the camps from the SS to the liberating forces and in caring for survivors. In Buchenwald the International Camp Committee helped the American army to understand the camp and establish order. The US commandant Captain Ball's order on 2 May for the Committee to be disbanded reflected the Americans' sense that they no longer needed its help, though it was probably also a response to the previous day's huge socialist-style May Day celebration that it had organised.[62] The committees, then, played a crucial role in certain camps in facilitating the transfer of power and initiating relief efforts. They also shaped mythical narratives of camp resistance, thus playing into the hands of the communists who were gradually imposing their brutal rule over Eastern Europe – an indication of the link between liberation and the shaping of postwar Europe. Yet this should not blind us to the fact that anti-fascist action was more than communist propaganda; rather, it was a deeply rooted, emotionally powerful part of many people's lived experience during and after the Second World War.

If Dachau, Buchenwald, Mauthausen and the smaller camps liberated by the Americans – most of which contained few if any survivors – gave rise to these now canonical reports and images, then perhaps the most iconic of all the liberations was that of Belsen.[63] This was not because, as was often misunderstood at the time and for decades afterwards, Belsen was an extermination camp; it was not. The reason it may have seemed so was that Belsen was the final destination of many of the death marches at the end of the war and, with administration in tatters, the thousands of camp inmates who inundated the thoroughly unprepared and inappropriate camp were left more or less to fend for themselves: 'The conditions in Belsen were at their worst six weeks before liberation. The camp was overcrowded. Typhus, tuberculosis, and other epidemics raged. In the hospital and throughout the camp about a thousand people a day lay on the floors, starving and dying.'[64] The famous mountains of corpses that greeted the British army when it arrived there were the bodies of people already dying of disease, weakness and starvation when they arrived at Belsen on death marches or who quickly succumbed to disease through lack of food, shelter and sanitation. It is because of the role played by the media in reproducing these horrific images, and the reports that accompanied them, that Belsen has long remained synonymous with the end of the Holocaust and the liberation of the Nazi concentration camps. In Britain, one of the most famous media events of the twentieth century was Richard Dimbleby's report of 19 April (although as broadcast it omitted the phrase about 'thousands of . . . Jews' included in the written report[65]). Today, the Imperial War Museum's

Holocaust exhibition in London is dominated by a massive reproduction of one of the most brutal images of Belsen corpses being bulldozed away.

The British army, represented by the 63rd Anti-Tank Regiment, entered Belsen on 15 April 1945. Captain Derrick Sington announced over a loud-speaker, to the sound of weeping and cheering from the women's camp, that the British were taking over and that the inmates were free. In his account of the liberation, Sington wrote: 'I had tried to visualise the interior of a concentration camp, but I had not imagined it like this. Nor had I imagined the strange simian throng, who crowded to the barbed wire fences, surrounding the compounds, with their shaven heads and their obscene striped penitentiary suits, which were so dehumanising.'[66] That evening the liberators brought in food and water, with medical relief workers starting their work on 17 April. The British discovered two camps: Camp One, the so-called 'horror camp', which contained some 40,000 dying men, women and children; and Camp Two, previously part of a large German training camp, which had recently been used as overflow for Belsen and in which the 16,000 inmates were starving but not ravaged by typhus. As the report in the *British Medical Journal* put it, 'It is impossible to give an adequate description on paper.'[67] Of the approximately 60,000 inmates discovered alive at Belsen, fewer than half were among those registered in the camp at the start of April (when there were about 40,000); 30,000 only arrived at Belsen a week before the liberation. Of the 37,000 people estimated to have died at Belsen, the vast majority perished in the spring of 1945.[68]

Those who saw Belsen immediately after liberation have, in retrospect, become the first builders of a national collective memory; even today some of their reports are almost unbearable to read. 'My God, the dead are walking!' exclaimed Leslie Hardman, the British military rabbi, upon entering the camp on 17 April. 'They are not dead', said the girl, a former inmate, who was accompanying him, 'But they soon will be.'[69] 'These once human beings, flesh and blood like you and me', Hardman went on, using imagery which would permeate the British consciousness for decades, 'were now reduced to hideous apparitions bearing no resemblance to man, but only witnessing to man's inhumanity.'[70] Brigadier Glyn Hughes, the chief medical officer of the 2nd Army who was held in veneration by the survivors for his efforts, wrote that 'it was a wonderful sight to see the joy of all those people although one felt that they were almost mystified at their good fortune. The troops themselves were incredulous, almost more so than horrified, that such things could be.[71] Journalist Leonard Mosley was among the first to see the camp; his description is fraught with a sense of his inability to set out what he saw adequately, with his text moving swiftly from 'the stench of death that hung around the camp' to the 'long stretches of grass covered with bodies, among which the SS guards were moving, gathering the frail lengths of skin and bone over their shoulders, three and four at a time, to take to the death pit.'[72] Sington called Belsen an 'inferno' and Hughes described in his memoir the thousands of inmates close to death mingling with the already-dead. 'Apart from the frightful conditions in compounds and huts', he wrote, 'there were many horrors – the enormous pile of dead lying everywhere, a crematorium, a gallows in the centre of the camp and signs of mass burial – one enormous grave open and half filled on our arrival.'[73] Lieutenant-Colonel M.W. Gonin wrote a devastating short report which reads like an earthly realisation of Hieronymus Bosch's hell:

> Piles of corpses, naked and obscene, with a woman too weak to stand, propping herself against them as she cooked the food we had given her over an open fire; men and women crouching down just anywhere in the open, relieving themselves of the dysentery which was scouring their bowels; a woman standing stark naked washing herself with some issue soap in water from a tank in which the remains of a child floated.[74]

'Life', journalist Patrick Gordon Walker accurately noted, 'had reverted to the absolute primitive.'[75]

Yet when Isaac Levy, the senior Jewish chaplain in the British army, came to the camp three days after the first British soldiers, the first people he saw were the relatively healthy, those who could still walk and who were excited to see the British arrive. Levy was therefore shocked when he was taken from meeting these people to what he called 'the hell of Belsen', the 'horror camp', where he found 'Heaps of corpses . . . lying in the main pathways. Those who still had a little life in them were crawling on all fours in search of scraps of food. Haggard, starved bodies, bulging eyes, pitifully appealing for help.' Entering the huts, 'The nauseating smell was unbearable. These wretched victims were lying in indescribable filth', and 'At first sight it was impossible to distinguish between the barely living and the dead, for those who still had the barest trace of life looked lifeless.'[76] As Derrick Sington also noted, it was impossible for those in this terrible state to reason: 'They were consumed by the famine which was burning them up, possessed only by the wild urge to eat and survive.'[77]

It is perhaps understandable then that sometimes the liberators, in anger at what they had seen, gave vent to feelings that make for uncomfortable reading today, since they come close to replicating what they found so upsetting. N.A. Midgley, photographer with No. 5 Army Film and Photographic Unit, wrote after seeing Belsen that 'It must be seen to be believed. I am now convinced that the Nazis are not human beings, but vermin that must be exterminated. This might have happened in England had Hitler's plans succeeded.'[78] Mosley noted that 'Many of my colleagues came away from Belsen raging against the Germans, and saying that they should all be wiped out for what had happened at Belsen; forgetting', Mosley reminded his readers, in the style of Victor Gollancz, 'how many of Belsen's victims had been Germans themselves.'[79]

Whatever the feelings of the liberators, there was little they could do to prevent more than 10,000 of the almost 60,000 living inmates dying in the first weeks after liberation; they were simply too weak to recover. 'Everything was done by the liberating forces to save them', wrote Josef Rosensaft, who did not mince his words when he wanted to criticise the British, 'but it was a hopeless task.'[80] The most basic of the sorrows of liberation was the fact that so many camp inmates died after it.

The first of the relief workers into the camps experienced the same jolt to their sense of self and humanity as the soldiers who preceded them by days. Francesca Wilson, an aid worker with UNRRA, was at Feldafing in mid-May 1945, shortly after the former Hitler Youth school on the Starnberger See had been taken over by the Americans as a camp for former inmates of Dachau, the first camp to be designated specifically for Jews.[81] 'As for the inmates of the camp', Wilson wrote, in terms that were unself-conscious in their frankness, 'at first it was hard to look on them without repulsion.' Although she had seen victims of famine before in interwar disaster zones,

> This was worse, for these people were victims of more than famine, they
> were victims of cruelty. They were wearing the convicts' striped blue

and white pyjamas, and had the shaven heads and the number tattooed on the left arm which were the marks of Auschwitz. Some were walking skeletons, most had hollow cheeks and large, black, expressionless eyes, which stared and stared and saw nothing. They had the furtive look and gestures of hunted animals. By years of brutal treatment, by the murder of relatives, by the constant fear of death, all that was human had been taken away from them.[82]

Others were more restrained and managed to contextualise their shock, realising that the survivors were not in conditions of their own making. In fact, although one can find some thoughtless and occasionally even anti-Semitic remarks by relief workers – who had to deal with people whose reactions and behaviour were sometimes far removed from 'civilised' norms – most of the people involved displayed remarkable generosity and compassion, and it is striking how quickly after the initial shock and outrage they appraised themselves of the situation. Charlotte Chaney was a registered nurse with the US army during the Second World War and was among the liberators of Dachau. She wrote letters home expressing her shock at the inmates' condition, stating in one that 'This is one place I will never forget as long as I live'. She describes in detail the care she and her colleagues gave to the survivors in the few weeks she was at the camp, revealing an instinctive sense of attachment to and compassion for her charges, especially the children. She recognised, though, that for all the care, 'their nightmare was over or maybe just beginning, either one way or another'.[83] The chief UNRRA nurse at Belsen, Muriel Knox Doherty, provided a no-holds-barred description of conditions in the camp in her letters home to Australia, as in this one of July 1945, which describes the scenes inside the barracks:

Masses of dead remained where they were or were pushed under the floorboards to make room for the living – who were beyond caring. Each of the two- and three-tiered wooden bunks held five or six living sick mingled with corpses, which owing to weakness and despair, the living were unable to remove; other sick lay naked on the polluted floor or were wrapped in rags foul with excreta and lice . . . Diarrhoea was rampant. Those lying in the lower bunks had no protection from the excreta dripping from above. On the floors the excrement was six inches deep, mixed with rubbish and rags. The walls were heavily contaminated also.

Knowing full well that her friends and relatives in Australia would balk at these words, she urged them on:

You may shudder at these descriptions – perhaps you will say it is sordid and unnecessary. Read on, my friends! The world should know what suffering and degradation this New Order in Europe brought to millions, lest it be quickly forgotten and rise again in yet another guise. It concerns us all – we must not forget – whether you can forgive, only you must decide.[84]

The Liberated

'I have survived and the general assumption is that for the survivor normal life again resumes at the end of the ordeal. How far indeed this is from the truth in the majority of cases and my own in particular.'[85] Trude Levi had more reason that most to feel that her 'liberation' had not exactly brought about her freedom. After collapsing on a death march she was able to hide in a barn where she met a Frenchman named Charles Oreste Paroldo, from Toulon, a POW who offered to stay with her until she was well enough to travel to France with him. This he did, but once in France he abandoned her at a Red Cross station in Toulon. When someone sent for Paroldo, he came and took Levi back to the flat he shared with his mother and sister. The two women were working as prostitutes and when Levi realised that they wanted her to do the same, she revolted and Oreste promised to take her back to the Red Cross. In fact, Levi found herself arrested, later to discover that Oreste had told the police she was actually former SS, and she was imprisoned for four months in Marseille alongside former *miliciennes* (female members of the Milice, the French fascist paramilitary force), Italian Fascist and German Nazi women. Only a chance encounter with a French former inmate of the Thekla camp near Leipzig, where Levi was sent before embarking on the death march westwards, persuaded guards that her story was true. She was released and set off for Paris where she went to live with her uncle and aunt. For Levi, then, and many like her, 'liberation' was neither a single, joyous moment nor a 'return' to content-ment. A regular and settled life would be some time coming.

For the survivors in the camps, by contrast, 'liberation' was more likely to be experienced as an actual event, though for them too it was not only joyful. Věra Hájková-Duxová, a Czech woman who had arrived at Belsen after a month-long death march from Christianstadt, a sub-camp of Gross-Rosen in Lower Silesia, noted in her 1981 memoir: 'The day of liberation is generally remembered with a feeling of triumph, satisfaction, boundless joy. Ours was a vague feeling of relief, but at the same time also helplessness and above all weariness. The coiled spring of desperately nourished hope came unwound.'[86] Jacques Stroumsa, from Salonika, was deported to Auschwitz, then to Mauthausen and finally to one of its sub-camps. When he was liberated with his friend Jacques Choel, he recalls, 'Our joy, however, could hardly overcome our despair.'[87] Eva Braun, from Slovakia, who had been at Auschwitz and Reichenbach and worked as a slave labourer at Philips and Telefunken factories, was liberated at Salzwedel. She remem-bers feeling overjoyed as the Americans arrived although she was too weak to stand, but at the same time, 'While I was elated by the freedom, there was tremendous fear. Who would I find? . . . It was euphoria, but it was a very ambivalent feeling. We were frightened.'[88]

Dachau was waiting for its liberation for several days before the Americans actually arrived. As Charles Y. Banfill of the USAF, who was assigned to observation duty with Brigadier General Linden and the Eighth Army, wrote in his report:

> the camp had been under extreme tension for many hours. The pris-oners did not know (a) whether they would be massacred by the Germans, (b) whether they would be caught in a fire fight between the German and American troops, or (c) whether they would be liberated by the timely arrival of the Americans. The sight of the few American uniforms that arrived . . . resulted in an emotional outburst of relief and enthusiasm which was indescribable.[89]

On seeing the camp on 30 April, Lieutenant Charles Rosenbloom, head of DP Team 115 which was sent by SHAEF to assist survivors, simply remarked: 'A lot to do.'[90]

He was not wrong. One survivor, Haim Rosenfeld, who was aged seventeen at liberation and had been sent to Dachau from Auschwitz, remembers 'only that I awoke to terrible shouts. I saw all the inmates standing by the fence and shouting. Outside the fence were American soldiers. I understood that this was the liberation, this was the end!' Rosenfeld recalls that many like him who were ill died soon after liberation, but marvels at the speed with which his own body recovered: 'I weighed 28kg. I couldn't stand on my feet, I crawled. A month later I went home on my own!' This is testimony to the care given by the Americans, but physical recovery could not take away the survivor's fear of the future. On liberation, says Rosenfeld, 'Here my second tragedy began. I didn't know who was alive and who was not.'[91] In the sub-camp of Allach, Polish Jew Ephraim Poremba and a friend decided to explore the area around the camp shortly after liberation. As they encountered Americans, he noticed that they 'looked at us as though we had landed from Mars . . . They looked at us as though we were not normal.' Indeed, compared with the Americans and the German locals, the camp survivors, garbed in strange clothes and in their emaciated state, were not 'normal'.[92]

In Buchenwald, the inmates' view varied widely depending on whether they were in the Upper Camp or the Little Camp, and on their state of health. Irrespective of where they were located, however, all those left in the camp were lucky to be alive, as some 25,500 were killed in the process of evacuation, and only the disruption of the end of the war and underground sabotage actions prevented the SS from emptying the camp completely. For those involved with the anti-fascist underground, the approach of the Americans was keenly awaited in full conscience of what was happening. Stefan Heymann wrote for the *Buchenwald Report* that the last day, 11 April, 'began with an ominous quiet' and that 'The tension grew from hour to hour'. As the sound of artillery fire came closer, there could be no doubt 'that the lead tanks of the Third Army were swiftly approaching'.[93] Karl Keim, a former *kapo* (or prisoner functionary) who would potentially have fallen under suspicion of having mistreated fellow inmates, wrote that he and other members of the 'camp police', as he called it, were 'proud of having been among those who formed the anti-fascist front and of having stood with weapons in hand at the outbreak of the struggle against the SS on April 11, at the approach of American tanks and the liberation that came with it.[94] The next day the celebratory roll call took place. For the survivors in the camp who had recently arrived on death marches or who were excluded from the ranks of the anti-fascist resistance, things looked somewhat different.

Mendel Herskovitz, for example, was fifteen years old in April 1945 and had been brought to Buchenwald from Łódź. Though weak, he was still able to walk, and at the approach of the Americans he and some other inmates ran out towards the tanks. On discovering, at machine-gun point, that Herskovitz was Jewish, one American soldier dropped his gun and 'jumped down to me and began to kiss me so that I have . . . that I didn't have the strength to hold out from the kisses that he gave me'. The soldier, whose name Herskovitz never learnt, promised to come back to the camp to see him; two days later, he did so, bringing with him cigarettes and chocolate. At the time of his interview a year later, Herskovitz was still speechless at this man's actions: 'And I didn't . . . he has . . . he has treated me . . . I have no words! And after that time I didn't see him any more because, naturally, he went on.'[95] Herskovitz, eighteen at the time of the interview, complained about having no 'poetical powers' to recount his experiences, but in the course of his narrative he nevertheless managed to condemn the German-appointed head of the ghetto's Jewish Council, Mordechai Chaim Rumkowski, for being '80 percent for the Germans', and explained how his family had been sent from the Łódź ghetto to Częstochowa, then to the ammunitions factory at Skarzysko-Kammienna, back to Częstochowa and finally, in January 1945, to Buchenwald. Herskovitz believed that he was the only survivor of the eighty-one members of his family.

Similarly, Henry Sochami, a Greek Jew from Salonika, was the sole survivor of a family of twenty-seven. His wife and three children had been killed when they arrived at Auschwitz in March 1943, while he had been sent to work in various commandos. He arrived in Buchenwald from a subcamp of Auschwitz after a three-day journey in a cattle truck without food or water, in the freezing cold. In the last days of Buchenwald's existence Sochami hid with some Russians, not telling them he was Jewish. When they left the bunker, Sochami was at first scared to do the same, until he saw that 'they were all kissing and embracing each other outside'. Then he emerged: 'I looked and I saw everybody was dancing because the Americans were coming, so I went out. I weighed only 38kg because of the famine, and

though I was falling down, I started singing and dancing.'[96] Willy Berler, a
Romanian Jew studying in Liège, was deported to Auschwitz, Gross-Rosen
and finally Buchenwald, which he reached in February 1945 after an excru-
ciating six-day journey with nothing to eat. When the Americans entered
the camp in April, Berler could hardly react: he had burned his arm a few
days earlier and the wound was gangrenous; and he could barely rouse
himself mentally. 'I should feel joy at the news that it is finally over, that our
SS torturers have no further power over us', he writes. 'But I feel nothing. I
probably can't feel anything anymore. History has moved forward faster
than my demise. If I am still alive, I cannot benefit from it spiritually, at
least not for now.'[97] Only a month later, during which time Berler also
assisted in caring for those sicker than himself, was he fit enough to make
the return journey to Liège, where he again fell ill.

Belsen shortly before liberation was a scene of utter devastation. Hanna
Levy-Hass, a Yugoslav-Jewish communist, condemned the process of
forcing the prisoners to die in so brutal a fashion: 'Better to put an end to it
all as quickly as possible, like a human being. Are we supposed to let
ourselves decay and perish, physically and psychologically, slowly but inex-
orably sinking into the void of total exhaustion, smelling of suppuration
and contamination, dying bit by bit like beasts? We die like animals here,
not like human beings.' No wonder Levy-Hass came to the conclusion that
'the vilest, most savage humiliation imaginable has turned life here into
something that no longer bears any relationship to life as we understand it.
In reality we are dealing with the barbaric annihilation of thousands of
human beings – of this there can be no doubt, *not the slightest doubt*.'[98] And
if a long-term inmate such as Levy-Hass could write this, then it is hardly
surprising that the Allies who liberated the camp, in the midst of an ongoing
war, could have thought that Belsen was a death camp.[99]

Gitla Borenstein, deported from Auschwitz-Birkenau to Belsen, could not
walk but only crawl at the moment of liberation. It took her days and days of
sleep before she was able to walk. She could barely eat, and describes the
process of beginning to do so again as unbearably painful, to the extent that
she wanted to die. Only after the Red Cross sent her and her seriously ill sister
to a hospital in Malmö, where she spent a few months, did her slow recovery
begin.[100] Another survivor, Fela Lichtheim from Poland, felt that she could
say far more about the few months she spent in Belsen than her previous

three and half years in captivity, but that it was too hard to do so: 'It is horrible. One cannot describe it in words, because words hurt too much.' Describing herself as looking like a seventy-year-old woman when Belsen was liberated (she was twenty-two), Lichtheim goes on: 'I was unable to move. I was all run down, emaciated, unwashed for weeks, without undressing. In that one dress and coat I was lying on the floor. I wanted some water for a drink, but I couldn't get it. I had diarrhoea for two months, and then I had typhus.'[101]

Likewise, Esther Brunstein, who was dying of typhus when the British arrived, was too ill to enjoy being liberated. Although she understood that being prevented from eating uncontrollably was the correct and sensible response, she nevertheless felt robbed of her dream of the previous five and a half years. She also 'felt cheated at not having the memory of experiencing the initial exhilarating moment of liberation'. And, as she reports, the first days 'were joyous and yet sad, confusing and bewildering. I did not know how to cope with freedom after years of painful imprisonment!'[102] Anita Lasker-Wallfisch sums up the experience of 'liberation' shared by many Belsen inmates. Hearing the sound of rumbling in the distance she dismissed others' suggestions that this might be the Allies approaching because 'I was more familiar with thoughts of death than with thoughts of possible "liberation".'[103] Elsewhere, echoing Primo Levi, she writes that 'When the first jeep finally rolled into the camp, we looked at our liberators in silence. We were so suspicious'. She goes on to say that 'After the tremendous elation of having survived came the sobering realization that one had lost everything – family, home, everything. And then one had to realize that one had to start over again.'[104]

Those who were physically strong enough to understand and take part in what was happening still struggled to comprehend it and often could not take it in. Josef Rosensaft, who became the *de facto* leader of the Jewish committee in Belsen, recalled in 1957 that 'We, the cowed and emaciated inmates of the camp, did not believe we were free. It seemed to us a dream which would soon turn again into cruel reality. In a sense, it still was a dream.' After liberation, which Rosensaft and the other inmates had dreamed about for so long, 'we saw before us a new kind of world, cold and strange'.[105] Norbert Wollheim, who subsequently became the head of the *Verband der jüdischen Gemeinden Nordwestdeutschlands* (Association of Jewish Communities in Northwest Germany) and was a colleague of Rosensaft's, later wrote that 'the joy which we felt' at liberation could not be expressed since it could not be shared with those closest to them: 'We were free from the whip and the pistols and the machine guns of the SS criminals – and yet the invaluable gift of the new freedom could not entirely make up for the sense of frightening personal isolation, the certainty of the infinite loneliness within ourselves, precisely because we were the last remnant of the survivors, because we were the men and women of the *Sheerit Hapleita*.' Thus began the process of searching for brethren and with it the possibility of 'overcoming the danger of seclusion and mental isolation by establishing new human contacts through the device of finding ourselves and others on grounds of a common task.'[106] But that would occur several days later. On the day of liberation there was certainly happiness but fear of the future and a sense of profound loss prevailed. Still, inmates such as Wollheim and Rosensaft who soon became leaders of the Jewish DPs were able to do so because they had already been involved in communal organisations before the war and/or in the camps and had the wherewithal and prestige to begin organising survivors immediately after liberation. Here again we see a link between the camps, liberation and the postwar period.

Compared with the few who were able to act, most of the survivors, even though they were free, continued to behave as if they were under SS guard, reluctant to move independently, shrinking from authority figures, hardly daring to believe that the food and drink being offered to them was real. In Belsen, some survivors unable to eat refused to take food intravenously, for they associated injections with Nazi execution. 'You came in with a tube and a needle and they all thought they were going to be slaughtered', as J.R. Dixey, one of the medical students, recalled.[107] The survivors had to 'unlearn' the camp experience.[108]

Others liberated in Belsen were fortunate still to be in a relatively robust physical condition. Hadassah Bimko, who in 1946 married Yosef Rosensaft, had been sent from Auschwitz to Belsen in mid-November 1944 as part of a nine-strong medical team to work in the camp hospital; she was appointed by Glyn Hughes and Colonel James Johnston to set up and run a medical team drawn from among the survivors. Rosensaft believed that she did not succumb to the diseases ravaging the camp just before liberation because she had developed immunity to them, having survived typhus and other epidemics in Auschwitz. Yet despite her pride in her work and her praise for the relief work carried out by the British medical team, who 'performed the superhuman task of saving thousands', recovery in a mental sense required time. When news broke that the war in Europe had ended, Rosensaft later recalled: 'Of course, we were glad to hear the news of the Allied victory, but we in Belsen did not celebrate on that day . . . We in Belsen did not dance on that day. We had nothing to be hopeful for. Nobody was waiting for us anywhere. We were alone and abandoned.'[109]

Elsewhere real scenes of joy did occur. Ernest Landau, in a piece with the sarcastic title 'Men versus Supermen', describes how on the approach of the Americans to their stranded deportation train in the Bavarian country-side, the prisoners attacked and overpowered the increasingly nervous SS guards. When the Americans arrived, 'We all run from the train. The American soldiers are surrounded, embraced, kissed, and raised upon our shoulders. We, until then prisoners, welcome our liberators with hysterical joy, with tears in our eyes.'[110] Alexander Donat, after almost two years in Majdanek and several small sub-camps of Natzweiler-Struthof, finally ended up in Allach, a sub-camp of Dachau. Like Landau, he too was placed on an open coal train in order to be deported away from the approaching Allied soldiers. After three days of aimless rolling over the Bavarian rail network and then forty-eight motionless hours on a siding in the rain, Donat and his colleagues finally saw Americans approaching:

> The soldiers of Patton's Third Army were shaken as the filthy skeletons in their striped uniforms embraced them, weeping, kneeling to kiss their hands, mumbling incomprehensible thanks. In that hour of libera-tion we wept as we had not wept during all the years of martyrdom; we wept tears of sorrow, not tears of joy. Our liberation came too late; we had paid too high a price. Only a few of us, in spontaneous gratitude, rushed to our American liberators to thank them; the overwhelming majority went to the supply cars and were soon parading around with a loaf or two of bread under their arms.[111]

Another survivor, the author Paul Victor, simply says that 'The joy expe-rienced at the moment of liberation is hard to describe' and suggests that his enthusiasm was tempered only by the news the next day of Roosevelt's death.[112] Anna Kovitzka, a Polish Jew interviewed by David Boder in Wiesbaden, describes how her death march, which was bound for Belsen, came to an end near Lippstadt when American forces overran the column and the SS surrendered. But amidst the dancing, cigarettes and chocolates, there was no escaping more pressing fears and concerns: 'The Ninth Army had not seen any Jews in Germany, and we thought that we were the only Jewish survivors, and we did not want to live. But they consoled us. They were telling us that there were many other armies that have reached other lagers which were liberated. That was liberation.' Shortly afterwards Kovitzka found out that her baby daughter, who had been hidden with a Gentile woman, had been murdered three weeks before the end of the war following a denunciation. After a year in Wiesbaden searching, Kovitzka found a niece in Belsen but no other members of her family. 'But my own people are no more. I am alone.'[113]

Of the concentration camps liberated by the Western Allies, Mauthausen was the most brutal. Created after the Anschluss with Austria, until 1944 Mauthausen mainly held criminals and political prisoners, as many as 80,000 in the main camp and its thirty sub-camps. After mid-1944 large numbers of Jewish slave labourers and deportees from the evacuated eastern camps arrived. As at Belsen, the death rate was very high, with 28,080 inmates dying between 1 January and 8 May 1945. Another 3,000 died in the days after liberation.[114] Under such circumstances, liberation was hardly a moment of unfettered joy, as one survivor who had been in the camp for six weeks when the guards surrendered, noted:

> I always thought and imagined a thousand times to myself that this moment would somehow be especially exciting, even shattering, but above all cheerful. I didn't feel anything of the sort! No happiness, no excitement, only desperate emptiness and a terrible fear, fear of going home and fear of the question of who I would find and for whom I would wait in vain, that is what occupied me at that moment . . . I was unable to be happy![115]

As happened with the camps liberated by the Red Army, many inmates of smaller camps and sub-camps in the west did not experience the sort of 'liberation' portrayed in the Allies' films. Max Sprecher, interviewed in 1946, explained that following three years in Sachsenhausen and two in Auschwitz, he was transported to Dachau in January 1945 and from there to

Tutzing, on Lake Starnberg. He was saved from further transport to the Tirol by the fact that the Americans had bombed the railway lines: 'we were unable to get through, and so by accident we remained alive'.[116] Lutz Hammer, a Berlin Jew who had been posing as an Aryan, was picked up by the Gestapo in November 1943 and sent to Auschwitz, then to Sachsenhausen, Ravensbrück and a small camp at Ludwigslust. Of the end, all he says is: 'On the morning of the 4th of May 1945 our camp had no guards and as we slowly dared to leave the camp, American troops came towards us.'[117]

At Gusen, a sub-camp of Mauthausen, the SS left the camp on 3 May and over the next twenty-four hours the inmates gradually realised that they were free. The Ukrainian political prisoner Petro Mirchuk, who had been in Auschwitz and Mauthausen, had been marched to Ebensee at war's end. Here he not only feared the unpredictable behaviour of the Nazi guards but was desperate for the camp to be liberated by the Americans or British rather than the Red Army, for in the latter case 'we knew the Ukrainian political prisoners would be sent to Russian concentration camps or executed – we were their political enemies too. We were political enemies of Communist Russia as well as Nazi Germany.' Even accounting for the Cold War context when Mirchuk was writing such claims (his book was published in 1976), it was certainly true that many Ukrainians – primarily forced labourers and collaborators – justifiably feared being returned to Soviet territory. Although that fate was not necessarily spared them, for inmates such as Mirchuk being liberated by the Western Allies was infinitely preferable to being liberated by the Red Army. If in all the confusion Mirchuk mistook the American five-pointed star for Soviet insignia and ran off into the town, nevertheless his 'liberation' before the US Army arrived was decidedly undramatic: 'On the morning of May 4 the roll call was different. The commandant of the camp and the SS guards were absent. In their place was a civilian who introduced himself to us as the mayor of the town Ebensee. He told us that the war was over, we were free, and were under the protection of the International Red Cross.'[118]

Yet Ebensee itself was in a catastrophic condition. The sub-camp had been established solely to use slave labourers to build and then work in the underground facilities of the Peenemünde rocket research centre. Conditions were disgraceful and became even worse at the end of the war when evacuees from other camps arrived. On the morning of 5 May, camp commander Anton Ganz tried to usher the inmates into the tunnels, assuring them that this was for their own safety in the face of the imminent American bombardment. But the prisoners refused, for the first time revolting against SS rule, and leaving them 'so happy that we hugged each other and shook hands with each other'.[119] On the same day, 7,566 of the camp's 16,650 registered inmates were reported as sick, and the photographs of the emaciated survivors reveal why. When the American troops of the 3rd Cavalry Group arrived from Steyr the next day, the scene was chaotic as jubilation mixed with horror. Among the many descriptions by survivors of the event of liberation at any of the Nazi camps, this account by Dutchman Max R. Garcia is among the most powerful:

> Soldiers in unfamiliar uniforms gaped in frank amazement from the top of their tanks at a mass of shrunken, ghastly scarecrows in filthy, striped rags, a reeking mass with their heads shaved except for a stripe in the middle. The soldiers stared at us and we stared at them . . . The silence of the first shock of our encounter was broken now, the gates somehow were opened, and we drew back to allow the roaring tanks and their small escort to roll slowly into the middle of our roll call square. Prisoners swarmed around the tanks, as the engines were switched off. The soldiers in and on their tanks seemed to be afraid. They looked as if they did not want to come down and mix around with us. Perhaps they just came from the latest battle, but we seemed to be too much for them. These hungry eyes. These sunken faces and skeletal bodies. These stinking subhumans. Us![120]

Garcia shouted to one of the soldiers in English and found himself hoisted onto the tank and subsequently given the job of guiding the sergeant and another soldier on foot around the camp. Afterwards they 'returned to their tank looking sick from what they had seen'.[121] Indeed, Staff Sergeant Bob Persinger of the 3rd Cavalry Reconnaissance Squadron recalls Garcia and his tour: 'Absolutely terrible. People lying on the barracks that would probably be more than half dead, because their eyes never made contact with you at all. Those folks were in very bad shape. Some alive, too, in there. If you were not sick and crying by now, you would be before you exited.'[122]

*   *   *

What many of the liberated wanted was revenge. Some were incapable of it, such as a young Jewish survivor of Buchenwald who admitted that he would have raped a German woman he encountered on a farm near the camp had he been 'a little more alive'. Others did carry out acts of revenge, such as Freddie Knoller, a survivor of Belsen:

> As I was looking for food (in this nearby farmhouse) I saw something sticking out from behind a wardrobe. It was a framed photo of Adolf Hitler. I took a knife and slashed it in front of the old farmer. That's when he came to me and said, 'Du sau Jude' – 'You pig-Jew.' I had the knife in my hand and I just stuck the knife in his stomach. I don't know if I killed him or not. The British soldier said, 'Come on, let's get back to the camp.' He didn't want anything to do with it. I would never have done that under normal circumstances, it was just that we were liberated and that a German continued to call us 'sau Jude.'[123]

Shlomo Venezia, who after being forced to work as a member of the Auschwitz *Sonderkommando* was liberated in Ebensee, admits that he assaulted an 'Aryan Pole' who had hit him earlier, and then outed him as a kapo to some watching Russians who beat the man to death: 'He didn't experience freedom and for me that was a great source of satisfaction, since he didn't deserve any better.'[124]

Another American soldier, Captain Barker, reported that in Dachau he and his colonel saw a stormtrooper's mutilated body, 'where a prisoner had been able to get a knife and relieve him of his head'.[125] And after holding his tongue for forty-six years, Harry Herder recounted in detail how a group of inmates had somehow left Buchenwald (then being guarded by the Americans), found one of the former guards, returned him to the camp and interrogated him, then placed a rope in his hands and forced him to hang himself. Herder and his colleagues, all armed and, as he says, able to stop the event, did not do so:

> We let them continue. In one way, we sanctioned the event. Ever since that day I have been convincing myself that I understood why the Buchenwald prisoners did what they did. I had witnessed their agonies. I had wondered how human beings could treat other human

beings as the prisoners at Buchenwald had been treated. I felt I knew why the prisoners at Buchenwald did what they did – so I did not stop them.

Still, Herder admits, 'When we returned to the barracks we did not tell anyone what we had witnessed.' He only did so many years later.[126] Another American soldier from the 20th Corps of the 3rd Army recounts quite calmly how he and his colleagues did not intervene while a former inmate of Buchenwald beat a German soldier to death.[127] Such encounters were possible because, unlike camps such as Buchenwald and Ebensee from which the SS had tried to flee, at many others the SS and camp guards (often Hungarian or Ukrainian) were still present when the Allied soldiers arrived.

Some went even further. How many we will never know, for obvious reasons, but some survivors have been willing to admit what they did. In his 1946 interview with David Boder, Benjamin Piskorz, a survivor of the Warsaw ghetto uprising, spoke openly and honestly about how he tortured and killed Germans, stating that 'I did the same thing as they did with us.' When Boder asked, 'For instance?', Piskorz replied:

For instance, I struck down a few people. I, too, tortured.

DB: Killed dead?

BP: Yes, killed dead. I, too, tortured a few people. And I also did the same things with the German children as the SS men did in Majdanek with the Po-. . . with the Jewish children.

DB: For instance?

BP: For instance, they took small . . . small children by the legs and beat the head against the wall so long until the head cracked and [the child] was killed.

DB: Did you do the same thing?

BP: I did the same to the German children, because the hate in me was so great, but only . . . maybe I would have in time forgotten all of this, if not [for the fact] that the Germans themselves had reminded me that when the Russians will enter they will be killed and they will be sent to Siberia and the same things will be done to them as [they did] to the Jews.[128]

Another survivor entitled his report for the Wiener Library 'Permission from the Russian Liberators to Take Revenge on Nazi-Murderers' and the centrepiece of his account is his murder, in Leitmeritz (Litoměřice), of an SS man from Theresienstadt (where the author was liberated) who was attempting to disguise himself as a Wehrmacht soldier.[129] But such confessions are rare.[130]

Yet others witnessed such acts but did not take part in them. Alexander Gertner, a young Romanian Jew who had been sent from the ghetto of Oradea (Nagyvárad in northern Transylvania, annexed by Hungary in 1940) to Auschwitz and then to Buchenwald, described the terrible scenes after liberation, as starving inmates fell on the food prepared for them by the Americans. He also said that as the camp could hear the Americans approaching, Russian prisoners disarmed about thirty or forty guards and 'pummelled and beat them' before putting them into 'the bunker', keeping them under arrest until the Americans' arrival.[131] And in Gusen, Leo Reichl saw three kapos murdered by surviving inmates who had previously sworn revenge with the words: 'If they survive the KZ, we will attack them with our own hands.' The Americans standing near them 'made an impression of indifference, whilst the KZlers were satisfied with their successful revenge.'[132]

Not only did former inmates give vent to their rage after liberation, soldiers, appalled by the scenes they confronted, also sometimes attacked the guards. Leonard Mosley reported how the soldiers became 'mad with rage' after witnessing Belsen:

> They beat the SS guards and set them to collecting the bodies of the dead, keeping them always at the double . . . When one of them dropped to the ground with exhaustion, he was beaten with a rifle-butt. When another stopped for a break, she was kicked until she ran again, or prodded with a bayonet, to the accompaniment of lewd shouts and laughs. When one tried to escape, or disobeyed an order, he was shot. Under the circumstances, it was impossible to have any sympathy for these guards. The cruelties they had practised, or the neglect they had condoned, were appalling. The punishment they got was in the best Nazi tradition, and few of them survived it; but it made one pensive to see British soldiers beating and kicking men and women, even under such provocation.[133]

The scene has also been reported by more than one camp inmate, as in this example:

> They turned with rage and contempt on the murderers, who stood around, and beat them up. They made them bury the dead at the double. They fed them on the rations the SS had given their prisoners. They made them run and run, urged on by sharp bayonet points. Some fell down and were swept up with the mass of corpses by a bulldozer and pushed into an enormous pit ... Then gradually the English rage subsided.[134]

In Dachau, one German soldier – apparently only recently posted there from the eastern front – surrendered to the Americans in full regalia and with a loud 'Heil Hitler'. The response was unsurprising:

> An American officer looked down and around at mounds of rotting corpses, at thousands of prisoners shrouded in their own filth. He hesitated only a moment, then spat in the Nazi's face, snapping 'Schweinehund,' before ordering him taken away. Moments later a shot rang out and the American officer was informed that there was no further need for protocol.

As General Eisenhower put it, 'Our forces liberated and mopped up the infamous concentration camp at Dachau. Approximately 32,000 prisoners were liberated; 300 SS camp guards were quickly neutralized.'[135] Percy Knauth also reported on how American soldiers attacked at random without checking to see whether their victims might deserve such vengeance. After leaving Buchenwald, Knauth says:

> I felt an almost insane desire to take an SS man, any SS man, and beat him till his insides spilled out of his body. I was not alone in that feeling. One evening when I was at the camp, some Buchenwalders brought in a few German prisoners, boys in *Wehrmacht* uniforms who had been picked up, unarmed, outside the camp. Before they could be properly put in jail, American GIs who had been through the camp that day fell on them and beat them bloody, just because they had on German uniforms.[136]

Indeed, William Cowling wrote to his parents that 'The Germans I took prisoner are very fortunate they were taken before I saw the camp [Dachau]. I will never take another German prisoner armed or unarmed. How can they expect to do what they have done and simply say I quit and go scot free. They are not fit to live.'[137] One German-born member of the 11th Armored Division involved in liberating Mauthausen also admits to coming close to killing German civilians after seeing the camp:

> I went crazy, I did. You know, when I went out into that field and I saw these farmers out there and I stopped them and said, 'What goes on in that camp?' and they said they didn't know. I carried a Thompson submachine gun, .45 caliber. I was just about ready to blast those people. Those people were in jeopardy, because that hatred was instilled in me at that point. And I had to kill people; why the hell couldn't I kill them? My jeep driver backed my gun down.[138]

Sometimes not only former guards but kapos or other prisoner functionaries were killed by the newly released inmates. In the Nazis' divide-and-rule strategy so cynically implemented in the camps, these people held positions of authority over other inmates and often maintained them with violence – and were encouraged to do so. Primo Levi described them on the one hand as 'a picturesque fauna: sweepers, kettle-washers, night watchmen, bed smoothers', and others who were 'poor devils like ourselves' but who, 'for an extra half-litre of soup, were willing to carry out these and other "tertiary" functions'. On the other hand, there were those who 'occupied commanding positions', from kapos of labour squads and barracks to those who worked in the camp administration and who sometimes held quite important posts. Though Levi explains they were not collaborators, he insists that the sort of power they were given left the functionaries 'free to commit the worst atrocities on their subjects as punishment for any transgressions, or even without any motive whatsoever'.[139]

In the midst of the anger which was released at the end of the war, the notion that prisoner functionaries were ultimately victims of the Nazis themselves was far too subtle. Besides, many had indeed treated fellow inmates with brutality. In Ebensee, for example, Drahomir Bárta reports that the pent-up rage against these men – perhaps aided by the fact that the

SS had left the camp – spilled out as the underground International Camp Committee took over: 'It was an unmerciful massacre and was done with everything they got into their hands, it was frightening and inhuman, but just', he writes. Some fifty-two camp functionaries were killed, according to Jean Lafitte.[140] One historian of Gusen, himself a former functionary in the camp and member of the underground, claims that a group of Polish and Soviet youngsters began revenge attacks before the liberated French (and other) prisoners, having just been informed by the first arriving American soldier that they were free, had finished singing the last verse of the *Marseillaise*. The attacks not only targeted the German and Austrian criminals who had acted as camp functionaries, and who were dragged out of hiding to be mercilessly murdered, but also killed innocent German-speaking inmates.[141] Spanish survivors tried to intervene to protect the German speakers from the Poles and Russians.[142] Another, more sensationalist account claims that the first American soldiers into Gusen found body parts lying in the mud; not victims of cannibalism, as they suspected, these were in fact the remains of kapos who had been torn limb from limb by the inmates after the SS had left the camp.[143]

Revenge on a large scale was exceptional, with the Nakam group (whose name is Hebrew for 'revenge' or 'the Avengers') being perhaps the best known. Led by former partisan Abba Kovner, they planned to poison drinking water in Hamburg and Nuremberg and bread in the SS internment camps in Dachau and Nuremberg. The latter plot was actually carried out in Nuremberg and resulted in a number of prisoners being taken ill and possibly some deaths.[144] However, for the most part, DPs talked about revenge but either did not carry it out or were prevented from doing so. Lieutenant-General James M. Gavin of the 82nd Airborne Division remarked that, 'of course, the first inclination' of DPs in Cologne, on discovering that the area had been taken by the Allies, 'was to break out of the wire and go loot German homes and get food. Anything like that. They hated the Germans and they wanted to kill them.' He stopped them, since he 'couldn't have them fighting the German civilians and killing each other'.[145] Similarly, at Landsberg DP camp, Irving Heymont forcibly prevented a mob from lynching a German whom they recognised 'as a former supervisor of a labour gang'; they were trying to drag the man out of his car and, Heymont says, 'The bitter hatred in their faces and their mad frenzy is beyond description.'[146]

*　*　*

Buchenwald was handed over to the Soviets on 4 July 1945 and the remaining survivors were evacuated with the departing Americans as the Soviets would not care for them. This meant some 6,000 'unrepatriables' were sent to hospitals or DP camps in the American zone of occupation. On 21 May the 'horror camp' at Belsen was burned down, 'to the relief of all those who had so strenuously fought against the ravages of diseases which had claimed so many victims' and 'amid cheers and cat calls which completely drowned the official cheering'.[147] The British erected a sign in English and German on the site of the camp which read:

THIS IS THE SITE OF
THE INFAMOUS BELSEN CONCENTRATION CAMP
Liberated by the British on 15 April 1945.
10,000 UNBURIED DEAD WERE FOUND HERE,
ANOTHER 13,000 HAVE SINCE DIED,
ALL OF THEM VICTIMS OF THE
GERMAN NEW ORDER IN EUROPE,
AND AN EXAMPLE OF NAZI KULTUR.[148]

The survivors were now in the DP camp, which contained 13,000 Jews who were now left waiting, most of them hoping to get to Palestine. Since Belsen had been burned down, the DP camp was in nearby Hohne. The British wanted to call the DP camp 'Hohne', but the Jewish survivors, recognising the powerful value of the Belsen name, insisted on retaining it. As the DP camp newspaper *Undzer Shtime* put it:

Belsen is a blot [*Schandfleck*] for the Jewish people for all eternity . . . By changing the name to Hohne one smudges the blot, one totally rehabilitates the murderers sitting in prison. Hohne means approval of National Socialist atrocities, a degradation of all those who fell in the struggle against National Socialism.[149]

On the basis of such strident statements, the survivors faced their liberators and the DP camps grew into communities in their own right.

CHAPTER THREE

Out of the Chaos

We orphans
We lament in the world:
Our branch has been cut down
And thrown into the fire –
Kindling was made of our protectors –
We orphans lie stretched out on the fields of loneliness.
NELLY SACHS, 'Chorus of the Orphaned'[1]

The most urgent problem facing the liberating Allies was the delivery of medical relief to the survivors or, as it has also been called, 'medical liberation'. The medical care offered by the military was extraordinary given that the war was still ongoing and given the massive logistical obstacles that stood in the way. Yet some people still believed that more could have been done. 'Inexcusable delay marked the delivery of the first relief shipments', wrote Jewish commentator Zorach Warhaftig. 'Months passed after the day of liberation before proper relief activities could be organized.'[2] This was not entirely fair: the charities, especially the JDC and JRU, organised themselves before the end of the war to send aid to the liberated survivors, and even if they could not quite appreciate the scale of the task at the start, it was not their fault that they were not permitted to enter the camps for several months after the conclusion of hostilities.

Particularly acrimonious debate has raged over the British medical relief operation, with some survivors and scholars offering sharp criticism. Ruth

Klüger, for example, who survived Christianstadt (a sub-camp of Gross-Rosen), Theresienstadt and Auschwitz, and who later became a professor of literature in the University of California, writes that 'in liberating the concentration camps the Allies had often been so careless and unprepared that people died because they couldn't digest the heavy food that was indiscriminately shoved at them, or because of a lack of medical care'. She goes on: 'You might say that wasn't the fault of the Allies, who couldn't foresee what they would find, but to me it seemed as if these last victims had died of Allied sentimentality'. Most cuttingly, she claims: 'Their liberators had been better at taking horrifying pictures of the living skeletons than at rescuing them.'[3] French historian Annette Wieviorka, in marked contrast to most British accounts, claims that despite the absence of SS violence, conditions in Belsen after liberation remained similar to those prevailing during its worst days.[4]

Another survivor, Joop Zwart, who was nominated by Belsen prisoners to act as their spokesman and who claims to have walked out to speak to Captain Derrick Sington when the latter first entered the camp, says that he asked the British to offer the survivors rice in warm water. Instead they gave them corned beef and allowed them to slaughter and cook the SS's pigs, with the result that several thousand died. According to Zwart:

> On the day of the liberation and the night following it from four thousand up to five thousand persons died in the camp, most of them because of eating too heavy food. It has taken us days to convince the British that a lean diet really was the best thing for the inmates of the camp. Finally they agreed, but then the catastrophe already had happened. We found young Ukrainians dead with a pork chop in their hands. Others had not been able to walk more than twenty meters away from the kitchen where they ate their too savoury meal. They died in the main street of the camp.[5]

Yet it would have been next to impossible to differentiate deaths caused by overeating from deaths caused by the state survivors were already in, and from which nothing would have saved them. As US Private William McConahey wrote in great frustration, 'In the camps the sick were still dying. We couldn't save them. We *tried* to feed some of these people, and really we *couldn't* . . . You couldn't save them. We felt *terrible!* They were dying under our eyes! Nothing we could do because they were so *close* to death. And you *couldn't* feed them.'[6]

Most contentious in his accusations is Rabbi Irving Greenberg. In his introductory remarks to a conference that took place in 2000 at the Holocaust Museum in Washington, DC, he claimed that inmates in Dachau continued to die after liberation thanks to a 'tragic lack of understanding of the condition of survivors'. He claimed that 'This mishandling reflected Allied ignorance and failure to plan, which in turn mirrored the democracies' lack of concern for the fate of the Jews. 'Even in Bergen-Belsen', Greenberg said, 'where the British appointed Dr Hadassah Rosensaft to lead a team of 28 prisoner physicians and 620 volunteers who desperately worked with military doctors to save as many survivors as possible, "the Holocaust claimed 13,944 additional victims during the two months after liberation".'[7] We now know that such claims are mostly unfounded, or at least need108

to be contextualised more carefully, especially if we are to understand why so many died after the British arrived. For as Anita Lasker-Wallfisch reminds us, 'What the British Army had to cope with was simply mind-boggling.'[8] The veracity of her remark becomes clear when one considers the facts. At the 'Belsen Trial' in September 1945 Glyn Hughes testified to the conditions at the camp when the British arrived; in response to the request to summarise the general health conditions in the camp, he said:

> I appreciated that of the inhabitants 70 per cent required hospitaliza-
> tion, and that of these at least 10,000 would die before they could be put
> in hospital. There were 10,000 corpses in the camp when we arrived
> there. Every form of disease was prevalent, but the ones mainly respon-
> sible for the frightful conditions were typhus, starvation and tubercu-
> losis. The cause of the disease was the privation and suffering which
> they had gone through.[9]

Although thousands died in Belsen after the liberation, this was in spite of the best efforts of the British and a result of the fact that so many were past the point of salvation. The decision had to be made 'to give the best chance of survival to the greatest number, and therefore to move out at once into the barrack area the supposedly fit and well, thereby making more room in the huts and supervision of feeding easier'.[10] Major W.R. (Dick) Williams, one of the first British soldiers to enter the camp on 15 April, was responsible for organising the first supply of food to come from the British. Shocked by what he saw around him, especially the 'rotting stacks of dry skin and bones', he reported to Glyn Hughes and requested the urgent delivery of food and water. The next day the food arrived and Williams and his team provided gruel and tea to the survivors. For those who could not walk, Williams explains that his team delivered tea to the huts but admits that 'I looked in the huts but never went in, unprepared for the sight of Hades where the living were lying with the dead in the stench-filled gloom.' His efforts sustained the living until 'more professional units from 2nd Army arrived and took over our RASC primitive arrangements'.[11] The RAMC's Lieutenant-Colonel J.A.D. Johnston and Lieutenant-Colonel F.M. Lipscomb took over the administrative and medical efforts on 17 April, just two days after the camp was liberated. At the same time the 10,000 corpses found in the camp had to be buried, which was one of the first tasks the liberators organised, making Hungarian guards dig the pits and SS men carry out the actual burial process. From 17 April, when the burials began, to 21 May when Camp One was burnt down, some 23,000 bodies had been buried in mass graves.[12]

On 25 April six Red Cross teams arrived. Their first weeks were spent organising emergency measures to save as many as possible, a herculean effort given that the war was still going on and that there were shortages of all necessary items, from bed sheets to bread. Muriel Doherty, who arrived in June, explained in her letters home how the nursing process was organised:

> A policy was adopted that the greatest number of lives would be saved by placing those who had a reasonable chance of survival under conditions in which the natural tendency to recover would be aided by suitable feeding and prevention of further infection, with rest in bed and elementary nursing for the very sick, and so it was decided to evacuate camp 1.[13]

Emergency feeding ensued and the survivors were placed on different rations depending on the severity of their condition. 'Many of the ex-prisoners had such sore mouths that they found it very difficult and painful to eat', wrote Doherty.[14] They were also terrified of being fed intra-venously, and feared being taken to be gassed when stretcher bearers came to bathe them or to move them to other huts for treatment.

At the end of April the twelve-strong Quaker Relief Team 100 arrived, followed soon after by Dr Meiklejohn of UNRRA and ninety-six RAMC medical students. At first, one report states, 'Little real nursing is done at all', since it was necessary to concentrate 'on trying to keep the patients clean, warm and fed – no easy matter when diarrhoea is prevalent and hot water almost unobtainable.'[15] They soon set up the so-called 'human laundry' where German nurses, reluctantly taken on because of the lack of alternatives, had to delouse and clean the frightened survivors, dust them with DDT, cut their hair, provide them with clean blankets and admit them into the makeshift hospital.[16] Survivors were terrified of them and although one British soldier claimed that the German nurses were 'the hardest working and most energetic body in the whole of Belsen', Muriel Doherty wrote in complete contrast that they stole supplies, were callous towards their patients, and had 'a passion for scrubbing walls and woodwork in preference to nursing the patients'.[17] With their contrasting views, both claims provide an early postwar illustration of the practical limitations on denazification – Germans had to be employed – and a hint of the kind of expediencies to which the authorities later resorted in the context of the rebuilding of Germany.

The Quakers re-established the water supply, the student doctors provided food and medical care and, in the 'horror camp', established a hospital. Their policy of feeding the survivors with intravenous hydro-lysates (a high-calorie mixture designed to enter straight into the blood-stream of those unable to eat) and a semi-liquid feed was sensible given that re-feeding, keeping people alive, was a prerequisite for establishing the inmates' other medical issues.[18] More than experimental nutrition mixtures, though, small amounts of food were what the inmates most needed. Michael John Hargrave, one of the medical students, wrote in his diary that where most survivors were concerned, if one could cure diarrhoea there was no need for any other treatment, 'as once you have stopped the diarrhoea the patients regain both their appetite and their strength'.[19] 'One week after the arrival of the students', writes Doherty, 'the death rate was halved, and in two weeks halved again. Within two weeks of the setting up of the hospital in Camp 1, 12000 patients had been washed, disinfected, admitted, treated and nursed.'[20] They worked in the 'huts' of the main camp until 21 May, when the last hut was burnt down. No wonder that medical officer Robert Collis, in his first report on the camp for the *British Medical Journal,* could write that the medical students 'have done and are doing a work of epic gallantry and are worthy of all honour'.[21] After the creation of the new camp hospital complex in the former Panzer training school the doctors and the nurses of the British Nursing Services were better able to work, although the number of patients per doctor and nurse was staggering: one medical officer to every 650 patients and a nursing sister for every 150, according to Lieutenant-Colonel J.T. Lewis, the man in charge of the Belsen hospital. This included Swiss, Italian and German doctors, the last of whom were POWs, as well as doctors who had themselves been Belsen inmates. Lewis credited the nurses especially for transforming the camp and for having 'shed a lustre on British nursing which will never be forgotten'.[22]

Though it has long been overlooked, the work of the nurses was crucial. Nor were only British or Commonwealth nurses present; there were also nurses of various nationalities who had been inmates of the camp as well as local Germans. Out of what now seems a misplaced sense of paternalism, female nurses were meant to be prevented from entering Camp One, the 'horror camp', as it was presumed to be too terrible for feminine sensibilities. However several nurses, including Muriel Blackman and Lyn Brown, did manage to get passes permitting them entry and the recollections of other medical staff indicate that women did go into in Camp One – quite understandably, given that their skills were badly needed there.[23] Many nurses attached to organisations such as the Friends Relief Society or the British Red Cross were involved in the first days of the liberation and the transfer of survivors to the hospital. It is rather startling today to hear that 'All the British people worked like niggers', but nurse M.F. Beardwell's description nevertheless provides some context for understanding the scale of the job facing the relief teams. Beardwell and another nurse, Silva Jones, were granted permission by Colonel Johnston to enter the 'horror camp' because, in his view, trained nurses 'could stand seeing the horrors better than those people who had no hospital experience'. It was, in Beardwell's words, a 'never-to-be-forgotten day':

The smell was terrible – the sickly smell of death mingled with the stench of excreta and burning boots, shoes, and rags of clothing. The camp, one square mile, had 60,000 people in it – 10,000 of these were lying dead and unburied. The few broken-down and derelict looking wooden huts were full of people – the dead lying on the living and the living on the dead; corpses were hanging out of the windows – heaps of dead thrown in grotesque masses – skeleton arms intertwined with skeleton legs and great vacant eyes staring up through the morass of sprawling dead. The majority of the living inmates looked more like animals than human beings. They were clad in filthy rags and were crawling and grovelling in the earth for bits of food. They took no notice of us or anyone – they vomited and stooled where they stood or sat – lavatories just did not exist – large square holes about ten feet square had been dug with a crude pole around, but most of the inmates were beyond getting to that pole.[24]

It is hardly surprising to learn that Beardwell and Jones were 'utterly stunned and without voice for several hours after our visit to the horror camp'. They soon discovered that 'nursing proper was impossible' until the inmates of the wooden huts had either died or been transferred to the Glyn Hughes hospital. Yet their work was undoubtedly crucial to the saving of many lives and to the organisation of Belsen into something approaching an operational hospital. So too was the work of the many survivors who also became nurses. Indeed, the work was especially hard for them given their immediate past. Jane Leverson, a member of the Quaker Relief Team which arrived in Belsen six days after the liberation, noted in a report written two weeks later that the story of one Polish nurse 'sums up the feelings of this camp, perhaps better than anything else': 'I was with an Austrian and a Yugo Slav, Jewish doctors, on the evening of the 4th May last, when a Polish nurse burst into our room, sobbing bitterly, that the War had ended, and she had no home, no family, no friends, where should she go?'[25] Following the implementation of the re-feeding programme the medical team – and we should not forget that as a percentage of the camp population the size of the team was wholly disproportionate to its tasks – was then able to focus on treating the other prevailing illnesses: tuberculosis and typhus. Since the two diseases produce similar symptoms, including fever and a rose-coloured rash, typhus (caused by faeces in the human body entering the skin where lice have bitten) was (and still is) often confused with typhoid (caused by bacteria transmitted in food or water contaminated by the faeces of an infected person). However, by testing negatively for typhoid in their mobile laboratories the RAMC could work on the assumption that they were faced primarily by typhus. Lipscomb recorded that 'No clinically definite case was discovered.'[26] In fact the British soldiers had been spraying the survivors with DDT since their arrival but they correctly realised that most of the deaths in the camp were caused by starvation. As Glyn Hughes noted, 'Typhus was on the wane and reached its peak in March. It is understood it commenced early in February . . . the medical members considered the worst was over.'[27] The strong likelihood is that of the thousands of sick inmates who died after liberation, most died not of typhus but of starvation and complications caused by starvation.[28]

The other major killer at Belsen in the liberation period was tuberculosis, which had also been prevalent in all the Nazi camps and ghettos and throughout wartime Europe. Indeed, it is likely that it was far more common than typhus, since the tubercle bacillus accompanies overcrowding and starvation. Tuberculosis was the main public health problem in Europe before it became treatable after the Second World War, and its ubiquity perhaps accounts for its having been little commented on in discussions of the camps. J.T. Lewis stated in a lecture held on 1 November 1945 in Belfast that TB was 'by far the greatest cause of death in Belsen' and that 'We came to the conclusion that 25% of all patients in Belsen were probably suffering from acute tuberculosis.' This, Lewis went on to say, was hardly surprising 'when one considers the degree of malnutrition and the appalling conditions in the original huts where the prisoners were packed, not only in one tight layer but often in several layers, with the dead forming a mattress for the living.'[29] There was a high incidence of tuberculosis among those who died after liberation, though it will never be established whether they died of tuberculosis or with tuberculosis. The working assumption was that if a starving patient did not improve after once more receiving a normal diet, or who had persistent anaemia, he or she probably had tuberculosis.[30]

The authors of one memoir, published soon after the war, proudly wrote of the British relief operation that 'Perhaps never in the history of medicine has a more gallant action been fought against disease than during the first few weeks which followed' the arrival of the medical relief teams.[31] Or as one of the student relief workers asked fifty years after the liberation: 'The question of whether the British forces did enough, quickly enough in Belsen is almost impossible to answer. In the circumstances what possibly could have been enough?'[32]

An indication of the efforts to which the British relief teams went – during a time in which the war was still on and the army's medical services were fully committed with dealing with the troops – is the description provided by Josef Rosensaft, who can hardly be regarded as a British patsy. Rosensaft describes Glyn Hughes as a 'great humanitarian' who, together with Colonel Johnston, 'another medical officer, conducted the desperate drive to save the liberated inmates of Belsen, and many were saved thanks to their efforts. A unit of the British Red Cross and a group of medical students from various British colleges under Dr Meiklejohn also worked in the camp with selfless devotion.' Rosensaft also praised the Swedish Red Cross.[33]

In fact, the medical relief operations at the camps liberated by the Western Allies accomplished a great deal, when one bears in mind the logistical difficulties of providing food, medicine and clothing whilst the war was still on. Paul A. Roy, briefly in charge of Dachau after its liberation, set out the scale of the challenge:

> We had more than 32,000 human beings on our hands who, for years, had been treated worse than animals. Our first job was their welfare. We had to nurse them back to health, and to rehabilitate them mentally. Many of them had been so completely starved that the fatty tissues surrounding their nerves had been used up, producing a kind of nervous short-circuit. They could not think consecutively. Some of them had lost their memories, and their mental reactions were very slow and childish. They were human wrecks who had to be salvaged.[34]

Similarly, in Buchenwald, the 120th Evacuation Hospital, a unit which specialised in treating battlefield casualties, was drafted in to help survivors. 'You do what you have to do', said Warren Priest, a surgeon with the

120th Evac. 'When you're faced with a situation where you can save people, you save them. And if you find a sign of life, then that is, in a sense, a measure of hope. And you try always to bring that hope back as fully, as vibrantly, as possible.'[35] Few survivors were strong enough to respond but the nurses and doctors did what they could. First Lieutenant May Macdonald, the head nurse of the 120th Evac, wrote a letter home on 28 April 1945 in which she described the survivors: 'With few exceptions, all were ragged, dirty and unkempt. Whenever we passed them in groups or singly, they saluted, smiled and in every way tried to show how much they appreciated us. We could see that they were dazed and happy, yet so weak that they could not show their enthusiasm.'[36]

These words need careful analysis. Although today it seems hyperbolic to hold (as do some survivors and their supporters in the Allied military) that the US and British armies treated inmates just as the Nazis did, it is equally important not to hero-worship the liberators and to understand what is meant when claiming that their actions were relatively effective. Priest, the surgeon from the 120th Evacuation Unit in Buchenwald, makes it clear that 'success' in this context meant not so much nursing the ill back to health but reducing the death rate. This the unit did by employing a few simple measures: within a few days they had 'stabilized [the survivors'] eating conditions so they could feed, and we were aware that the best thing we could do was to give them whole blood, especially those more severely impacted, that they couldn't tolerate food in the stomach; they could tolerate whole blood with some nutrients from a healthy person, which we did. We had to get blood from everybody we could. I think all of us gave some blood.'[37] Medical relief, in other words, was at first an emergency measure, it did not mean that those who were dying when the liberating soldiers arrived would recover and survive.

Many who did survive commented on the skill and rapidity with which medical care was delivered. Jörn Gastfreund, for example, a German Jew who had been in Auschwitz, Dachau and Gross-Rosen, was liberated in a camp in Mühldorf at Ampfing, and there contracted 'spotted typhus from lice'. When the Americans arrived on 2 May Gastfreund was sick with fever, but he was fortunate: 'The Americans cared for us very, very well. The medical treatment was excellent.' And although he suffered a relapse two weeks after getting up, he again received proper medical attention:

While in the lager we didn't receive any medicine or any means of prevention of disease; here spotted typhus was treated altogether differently. We were given tablets, we were examined by the physician three or four times a day, our temperature was taken, and so it was no wonder that we soon recuperated. I may say, in general, that only a few of the people who were liberated by the Americans died afterwards.[38]

His words are corroborated by another survivor of Mühldorf, Jürgen Bassfreund, who, also suffering from fever at the time of liberation and unable to celebrate, recovered quickly in the hands of the Americans, whom he praised for treating the survivors 'very, very well'.[39] A longer period of recuperation was required for Isaac Neuman, who was close to death when the Americans liberated Ebensee, where he had been marched first from Gross-Rosen via Mauthausen. Dying of starvation and tuberculosis, Neuman spent eighteen months in a DP hospital in Bad Goisern and then close to Linz before he was assisted by the JDC to immigrate to the US in 1950 and, eventually, to train as a rabbi.[40]

In Dachau, as Joel Sack put it, 'liberation hurt'; one could hear 'expressions of happiness at having found someone, of the excitement of being liberated, and of sorrow over losses of family and friends'.[41] The American military offered medical care to the extent that it was able in May 1945, but many inmates alive on 29 April still died afterwards. In Mauthausen, the Americans 'faced a formidable task when they took over . . . and on looking back, it is clear that it was well and ably carried out'. After supervising the filling in of the enormous communal grave (it contained 10,000 bodies) and the burial of a further 5,000 in the SS football field, the American medical authorities set about caring for the living. Evelyn Le Chêne reports that many American soldiers donated blood, and against poor odds, very many survivors were nursed back to health. Still, some 3,000 died after liberation. Le Chêne suggests that:

Many died from sheer joy. They had lived on hope, on fear and on their nerves for so long that the sudden relaxation of tension, when it came, was too much for them. Many people died because they left the camp before they were strong enough. The Americans warned them against doing so and encouraged them to stay on, but the pull of their homelands was too powerful. Trains were sent, particularly from the USSR, to repatriate nationals and anyone else who wished to return eastwards to his homeland.[42]

In the camps liberated by the Americans, too, nurses played a vital role in helping the sick. One former nurse at Gusen, Phyllis LaMont Law, recalls her shock on seeing the state of the inmates and how some of them died whilst in the process of receiving blood transfusions. 'The situation is kind of hopeless', she said. 'You just hope you can save a few.'[43] As in Buchenwald, in Mauthausen the former underground Camp Resistance Committee also played an important role, not just in medical relief but in coordinating the collection of testimonies to be used against war criminals. By June, most of those liberated had left the camp to make the arduous journey home; but there were still 5,200 former inmates there, including 1,621 still receiving medical attention.[44]

With respect to the role played by dedicated nurses, their caring for children deserves special mention. In 1945, Gitta Sereny, who later became Albert Speer's biographer, was working for UNRRA and was assigned to work as a child welfare officer in occupied Germany. Her first task was to care for child survivors of Dachau. 'Was it thinkable', Sereny asks, 'that they would have sent children to these places? It was: children of all ages, all religions, many nationalities, including Germans.'[45]

As in Dachau, no aspect of Belsen elicited greater sympathy and interest than the children, some 500 of whom were in the camp when it was liberated. In the 'children's home', as it was known, 100 Dutch orphans were cared for by Luba Tryszynska, 'the angel of Belsen', and Hermina Krantz, nurses who had been sent to Belsen from Auschwitz. There they worked under Hadassah Bimko and devoted themselves to these children of prominent Dutch Jews who had been spared the worst of the starvation and disease that prevailed in the camp's last months. In July 1945 the children were returned to the Netherlands. Bimko herself quickly established herself as a prominent leader and very competent physician in the concentration camp following her arrival there in November 1944; after the liberation she played a crucial role in the medical relief efforts as the head of a medical team and, following her marriage to Josef Rosensaft, she was at the centre of DP politics for years after the war.[46]

The rest of Belsen's children were not so lucky. Their condition can be appreciated in the words of nurse Joan Rudman: 'The children's ward', she wrote, 'would break your heart, tiny little scraps in a bed with two big eyes staring out of a sunken face and little babies just like birds. I want to cry every time I go near the place to think that innocent little children should have suffered so much.'[47] Indeed, the suffering of children was and is the most incomprehensible aspect of the Holocaust. According to one report, when David Ben Gurion visited Belsen DP camp in October 1945, he too found the children's block hard to bear. Viewing the crematoria and mass graves or listening to the views of the Pioneer youth groups, Ben Gurion was attentive and took notes. But when he visited the children's block he behaved differently. 'When he heard that these were children who had only been saved by a miracle, he was very moved. It seemed as if he had only understood the depth of the Jewish tragedy at this moment. This time he took no notes and tears flowed from his eyes.'[48]

DP care worker Zippy Orlin describes the eighty orphans in Belsen's children's home who 'had been dragged from one country to another, from one concentration camp to another', some of whom did not even know their names or where they were from: 'At mealtime they stuffed themselves hurriedly and anything that was left on the table was put into their pockets, and later hidden under their pillows. But after many months of careful and patient training they learnt that there would be more food tomorrow, and the next day, and every day until they left Belsen for Israel.'[49] The phrase 'after many months' disguises a great deal of what went on in the period following liberation to bring some sort of order to the child survivors' lives as they became ensconced in DP camps, waiting to go somewhere else. 'Most children were too ill and numb to remember anything about the day' of liberation; only gradually were some of the children able to be returned to health. There then followed a perhaps even harder period of helping the aimless children to give their lives some purpose, as kindergartens, schools and training centres were opened in the DP camps.[50]

As the Belsen children's condition improved they offered a sense of hope to the adults in the camp, both survivors and relief workers. Those on the cusp of adulthood, especially, provided a glimpse of hope for the future:

One morning there was great excitement on the ward when Hannah Sachsel started her first period. She was fourteen and had managed to survive with her seventeen-year-old sister Eva. Everybody loved them as they symbolised the immortality of youth and hope. It was celebrated like a miracle as no-one had menstruated since entering the camp.[51]

Of course, the fact that menstruation should be celebrated in this way reminds us that conditions were far from normal and that suggestions of 'hope for the future' were coming from a very low starting point. Still, the improvements in the children's lives were real and were realised by the dedicated staff. 'I could write a paean of praise', wrote American relief worker Vida Kaufman, 'to the teachers and supervisors of the schools, for it is their goal to bring normalcy into the lives of the children, to do everything possible to make them forget the horrors and travails of the preceding years.'[52]

According to Robert Collis, the children's blocks were 'the happiest in the whole camp'. This might seem a strange claim when he also noted that of the approximately 500 children in the camp, 'about one hundred died and two-thirds were affected with typhus or tuberculosis to a greater or lesser degree.'[53] What he meant was that:

Many of the children are emaciated, showing the utmost marasmus, and many are sick; but also many are now beginning to recover, and, strange though it may seem, these, particularly the children under 7, do not show the terror symptoms which are perhaps the most terrible aspect of the adult patients' mental state. Already they are laughing and smiling again. Many are going to recover altogether.

'But', Collis went on, recovery in a physical sense would not be the end of the story. Instead, 'our responsibility will not end then, for most have no homes to go to, no parents, no ordinary future. Surely somewhere in the world there are people who will come forward and care for these children and give them a home again.'[54]

The initial medical relief operations had brought about a situation where the survivors could begin to consider their lives. Hence the emerging problems with the DP camps: those inside them did not want to be left languishing but their aims and ambitions – especially to emigrate, bound for Palestine or the US – did not always square with those of their liberators. Leo Schwarz describes this developing sense of agency with characteristic hyperbole, omitting to mention the existential crises that lay behind it:

> Again at the concentrations of enslaved masses such as Buchenwald, Dachau, Bergen-Belsen, Mathhausen and Theresienstadt, medical units of the British, American and Soviet Armies, working with selfless exertion, launched what was probably the largest scale administration of blood transfusions, glucose injections and anti-typhus prophylaxis ever undertaken. Nevertheless, the objects of these splendid humanitarian endeavours soon realized that liberation in itself was not necessarily tantamount to freedom; only initiative and persistence, even beyond that exerted for survival in the preceding years, could transform their lives.[55]

Very early on, Robert Collis gave a more accurate analysis of the increasingly obvious problem for the survivors, now growing physically healthy but still mentally extremely frail, in a tough but humane assessment:

> Finally comes the immense problem of rehabilitation of these poor, abused, broken people. First the demands of their bodies must no doubt be met, but many are as wasted in mind as they are in body ... The problem of what to do with these forsaken, almost lost, souls is immense, but one which if not tackled and solved will make all our efforts here a mere waste of time, for then it were kinder to have let them die than to have brought them back to mere existence and more suffering in a hostile world where they have no longer even a hope of being able to compete in the struggle of the survival of the fittest, and must inevitably go down.[56]

Nevertheless, that Schwarz and Collis, in their different ways, were able to think along these lines at all was thanks largely to the work of those involved in providing medical care following the liberation of the camps. Their work paved the way for others who sustained the survivors over the longer term – survivors who had now become DPs.

*   *   *

Who were the people who did this work? The various Jewish aid organisations to which many of them were attached have been criticised for their late arrival at the camps. This was partly a result of military restrictions, partly a failure of the organisations themselves to realise the scale of the task facing them and to recruit personnel quickly enough. The lack of response that Zalman Grinberg got to his requests for aid from the US military and Jewish organisations in the US shocked Robert Hilliard, who helped the survivors at St Ottilien.[57] When they did arrive, the aid organisations, well-meaning though they were, did not always win the survivors' admiration. Josef Rosensaft, for example, praised the relief work of the JDC, HIAS (Hebrew Immigrant Aid Society), ORT, JRC (Jewish Relief Committee) and JAP (Jewish Agency for Palestine), and Joseph Schwartz in particular, but he reserved especial praise for the World Jewish Congress because it 'engaged itself in political aid, which was given us not in the spirit of pity on poor Jews in reduced circumstances, but in true brotherly fashion, in full co-operation with us and through continuous consultations as between equals. This is what made the assistance of the World Jewish Congress so different from that of other Jewish organisations.'[58] His assessment of the WJC implies a rather negative view of the other organisations, which Rosensaft regarded as looking down on the survivors, forgetting that they had had lives before the war and were in fact not mere 'human dust'.

After September 1945, the JDC became the single largest provider of aid in the American zone, at first in several camps and eventually in just one: Föhrenwald. Criticised by many survivors (and historians) for its tardy arrival, criticised too for patronising the survivors,[59] the JDC nevertheless took on the massive task of caring for the survivors of Europe's Jewish communities. It first began operating in Buchenwald on 13 June 1945, then in Feldafing in August. The main new camps that were set up by the Americans were those at Landsberg and Föhrenwald. Major Irving Heymont, a Jewish officer (though neither the DPs nor the American soldiers knew at the time he was Jewish), was responsible for ensuring that the inadequate and inappropriate living conditions at the former military barracks at Landsberg were made suitable for the 6,000 Jews who were there in August 1945. If the JDC focused its energies on Föhrenwald, which became a Jewish camp in October 1945, it was because the camp was more suited to civilian use and because it was used for the registration of Jewish children. For the first few months the JDC was stymied by army regulations which prevented the organisation from sending its own people into the camps and, more importantly, forbade it from sending supplies for civilians.[60] And in Bavaria supplying food was also harder than in some other locations.

These difficulties did not stop the authorities from trying to help the DPs, though they were often insufficiently sensitive to their needs or were unable to understand what they had been through. Sometimes, one gets the impression that they both did and did not understand at the same time. In September 1945, for example, Major Heymont addressed survivors in Landsberg with the intention of improving their morale and overcoming the effects of their persecution through a rediscovery of the work ethic:

> I know better than to accuse you of laziness. Under the Germans, work meant death for you. The harder you worked, the weaker you got on the few hundred calories you were fed. Every bit of work you did strengthened your oppressor. Even now you are reluctant to do any work in the camp. You think – 'why work in the camp. We won't be here forever' . . . All of that is true. But now is the time to relearn the habits of work and industry. Now is the time to relearn how to be self-respecting civilised persons. No man can ask you to forget what you and your families have been through. However, you can't live in the shadow of the past forever.[61]

Such efforts were well intentioned but hardly took cognisance of the fact that the DP camps seemed, to those stuck in them, to be a continuation of their imprisonment, this time at the hands of the Allies and UNRRA, and that such disillusionment bred 'a sense of abandonment' which led many to 'despair, depression, bitterness and resentment'.[62]

In the British zone, the combination of the authorities' reluctance to implement the reforms the DPs demanded – in particular, separate Jewish camps to put an end to hostility between Jewish and non-Jewish DPs – and the 'late arrival' of civilian relief teams, led to increased tensions between the DPs and their British liberators. What the DPs did not know was that the delayed arrival of civilian (especially Jewish) relief teams was caused by the British military's wariness at allowing them into Germany; but the result was that the Jewish DPs 'felt abandoned by their own people', setting off a vicious cycle whereby British policy exacerbated the perceived need for the relief teams that were being prevented from entering by those same policies.[63]

The most important of the relief organisations in the British zone, when they were finally admitted, was the Jewish Relief Unit (JRU), a formation of the JCRA, which had been founded in January 1943 in anticipation of the war's end.[64] Under Leonard Cohen and Lady Rose Henriques, the JRU arrived in Belsen in late June 1945 and was the first relief unit on the scene after the British army. Other Jewish bodies also sent teams to Belsen – the JDC, for example, arriving in early July 1945, and the JAP in March 1946, but the JRU provided the bulk of the manpower and resources. By April 1946 there were sixty-eight JRU workers in Germany, rising to ninety-two by the summer of that year.[65]

In the early days after liberation the JRU was struggling against the odds. The sources suggest a heroic effort on the part of British amateurs, which makes quite understandable the annoyance of those who have argued that the response of the British authorities was inadequate. Jane Leverson, at the time the only female Jewish relief worker in Belsen, wrote in May 1945 to the headquarters of the JCRA in London explaining that she and the other relief workers were engaged in 'an impossible task'. 'It really is a phenomenal battle against death', Leverson wrote, 'and we have no hope for anything but a comparative handful of lives.'[66] She was clear in her assessment of the state of the Jewish survivors: all were damaged physically and mentally, fearful of the present and the future, ready to grumble and complain at the slightest inconvenience, and desperate to find relatives and friends. She argued that if the cycle of increasing resentment of both parties (the survivors and the British liberators) was to be broken, the only solution was to allow the Jews to go to Palestine. 'Work amongst these Jews is heart-breaking', she concluded, 'unless one can offer them good grounds for hope with regard to their rehabilitation.'[67]

A few months later, however, the situation was improved, if still far from satisfactory. In July Rose Henriques reported that in the camps other than Belsen (which she described as 'well housed'), the 'crowds' were still 'waiting for "something to be done."' This 'something', she thought, included most basics: decent housing, proper clothing, decent food, adequate medical services, social amenities.[68] She explained too that the camp survivors were still very fragile and in need first and foremost of reuniting with family members.[69] In Celle, Henriques had to appeal to the army to do something about the increasing numbers of Jewish travellers searching for family members being forced to sleep rough.[70] Yet such appeals indicated that conditions were improving to the extent that such travel was possible at all, and Henriques also reported that DPs were in receipt of clothing and food, that DPs in hospital were being visited, that cultural and vocational activities were up and running, that a communal kitchen and children's play centre had been set up in Celle, and that the JRU had offered food parcels to those travelling in search of relatives.[71] Winter clothing was the next pressing need.[72] In contributing to the establishment of semi-permanent social needs, the JRU was in effect contributing not just to the relief of the DPs but to their entrenchment into communities.

Despite the relief workers' best efforts in the face of adversities beyond their control, the JRU's work was not always well received. Hadassah Rosensaft, for example, was quite critical of the JRU's efforts. For the 'assimilated Jewish woman' Henriques, Rosensaft writes, 'this was a team of social workers, and she showed little understanding of our tragic experiences'. This seems somewhat unfair, but Rosensaft was of course not privy to the extent of Henriques' efforts to secure supplies for the survivors and DPs. She could not have known that Henriques protested about British policies which were pushing Jews in the British zone 'into a life of crime in order to exist', by which she meant engaging in the black market and, in concentration-camp slang, 'organising' (i.e. stealing) food, material and equipment.[73] And she is unlikely to have seen Henriques' last report as leader of 132 JRU, in which she offered to the British military authorities, the Red Cross and UNRRA her barbed thanks 'for the help they have given and the patience with which they have listened to my many requests, even though it may not always have been in their power to grant them'.[74] Isaac Levy, despite initial protests about the JCRA's slow reaction and failure to inform him of their movements, was eventually more appreciative, saying that the JCRA was 'doing an excellent job . . . and although hampered by lack of materials, were making a decisive impact'.[75] Next came the JAP, HIAS, ORT and the JDC, which 'brought us the first supply of food in July 1945'.[76] Rosensaft has more praise for the JDC, but then it was far better equipped and resourced than was the JRU. 'Everywhere', said the author of one report on the first news of the fate of survivors, 'Jewish refugees asked after the Joint'. This statement confirmed that, as he also said, 'the job was much too big for the

Army and the arrival of Unrra DP teams had not yet relieved the situation.'[77] It also indicates the JDC's status in Europe. The same report offered a thorough survey of the needs of the DPs in camps in Salzburg, Augsburg, Dachau, Allach, Ebensee, Linz and Freienberg, and also included some comments on the situation in Poland. Overall, it was clear that there was a general shortage of clothing, that the food rations were inadequate, and that Jewish survivors regularly faced anti-Semitism from non-Jewish (especially Polish) DPs. The JDC was facing an enormous task.

JDC worker Zippy Orlin, for example, came to Belsen in July 1946 after first stopping off at the organisation's Paris headquarters. Not long before (in May) the DP camp at Belsen had become a Jewish-only camp, with a large number of new incomers fleeing anti-Semitic violence in Poland. In August 1946 the DP camp had 11,139 residents, its largest population.[78] That number was partly a result of the Jewish inmates refusing to leave for their nominal 'home' countries. Leslie Hardman, attempting to help return Polish Jews to Poland shortly after the establishment of Belsen's Camp Two, was dressed down for 'spreading Zionist propaganda' after he reported that the Jews in the camp 'don't want to go back to their former homes. They want to go to Palestine, and nothing will stop them.'[79] Hardman maintained that he was simply acting as a go-between, bringing the people's fears to the attention of the British authorities. But it was not what the authorities wanted to hear, despite being true. It set the scene for the difficult relationship between the survivors – grateful for the care they received but anxious to be allowed to choose where and how to make their future lives – and the British authorities, sympathetic to the plight of the surviving Jews but annoyed that their care and attention was being repaid, so they thought, with resentment and contumacy. As Josef Rosensaft put it, 'Many months went by before we were recognised as Jews ... As late as September 1945 there were still fifteen thousand Jews in Belsen who were suffering from the curse of national anonymity.' The key galvaniser, as we shall see, was the American initiative known as the Harrison Report. Reluctant though they were to follow the Americans' lead, the British eventually did so in the summer of 1946 by turning Belsen into a Jewish DP camp. In doing so, as Hadassah Rosensaft writes, 'The British finally came to understand and respect us because the issues were not of trivial import but related fundamentally to principles of human justice and political liberty.'[80]

In the American zone, change occurred faster. The JDC arrived at Buchenwald in June 1945 and the JAP arrived in the US zone in December. Yet because of the obstacles that the military authorities placed in the Jewish aid organisations' way, it was not until six months after the liberations that they were really able to start making a difference to the lives of survivors – that is to say, at a point when the worst was already over. And it was not until almost a year after the liberation of the camps, in spring 1946, that a regular and sufficiently large supply of food and goods was flowing in. In the immediate post-liberation period, 'the all-important helpers', one historian reminds us, 'were courageous individuals who happened to be Jewish and who happened to find themselves in a place or position where they could assist Holocaust survivors'.[81] In order to understand why it took so long to establish a regular and systematic form of support, one has to set the Allies' policies towards the DPs in a wider context of intra-Allied tensions over empire, Palestine, immigration, domestic political concerns, occupation policies and the emergence of the Cold War.

*　*　*

In April 1943 Jacob Robinson, the director of the New York-based Institute of Jewish Affairs, published a short article outlining the problems that would face the Jews who survived the war and those tasked with assisting them. Arguing that the most pressing need would be for food, emergency medical care, clothing and shelter, the checking of disease and the restoration of physical strength, Robinson observed that such an effort 'will demand the full coordinated effort of governmental and other relief and rehabilitation agencies, as well as Jewish child aid organizations'.[82] He argued in favour of complementing these efforts with programmes to reintegrate Jews into education and economically useful activities, but noted that 'the conditions under which relief work will be done in liberated Europe will be unprecedented', thanks to the scale of the war, the extent of the Nazi attack on the Jews, and the survivors' dispersal throughout Europe. Above all, he recommended that those who wanted to should be allowed to enter Palestine. All of Robinson's recommendations presented difficulties for the Western Allies.[83]

Clearly, the sorrows of liberation weighed heavier on the survivors than on the population at large. Zalman Grinberg, formerly head of the Kovno ghetto and a doctor who had established a hospital for 800 survivors in the St Ottilien monastery near Dachau, spoke for many when he declared the survivors to be 'living corpses'. At a ceremony in Munich on 10 June 1945, Grinberg claimed that the survivors were not really alive but were in fact delegates of the dead. He went on, in a speech that indicates the depth of despair felt by many even as they were amazed to be alive, and even amongst the most active of campaigners:

> We are free now, but we do not know what to begin [sic] with free but unhappy life. It seems to us, that for the time being mankind does not comprehend what we have gone through and what we have experienced during this period of time. And it seems to us, neither shall we be understood in the future. We unlearned to laugh, we cannot cry any more, we do not comprehend our freedom yet, because we are still among our dead comrades.[84]

The Allies devoted considerable effort and resources to housing and caring for the liberated and for those who later entered the DP camps even though the latter did not, strictly speaking, qualify as DPs. Yet, as Ruth Klüger writes: 'The free world didn't welcome us as brothers and sisters, long lost but found again, liberated from evil forces and now to be jubilantly included in the Family of Man. That was the picture my childish yearning had painted. In reality we were a burden, a social problem.'[85] The survivors, as one Jewish commentator noted, had not benefited as much as they should have from being freed from Nazi rule. 'There has been little improvement in the situation since the day of liberation for the Jewish displaced persons, dispersed all over Europe', argued Zorach Warhaftig. 'They have been liberated from death. They have not been freed for life.' Indeed, he went so far as to claim that:

> In a sense, their situation has deteriorated since the day of liberation. They have experienced the most bitter disillusionment a people can have. Their faith in mankind has suffered a terrible shock. During the years of stagnating behind the barbed wires of Nazi camps they nourished the hope of liberation . . . In stark contrast, however, they encountered an indifferent, at times a cold, if not hostile, reception. Eighteen

months after V-E Day, and all the beautiful dreams have faded … A fearful feeling of helplessness and hopelessness, of being abandoned by democracy and humanity is growing. The peril of tragic catastrophe pends. They [the DPs] are firmly convinced that the world which could not prevent the slaughter of the overwhelming majority of European Jewry owes the pitiful remnants, at least now the war is over, assistance and a permanently fair solution.[86]

Most of the Jewish survivors had believed that they would receive help and compensation for their suffering. In reality, they were not offered new homes in new countries and often found themselves unwanted, and sometimes even attacked, in their countries of origin. There quickly arose a contradiction between UNRRA's policy of repatriation and the insistence of many of the Jewish survivors – mostly those from Eastern Europe – that they could not return 'home'. Lucie Adelsberger concurred: 'After so much brutality and so much cruel misfortune, one expects an excess of kindness and good fortune, and that's just not the way it is in this world.'[87]

So the Jewish survivors of the war became a burden that the Allies reluctantly and gradually took on, although the sense that they were a nuisance never quite escaped the officials' way of thinking. They were housed in assembly centres, often in the places where they were liberated, which soon became known as DP camps. They varied enormously both in size and conditions. The Jews themselves graduated from being 'survivors' to 'DPs', thanks largely to UNRRA's arrival with newly provisioned legal definitions for handling Europe's massive displaced population. Some Jews were housed in former Nazi camps or, as in the case of Belsen, close enough to retain the symbolic name. Others were in former barracks, hospitals, garages, hotels and apartment blocks.[88] At first, these places could only be described as basic. In Munich's Funk Caserne, a former Luftwaffe base, Ira Hirschmann found a three-storey garage that the Germans had used to store coal and wood; inside, 1,800 men and women 'were herded together like cattle in an abattoir'. At Zeilsheim, near Frankfurt, in 'nondescript huts and primitive, weather-beaten wooden barracks which once housed Russian slave-laborers, I found more than 3,000 Jews living in a miserable and frustrating environment'. At Kloster Indersdorf, the children's DP centre in Munich, he discovered that ill children could not be treated because of a lack of medicine.[89] The DP camps at this stage were being run by the military authorities because UNRRA wanted to concentrate its energies on repatriation. The military's concerns about civilians entering and travelling around newly-occupied territory meant that aid organisations could not provide assistance to the DPs until summer 1945, a fact which caused considerable bitterness but also meant that the DPs became self-directed and organised, not to mention ready to object to what they regarded as the patronising attitude of the charities when they did arrive. The DPs, many of whose leaders had considerable administrative experience from before and during the war (for example, in the ghettos of Poland), were not prepared to be regarded as charity cases.[90]

Before the charities and aid organisations were allowed in, survivors depended, as we have seen, on the military; Jewish military chaplains and soldiers were often the most important source of help for Holocaust survivors in these early days. Jewish chaplains in the US and British army went beyond the call of duty – literally, they often exceeded their official mission and risked reprimand – in assisting the survivors with providing food, speaking on their behalf with the authorities and, vitally, helping to contact relatives. The latter was especially important as the survivors had no postal service, and these efforts formed the basis of what soon became the Allied-operated tracing service, which in 1955 became the International Tracing Service under the aegis of the Red Cross.[91] In particular, Reform Rabbi Abraham J. Klausner helped to organise survivors in southern Germany and Leslie Hardman did the same at Belsen. Individual soldiers, from officers to privates, also played important roles, from local organisation of supplies to writing letters back to friends, relatives, and community publications at home denouncing official policies. Soldiers in the Jewish Brigade, 'by their insignia and their very presence inspired the survivors, and especially the first elected leaders there'; equally, many non-Jewish soldiers also simply offered help and support in ways that carried them far beyond their official roles.[92] In terms of what is usually referred to as 'rehabilitation', the DPs needed food, medicine and shelter. Then the Jewish DPs in particular wanted help with tracing relatives and finding new homes. The difficulties in the way of the latter, in particular the ways in which the fate of the DPs became entangled with the geopolitics of the British Empire and the early Cold War, ensured that the DP camps lasted far longer than anyone could have believed possible at the conclusion of hostilities.

*   *   *

The 45,000 or so Jewish survivors of the Nazi camps who were still in DP camps at the end of 1945 (some 36,000 of them in the US zone) were soon to be joined by tens of thousands of new arrivals. The near-impossibility of Jews continuing to live in their former Eastern European homes – as made stunningly clear by the Kielce pogrom of July 1946 – contributed to a vast westward migration, swelling the numbers of Jews in liberated Germany in May 1945 with former Polish Jews who had spent the war in exile in the USSR, and a smaller number of Jews who had survived in hiding or by passing as Aryan, the majority of whom made their way to the DP camps. Here they formed representative organisations and, despite the many national, religious, linguistic and other differences between them, set about trying to speak together so as to be able to defend their interests with a unified voice. In the US zone Zalman Grinberg emerged as the leading spokesman, and in the British zone, Josef Rosensaft, who had already taken on a leadership role in the concentration camp. Though the men competed with each other as well as with the authorities, they also held joint con-ferences and sought to represent all the Jewish DPs. This was not always successful, thanks partly to travel restrictions between the zones and partly to cultural differences between the DP leaders, whose backgrounds – Lithuanian-intellectual in the case of the US zone, Polish petit-bourgeoisie in the British – was a traditional source of tension. The British authorities also resisted any attempts to unify the leadership of the Jewish DPs and the German Jews living in towns and cities, though Rosensaft and Norbert Wollheim, who represented the German Jewish communities in the British zone, worked well together. The DP leaders in the US and British zones shared a condemnation of the way in which the Jewish DPs had been 'aban-doned' and both argued that allowing emigration for Palestine was the only real solution. As Grinberg said in his closing speech to the Liberated Jews in the American zone's Munich conference in January 1946, 'We cannot possibly be expected to contribute to the reconstruction of Germany, we want to get out of Europe, we want to go to Palestine.'[93] The *Brichah* (Flight) organisation helped spirit over 100,000 Jewish Holocaust survivors from Eastern Europe to Palestine. But for the rest, the DP camps in Germany were the best option, and as their numbers grew during 1946 so did the tension between the DPs and the authorities.

By the end of 1946 there were some 141,000 Jewish DPs in the American zone and, according to a Joint estimate, a further 50,000 in the British zone. There were also about 1,200 Jews in the French zone, only half of whom lived in camps. Until the summer of 1945 Jewish DPs had no choice but to live alongside forced labourers, volunteers for work in Nazi Germany and, at worst, collaborators, including former camp guards. As a result, conflict, including physical violence, between the Jewish and non-Jewish DPs became a regular occurrence. For instance, Polish DP police burnt a synagogue during the Jewish festival of Hannukah in December 1945, at which point the British authorities permitted the Jewish DPs also to establish a camp police force.[94] In the British zone most of the Jews were housed in Belsen-Hohne, along with some 10,000 non-Jewish Poles who refused to be repatriated. The latter were rehoused on 22 August 1946 as a result of the tensions between the Jewish and non-Jewish DPs, whereupon Belsen became a Jewish camp. Although Belsen was by far the largest Jewish DP camp in postwar Germany, most Jewish DPs were located in the American zone, where DPs were at first also housed by nationality, suffering the same problems as at Belsen.

This policy of placing surviving Jews with forced labourers, volunteers and others according to nationality was not unique to the DP camps, although it was particularly marked in the British zone. Indeed, a reluctance to separate out categories of victims was common throughout Europe, in the east because the authorities were spreading a message of unified, communist, anti-fascist resistance, and in the west so that new conflicts between different constituencies, including collaborators and forced labourers who had not been treated so badly, would not disrupt the process of rebuilding functioning societies. Richard van Dam, for example, was a Dutch Jew who was taken to Auschwitz as a political prisoner (the Nazis did not discover he was Jewish) in spring 1943, where he was eventually employed as a medical orderly. Later he was transferred on a death march to Mauthausen, and then finally to Ebensee. There, close to death following an industrial accident which had bored a hole in his foot and caused infection, he was liberated. He was operated on by the Americans and, during his recovery, worked for the US troops as a translator. When he was well enough to return to the Netherlands, via Paris and Brussels, he was sent to a reception centre in Tilburg where 'he and his fellow-prisoners were assigned to billets in a school where a large number of repatriated Dutchmen were who had voluntarily worked in Germany'. Van Dam refused to enter and, following a row with the Dutch official in charge, was finally billeted in the home of a factory owner, with whom he became close friends. He returned to his home town of Rotterdam in July 1945, but in the context of a country that was not yet ready to grapple with the differences between the experiences of those who had volunteered to work in Germany, those who were forced labourers, and those who were concentration camp survivors.[95]

The Americans were unsure what to do with the different groups of DPs or how to deal with the rapidly growing problem of overcrowding at the DP camps. The solution to the flawed policy that saw Jews and their tormentors living side by side came in the shape of the Harrison Report. In response to the tensions, centred upon the DPs' housing situation, between the DP groups and between DPs and the American army, in July 1945 President Truman commissioned Earl G. Harrison, dean of the University of Pennsylvania Law School, to visit the camps and produce a survey of prevailing conditions. This he duly did in August, accompanied by Joseph Schwartz, the head of the JDC in Europe. Harrison's report was explosive. He took the Jewish DPs' view of matters at every turn, explained why they felt so neglected, and made recommendations that would not only improve their situation but which would create further friction between the Americans and their British allies over the question of Palestine. As we will see, the British wanted to keep the DP question separate from their role as mandatory rulers of Palestine, whereas the Americans insisted that allowing immigration into Palestine would resolve the problem.

Harrison began by noting of the victims of Nazi persecution that:

> Up to this point they have been 'liberated' more in a military sense than actually. For reasons explained in the report, their particular problems, to this time, have not been given attention to any appreciable extent; consequently they feel that they, who were in so many ways the first and worst victims of Nazism, are being neglected by their liberators.[96]

The report described the efforts that had been made to feed and clothe the survivors but criticised the failure to rehabilitate them, with the result that their morale is 'very low'. In the absence of any plans for their future,

> they wonder and frequently ask what 'liberation' means. This situation is considerably accentuated where, as in so many cases, they are able to look from their crowded and bare quarters and see the German civilian population, particularly in the rural areas, to all appearances living normal lives in their own homes.[97]

Harrison, deliberately taking on the policy of grouping the DPs by nationality, argued that Nazi targeting had made of the Jews a special group whose needs were different and greater than the non-Jewish DPs. Even further, Harrison's report contentiously suggested that the British 1939 White Paper on Palestine should be modified so as to permit more Jewish DPs to enter. Harrison claimed that he made this observation 'on a purely humanitarian basis with no reference to ideological or political considerations so far as Palestine is concerned', but he was not exactly reticent in noting that 'To anyone who has visited the concentration camps and who has talked with the despairing survivors, it is nothing short of calamitous to contemplate that the gates of Palestine should be soon closed.'[98] Finally, in an oft-cited passage, Harrison claimed:

> As matters now stand, we appear to be treating the Jews as the Nazis treated them except that we do not exterminate them. They are in concentration camps in large numbers under our military guard instead of S.S. troops. One is led to wonder whether the German people, seeing this, are not supposing that we are following or at least condoning Nazi policy.[99]

As has been noted, the 'passionate outrage' of Harrison's report 'was hyperbolic and unfair to the substantial efforts that had been made by the US military', but it pushed General Eisenhower to appoint an advisor on Jewish affairs.[100] Judah Nadich, who took up the post on a temporary basis, produced a report every bit as scathing as Harrison's – which he described as having thrown 'a bombshell into American government circles' – on 16 September. He criticised the insufficient food rations, the physical conditions of the camps, and the army's failure to distinguish concentration camp survivors from voluntary or involuntary labourers in Germany.[101] But neither Harrison nor Nadich was as critical as the authors of a letter from St Ottilien. Two privates, Edward Herman and Robert Hilliard, took it upon themselves to stir up outrage at what Hilliard later called America's 'genocide by neglect' after the war. The letter they sent to over 1,000 individuals and institutions in the US in August 1945 began simply:

> Friends:
>
> The Jews of Europe are a dying race. Even now, after the defeat of Hitler and Nazism, they are slowly being exterminated from the face of the earth.
>
> YOU ARE TO BLAME!
>
> If you consider yourself a human being, a member of the human race, then you are – although perhaps unwittingly, yet nevertheless certainly – a murderer.
>
> For you are carrying out Hitler's plan of destruction of the Jewish race. By your unconcerned neglect, you are just as responsible for the present death of the European Jews as the most diabolical of Nazis was in the past.[102]

In his memoir, Hilliard claims that the letter reached the US President and that its charges were the reason for Truman's decision to ask Harrison to investigate the DP camps.[103] Whatever the case, the immediate upshot of Harrison's report and the subsequent appointment of an adviser was that the US government agreed to establish separate camps for Jewish DPs, to raise their food rations and to grant them some measure of autonomy within the camps. In retrospect, Nadich wrote that in the wake of Harrison, 'Everyone concerned with the problems of the Jewish DPs saw the necessity for placing Jews in separate DP camps. The Jews had suffered far worse at the hands of the Nazis and, therefore, as a group required special treatment.'[104] That 'everyone', however, did not include the British, who refused to follow suit straight away; however, after incidents involving Polish DPs attacking Jewish DPs they did eventually separate the Belsen inmates into two sections, one for (mainly) non-Jewish Poles and the other for Jews, thus creating in Belsen a *de facto* Jewish camp alongside the Polish one. And although the British non-fraternisation rules remained in force, meaning that German

Jews were evacuated from the camp into the German community, the rise in the number of new arrivals from Eastern Europe meant that the British were forced to treat these people as DPs.[105] Nadich was very critical of the British, claiming that 'in their keen desire to be unlike the Nazis and not to treat the Jews as "a separate race," [the British] were unrealistic enough to lose sight of the fact that the Jews, because the Nazis had thus singled them out for special barbarous attention and savage treatment, now stood in dire need of special rescue and rehabilitation treatment.'[106] This was correct, formally speaking, but in fact a very British approach ensued, whereby the authorities did adapt their practices to meet the changing circumstances and the American criticisms, but left the rules unchanged.

So by 1946, as one commentator noted of Jews from Eastern Europe arriving at the DP camps in occupied Germany, 'The persistence and resolute determination of the fleeing Jews to disregard all hardships and obstacles, combined with the utter impossibility of removing the causes of the flight, have contributed to the reluctance of the governments concerned to combat this unauthorized movement. Moreover, a certain amount of tacit compliance with this flight has been implied.' The reference was to governments such as those in Poland and Romania. The Polish government, trying to ingratiate itself with the population in the process of building communism, cynically advocated a policy of granting the Jews special status as refugees. Doing so accorded with the Allies' policy of removing ethnic minorities, and allowed the Poles to present the move as a philosemitic gesture. The Romanians wavered, sometimes like the Poles encouraging Jews to emigrate, sometimes preventing them from doing so, but ultimately they did allow large numbers of Jews to leave for Palestine at certain points in time.[107]

The Jews were going to keep coming, yet a clear policy for dealing with them was lacking. As Zorach Warhaftig went on to observe:

> The attitude of the authorities in the receiving areas varied. The attitude of the American military authorities has been the best by far. Individual fleeing Jews may find a haven in many European countries as well as in the British or French occupation zones, but it is a matter of good luck as to whether they can get in, or whether, once in, they can remain. It is only in the U.S. zone that the newly arriving DP's are made welcome, are received and cared for on an organized basis. The military governor of

the British zone in Germany announced on August 9, 1946, that *exhaustive measures* had been taken to seal this zone against further infiltration of unauthorized refugees from the East, including Polish Jews. About five thousand such refugees who were in the British zone at that time were denied food ration cards. The British, while resolved not to turn back the 'illegal entrants', did consider the denial of all DP privileges to these people as an effective measure to check the 'illegal movement' of Eastern Europeans into the British zone.[108]

Indeed, the Americans were here simply conforming to the recommendation from UNRRA of 27 January 1946 that people who arrived at DP camps after the end of hostilities should still be considered Displaced Persons and treated accordingly. As UNRRA Director General Fiorello LaGuardia said: 'A persecuted people leaving a country, and that is the case of the Jews leaving Poland, are entitled to benefit from all the help and assistance that UNRRA is permitted to give to displaced people.'[109]

Yet January 1946 was more than half a year after the last liberations. This generous attitude to and expansive definition of DPs developed slowly over the immediate postwar months, glacially so from the point of view of the DPs themselves. So although their situation and the authorities' understanding of their plight gradually improved, one can understand why the Jewish DPs became so deeply disenchanted with the same people who had saved them only months before. In the case of those in the British zone, this disenchantment was compounded by the British distrust of the DPs' emerging Zionism, a distrust that ironically only helped to strengthen that which it wanted to suppress: Jewish national aspiration. As Rose Henriques noted at the end of December 1945, British policies, including requiring Jewish DPs to remain in camps and not permitting them freedom of movement (ostensibly for their own protection), alongside the official position on Palestine, were 'not merely creating present discontent and discredit of British rule, but they are putting the Jewish D.P.s into the wrong frame of mind in which to await the announcement of their future fate, which decision must, obviously, still be delayed a while'. These people, who were growing increasingly contemptuous of British rule, went on to form the backbone of the Brichah movement, whose existence and persistence fuelled the war of 1948 which brought about the state of Israel.[110] Indeed, as Henriques noted in the same report, 'If there is trouble amongst the Jewish D.P.s, we shall have brought it upon ourselves, by our unimaginative and bureaucratic attitude to them in this first year of release, when we have curtailed their liberty, so very precious to them, as much instead of as little as possible.'[111] By this she meant primarily preventing the Jewish DPs from emigrating to where they wanted to go, but it was also a reference to the many everyday problems, from demands for more and better food rations to more help with tracing relatives and allowing increasing levels of administrative autonomy within the camps.

As late as August 1946, a year after the Harrison report, life in the DP camps had improved insofar as the Jews no longer had to share their quarters with former persecutors, but things were still difficult. As Dr Jacob Oleiski, an official of the Central Committee of Liberated Jews in Germany and working as a representative of ORT, told David Boder in an interview in Paris:

> The largest part of the Jews live in lagers in the American zone. These lagers are former armouries, or transient homes, and former factories which had many workers. A smaller part lives in [small] towns . . . in cities and towns. The dwellings of the people are not happy, not decent and not pleasant. Several families are compelled to live in one large room; people are compelled to eat in large refectories, it is impossible to create that genial [way of] life . . . under which that great mournful past which the people have experienced could be forgotten.[112]

In other words, starting a 'new life' was not something that happened overnight. For some survivors the process took many years. Paysach Milman, for example, liberated by the Americans in the process of being transferred from Dachau to the Tirol, remained in a hotel, paid for by UNRRA, and survived by taking menial jobs as they came along until November 1949. Only then did the Radomir Committee, a local aid society (*landsmannschaftliche Hilsorganisation*), arrange for him to immigrate to Melbourne.[113] Such stories remind us that far from being allowed to go where they wanted after their liberation and recovery, many Jewish DPs, contrary to what they had expected, were held in DP camps for years. What these camps were like will be the subject of Chapter 4.

Before we turn to them, it is worth reminding ourselves of the real people who were affected by these geopolitical machinations and whose

1 German civilians forced to wait in line to view the Buchenwald concentration camp, 1945.

2 German prisoners of war are forced to watch an atrocity film about the German concentration camps. The looks on the POWs' faces indicate the range of emotions experienced by Germans at the end of the war.

3 The British sign erected in English and German at Bergen-Belsen concentration camp. The sign was put up following the torching of the 'horror camp' on 21 May 1945.

4 David Ben-Gurion addressing the Central Committee of Liberated Jews in Munich, 27 January 1946.

5 Children in Rosenheim DP camp. Such protests were a regular occurrence and the involvement of children was a clear attempt to try the world's conscience.

6 The Landsberg and Föhrenwald football teams. Sport was of great importance in the DP camps, both in encouraging a return to physical health and in shaping communities.

7 Sonia Boczkowska performs the poem 'Shoes from Majdanek' at Belsen DP camp. Boczkowska, who had worked as an actress before the war, survived the Łódź and Będzin ghettos, then the slave labour camp Annaberg (a sub-camp of Gross-Rosen), Mauthausen and finally Belsen.

8 A scene from *Partisans* played by Katzet-Teater, Belsen DP camp. *Partisans* was one of the more popular pieces, giving surviving Jews a sense of agency and shifting the focus away from victimhood pure and simple.

9 The Yiddish Youth Theatre during a performance at Belsen DP camp.

10 Sally Katz of the Katzet-Teater performing in *Die Mutter* (The Mother) in Belsen DP camp. The piece dealt with a mother's suffering following the murder of her child in a camp.

11 An effigy of Hitler during a Purim celebration, Landsberg DP camp.

12 Such re-enactments as this, at Landsberg DP camp, in the context of Purim both incorporated recent events into Jewish history and permitted the acting-out of revenge fantasies.

13 Students studying Talmud at a *yeshiva* in Zeilsheim DP camp, 1945. A remarkable number of survivors clung to the religious life they had followed before the war.

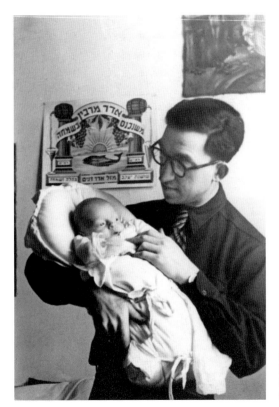

14 Zvi Silberman holds his newborn son in a DP camp in Austria. The sign behind him reads, 'When Adar comes happiness is multiplied'. 'Adar' is the Jewish month in which Purim falls.

15 Clothing produced at an ORT-UNRRA school, probably at Landsberg DP camp. ORT provided large numbers of survivors with training in new professions.

16 Kibbutz Nocham, Belsen DP camp.

17 *Exodus 1947* on a Jewish New Year greeting card. The travails of the *Exodus* provided a golden opportunity for Zionist propaganda.

18 A protest in Belsen DP camp against the treatment of *Exodus 1947* passengers.

19 The 'British Floating Dachau' protest sticker.

20 Detention Camp no. 55 in Cyprus, the first of the camps in Karaolos to be opened to house illegal immigrants to Palestine. Inmates were housed in Nissen huts (visible in the background) and tents in two main sites on the island.

21 A wedding portrait in a Cyprus detention camp. Normal life continued as the refugees waited for their opportunity to leave for Palestine.

lives were made and broken by their ability to get through the initial postwar period and then to cope in the DP camps. Not everyone was able to tolerate further internment on an open-ended basis.

Among Rose Henriques' papers relating to the administration of relief for the Jewish survivors in the British zone, one can find numerous small reflective pieces. They appear to be exercises in emotional release for Henriques, whose daily reality obviously took its toll on her mental and physical state. As order was established in the concentration camps and the newly formed DP camps, so the survivors of the camps and the other Jews from Eastern Europe whose arrival increased so substantially the number of Jewish DPs, began to rebuild their lives. As the next chapter will show, the DP camps were sites of communal renewal, and had the highest birth rate in Europe. But these signs of rebuilding were always accompanied by inescapable reminders of sorrow; indeed, sorrow and joy did not just coexist, they reinforced one another. A joyful event would always be shadowed by the recent past; anything else would have been unimaginable. Just such a dialectic is indicated in Henriques' short story, 'Calico and the Little Men', which she wrote at the end of July 1945 and which, despite its mawkishness, offers insight into the inseparability of the opposing but intertwined emotions with which the DPs lived.

They came from the same village – they had gone through five years of hell – they were liberated together – they were the same age – 18.

Liberation brought calico to both. To one, so deathly ill that she was borne to the hospital, it brought a faint chance that the loving care she received there would help her to cling on to life, even if it would never enable her to be robust. To the other it brought a lover, a boy old in suffering but young in ardour. They wooed, they loved, they planned their wedding.

Then came the Great Day.

To one it brought a bridal gown made of common white mattress calico, lovingly and cunningly made by her camp-sisters – buttoned with linen underwear buttons taken from essential garments. Her veil was of gauze filched from the First-Aid box – her bouquet of flowers from the camp garden. Trembling yet radiant in her coarse-grained virginal robe, she embodied the miracle of life arising ever triumphant from the ashes of destruction.

To the other it brought eternal stillness – her wasted frame had spent its last mild effort in maintaining the spark that flickered and then went out. She too had a robe of calico, folded lovingly round her by tender sister-hands. Even its simple folds could not disguise the bony nothingness that was meant to represent a human frame. Her veil was of coarse wood, roughly put together by the sexton, her flowers two sprigs of fir tree placed in her cold skeletal hands, scarce more colourful than the calico that enshrouded her.

Aloof and serene she embodied the dignity of Eternal life when dust returns to dust and the spirit flees to its rest.

The little men who had suffered laid gentle hold of the planken coffin, bore it tenderly to the grave hewn in the ancient cemetery of her Faith, on the little hill in the outskirts of the little town.

Her camp sisters wept around the grave. The little men quietly filled it in.

The little men departed – the little men made haste to return to their Home of worship.

They awaited the arrival of the bride. They read the prayers – they held the canopy, they tendered the wine – they produced the glass. They cleared a way for the bride and groom to pass out.

The little men had eaten nought – the day had been busy, evening was upon them.

To their little attic they withdrew – fetched out their bread, their morsel of cheese, their cup of tea – said the blessings, and laid their feast gratefully on their square yard of calico.[114]

Although this story might suggest that Henriques was unable to choose whether happiness or joy was the predominant emotion in the post-liberation period, others were more decisive. In May 1945, before the huts of Belsen's Camp One had been burned, Jane Leverson summed up the situation:

Considering the immensity of the task here, my own view is that, although there are small ways in which the British might have done better, on the whole, and within a very short period, the British have brought a remarkable amount of order into this area of chaos.[115]

CHAPTER FOUR

Displaced Persons or Betrayed Persons? Life in the DP Camps

We, the rescued

From whose hollow bones death had begun to whittle his flutes,

And on whose sinews he had already stroked his bow –

Our bodies continue to lament

With their mutilated music.

We, the rescued,

The worms of fear still feed on us.

Our constellation is buried in dust.

NELLY SACHS, 'Chorus of the Rescued'

'. . . this residue left after all the people *with* countries and homes have gone off to them, they really are a heartrending tribe.'

ROSE HENRIQUES[1]

Of the 6,000 people in Landsberg DP camp in September 1945, 5,000 were Jews and the rest were Hungarians and Balts, at least according to US infantry officer Irving Heymont, for whom the camp was 'filthy beyond description' at that point.[2] Heymont immediately set about trying to get the camp turned into a self-governing institution; 'the Army came to Europe to fight the Nazis and not to stand guard over their victims', as he put it to the camp committee.[3] At this point in time, the DP camps – which varied from large former barracks to small apartment blocks – were UNRRA's responsibility rather than SHAEF's (which ceased to operate in July 1945), and the DPs still existed in a kind of 'protective custody'.[4]

Heymont's righteous anger at the existence of DP camps reminds us that, in retrospect, we should not regard them as being inevitable consequences of the war and the end of the Holocaust. There were other options, but the 'non-repatriable' DPs, and especially the Jews, the 'human debris' of the war, became the victims of international politics.[5] So whilst there were people who regarded the camps as an outrage, they nevertheless continued to exist for far longer than anyone had anticipated in 1945 and, as a result of the influx of Jews from Eastern Europe, grew larger and became communities in their own right, with a unique social, economic, cultural and intellectual life. Most of the Jewish DP camps were in the American zone of Germany (thanks to the US policy of granting DP status to newcomers), the largest at Feldafing, Föhrenwald and Landsberg, all near Munich, though none was as large as the DP camp at Belsen in the British zone. There were also a handful of DP camps in the French zone. By the end of 1945 there were about 150,000 Jewish DPs housed in the American zone, about 15,000 in the British, and 2,000 in the French.[6] Additionally there were some DP camps in Austria and Italy; although small in number, the DP camps in the latter, especially in the south of the country, presented the British with the headache of 'illegal' immigration to Palestine.

Forced labourers, especially from Western Europe, were able quickly to return home. Gilbert Coquempot, for example, who had been imprisoned at Flossenbürg as a member of the Resistance, was liberated at the sub-camp of Ganacker, a Messerschmitt factory. He recalls that he got back home at the end of May or beginning of June. Although he 'was totally dispirited' and 'had nightmares all the time', he started work again in December 1945 and formed a jazz group with old friends from music school.[7] Another French internee, Robert Deneri, imprisoned for 'the manifestation of sentiments hostile to Germany', was sent to Sachsenhausen and Flossenbürg, and was one of very few survivors of a death march massacre carried out by the SS as the Americans were approaching. He had to convalesce until the autumn of 1945 and spoke of a 'sad remembrance' that is always with him; at the same time he recalled that 'There was no problem with my family: everyone had survived, and there was great joy in France at having thrown off the German yoke. I wasn't yet 23 and life was ahead of me. I felt good.'[8] For the 'non-repatriables', the outcome of liberation was different.

Only nine days after the liberation of Buchenwald, Jewish survivor Abraham Ahubia gave voice to his frustration in his diary: 'The Frenchmen and the Belgians are going *home*. Yes indeed, they are going *home*, to their relatives, families and neighbours. They go to those whom they love and who return their love. They are returning to their former lives. And I – where will I go? Where shall I seek my home? Where shall I find my family and relatives? I have neither.'[9] There were many DPs in Central Europe at war's end, but within months most of those who remained were 'non-repatriables'. Proportionally, the approximately 500,000 non-Jewish Poles constituted the largest group of non-repatriables, but the Jews were the biggest 'problem'. The former, to use Ira Hirschmann's useful distinction, were political dissidents who did not want to return to communist-controlled Eastern Europe; the latter were, like Ahubia, persecutees without a home to return to and in need of care and rehabilitation.[10] Or, to use David Boder's psychological vocabulary of the early 1950s, the refugees from the east were people whose trauma consisted more often in fears of what could have happened to them, whereas the camp survivors reported their trauma 'in terms of occurrences that have actually struck them in person'.[11] The same applied to Jews who returned from exile in the USSR to find destroyed communities. As Rose Henriques said in a letter to her husband, 'I do not know enough about the situation to judge whether they [i.e. Jews] should be mixed with non-Jews, because their category is really a different one, they are ex-concentration camp and the others are merely Displaced Persons and although they also need care and attention, they have not to be built up physically and mentally as have the wretched ex-concentrationaires'.[12]

The problem was that over time – that is to say, as the Cold War unfolded – the DPs became, as Hirschmann noted, 'pawns on a political chessboard'.[13] Poles and Balts were being, as he put it, 'soft pedalled', because they were anti-communist and could be useful to the West in the future. Their experiences as DPs were often traumatic, for they had to negotiate fear at being returned to the Soviet Union (or, with respect to the Balts and eastern Poles, areas and countries which had been incorporated into the Soviet Union at the end of the war), the interrogations of UNRRA officials, and the changing complexities of Western countries' immigration policies. Many had lost their homes and, often, some of their relatives through brutal Soviet and Nazi occupations (especially in Poland and Belarus), fighting and expulsion. When they finally arrived in their destination countries, they often faced years of disorientation, unpleasant living and working conditions, and isolation, especially if they met few compatriots or found learning a new language difficult. Yet on the whole, considered as national communities, they had not been decimated as had the Jews; they were not as psychologically disturbed and in need of rehabilitation assistance. Nor were they regarded by the Allies or the surrounding population in Germany and Austria with as much suspicion as were the Jews while they remained in the DP camps. Jewish survivors of Nazi genocide were assumed to have compromised themselves in some way in order to survive, and, partly because Jews were 'difficult' to deal with thanks to their traumatised condition, they were regarded as a problematic group. 'It is difficult', wrote Ralph Segalman, who had directed the JDC's activities in the Vienna area, for UNRRA and military officials 'to understand (and emotionally accept the idea) that those who exhibit such negative behaviour are those who need the most patience and help. More often', he went on, 'instead, the Jewish Displaced Person is characterized as ungrateful, unclean, lazy or unambitious.'[14] Ironically, the non-Jewish DPs – among whom not an inconsiderable number of voluntary labourers and collaborators were to be found – were considered better 'material' for emigration than the Jews.

One can thus understand why it was that Ira Hirschmann noted that the DP camps inhabited by non-Jewish Poles and Latvians, such as in Schutzenberg and Blomberg, were well cared for by UNRRA and enjoyed 'a community life which lacked the nervous tensions typical of a Jewish camp'. After talking with many of the DPs, Hirschmann concluded that among them were many who had come voluntarily to Germany and who now 'posed as war victims and exploited the charity of UNRRA'.[15] Ironically, the comparatively pleasant surroundings of the DP camps for non-Jews were in inverse proportion to the longevity of those camps. The Jewish DPs were the ones who ended up in the camps for longer. One commentator, writing in 1947, observed that:

the most striking contrast between Jewish DP camps and those of Poles and Balts is in the atmosphere of impermanence in the Jewish camps.

Here you see no neat little gardens, no green lawns and flowers, no attempts at community decorations and small luxuries to make life easier. In the center of each Jewish camp, there is only the stark little memorial to the six millions who died, and nothing else.

Bernstein partly explained this state of affairs by suggesting that 'the Jewish DPs are mostly from the cities, and have never had the pleasant habit of tending a piece of land of their own'– a claim which even he obviously found of limited use. For 'the real reason lies elsewhere', he went on: 'in the burning desire to get out, and to shut out any implication that they may have to remain where they are for any serious length of time'.[16]

Another view of the Jewish DPs was set out by Francesca Wilson, who worked at Feldafing until July 1945:

Feldafing remained a tragic place: everywhere one saw unsmiling faces with haunted eyes. It was clear that, if nothing were done to solve the Jewish problem, camps like Feldafing would become forcing-beds for Terrorists and Stern gangsters, who would somehow or other find their way into Palestine.[17]

It was this fear, as much as humanitarian compassion or a realisation that Jews could not be treated in the same way as former forced labourers, which persuaded the British to follow the Americans' lead and establish Jewish-only camps. In contrast to the US zone, where many DPs engaged with the local economy, the DPs in Belsen were for the most part dependent on the aid agencies and thus the camp remained 'something like an extra-territorial island detached from its vicinity'.[18]

Not all Jewish DPs lived in camps: German Jews especially, and groups of 'free livers', inhabited towns and cities across occupied Germany and Austria, or settled in *hachsharot*, pioneering farms that aimed to train members for life in Palestine. But they still retained their DP status, and most had connections with the DP camps through trade, social life, sport, employment or participation in the political organisation of Jews in Germany.[19] German Jews who had survived in hiding in Germany (including more than 1,000 in Berlin) or who had returned from camps, made a start at rebuilding Jewish communities. According to the October 1946 census, the first in occupied Germany, there were 44,692 Jews living in German society outside of camps. Only a small number of those were people who had lived in Germany before the war, for the German Jewish communities had been destroyed. Thus, although the *jüdische Gemeinden* (Jewish communities) began to rebuild, in stark contrast to the aid offered to returning German POWs they received no help from the authorities, as their representatives complained. The Dortmund Jewish community wrote to the regional prime minister in 1946 saying that on liberation 'No German authority, no German organizations took any notice. Nobody acted to fetch us, German citizens of the Jewish faith, from the concentration camps. We had to find our own way. We had to find our own way home.' Karl Marx, the editor of the *Jüdisches Gemeindeblatt*, stated that 'In Germany, not a single group emerged to help people who had been robbed of everything and who had been the first victims of National Socialism as well as the last. They received not the slightest help in furnishing a home or finding work to rebuild their life. No German body seized the initiative.'[20] The Jewish relief organisations picked up on this too; with respect to Jews who had survived in hiding in Berlin, for example, one JCRA report claimed that: 'They are deeply disappointed that liberation has not fulfilled the hopes which it had raised. What mortifies them most is the indifference shown by the British and American authorities . . . The survivors feel that little has changed since the Russians entered Berlin, except that food is even shorter. They are still a stricken minority, unrelieved and uncared for by anybody, which is rapidly nearing the limits of human endurance.'[21] The German Jewish communities did gradually rebuild themselves but in the first years after liberation their links with the DP camps, which remained the key centres of Jewish life, were crucial.

Hirschmann recounts how General Joseph T. McNarney, Eisenhower's successor as chief of USFET, told him that the Jews constituted the biggest problem: 'If I were in their place,' McNarney said, 'I wouldn't want to lay a finger on anything which would rebuild the Germany that had murdered my family. There is no future in Germany for them. I do not blame them for their attitude and their insistence upon leaving this country.' Again, the British and their Palestine policy were the principal culprits for this state of affairs.[22] As the historian of the JDC notes, despite all the effort (and money) being spent on housing and feeding the DPs, then schooling and rehabilitating them, 'these places were not easily emptied'.[23]

If ultimately the Americans appointed an Adviser on Jewish Affairs and the British and French reluctantly recognised the need to treat the Jewish survivors differently from the non-Jewish DPs, this was 'largely due to the efforts of the few Jewish Chaplains and Relief workers who have been enabled to bring relief and comfort to the inmates', as one JCRA report noted early on.[24] This meant people like Harrison, the many military chaplains such as Klausner and Levy who helped survivors, officers such as Heymont, and soldiers such as Robert Hilliard and Ed Herman, who sent over a thousand copies of their letter to friends and relatives in the US requesting help for the survivors. Another example is the Jewish soldier Jerry Himmelfarb, from Buffalo, New York. Stationed in Munich, he wrote to his rabbi in August 1945 urging him to secure the financial assistance of his congregants in order to help the JDC's operations in Europe. The letter was published in the *Buffalo Jewish Review*. Opening with a description of the atrocities discovered at Dachau, Himmelfarb went on to explain that the money would be well used, that supplies were getting through to those who needed them – not being siphoned off along the way, as so many thought – and that more money was needed:

> Jolt them right off their seats. Tell them to do something about the crocodile tears they have been shedding for the past ten years. Tell them to stop that, 'how awful, tsch, tsch' talk and start some real talk. Money talks. Don't give them a chance to say, 'But –'. It's too late for 'buts' now. Talk is O.K. in its place. The place isn't here.[25]

George Vida, who later served on the Anglo-American Commission of 1946, was a US army rabbi originally from Hungary who was assigned in August 1945 to take care of Jewish army personnel in the Frankfurt and Wiesbaden area; he was told that in his 'spare time' he could assist Jewish DPs. In practice, he helped to provide supplies for the Zeilsheim DP camp, in which 'living conditions were beyond description' in the summer of 1945, and to help the DPs organise their religious and cultural needs.[26] As his work on behalf of the DPs began to take precedence over administering to Jewish army personnel, 'I was always guided by the realization that but for the grace of God, my family and I would also be among them today.'[27]

These were the people who got the DP camps to start functioning and helped the survivors make it through the first weeks, when food, medicine, shelter and friendship were all in short supply. After this initial period, however, the complaints did not cease. In October 1945, Shea Abramovicz, a JCRA worker seconded to the JDC and working at Föhrenwald DP camp in the American zone, argued that the UNRRA personnel in the Feldafing and Landsberg DP camps (which he had just visited) were 'not too fit for the job', claiming that the Americans 'have taken the best administrative jobs for themselves and sit in warm offices sipping coffee'. Of course, he was writing from the American zone, which somewhat mitigates Abramovicz's gripe, but his next letter's claims that the 'people in the camps do not understand the Jews too well. Even now there still exist mixed camps' reveal that there was a long way to go. While the DPs were starting to organise themselves there was as yet no strong match between their self-generated activities and those being provided for them by UNRRA or the military authorities.[28]

Besides, the very existence of DP camps seemed to contradict the notion that their inhabitants had been liberated. Simon Schochet, author of a memoir of his time in Feldafing DP camp in Bavaria, observed that 'Feldafing is growing up into a strange and separate community, organized as if it were intended to remain so for a long time to come.'[29] And when Derrick Sington completed his book on Belsen, he noted that in October 1945 there were still 8,000 Jewish and non-Jewish residents there, all of whom wanted to resume a normal life:

> They were frustrated and demoralised by the life of the camp. Their complete economic dependence on the British authorities was humiliating for men and women officially declared to be free. Their status resembled too closely that of paupers in an institution.
>
> Can one wonder, then, that these eight thousand Polish and Jewish exiles in Belsen faced the winter of 1945 with sadness?[30]

Yet not only would the Belsen DP camp not close, it would get considerably larger and continue to exist until July 1950. The JCRA only held its last meeting and ended its operations in October 1950.[31] Even then the last few hundred inhabitants, most of them ill, were transferred to Jever, near Wilhelmshaven, where they were obliged to spend another year until

August 1951.[32] Given the basic fact that the authorities considered it accept-
able that the Jewish survivors of the Second World War should be housed
in camps indefinitely until their forward passage could be arranged, it is
worth considering how those camps became important centres of Jewish
life. Ironically, the heart of Europe, amidst the ruins of the Third Reich, in
camps where the Jew's liberators forced them to live and from which they
intended to leave as soon as they could, became the setting for the revival of
Jewish life and culture.

Rebuilding Lives

Abraham Levent, who was taken to Feldafing after being liberated
near Dachau, recalled: 'And after a while you start – even right after
the liberation – people start to make committees, to start learning, to
make a newspaper. All kinds of little things show to you that's how fast
the people – the Jewish people – are rising up from the ashes and right
away they start building up a home.'[33] That of course meant a home in a
DP camp. Visitors to the DP camps were often struck by finding the
inhabitants to be in quite good health. As Judah Nadich explained, the
explanation was a very simple one: 'had these people not been physically
strong, they would have been among the six million Jewish victims of
the Germans'.[34] These were the self-styled 'she'erit hapleitah', or saving
remnant, a designation that clearly indicates the difference between
Jewish and non-Jewish DPs, the former being conscious of the fact that
they represented the last survivors of a destroyed culture.[35] Even accounting
for the fact that by late 1946 the majority of DPs were 'infiltrees' from the
east and not liberated camp survivors, the idea of the 'saving remnant' was
one to which almost all adhered, giving their struggle to cling on to life in
the wake of the Holocaust some sense of dignity. It was based above all
on the survivors' sense of Jewishness: having been attacked on that basis
they now made their Jewish identity the single most important fact of
their lives. According to the sociologist and former spokesman for the DPs
of Landsberg, Samuel Gringauz, the she'erit hapleitah regarded itself as 'a
herald of the indivisibility of Jewish destiny' as well as a harbinger of revenge
against Nazism in the shape of 'a defiant affirmation of life and national
rebirth'.[36]

This vision entailed an emphasis on Jewish self-help. This was a notion that, at first, brought the Jewish DPs together; indeed it did not take long for the survivors to start organising themselves. As a result the DP camps became sites of Jewish history which were not just objects of the occupying forces' policies. The camps' history became one of interactions – albeit often contentious and ill-tempered – between the inmates, the Allies and the German population.

Naturally, the emergence of self-help did not do away with distinctions between different Jewish groups; rather, it encouraged them. Although in the early days religious distinctions between the Jewish survivors were irrelevant, they soon became one of the main sources of discord and differentiation. The re-emergence of such divisions – natural, after all, in every Jewish community as well as non-Jewish ones – is no doubt an indication of the return of 'normality'. It was encouraged, inadvertently, by the relief groups' policies. As well as essential material goods such as clothing, the Jewish relief workers were especially eager to provide DPs with religious items.

Rose Henriques, for example, was delighted to see how everyday items transformed the lives of survivors, writing in a report of August 1945 that 'All the lovely Woolworth toilet articles are needed as a real piece of "luxury".' 'For instance', she went on,

> the other day we were able to give 120 Czech women who were being repatriated each a complete outfit of dainty toilet articles and a box of assorted sewing materials which we had put together out of the boxes we brought out with us. For someone who has had to do without even the faintest sniff of scent for six years and who has only occasionally had a whole piece of soap to herself, the receipt of pink perfumed soap, pink more strongly perfumed powder and a pink pliable elastic suspender belt, together with about two dozen other items falls little short of a miracle.[37]

Henriques' claim about the importance of ordinary things is confirmed by the survivors themselves. Auschwitz and Ravensbrück survivor Lucie Adelsberger wrote to a friend to thank her for sending stockings and cigarettes, gifts which spoke of 'an exceptional talent and love'. Indeed, barring black shoes and a *Hüftgürtel* (corset), which she asked her friend to try and find, Adelsberger claimed she had all she needed. Yet, she readily admitted, she only had to close her eyes in order to see 'suffering, despair, death and a terrible Jewish fate'.[38] Simon Schochet remarked, less than two months after his liberation: 'I received a comb today. What a luxurious and civilized feeling it is, to be able to use one again.'[39]

Others were less easily placated. In Belsen, Hadassah Rosensaft, who had helped save Jewish children in the camp's last months, then had run a survivor-led medical team after liberation, and who was now among the leaders of the DPs, spoke at the first Congress of Liberated Jews in the British zone of occupation in September 1945. After appealing to British Jewish soldiers stationed in Germany to visit the camp and spend time with the orphans, she then criticised the British delegation:

> We were receiving packages of clothes from Jews in England. They were sending us long evening dresses from Victorian times, and gold and silver evening shoes with very high heels and bows. I could imagine the old ladies opening their chests full of mothballs and getting rid of those items, satisfying their consciences by giving to charity. I said that we were deeply insulted. We did not want these things, and we did not want pity. We had not been born in Auschwitz or Belsen; we had homes, families, love, education, and beautiful clothes, and we still had our pride. I made an exhibition of these ridiculous clothes in the office and invited the British delegation to see it. They did not say a word, but clearly they were shocked and ashamed.[40]

For the relief workers, supplying religious items was therefore not only in certain respects 'safer' – they were less likely to offend survivors in the same way that offering them cast-off clothing might – but was also well received. Meeting survivors' spiritual and physical needs, or what relief workers perceived such needs to be, therefore went hand in hand. If, as historian Lucy Dawidowicz put it in her memoir, 'Going to work among the surviving Jews would be like embarking on a pilgrimage of homage to the dead', then one can well imagine that the relief workers' expectations and the survivors' were not always the same.[41]

In October 1945, for example, Shea Abramovicz was pleased to report that schools had been set up in Belsen, where instruction in 'Hebrew,

Religion, Bible, English, Maths, Drawing, Gym, Music etc.' was under way. On his list of requested items to be sent – and he noted that the 'Chief Rabbi's Emergency Council has not sent me anything so far' – Abramovicz placed most emphasis on religion: 'I need all kinds of Religious supplies, Tfilen, Tztizit, Chumashen etc. and Sefer Torah.'[42] The rebuilding of lives was by no means just a physical or physiological process and almost a year later Abramovicz was still asking for the same items, saying that although the camp library had grown, they were still very short of bibles and religious requisites.[43]

All of these efforts to provide schools, vocational training and leisure facilities, and to facilitate religious, political and social activities, make the camps sound almost pleasant places to be. Yet, as a September 1952 *Jüdische Rundschau* article on Föhrenwald, the last remaining DP camp, put it, 'If one hears such a report about Föhrenwald, conditions there sound almost idyllic, if one does not know the sometimes tragicomic but also very often tragic and sad atmosphere.'[44] One especially obvious (or at least oft-discussed) indicator of this kind of unhappy atmosphere was the problem of DPs' involvement in the black market and the ways in which this activity soured relations with Germans. The problem was vastly exacerbated by the tendency of many Germans to associate Jews with criminality – a connection that had been a mainstay of Nazi propaganda. Indeed, what made the image of the Jewish DP criminal so powerful was its connection with familiar, long-standing Nazi and even pre-Nazi anti-Semitic imagery.[45]

In autumn 1945, Jacob Biber travelled from Föhrenwald DP camp to Furth to attend a teachers' conference organised with the help of UNRRA and the JDC. On the way back, whilst changing trains at Nuremberg, the group of a hundred or so Jewish men and women were surrounded by military police who searched their briefcases. On discovering the cans of food they were carrying for the journey, the police arrested them and forced them onto a train, to the great amusement of watching German travellers who pointed at them and called them '*Juden Schmugglers*' (Jew smugglers). They were only freed at 2am after the intervention of UNRRA and JDC officials.

Biber's story is unremarkable. Schochet also comments on the increase in searches of DPs by American military police, remarking that being 'singled out and searched in front of the Germans and by our liberators to boot is strongly resented by all of us'.[46] *Undzer Shtime* reported at the end of 1946 of a British military police raid on a fishing kibbutz at Blankenese near Hamburg, during which the inhabitants were stripped and searched, several were wounded, and all were forcibly removed, accompanied by 'the satisfied smiles of the Germans in Blankenese, who were rid of the Jews with the help of the English'.[47]

Germans who had lived through a regime that touted the ubiquitous notion of 'the Jew' as a parasite and a thief were unlikely to abandon such views overnight. What is interesting is Biber's suspicion that the military police who carried out the raid 'were influenced by the Germans', in other words that Americans were susceptible to the same pervasive stereotypes. One historian argues that the British military government was equally prone to such thinking, and 'soon agreed with the Germans that the displaced persons were the cause of all difficulties in the field of law and order'. Their collusion with the new German civil police, which derived from fear that they might be perceived by the Germans as weak occupiers, drove the British, according to this highly critical interpretation, to work 'against a group of population who as victims of Nazi oppression had originally been taken under their special protection and care'.[48] This problem was no doubt a result of how 'normal' the Germans seemed in comparison with the Jews. It was undoubtedly the case that some Jews were involved in the black market, though certainly not to the extent many Germans believed and most likely in lower numbers (as a percentage of the population) than Germans. As Biber also noted, 'Survivors who were not interested in social activities turned their talents to illegally buying and selling all kinds of goods, dealing with American military and with Germans. They dealt with food, clothing, cigarettes, and jewelry. It helped them relieve some of the tedium of the hardship of camp life.'[49]

For the most part, the DPs were uninterested in integrating into the German economy, preferring to engage with it on an ad hoc basis as the need arose, which is why the camps became largely self-sustaining. The black market was simply a fact of postwar European life, but the involvement of DPs in it provided the opportunity for anti-Semitic stereotypes to come to the fore. It was commented on regularly by the relief workers in their reports and gave rise to much concerned comment. 'By many Germans', wrote Simon Schochet, 'we are viewed as criminals, since we were formerly prisoners and must be therefore guilty of some criminal offence.'[50] Schochet's claims are backed up by the work of Oscar Mintzer, the JDC's legal adviser in Germany. He noted that Jewish DPs were regularly arrested in Munich for black-marketing, possession of American property, possession of foreign curren-cies, entering the American zone without authorisation and improper identification papers. As he added: 'Many times these charges are brought unjustly, unintelligently, or frivolously.' They were often made on suspicion alone, 'simply because in the mind of the police officer the accused possessed "too much money" or "American commodities", when the articles in question could have been held entirely legally.'[51] On occasion this stereotyping led to unpleasant incidents, even some years after the establishment of the DP camps when, following the introduction of the Deutsch mark, the West German economy was picking up. For example, although the DP camps were supposed to be off-limits to them, in 1952 the Bavarian customs police entered Föhrenwald in a raid, according to the *Manchester Guardian*, 'which bore all the trade-marks of Nazi descents on the ghettoes of Berlin and Frankfurt in the past'. The newspaper reported that, according to the camp committee, 'policemen yelled such slogans as "The crematoria are still there", "The gas chambers are waiting for you", and "This time you really will get it in the neck, you damned Jews".' And whilst the incident ended with the police, stones raining down upon them and inhabitants lying in front of the trucks, having to leave the camp without conducting their search, the *Guardian* used the incident to remark on the shocking fact that DP camps still existed in mid-1952. Although 'With their racial thrift and energy the Jews here have opened a restaurant and half a dozen little shops in the camp', and despite the fact that the camp was generally clear and well cared for, 'Almost to a man they want to get out of Germany, away from the smell of the slaughterhouse.'[52] It was indeed 'a savage irony that Nazis were held accountable for only a fraction of their crimes, while a more genteel version of anti-Semitism in the postwar order nurtured the "crooked" taint of Jewry'.[53]

Psychological Problems

According to one commentator on the Jewish DPs, 'In most camps, life for most of the people continued as it had existed in the past, except of course for the addition of somewhat increased rations (still under minimum bodily requirements), and the elimination of torture and extermination and work.' Small wonder, then, that Segalman could go on to claim that the DPs had become bitter towards the rest of the world, especially towards the liberators and the local German population.[54] Similarly, one JCRA report noted that the 'physical hardships' of the DPs were accentuated by 'grave psychological and social problems' and insisted that the DPs 'continue to be mere numbers in what are for them – in spite of the absence of torture and cruelty – still concentration camps.'[55] The British authorities were especially blamed for this state of affairs; the British directive that 'no discrimination on religious grounds can be permitted' meant, in the view of Londoner Rabbi Munk who was a relief worker in the British zone, that 'it is difficult to make the Military Government realise the specific Jewish needs.'[56] Oscar Mintzer wrote of a DP camp near Frankfurt that 'The hand of the Nazis is on these people – and will always be there, as long as they live, and even on their children. They aren't normal, in the sense we use the word, and their lives these past 12 years have done this to them.' He went further, in the spirit of the Harrison Report, claiming that although the Nazis were partly to blame for this state of affairs, it was 'mostly ourselves' at fault, for the Allies had 'made a mockery of Liberation, and destroyed any faith and hope which may have been left.' He particularly criticised the British, who, he had heard, 'have in many respects been bigger bastards than the Nazis.'[57] Such reports were repeated over and over, with increasing urgency, and reflect the grave disappointment felt by the Jews in the British zone that their liberators were now, as they saw it, acting as their jailers by preventing them from emigrating.

Even when they were no longer sharing quarters with non-Jews who were often anti-Semitic, Jewish DPs faced psychological problems as a result of the policies that had been directed towards them. In Belsen, survivors were scared of being moved or of being fed intravenously, and Jewish residents of DP camps more broadly feared being transferred on because of what 'transport' had come to mean under the Nazis. As late as October 1945, Irving Heymont was just beginning to understand 'why the people of the camp are so reluctant to move to Föhrenwald':

To most of the people of the camp, the very mention of a 'transport' or move brings back bitter memories of when a transport or move to another camp meant that many were to die. Under the Nazis, a transport usually meant gas chambers and starvation for many of those being moved. Psychologically, the people are still unprepared for any shifts of camps.[58]

Heymont's claims are substantiated by Miriam Warburg's report, which described how the children of Feldafing who were to be relocated to Föhrenwald for schooling refused to go. 'As they were used to being dragged out of their beds at night and carried away by force', she wrote, 'many spent the whole night in the forests which surrounded the Camp in a torrential rain.'[59]

In Föhrenwald itself, for survivors such as Jacob Biber 'sleep was not a respite, but a reliving of tragedy in our nightmares . . . Night after night, the same nightmares, filled with concentration camp survivors in the huge theatre hall.'[60] How could it be otherwise when, initially at least, the survivors spent so much time comparing stories, 'listening to each other's tales of devastation'? As Biber noted, many survivors 'suffered serious psychological reactions beyond control'.[61] DPs became attached to anything that suggested security, such as letters from relatives, food items, money, small portable possessions and so on. Segalman described their behaviour as infantile, ironically with the exception of the children, who often appeared older and more cynical than their years.[62] He argued that the only likelihood of restoring some semblance of individual and group psychological normality to the DPs was for them to be allowed into Palestine, where 'the readjustment of the Jews is within the realm of possibility' in a way that it was not in occupied Germany.[63] Those who could not cope often found the consequences only exacerbated their problems; they could be sent to a German asylum, where their 'disturbances, expressing themselves frequently in visions of their near and dear ones being slaughtered by Germans, are expected to be cured by German doctors'. As Shea Abramovicz concluded: 'Nothing need be added.'[64]

Koppel Pinson, the professor of German history who as the JDC's education director worked in DP camps in Germany for a year from October 1945, noted in an article published in 1947 that DPs were characterised by 'emotional restlessness', an 'almost mad hunt for family and friends' and other 'physical and psychic effects of the harassed life they led'.[65] The manic edge which tinges Pinson's description is an accurate reflection of the disastrous events through which the DPs had lived. They might break into tears unexpectedly and they were for the most preoccupied with their immediate past. Yet Pinson nevertheless claimed that these scars were 'not necessarily permanent in character'; rather, most of the DPs were 'ordinary normal people who have suffered more and are therefore more emotionally tense, but given once again normal surroundings and community life these exaggerated and intensified personality traits can easily be reduced to something approximating normal'.[66]

Echoing Pinson, Jacob Biber claims that 'Within a short time, Camp Föhrenwald began to function like a normal *shtetl*'.[67] Given the inhabitants of the camp and their recent past it is hard to believe that Föhrenwald was ever 'normal'; what Biber referred to was the large range of social and cultural activities that had sprung up. From schools to libraries to newspapers, musical and theatrical performances and sports clubs, to religious and political organisations, the DP camps – aided to some extent by the fact that their inhabitants were partly isolated from the world around them – became veritable hives of activity. It was a natural process of restarting a normal life, but it was also a way of trying to keep the darkness at bay. Biber, who kept himself occupied with the camp school, admits that when alone in his room, especially on the Sabbath, 'I sat in a corner of the room in a sad mood'. He was recalling his family, as did every other survivor: 'The longing for our loved ones, thinking about their deaths, tortured my mind near explosion.'[68]

If anything resembled Jewish normality in the DPs camps, it was the disintegration of the Jewish unity experienced in the immediate aftermath of liberation. People of different national, linguistic, class, religious and social backgrounds were thrown together in the camps for the sole reason that they were considered by the Nazis to be Jews.[69] Gringauz claimed that the *she'erit hapleitah* felt itself to be 'the embodiment of the Jewish experience: Jewish unity for them is no political program but an actual and living fact of experience'.[70] Yet the paradox of attempting to create a stable society when that society was geared towards transition to another place, and when the occupation authorities were not facilitating that transition quickly, made itself felt: post-liberation unity soon broke apart, ending in the much more common situation of competing versions of Jewish life trying to make themselves heard.[71]

DP Newspapers and Historical Commissions

This scramble to be heard is evident in the many Jewish newspapers which very quickly began appearing in the DP camps. These were mostly in Yiddish, which was used not only as the common language of the Eastern European Jews (though large groups, such as the assimilated Hungarian Jews, did not speak it) but also as a marker of Jewish national aspirations. Until Hebrew typefaces became available at the end of 1945 the newspapers used Latin characters, but they often also ran advertisements and summaries in English and Hebrew, again marking a break with Europe and a making statement of national aspiration, as in the case of the regional newspaper *Undzer Veg* (Our Road), the weekly organ of the Central Committee of Liberated Jews in Bavaria. Over a hundred such publications appeared, such as *Undzer Vort* (Our Word) in Bamberg, *Undzer Hofenung* (Our Hope) in Eschwege (Kassel), *Dos Fraye Vort* (The Free Word) in Feldafing, the *Landsberger Lagertsaytung* (Landsberg Camp Newspaper), and *Undzer Shtime* (Our Voice) in Belsen, the first of the newspapers to be produced.[72] At its peak, Samuel Gringauz's *Landsberger Lagertsaytung*, which changed its name in 1946 to the *Yiddishe Tsaytung* to indicate that it was meant for Jews throughout Germany, had a circulation of 15,000.[73]

As well as reporting on events in Europe and the Middle East – crucially important given that the surviving Jews had not had access to a free media for years, or any media at all in many cases – the journals published memoirs, accounts of the ghettos and camps, reports on the activities of the historical commissions, and reports on developments in the DP camps with respect to emigration, military and medical relief, and the changes in the local surroundings. *Undzer Shtime*, for example, ran a regular column entitled '*Fun Undzer Lebn*' (From Our Life), which recorded incidents from the desecrations of gravestones in Osnabrück (30 October 1947) and Lübeck (15 May 1947), to the election of a new Jewish Committee in Braunschweig (15 September 1946) and the availability of kosher food (1 January 1946). Additionally, and in contravention of copyright laws, the DPs published books, including lists of survivors, photographic records of the Holocaust, and anthologies of songs from the ghettos and camps.[74] Yiddish was not, however, the only language of publication and journals appeared in Polish, Hebrew, Hungarian, Romanian, Lithuanian and German. Starting life as carbon copies of handwritten sheets, they became more professional as printing presses found their way into the DP camps, including that which had been used to print Julius Streicher's notorious Nazi newspaper *Der Stürmer*, now sequestered for DP use.

Among the survivors were not just journalists but also scholars. One of the most significant endeavours that took place in the DP camps was the beginning of historical research into what we now call 'the Holocaust' but which was known to many of the survivors as *die letstn Khurbn*, or 'the latest destruction', using the same word (*Khurbn*) that designates the destruction of the first and second temples in ancient Israel. Indeed, one commentator stated that survivors began collecting and documenting 'at the very same moment when they opened the first public soup kitchens to cook thin little soups'.[75] Historical commissions were set up by survivor historians in Poland (first in Łódź and then in twenty-five branches, which merged into the Jewish Historical Institute in Warsaw in 1947), Budapest, Paris, Prague, Linz and elsewhere, with the aim of collecting documents and recording testimonies. Among their number were historians, some already well known before the war, who are regarded today as founders of Holocaust history, such as Philip Friedman, Joseph Kermisz, Isaiah Trunk, Ber Mark, Joseph Wulf and Rachel Auerbach. In Munich, the Central Commission of the Central Committee of Liberated Jews was established in December 1945. It carried out a great deal of work in the DP camps and its journal, *Fun letstn Khurbn* (From the Latest Destruction), which ran to ten editions over three years, had a circulation of 12,000, though it was not avidly read.[76]

The first of the DP camp-based commissions was that established in the British zone at Belsen. Its founders' first announcement insisted that 'Every single fact of Jewish life under German occupation, of the time of the ghettos, concentration camps and crematoria is of infinite importance for us. We must fulfil this holy task with all our means.'[77] As the terminology suggests, this was by no means a dispassionate act of scholarship; for these historians their work was a holy duty, for they believed that 'every document, picture, song, legend is the only gravestone which we can place on the unknown graves of our parents, siblings, and children!'[78] The importance was not lost on either the DPs or those who worked with them, with Koppel Pinson, for example, noting that 'The pattern of cultural institutions in a

DP camp is rounded out by a sport club, which is usually the most popular activity in the camp, a dramatic group and an historical commission.'[79]

Over 10,000 testimonies were collected by the historical commissions in Poland, the DP camps, Budapest, Lithuania and elsewhere. They were given and collected with the aim not just of recording what had happened but of bringing perpetrators to justice. Historian Rachel Auerbach, who had been part of the Oneg Shabbat team in the Warsaw Ghetto (which conducted huge amounts of scholarly research into all aspects of ghetto life)[80] and was subsequently based at Yad Vashem, was well aware of the problem of using testimonies for historical research – documents given after the fact are often regarded suspiciously by historians – but argued that they were vital given the paucity of Jewish sources. 'It is the surveys of Jewish imagery', she emphatically stated, 'that give us a picture of the situation with which it is possible to fill in the outline based on official documents.'[81] Philip Friedman concurred, arguing in a lecture at the end of 1948 that the Nazi sources, which were abundant and easily accessible, 'endeavour to hide or diminish the true dimensions of the Jewish tragedy', whereas the harder-to-acquire Jewish sources 'give us a life-size picture of the catastrophe'. Recognising that Jewish sources were also biased and likely to be emotional and partial, he nevertheless issued a warning that is still relevant for the history of the Holocaust: that Nazi sources alone cannot provide a complete picture.[82]

The historical commissions' main approach to acquiring testimonies was to use a questionnaire. At the time, recording oral interviews was difficult and expensive. So David Boder's interviews were not only quite unlike many of the historical commissions' templates for written testimonies, they also capture something of the provisional and as yet undefined nature of the survivors' experiences, as they struggle to explain what they have lived through and as Boder struggles to understand. Most of those who worked for the commissions and designed their questionnaires were survivors. Boder, though he had been born in Eastern Europe (in Liepaja, Latvia) and studied in St Petersburg, immigrated to the US after the First World War and had not experienced the Holocaust. His interviews are notable for the fact that he often cannot follow what his interviewees are saying, for he had no frame of reference to make sense of their talk of camps, kapos, slave labour and all the rest – things that were instinctively understood by those who had lived through the Nazi occupation.[83] His interjections and demands for clarification are invaluable to historians now, for we can see the process whereby those who had not lived through the Holocaust were beginning the long process of trying to grapple with what had happened, and those who had were facing the problem of finding the words.

Apart from the historical commissions the most significant publications dealing with the Holocaust were memorial volumes, or *Yizker-Bikher*. These were volumes compiled by *landsmanshaftn*, surviving members of a community (town or village) who had direct links with the dead, and combined personal accounts and historical analyses. They varied considerably, not just because of the differences in the size of the original communities to which they were devoted but because of the vagaries of individual survival rates and the availability of sources such as photographs and official documents. These were mostly produced in Israel and were published for the most part by left-leaning kibbutzim, which placed a strong emphasis on resistance (especially the Warsaw ghetto uprising) and Zionist patriotism. But their origins were in the DP camps, and nine were actually published in the US zone.[84]

Education: 'If only the world would send us books, books, books!'[85]

The child survivors, DPs and, very soon after liberation, those born in the DP camps were a central focus of the central committees and the relief workers. In postwar Europe, the fate of so-called 'lost children' was one of the most pressing concerns for UNRRA and the IRO. Not only were hundreds of thousands of such children anxiously sought by their parents (and vice-versa) but the practice of determining to whom children belonged not only led to conflict between different families, groups and institutions, but intersected awkwardly with notions of nationhood and religion, as children were sometimes forcibly relocated, often taken away from homes in which they had grown up believing they were one thing only to be told they were in fact something else. They included Polish children kidnapped and fostered by German families, and Jewish children hidden with non-Jewish families or in institutions such as convents across Nazi-occupied Europe. The result was often deeply traumatic as children had to get to know their 'real' families, learn new languages and acquire new identities, ones which

often clashed irreparably with what they had previously known. Uniting all
of these cases was the fact that, once again, the international relief teams
organised the children according to nationality, thus continuing after the
war one of the principal lines of division that had fuelled the conflict.[86]
Given that the DPs also chose to organise themselves along national lines,
it was challenging to do things differently. In unusual cases, though, the
effort was made to support multinational institutions, as in the UNRRA
University in Munich which promoted a liberal humanist education to its
displaced students.[87] Another was the remarkable Kloster Indersdorf children's centre run by Greta Fischer, where children of all backgrounds were
cared for together. Some peculiar problems ensued. One nine-year-old
Polish boy, who had been used as a mascot by a German officer, walked the
corridors of the children's centre shouting 'Heil Hitler!' Fischer recorded
that the Jewish children, who were deeply upset, almost killed him, and she
had to throw herself into the fracas to save the boy. It took a long time to
explain to him that he had to stop doing it.[88]

For Jewish children, education meant an orientation towards Zionist
aims. Support for such aims in education was fuelled by the post-liberation
situation in the DP camps. Shea Abramovicz cited the case of one girl who
said to him:

> When we lay on our bunks in the camp we sometimes began to dream
> of a day when liberation would come. But all this we knew was only a
> dream. Of one thing we were certain however; that if we should ever be
> saved then the world would do everything to compensate us for our
> suffering . . . Now we see how different it is. So many months after
> liberation we are still in camps, still being given 2000–2500 calories, still
> wearing striped 'Kacet' pyjamas, S.S. uniforms and Wehrmacht clothes,
> because we still have no other clothes.[89]

With youngsters in this frame of mind, education became a pressing
priority and Zionism as a form of rejectionism becomes understandable.
Acquiring a group mentality was, according to exiled psychologist
Ernst Papanek, also necessary for the children to feel able once again to
function in society. 'More than other children', he wrote in 1946, 'they
must regain the conviction that they are accepted, that they are members

of a group, that they are no longer an object to be handled but human beings able to co-operate and share in democratic decisions.' Most important, Papanek stressed that it was irresponsible to neglect the children's education now in the expectation that it could begin once they were relocated to a new country. 'The period between their liberation from Nazi terror and their final placement', he argued, 'is decisive, in the future development of displaced children, in determining whether they will become healthy, happy individuals or delinquents and neurotic wrecks – whether they will prove an asset or a danger to society.'[90] Besides, as one teacher explained in response to the criticism that the curriculum was one-sided:

> Maybe it's not good pedagogy to present only one side of a case . . . but we can't afford such luxuries. The children have nothing, nothing. What should we talk about – the blessings of Poland? They know them. Or the visas for America? They can't get them. The map of Eretz [Israel] is their salvation . . . Indoctrination may not be good for normal children in normal surroundings. But what is normal here? . . . *Auf a krumme fuss passt a krumme shuh.* (A crooked foot needs a crooked shoe.)[91]

Education was not just restricted to young children, however. The JDC's Oscar Mintzer was told that, more than anything else, the DPs 'want books and teachers, for children and adults. The teachers, the professionals, were all killed.'[92] Adult education, one historian remarks, was 'the stepchild of the DP school system'.[93] Indeed, it was hardly possible only to teach youngsters given that just 3.6 per cent of 25,000 survivors surveyed in Germany and Austria in July 1945 were aged under sixteen. In Belsen there were at first sixty children in the kindergarten, 200 in the elementary school, and sixty in the high school. Within a year this had changed dramatically so that in the American zone at the start of 1947 there were over 10,000 children attending day schools and another 3,000 at religious schools (*yeshivot*).[94] Many had missed out on vital years of schooling because of the war. 'What pleasure it is', Abramovicz enthused, 'to enter a school room and hear the "children" of 20 or so speaking English or learning geography in Hebrew.'[95] Föhrenwald, where Abramovicz was based, was a particularly important centre for education because Jewish children from across Bavaria were gathered there because of its better living conditions. A report on the early days of schooling at Föhrenwald sent to London by Abramovicz's colleague Miriam Warburg, the general secretary of the Children and Youth Aliyah Committee, working in Germany with the JDC, gives us considerable insight into the trying nature of educating child survivors.

The children, Warburg wrote, were 'very eager to learn something' given the wartime interruption to their schooling. But they were not exactly in the right physical or mental shape to do so. The first thing Warburg and her colleagues had to do was to find a way of doubling the children's bread rations so that they were less hungry; the second was to accommodate themselves to the terrible fact that some of the children (mostly boys) in their teenage years did not know how to hold a pencil and were unable to do simple arithmetic. 'When I distributed pencils one boy turned to me and said, "This is the first time in six years I have had a pencil in my hand." Many ten-year-old children cannot read or write', Warburg reported.[96] Nevertheless, after the first class, on 20 September 1945, Warburg said that 'I have given many lessons in my life, none so strenuous and none so satisfying as those I gave today.' Indeed, the children, Warburg wrote, 'were in despair when the lesson was over and they wanted to know more and more'.[97] Beginning with Hebrew, English and arithmetic, Warburg extended her teaching to include geography and Jewish history, helped by a handful of teachers recruited from among the camp inmates, all of whom were desperate to hold a book in their hands for the first time in years.

Apart from catching up on formal education in languages, history, geography and mathematics, the most important organised activity in the DP camps was sport. Numerous teams were formed in various sports, including football, table tennis and boxing. Sport associations were often organised along political and religious lines; in Belsen, for example, there were six different groups, whose affiliations ranged from Revisionist Zionist (*Betar*) to left-Socialist Zionist (*Ha-Shomer Ha-Tsa'ir*).

Sport was vital not only for physical recuperation but – in the manner of prewar athletics or boxing clubs – for the physical and spiritual renewal of the Jewish people as a whole. The 'muscle Jew' of early Zionist lore was revived in the camps, and sport combined fun and fitness with a sense of preparation for life as a pioneer in Palestine. A 'call to Jewish youth' of 22 November 1945, for example, makes this clear:

We still have the horror of hunger, of agony, of death and the crematoria before our eyes. Thus we want to revive our old traditions for a new life, using sport to develop the soul's new physical and moral strength ... Our future generations should be both physically and mentally strong.[98]

The *Yiddishe Sport Tsaytung* proclaimed that 'We sportsmen must prove that we are the avant-garde of our people.' It went on, making the point particularly clear: 'From our ranks the heroes will come who will carry the flags of Eretz Yisrael's liberation and independence. Jewish sportsmen, military service is your duty!'[99]

Theatre

Sami Feder's 'Katzet-Teater' in Belsen, which gave its first performance on 6 September 1945, proves that the development of musical and theatrical groups in Belsen was 'more than a mere peripheral phenomenon [*Randerscheinung*] of everyday life'.[100] In fact one relief worker affirmed that, amongst all the cultural activities springing into life, 'The finest camp effort is undoubtedly the Theatre Group.'[101] The Katzet-Teater presented plays dealing with the recent experiences of the Jews as well as works from classical Yiddish theatre. Likewise, films and concerts served the dual purpose of rehabilitation and spreading knowledge of Hebrew.[102] Feder himself, a professional actor before the war, was one of the founding members of the Central Jewish Committee, the first congress of which was held at Belsen on 27 September 1945, and was head of its Cultural Department.[103]

One of the key members of Feder's troupe was Sonia Boczkowska. Born in Łódź, Boczkowska survived the Łódź and Będzin ghettos, then the slave labour camp Annaberg (a sub-camp of Gross-Rosen), Mauthausen and finally Belsen, where she was deported in January 1945. Here she found Sami Feder, with whom she had previously worked in Będzin. Together with Hermann Helfgott they decided to found the Katzet-Teater theatre group. She was one of the first to perform *Lieder* in the camp and, later, on tour with the Katzet-Teater.[104]

Among the Katzet-Teater's more popular pieces in Belsen was *Partisans*, written by Feder, in which a cabaret singer seduces German officers and steals their weapons to pass on to the renegades. Like other popular pieces dealing with resistance or immigration to Palestine, *Partisans* gave the audience the chance to feel as though they had regained some agency and were not simply victims.[105] That included those present who had not been inmates of the camp: 'Tonight I am invited to a theatre-play', wrote Miriam Warburg, 'written by one of the Jewish teachers. It is about the life and sufferings of Jews in the Ukraine and their activities with the Partisans. They have a beautiful Jewish Partisan-song which they promised to write down for me.'[106]

Similar troupes were established at many of the other DP camps, with the one at Föhrenwald also founded soon after the end of the war under Jacob Biber's direction. Their first performance, a variety show on 28 October 1945, was well received and the group was invited to perform at Feldafing. That performance, in front of most of the DPs including rows of sick still in their hospital cots, was a moving experience for Biber:

> When the show was running, I looked out from behind the curtain and saw pleasant smiles on their skeletal faces. Some of them were still wearing their striped concentration camp clothes. Others were covered with white sheets but their eyes peering out from the covers expressed their eternal gratitude and satisfaction once again to see Jewish children performing.[107]

With outfits and scenery 'organised' from the military authorities or acquired on the black market, these theatrical troupes proved immensely resourceful in putting on performances, and not just because the actors themselves were still in a poor physical shape. Their willingness to jeopardise their right to emigration by engaging in such activities in order to realise their ambitions – if they were caught stealing they risked having their applications for visas rejected – indicates the extent to which theatre was not just a matter of entertainment. Plays graphically re-enacting aspects of the ghettos and camps, probing deeply into the survivors' traumatic memories, reveal that theatre was a way of confronting the recent past. Certainly, acts such as *Ein, Zwei, Drei* at St Ottilien DP camp, which dealt with selections in the camps, or *Ich Leb* (I'm Alive), a '*Heldendrama in drei Akten*' performed by the MIT (Minchener Idisher Teater) which 'produced the horror of recent years on the stage',[108] were very popular. Whether they allowed survivors to 'work through' the past or simply allowed them to share their grief together is hard to say.[109] Theatre in the DP camps can be regarded as a form of therapy but above all it bespeaks a fierce determination on the part of the DPs to choose their own way of living when they were not yet wholly able to do so.

Religion

Religious celebrations were also opportunities to confront the recent past. Purim, especially, a raucous festival commemorating the deliverance of the Jews of the Persian empire from Haman's plan to destroy them, offered a chance to grapple with the Nazis in the context of long-term Jewish history. At Landsberg DP camp in 1946, DPs dressed up as Hitler and were 'arrested', and effigies of Hitler were hanged. Jewish rituals, whether carried out as a matter of observance or not, anchored DPs in the cycle of daily routine. For some, they reaffirmed the existence and persistence of the Jewish people, and for others they were the natural place to turn to find a way of marking significant events.

Regular markers of Jewish practice, though less eye-catching than these carnivalesque ceremonies, were important for making the movement of time once again seem regular and predictable. In October 1945, for example, relief worker Shea Abramovicz noted the first circumcision in Föhrenwald. He arranged too for schnapps and 'a feast' to be laid on the Jewish festival of Simchat Torah and remarked: 'A wonderful sight to see the people dance.'[110] Whatever had happened to their faith during the Holocaust, many DPs valued the sense of simply being permitted to enjoy familiar routines once again. With respect to the saying of the *kaddish* (the prayer for the dead), for example, or Sabbath rituals such as lighting candles, as well as less chronologically-fixed occurrences such as circumcisions, weddings or the erection of small monuments to the dead, religious observance 'created a space for the performance of this ethnic identity and its political expression, Zionism'.[111] If ordinarily one would not expect to see such a clear correlation between Jewish religious practice and Zionism, in the specific conditions of the DP camps this was the case: the affirmation of religious identity in the context of the authorities' refusal to permit Jews to emigrate drove the two spheres close together.

Religion was not only a form of consolation, of course. Many Jews among the survivors were observant, especially once the infiltrees arrived, many of whom came from traditional Polish-Jewish backgrounds. In early 1946 orthodox Jews comprised perhaps 40 per cent of the DPs in the camps. Hence among the schools established at the DP camps there were also *yeshivot*, religious schools that emphasised the study of Torah. In stereotypical fashion, the students devoted themselves to their studies and neglected everything else. At least that is how Zippy Orlin recalled the *yeshiva* at Belsen. Claiming that she often 'tried to improve the conditions under which the students lived and worked', she equipped the *yeshiva* with cutlery, crockery, linen and furniture, and had the rooms painted: 'but alas, no one was prepared to accept responsibility of looking after these things – all sat with their heads buried deep in their books, and swayed and chanted far into the night'.[112] The influx of orthodox Jews also had practical implications, such as the need to build new *mikvaot*, or ritual baths, for women; this became especially important as weddings and births started to take place in large numbers and rituals of purification had to be observed.[113] Orlin's tendency in retrospect to see her time in Belsen DP camp through somewhat rose-tinted spectacles overlooks the extent to which conflict existed between the orthodox Jews and the camp's other residents. On occasion this led to clashes, such as over whether the camp's streets should be closed to traffic on the Sabbath.[114] Yet even these altercations were, to some extent, a sign of the return of 'normal' life.

'Normality' did not quite resume with a return to religious tradition. Apart from the uncompromisingly orthodox, many DPs found that the form of the prayers and rituals could hardly compensate for the substance which they now felt was missing. Tradition, too, was altered in the face of new realities. In a September 1945 speech at the Landsberg DP camp synagogue on Yom Kippur (the Day of Atonement, the holiest day the Jewish calendar), Samuel Gringauz announced that the rules governing the reciting of the *yizkor* prayer (the sombre prayer for the dead that closes the Day of Atonement) no longer applied, because 'Our *yizker* is a constant and uninterrupted one. We say *yizker* in the morning and in the evening. We say *yizker* by day and by night. We say *yizker* while awake and in our dreams. Our heart beats to the rhythm of *yizker*, and in our brain its melody plays incessantly. We require no special *yizker*.'[115] With a rhythm that recalls the *shema*, the Jewish daily prayer, Gringauz made clear not only that commemorating the dead is a continuous and unavoidable process, but that the prayer for the dead had dislodged the *shema* as the Jews' main daily religious obligation. Given that the dead were still being buried in large numbers after liberation and in the DP camps, this was no theoretical matter. Whether bringing the dead into the centre of religious and political life in this way was a form of comfort, however, is debatable. In the DP camps, the traditional role of mourning rituals in enabling a gradual, tolerable separation between the living and the dead was seriously compromised, as is suggested in this account of a memorial service for the Jews of Rivne (Ukraine) at Föhrenwald:

> The assembled rise in honour of the martyrs. The cantor intones the memorial service ... When the cantor recites the words 'the souls of the murdered who relinquished their souls for the sanctification of God's name,' the assembled see the souls of their dear ones in the burning candles, and their hearts fill with tears; the assembled cannot restrain themselves, and the hall erupts in a wailing lament by all the assembled. The assembly of bereavement is over, [but] the people cannot move, tears gush, the heart is in pain. *Great is the wrath.*[116]

Family

It was not what the Nazis had intended: the Jewish DP camps in Germany had the highest birth rate in postwar Europe. At Belsen in the first two years after liberation, 1,438 marriages had taken place and some 500 circumcision ceremonies had been carried out.[117] The first wedding at Feldafing was that between Ernest Landau, one of the leading spokesmen for the survivors, and his wife, a Jewish deportee from Hungary; they had met in a concentration camp. Landau describes the wedding as 'a real event', with journalists there to record it. With the help of a German informer and the American Jewish army chaplain, Major Max Brauder, Landau and some colleagues confiscated the cellar of the Dallmayr Gourmet Store, so that at the wedding 'every single inmate got a bottle of wine'.[118]

But these marriages were not entered into on the same basis as before the war. 'I was lonely and she was lonely', said one man. 'Perhaps together, we'll be only half as lonely.'[119] Nor were the weddings carefree, joyous occasions. 'Weddings were performed, children were born, anniversaries were celebrated, but not with a normal happiness; more like a forced smile.'[120] Weddings were often rather sombre affairs at which 'the memories of the dead were vivid'.[121] As American rabbi Max B. Wall wrote of a wedding he performed in October 1945 in a hotel in Alt-Otting where some 165 Jews were living: 'Tears flowed quite freely and it was obvious that not all the tears were tears of joy.'[122] 'Everybody', as Jack Werber, a survivor of Buchenwald writes, 'wanted to feel connected again to the world that once was.'[123] One relief worker reporting in summer 1946 on the orderly nature of Admont camp in Austria, which seemed akin to a small, well-run country town, nevertheless noticed that among the 'problems and difficulties of DP life' were the 'mothers who don't want their children and babies to be born, and grow up, in a "Lager".'[124] Nevertheless, those babies were being born in large numbers.

Until the DPs themselves started having so many children, the concept of 'family' was one of the bitterest for the survivors. When the DP camp at Zeilsheim opened in summer 1945 there was not a single child there.[125] Shea Abramovicz wrote in a report of October 1945 that in Landsberg, where he had spent Yom Kippur, 4,000 people gathered for prayers, amongst whom 'there was no one present who had not lost the majority of his or her family'. There was only one child present, a sickly girl of three who had been born in the woods in hiding, who could neither speak nor walk. 'Every child', Abramovicz went on, 'is looked upon as a treasure and in such a gathering the agonized cry of Yiskor ['remember'] must have rent heaven itself. The Yiskor for murdered babies, mothers, Jewish intellectuals, Jewish workers, the Jewish people ... No sermons were necessary to move the people, we all cried, we wept to ease our heavy hearts. These people can never forget what they have suffered.' Hardly the words of an objective report, Abramovicz's description, with its telling shift from 'the people' to 'we', indicates the extent to which Jewish families had been decimated. It was perhaps the single most emotive issue for the survivors and the relief workers.[126]

If in 1945 the DP camps were striking for the absence of children, a few years later they were noteworthy for having so many. A Joint report of 30 May 1948 recorded a total population of 3,419 people in Föhrenwald, of whom 194 were babies under one year old, 397 were children aged between one and six, and 191 were youths aged seven to seventeen. Additionally, amongst the 1,132 women in the camp, ninety-three were pregnant.[127] In Belsen, around fifteen children were being born every week by 1947 and the birth of the thousandth baby was marked in February 1948.[128] One Joint worker noted that 'by the spring of 1946, every third woman was either pregnant or pushing a baby carriage'.[129] The claim was backed up by Zippy Orlin, who recorded what happened next: 'The staff of the maternity section of the hospital was kept busy all day as the birth-rate was extremely high. The "mohels" [circumcisers] in Belsen often worked overtime.'[130] What was behind this baby boom?

First of all, the babies were a sign that people wanted to have families again. Second, many women feared that their experiences had left them infertile and many sought to become pregnant as soon as they could. Often they did so before they were physically ready and with little experience of motherhood, since usually they were still young and their own mothers had been killed. Third, having babies has been understood not just as a reassertion of normality but as a variety of 'revenge' against the Nazi desire to wipe out the Jewish people. They were, in other words, 'messiah children' (*Maschiachskinder*), since they spoke to the salvation of the Jews. They were proof that '*mir szeinen doh*': we are here. This slogan – highly ideological, as Atina Grossmann notes – was a kind of overstated compensation for the fact that the new reality of marriage and babies was by no means a replacement for what had existed before.[131] Rather, the two lives coexisted so that the willed joy and charged symbolism of the new life existed alongside the permanent sorrow of those that had been lost. Hence so many survivors, especially women, faced psychological difficulties with raising their children, from practical issues such as not knowing how to feed an infant, to those more obviously related to their trauma such as an inability to cuddle their child. These were long-term problems, often passed on to the next generation.[132]

Training and Rehabilitation

Given the general despondency among the DPs, the significance of vocational training should not be underestimated; it provided a way of giving people the hope that their lives would acquire meaning. Key to this process was ORT, whose official position was that 'Our organization felt the moral obligation to assist the most stricken Jews in the DP camps by providing them with vocational skills.'[133] One of ORT's historians claims that 'The presence of ORT inside the DP camps made the immediate post-war months and years bearable ... It was the diligence and initiative of the workers of World ORT that was responsible for instilling self-worth and purpose back into the lives of the newly liberated concentration camp survivors.'[134] ORT's mission to equip survivors with the skills necessary for a productive life was applied, with UNRRA's agreement, across the western zones of occupation and Italy. A.C. Glassgold, for example, was assigned to Landsberg:

> Though I had heard and read about the tragic lives of these people in German concentration camps, I was not quite prepared for the shock of seeing the tattooed blue numbers on their left forearms ... It was here in Landsberg that I witnessed the miracle of the human spirit; saw it revive from the ashes of the gruesome past to rise above the obstacles of the present and soar above the bleak promises of the future.[135]

Indeed, at Landsberg ORT's work was forwarded by Jacob Oleiski, a survivor of the Kovno ghetto who had previously run ORT Lithuania. He was now, as Irving Heymont noted, 'preaching and putting into practice his credo of salvation through work'.[136] This meant not just enjoying a useful future but partially overcoming the grief of the recent past: 'it is only through productive, creative work that we can lessen our anger at having lost so many years', Oleiski wrote.[137] And at Belsen, another important ORT site, the director Joseph Mack developed a 'workshop' system offering a wide variety of training from sewing to electrical engineering.

The significance of ORT is illustrated in a report written by Leonard Cohen following a visit to Western Europe in June 1945. Whilst in Paris he visited the ORT Training School and was impressed by the amount and the quality of activities on offer. Cohen referred in particular to one girl, an orphan who had spent six months in a mental health institution following a breakdown. 'She had now recovered', Cohen was pleased to report, 'and under the care and individual attention of her teacher she was learning to take her place in society.'[138] He eagerly recommended that the JCRU should grant £3,000 for the purchase of machines, tools and materials for this ORT school and a further £2,000 for a projected ORT school in Belgium. ORT also continued to run its operations in Eastern Europe, assisted financially by the JDC. In Bucharest, for example, ORT ran many training schools, including in metalwork, welding, carpentry, watch-making and agriculture, until these were all shut down by the communist government in March 1949.[139]

ORT was a haven for a minority of DPs. It could not erase the scars of the recent past. Nevertheless, according to one postwar report, as of 31 May 1948, 10,400 students were enrolled on ORT vocational courses.[140] The JDC also ran vocational courses in the DP camps, as did UNRRA. Writing from Föhrenwald as early as November 1945, Shea Abramovicz, the head of the camp's various schools, workshops and training centres, totted up that he was responsible, among others, for a tailoring school, a metalworking school, hairdressing, electrical and carpentry workshops, and he was 'working on a scheme of agronomy and agricultural school (for 100), electrical and radiological school etc.' He proudly proclaimed that 'We have outstripped every other camp in the vicinity that had tools instructors and started weeks nay many months before us.'[141] Even so, when the vocational schools started to struggle to acquire materials in 1946, ORT stepped in to help, on condition that the school would include 'ORT' in its name.[142]

Whether through vocational schools or adult education, such as at the Landsberg 'Popular University', many young DPs thus fulfilled their aim of obtaining a skill that would prepare them for a life elsewhere once they were able to realise their ambition of leaving the DP camp. For the most part, that 'elsewhere' meant Palestine, and many of the DPs organised themselves into kibbutzim in order to isolate themselves from their German surroundings and to live as if they were already in their chosen land.

Zionism

Zionism was not the default position of all DPs. However, it was helped along by the British authorities' anti-Zionist attitude, which had the effect of hardening the DPs' resolve. At the first Congress of Liberated Jews in the British zone, which was held at Belsen in September 1945, the call was made to permit the survivors to enter Palestine, and this resolve was maintained throughout the DP camp's existence. As one British military report noted, 'Despite a few enthusiastic anti-Zionists the meeting was overwhelmingly in favour of the opening of Palestine to such as wished to go there'.[143] Hanna Yablonka calls this 'an instinctive "gut" Zionism rooted in a loss of faith in the European emancipation and the profound sense of humiliation that [the Jews] felt during the years of destruction'.[144] Yet Zionism was not just a fallback position of Jews who were waking up to the fact that they had no other option. Nor was it forced upon the *she'erit hapleitah* by a cynical Yishuv seeking to capitalise on the survivors' weaknesses. Rather, for the majority of the DPs, as Samuel Gringauz argued, this Zionism was 'a historical philosophical Zionism felt as an historical mission, as a debt to the dead, as retribution toward the enemy, as a duty to the living. It is, moreover, a Zionism of warning, because the Sherit Hapleita feels that the continuation of Jewish national abnormality means the danger of a repetition of the catastrophe.'[145] Or, as Koppel Pinson remarked, 'Anti-Zionism or even a neutral attitude towards Zionism came to mean for them a threat to the most fundamental stakes in their future.'[146]

It has often been remarked that the Israel Defense Forces regarded itself as the heirs of the Warsaw ghetto and that the State of Israel was able to come into existence when it did because of the Holocaust. The Jewish DPs provide the link between the Holocaust and Israel. Their Zionism, with American support, forced Britain's hand on Palestine; and the presence of the survivors in such numbers in post-1948 Israel (comprising perhaps a third of the population) meant that Israeli institutions were not just imbued with a sense of emotional connection to the world of the Holocaust but were actually linked to it by the people who ran and staffed them. Half the soldiers who fought in the War of Independence, for example, were Holocaust survivors.[147]

The survivors' Zionism was deeply felt, sometimes to the extent that Palestine was chosen over proximity to close relatives. Edith Feuereisen, a sixteen-year-old Hungarian survivor of Auschwitz, could have gone to live with her father in the US. Her devotion to the Zionist cause, however, won out:

In America we may be comfortable for a year, for two, for ten, but the end will be the same – we will be driven out. I have learned a lot of things in Auschwitz and one of them is that unless we have a National Home, we will perish as a nation. I am young in years, but I am very old in experience. I am still strong and I want to work for my people.[148]

The clearest illustration of this burgeoning Zionism, especially amongst the young, was the emergence of the kibbutz movement inside the DP camps.

At the end of 1945 there were sixteen kibbutzim – institutions in which members live and work together, sharing their possessions and food – at Föhrenwald containing nearly 1,000 people. It was one of the central ideas of early Zionism and, as preparation for life in Palestine and often in protest at the lack of focus in DPs' lives, many groups in the DP camps organised themselves along kibbutz principles. They had a huge impact. As Shea Abramovicz noted of Föhrenwald, 'The Palestine question and Bevin policy have a great effect on the daily life.'[149]

One of the earliest kibbutzim to be founded, and the earliest of the *hachsharot* (agricultural kibbutzim), was Kibbutz Buchenwald. Devised in the former concentration camp by survivors of the death marches, the nascent kibbutz was granted permission by the American military authorities to settle on Egendorff Farm near Blenkenheim, some nineteen miles from Buchenwald. The first group of sixteen men arrived there on 3 June 1945, followed over the coming weeks by more camp survivors who wanted to join the group.[150] When the Soviets took over jurisdiction of Thuringia from the Americans the kibbutz relocated to Geringshof, near Fulda. The members' stated aim was to take control of their destiny and not allow others to make decisions about their lives, as had been the case under Nazism: 'Through our physical labour in this kibbutz, we have meant to demonstrate that we are not yet destroyed, but that we have a will to live and to build. We have meant to demonstrate our dislike of continuing to live in the camp, even as liberated people, and our dislike of philanthropy and dependence on others.'[151] The use of the word 'yet' – as in 'not yet destroyed' – is, despite the forceful tone, highly revealing. One of the kibbutz members' main points was that time was not on their side.

Located for the most part within the DP camps, the kibbutzim were set apart both physically (they usually had their own building) and mentally, in terms of their tightly organised structure and their devotion to the cause of preparing for life in Palestine, especially in agriculture. In general, the discipline shown by the *kibbutzniks* in studying Hebrew, Jewish history and geography was quite remarkable. Richard Crossman, the Labour MP who was a member of the Anglo-American Committee of Inquiry on Palestine in February–March 1946, remarked also on the psychological effect of the kibbutzim during his tour of the DP camps:

> We had observed that morale was always highest in the centres where a Kibbutz (a group community training itself for the new life in Palestine) had been organized . . . To destroy the Kibbutz would be to break the only values which prevented these people from degenerating, as many in the concentration camps had degenerated, into sub-human beastliness.[152]

Yet the kibbutz *hachsharah* was a special case, since establishing them required expropriating land from Germans. This was straightforward in the case of former Nazi landowners but more complex when German land-owners remained *in situ* or when German agricultural trainers had to be employed due to lack of expertise within the DP community itself. Nevertheless, by summer 1946 there were twenty-four such agricultural kibbutzim with over 2,000 members.[153]

The kibbutzim varied widely in terms of composition and politics, though the majority of members were young and single. They aimed to live in harmony yet, as is hardly surprising given Jewish history in general and the traumatic experiences their members had undergone in particular, such consensus was hard to maintain, especially when confronted with what the historian of Kibbutz Buchenwald calls 'the schismatic political heritage of the Yishuv' when transplanted to Palestine.[154] A group of eight ultra-orthodox women, for example, left Kibbutz Buchenwald to join the more homogeneous Kibbutz Hafetz Hayyim near Zeilsheim in October 1945.[155] The majority of kibbutzim were from the start affiliated to a religious position or political party, and many of them were temporary in nature, formed solely with a view to coordinate immigration to Palestine (so-called *aliyah kibbutzim*).[156]

By the start of 1947 there were 276 kibbutzim with 16,328 members.[157] Often the members were youngsters who had been badly damaged by the war, both physically and mentally. 'A fifteen-year-old boy often possesses the verbal proficiency of a first-grader in Palestine, the general education of a ten-year-old, and the life experiences of an adult', wrote Joint worker Akiba Lewinsky in April 1947.[158]

Backbone of the new state of Israel though they may have been, but the kibbutzim, full of youngsters in a hurry to get out of Europe and begin life afresh in Palestine, might not always have been the healthy environment their devotees claimed – even if it is easy to understand why people chose to join them. By bringing together members with their experiences of suffering, the kibbutz acted as both a protector from and incubator of trauma. The group could share its grief but at the same time that shared grief became its common denominator, underlying the members' aims and hopes. This double-edged nature of the kibbutz might also help to explain why Israeli politics and culture rapidly became suffused with apocalyptic imagery.

Despite the existence of the kibbutzim, and despite the noisy demonstrations against British policy in the DP camps, by no means all the DPs devoted themselves to Zionism. The desire of a large minority to gain entrance to the US and other countries should not be overlooked. In fact, this ambition helps to explain why Jewish DP camps existed at all after the middle of 1948 when the State of Israel had been proclaimed. For Jews who came from a Bundist or communist tradition the US might not have been wholly attractive, but neither were they likely to be wholehearted Zionists. For many, Palestine was simply the geographically closest viable option and there were organised ways of getting there.[159] As the Kibbutz Buchenwald group diary put it: 'Most of us are Zionists of old; the rest, through prison and suffering, have come to the realization that the only place for us is in our own national home.'[160] Indeed, for the majority the desire to reach Palestine was overwhelming; youth groups especially spearheaded this 'Palestine passion' through the kibbutzim.

BPs?

Ira Hirschmann noted that at Landsberg, thanks to the efforts of A. Cook Glassgold, the director of the DP camp, and his team, 'there was a wonderful spirit among the Jews in spite of their living under the most trying circumstances'. This did not stop him regarding the Jews – 'souls snatched from slaughter' – less as DPs than as 'BPs', betrayed persons, for ending up in such camps in the first place.[161]

The same belief permeates an important report sent by Shea Abramovicz to the grandees of the JCRA in March 1946, summarising his six months at Föhrenwald. He went into considerable detail explaining how he and his colleagues had made every effort to better the lives of the DPs, and he proudly asserted that they had achieved a good deal, from improving the DPs' health to providing opportunities for education and training. Yet, as he admitted, the whole enterprise felt very fragile, such that 'there is always a question present in the minds of all the people'. That question could be simply put: 'What is going to happen to us?' He went on: 'This life they lead is so unstable, so purposeless. They see no future anywhere except in Palestine. They trust no one. Everything is temporary and therefore no one is interested except in matters that will assure one's future ... They feel themselves neglected, forgotten.'[162] Or, as Schochet put it after nearly a year at Feldafing: 'We are an unfortunate anachronism. We are an unpleasant burden and a constant reminder of the horrors of war and of man's bestiality. As a result of having been forced to live grotesquely, we are a group which appears grotesque in dress and behaviour. Perhaps we will acquire a new look when we once again live as equals amongst our fellow men.'[163] American journalist I.F. Stone was more dramatic when he warned that the 'American zone of Germany, with its hundred thousand restless Jews, still homeless and still far from free a year and a half after the liberation, seemed a human volcano in which bloody battles might break out at any time and spread from town to town'.[164]

Another year later, patience was running out and commentators were starting to reappraise the DP camps in quite harsh terms. A spokesman for the Jewish community in the Rhineland-Palatinate claimed that when even though the Jews had all had quite different visions of what liberation would be like when they dreamed of it during the war, 'even the most extreme pessimist did not envisage a time like today'.[165] Another commentator reported that 'the DP regards the activities of the Allied armies and their military governments with fear and apprehension'; it was logical, then, 'that his morale in the day-to-day existence of the DP camps is at a low ebb'.[166] The DPs were regarded suspiciously by the military authorities and the feeling was mutual – hardly surprising when DPs were subject to capricious and often incomprehensible demands, raids, searches, confiscations and forced relocation, not to mention a host of petty regulations, even if at the same time they were being kept alive. Alongside these tensions, and the mistrust between DPs and the wider German population, Gringauz noted in 1948 that the 'anti-German sentiment of the Jewish DPs in the occupation zone clashes with the American policy of supporting a West German state'.[167]

At bottom, the DPs' state of mind was affected by not knowing what the future held for them. 'Aware', as Berger went on to say, 'of the apparent unwillingness of most countries to offer them opportunities for migration, they are torn between alternating fears of forcible repatriation and of abandonment to the tender mercies of the native German population'.[168] Abramovicz wrote: 'If the people have to stay here very much longer their nerves are bound to get even more strained and then we can expect anything ...'[169] Hirschmann was right to say that the term 'displaced persons' was 'a smooth, diplomatic term which, particularly for the Jews, ridiculously failed to express the utter tragedy it encompassed'.[170] By the start of 1948, commentators were openly wondering how much time was left to save the DPs from despair.[171]

CHAPTER FIVE

Transitions:
DPs in a Changing World

'I'd like to note here that for us Jews the closing down of the concentration camps (or internment camps) is the most important political
demand of all. It's clear that it is a question of basic existence . . . everything that's happening now – that is, the migration from German DP
camps to the Palestinian Atlit Camp and to the concentration camps on
Cyprus – is possible only because the whole world sees it as 'humane' in
comparison to Auschwitz. Apart from all the speeches and declarations,
one consequence of the death camps is that Jews are regarded a priori,
so to speak, as potential inhabitants of concentration camps.'
HANNAH ARENDT, 1946

'As a European I found it hard to accept the inevitable conclusion. Could
it really be true that, apart from the western democracies where the
Jewish communities had always been insignificant, no single European
country could be expected to revive its Jewish community? Could Hitler
really have accomplished his aim?'
RICHARD CROSSMAN, 1947[1]

When Jewish DPs took over the farm that had belonged to Julius Streicher,
the infamous Jew-baiting editor of the Nazi newspaper *Der Stürmer*,
they found a sign hanging over his villa which read: '*Ohne Lösung der
Judenfrage gibt es keine Lösung der Weltfrage*' (Without a solution of the

Jewish question there is no solution to the world question). According to Koppel Pinson, who worked as Education Director for Displaced Jews in Germany for the Joint between October 1945 and September 1946, the DPs left it in place.[2]

The Jewish DPs, in other words, were absorbed by their suffering and understood the world through it. 'The Jewish problem is identical with the DP problem and the world problem with the Jewish problem', wrote Pinson.[3] And it seems that the DPs who took over Streicher's farm really did think this way; thus argues the historian of Kibbutz Nili, which operated from the farm: 'For the kibbutzniks this statement was connected to the creation of a common Jewish way of life [jüdischen Gemeinwesens]. The "Jewish question" in the She'erit hapleitah's sense could only be solved by the foundation of the State of Israel.'[4] This might not have been true for all DPs but their future was indeed intimately tied to broader questions of world politics. With the reconstruction of West Germany in the context of the emerging Cold War, the creation of NATO, the decline of the British Empire and conflict over the future of Palestine, the apparently minor (in world-historical or geopolitical terms) issue of the Jewish DPs took on considerable significance.

The DPs did not bring about the creation of Israel by themselves. Of greater significance were the actions of the major powers, most importantly the Soviets' harrying of the British Empire and its allies in Greece, Iran and Turkey; the impact of the war on Britain's ability to control former imperial possessions such as Singapore where Japanese-inspired anti-colonial movements had gained ground; and the impact of Jewish terrorism in Palestine which, within the frame of imperial decline and in the face of American opposition, weakened the British government's determination to maintain the Mandate. The policies of UNRRA and its replacement, the IRO, which eventually acknowledged that Jewish DPs constituted an extraterritorial collectivity with the right to migrate, lent international legitimacy to Jewish claims to nationhood.[5] All of these developments hastened the British decision to leave Palestine, as did, crucially, Britain's increasing financial dependence on the US. Indeed, as we will see, more than any other factors, American actions – and inactions – after the war were responsible for the creation of Israel. Yet every development was intimately related to the fact of liberation, for without the liberation from Nazi rule and the events which followed it, it is questionable whether the state of Israel would have been created.

The DPs' activities contributed to the process in important ways: their fear of remaining in Europe, their rage at what they perceived as the world's failure to help them, and their desperation in the face of continued incarceration in DP camps all tie the story of liberation to the events of the postwar world. From the liberators' side, the British response to illegal emigration across the Mediterranean Sea not only created the unfortunate image of a harsh great power cracking down on luckless and desperate survivors of genocide, it also meant that the British devoted resources to intercepting the boats and interning the migrants in camps on Cyprus, in another wasteful diversion of naval resources from more pressing commitments. So if the DPs and their helpers in the underground *brichah* movement – including the JDC and US army chaplains such as Judah Nadich – did not on their own force the British out of Palestine, they certainly speeded on the decision to do so.[6]

Strained Alliance

When, after the Harrison Report, the US changed its policies towards Jewish DPs, the decision coincided with the largest influx of Jews to Germany yet, as the Polish returnees from Soviet exile made their way westwards. Most of them deliberately sought refuge in the US zone, where they knew they would be treated as DPs. By November 1946, there were some 157,000 Jewish DPs in the American zone. Although Belsen remained the largest DP camp, only small numbers of 'infiltrees' – the term is itself revealing of official attitudes towards these refugees – sought to settle in the British zone. The disagreement between the Americans and the British over Jewish-only camps was framed from the British perspective as an ethical policy of not replicating Nazi thinking by singling out specific groups according to race or religion. Although the claim might have been well-meaning at the outset, it quickly became a mantra that disguised the real British fear: Palestine. The British were not only jumpy at the local level about the presence of Jewish military rabbis and other military personnel in Belsen, some of whom were reassigned because of fears they were or would become Zionist agents. They also feared that American and UNRRA policy was aimed at forcing their hand over Palestine, with the intention of stemming immigration to the US on the one hand and solving an expensive refugee problem on the other.

In order to try and mitigate these fears and to alleviate some of the ill-will that was disrupting US–UK relations in the wake of the Harrison Report, in November 1945 the British government set up the Anglo-American Committee of Inquiry on Palestine (AACI) to investigate Harrison's claims. The group of six Americans and six Britons visited DP camps in February 1946 and Palestine in March, with sub-committees travelling to several Arab capitals to take representations there. One member, Labour MP and socialist intellectual Richard Crossman, noted in his account of the Committee's visit to the DP camps that 'each of my colleagues had undergone that violent personal experience . . . They had smelt the unique and unforgettable smell of huddled, homeless humanity. They had seen and heard for themselves what it means to be the isolated survivor of a family deported to a German concentration camp or slave labour.' He had come to understand, on the basis of these experiences, why it was that 'Policies which seemed sane enough in the White House or in Downing Street struck these wretched people as sadistic brutality.'[7] Another member, prominent American lawyer Bartley Crum, was even more impressed than Crossman by the survivors' determination to get to Palestine. 'The displaced persons must be permitted to go where they wanted', he told a press conference in Vienna, 'and if that was Palestine, so be it. If they did not get out, I said, they would be utterly demoralized.'[8]

The members of the Anglo-American Committee did not all share the same outright support for the Jewish DPs expressed by Crossman and Crum, but when they wrote up their report in Lausanne, which was published in May 1946, they reached a consensus that ran counter to Bevin's intentions. As well as recommending an expeditious restitution of Jewish property and urging European governments to make staying on in Europe as attractive as possible for Jewish (and other) DPs, the Committee agreed with Harrison that the DP camps provided only inadequate housing and, in its April report, reiterating Truman's earlier suggestion, recommended allowing 100,000 DPs to enter Palestine:

> We know of no country to which the great majority can go in the imme-
> diate future other than Palestine. Furthermore that is where almost all of
> them want to go. There they are sure that they will receive a welcome

denied them elsewhere. There they hope to enjoy peace and rebuild their lives.

We believe it is essential that they should be given an opportunity to do so at the earliest possible time. Furthermore we have the assurances of the leaders of the Jewish Agency that they will be supported and cared for.

The Committee was very careful not to antagonise any interested parties. Rejecting partition, they insisted that Palestine should be neither a Jewish nor Arab state nor a land governed by 'narrow nationalism'; rather it should be a state 'which guards the rights and interests of Moslems, Jews and Christians alike.' They further argued that in order to forestall the possibility of one side trying to dominate the other in a way that 'might threaten the peace of the world', the British Mandate should be continued 'pending the execution of a trusteeship agreement under the United Nations'.[9] These words of caution notwithstanding, Attlee and Bevin were displeased. Seeing only the headline statement that 100,000 Jewish DPs should be permitted to enter Palestine, they felt that Truman had betrayed them.[10] Attlee told Crossman that he had 'let us down by giving way to the Jews and America'.[11] And at a press conference on 13 November, Bevin said, in a statement which has given rise to much debate about his views on the Jews, that:

> I am very anxious that the Jews in Europe shall not over-emphasize their racial position. The keynote of the statement I made in the House [on the establishment of the AACI] is that I want the suppression of racial warfare, and therefore if the Jews, with all their sufferings, want to get too much at the head of the queue, you have the danger of another antisemitic reaction through it all.[12]

Stalling on Truman's proposals for further conferences between the Jewish Agency, the US and the Arab states, Attlee and Bevin reiterated the government's longstanding position that Jewish immigration to Palestine could continue at a rate of 1,500 per month and that higher numbers were impermissible without the approval of the Arabs and without the Jewish underground movement laying down its arms. Britain's attempt to persuade the US to share its desire to deal with the refugee problem without involving Palestine failed, and Bevin 'was forced to retreat – albeit with threat and bluster – step by bitter step'.[13] Even the editorial position of *The Times* indicated that Attlee and Bevin were out of step with world opinion. In its appraisal of the year 1946, it noted that:

> The suggestion that 100,000 Jewish refugees should be admitted to Palestine as soon as practicable caught the imagination of humanitarian circles both in Britain and the United States, and Zionist opinion in the United States as well as in Palestine was greatly encouraged, and shows signs of even more dangerous impatience at British endeavours to prevent all Jewish immigration not sanctioned by the small minority quota.[14]

This retreat from Palestine was a slow process, however. Receiving the Anglo-American Committee's report enthusiastically at first, the DPs soon realised that its recommendation of a cessation of underground activity and a laying down of arms made highly likely both the perpetuation of the British Mandate and a delay in any possible exodus from the DP camps. The DP camps did not begin to close; rather as we have seen, they consolidated, becoming hives of activity mixed with increasing despair as opportunities to leave were dangled and then withdrawn. A radicalisation of illegal emigration methods ensued along with a continuation of resistance to British rule – the Irgun Zvai Leumi blew up the King David Hotel in Jerusalem on 22 July 1946, killing ninety-one people – and Arab-Jewish conflict in Palestine. The British, frustrated by the Jewish Committee in Belsen as well as by American policy, lashed out, calling Josef Rosensaft the 'chief nigger in the woodpile' for his alleged communist sympathies and for assisting the DPs with illegal immigration. When Rosensaft and Wollheim complained about the British failure to help the liberated Jews enter Palestine, relations between the British authorities and the Jewish Committee reached a new low. Rosensaft was blamed directly for the dreary state of affairs, with one letter to the Foreign Office stating that 'the difficulties our authorities have had in dealing with the Jewish DPs in the British zone are in large measure attributable to him'.[15] This personalisation of a much wider problem contained a kernel of truth but was hardly an adequate response to an issue that had international ramifications.

These dilemmas and conflicts were played out most spectacularly in the British response to the illegal ships of DP migrants trying to reach Palestine.

In August 1946, following Truman's rejection of the Morrison–Grady plan to partition Palestine under British control, Bevin announced that the government would henceforth deport illegal immigrants to detention camps on Cyprus. The government blamed the Jewish Committee in Belsen, the JDC and the underground Zionist movement for exploiting the DPs in order to further their goals and for fanning the flames of conflict between Arabs and Jews in Palestine. The Arabs agreed with the government's assessment and further pressed the British to prevent illegal immigration, but to no avail: the ships kept coming, the French and Italians turned a blind eye, and the threat of detention on Cyprus was regarded by the DPs as but the latest inconvenience in their long-running saga.

I.F. Stone gives a vivid account of one such crossing on a boat manned mainly by American Jews, some of whom had been born in Eastern Europe. The passengers were mostly Polish and Czechoslovak Jews, with other Jews from all over Europe from Latvia to Greece, which made the ship something of 'a floating Babel'. There was also a group of Dutch youngsters (in fact, many of them German and Austrian who had been refugees or hidden in Holland) who 'were not fleeing Holland – they were going to Palestine'.[16] Packed into the hold 'like the cargo of an African slaver', the refugees endured a week of calm travelling until they transferred to a Turkish cargo ship and were then intercepted by a British destroyer. Although the ensign asked if the boat's passengers were willing to be towed into Haifa harbour, he returned to his ship and it sailed off, leaving the would-be immigrants stranded on the high seas south of Cyprus. They headed uncertainly for Haifa where the same ship that had abandoned them at sea received them 'with a bit of gallantry', dealing politely with the refugees – until they were placed under quarantine after two cases of bubonic plague were found on board. Discovering that the cause of the swollen glands was not in fact plague, and seeing that the British were using the suspected disease as a way of keeping the refugees on the ship for as long as possible, Stone managed to furtively disembark in his US military correspondent's uniform and began his journey home. His travelling companions were also lucky, 'for they were among the last shiploads of illegal immigrants permitted to land. They were not sent to Cyprus.'[17]

The most famous case of attempted illegal immigration was that of the *Exodus 1947*, which set sail from Sète in southern France on 10 July 1947

with 4,530 DPs on board. On 17 July, just before reaching Palestinian territorial waters, the ship was captured by the British navy and towed into Haifa
harbour. The passengers were then sailed all the way back to Hamburg on
board military transport ships and interned in transit camps at Pöppendorf
and Am Stau near Lübeck. Their fate – ending up in Germany in heavily-
armed camps – sparked protests around the world, including two occasions
in Belsen on 23 August and 7 September when DPs marched to show solidarity with the returnees. Although the British, contrary to their usual
policy, treated the refugees as DPs, the damage done to British standing was
considerable.[18] The Jewish Historical Society of Greater Washington, for
instance, produced a sticker which was seen in protests at the British
Embassy, reading 'S.S. EXODUS 1947: BRITISH FLOATING DACHAU'.

Once again, Jews found themselves in camps, this time in Cyprus. The
propaganda value of this British decision was, for Ben-Gurion and the
Yishuv, exactly what they wanted. But for the DPs, their renewed internment proved Hannah Arendt's point that Jews were now regarded as people
who were fit to be held in camps. Their separation from 'normal' human
beings had not yet ended. The fact that the Cyprus internment camps, like
the DP camps in Germany, were not 'as bad' as Nazi concentration camps
did not remove the symbolic resonance of what was happening. 'Liberation'
meant, as far as many Jews were concerned, simply a prolonged internment. 'Standing on this sun-baked forlorn island', wrote Ira Hirschmann,
whilst waiting for a plane in Cyprus in May 1946, 'how could one imagine,
even in his most sinister dreams, that within the next few months it would
become the prison of more than 30,000 Jewish refugees, seized by His
Majesty's Royal Navy, taken from tiny, leaking ships bound for Palestine,
and that the British government would so soon take over Hitler's role as
keeper of the concentration camps, and immortalize Cyprus along with
names like Dachau, Belsen and Maidanek?'[19]

Held partly in tent camps, partly in Nissen huts (much like the American
Quonset huts), the camps were mostly on two sites close to Famagusta (in
Caraolos) or Dekhelia (in Xylotymbou). As in Germany, the Cyprus camps
developed schools, vocational training centres, theatres, religious centres,
sport clubs and political parties, not to mention the contacts with the
Aliyah Bet, Mossad's illegal immigration arm. Among the Jews interned in
Cyprus were a small number from Morocco and larger numbers from the

Balkans and Eastern Europe. Some 60 per cent, however, had been in the DP camps of Germany, Austria and Italy. Among them were, according to a report of June 1947, some 1,775 children, 985 of whom were orphans, housed in the 'Children's Village'.[20] From November 1946 until May 1948 the Cyprus internees were allowed to enter Palestine at the rate of 750 a month, half the British monthly visa quota. In that period, some 26,000 of them made up 67 per cent of Jewish immigrants to Palestine.[21] As their efforts to try to get there illegally might suggest, they were among the most determined to reach Palestine, and their further incarceration heightened both this necessity and the trauma that accompanied seeing it unfulfilled. As the Palestinian Arabs noted, Cyprus, being only just over 200 miles from Palestine, was 'another springboard for Jewish immigration to Palestine'.[22] The internees agreed; they referred to Cyprus as *Erev Eretz Yisrael*, the eve of Israel.[23] The island's local left-wing movement AKEL made its own anti-colonial (i.e. anti-British) message clear in the assistance it gave the Jewish internees, providing them with clandestine deliveries of food and helping with illegal immigration, for example by showing escapees the whereabouts of caves near the coast.[24] Yet the length of the detention, enduring a seemingly interminable wait, was psychologically painful for the DPs, especially as it was enforced on them by their liberators. As one survivor and Cyprus detainee interviewed in later life noted:

> I would like to point out that the trauma that remained with me from Auschwitz increased with the capture of our boat when we were brought to Cyprus. And that night in which they informed me: 'You are going to captivity.' This left a trauma until this very day. I dream often about concentration camps, and I cannot see anything connected with war . . . or with violence. It always reminds me of my past.[25]

The process of detention was also difficult for those trying to help the Jews, often placing them in an invidious position. Morris Laub was the director of JDC's Cyprus office during this period. He recalls how when one ship, the *Rafiah*, crashed against rocks in Greece, its 785 passengers were picked up by a British boat and brought to Cyprus. When the passengers refused to leave the hold, saying that they would only disembark at Palestine, the British asked Laub to talk with them, which he did, in

Yiddish. On attempting to persuade them that their position was hopeless and that there was no point resisting, they hissed and booed and accused him of being a British agent and a traitor. The British soldiers then brought them out with the help of tear gas.[26] But some of the British also considered their tasks unpleasant, or absurd – such as only allowing the children to swim in the sea if they were escorted there and back by tanks. Colonel Widdicombe, the first supervisor of the Cyprus camps, told Laub that 'This is no job for a soldier. I don't want to be the jailer of women and children.'[27]

Even after the UN voted to partition Palestine in November 1947, the British continued to divert ships to Famagusta. Indeed, their efforts to do so increased, so that in the six months following the partition decision until the Israeli declaration of independence in May 1948, the British deported 22,384 illegal immigrants on twelve ships to Cyprus. In total the British succeeded in diverting to Cyprus some 51,000 of the approximately 70,000 Jewish DPs who sailed for Palestine illegally on sixty-five mostly unseaworthy ships.[28] If this was considered a success by the British, insofar as it kept Arab passions in check, it was also hugely costly to accommodate the refugees on Cyprus, and the negative press generated by turning back the ships not only kept the DP issue alive in the world's media but did so at considerable cost to Britain's reputation. Zionist organisations accused the British of 'Nazi practices ... in order to complete the transformation of Palestine into an armed fortress to safeguard British imperial interests'.[29] Demonstrators at the Cyprus camps made the same point, waving banners reading 'We want to go home!' and 'Down with Bevin, the successor to Hitler!' 'The intensification of Britain's anti-Zionist policy', writes Yehuda Bauer, 'gave the Zionists a golden opportunity to put pressure on the Americans and on public opinion in the Western world.'[30]

The DPs were angered by the British government's intransigent position on Jewish immigration to Britain and Palestine. Sir Frederick Morgan, the head of UNRRA operations in Germany, may have been extreme in his provocative claim that a Zionist conspiracy was at work to persuade Polish Jews to leave their homes but, as David Cesarani notes, his statement 'reflected Foreign Office policy to keep Jews out of the British Zone of Occupation and the British sector of Berlin for fear that they would become an embarrassment by then demanding the right to emigrate to Palestine'. The Foreign

Office continued to maintain its stance that Jews who entered the British occupation zone 'illegally' should not be entitled to rations or accommodation.[31] Many British diplomats criticised the American position, with Lawrence B. Grafftey-Smith in Jeddah warning that:

> The Middle East is for us what the Balkans are for Russia or South America for the United States. It is the enemies and not the friends of the British Empire who seek to establish this irritant of non assimilable elements of Eastern European outlook and dubious ideology in a dominating position across our Imperial communications.[32]

He condemned the Anglo-American Committee's report as 'disastrous' where Britain's relations with the Muslim world were concerned and, like many civil servants and government ministers, feared the Arab reaction to it.[33] The receptiveness of wider society to such attitudes was made clear in August 1947 when, in response to the government's policies, the Irgun murdered two British soldiers in Palestine and anti-Jewish riots erupted in cities across the UK.[34] When one considers the sympathy that the liberated Jews of Europe had received (and were still receiving) in Britain, the anti-Jewish sentiment of 1947–48 indicates the extent to which the government had exacerbated an already complex situation.

In contrast to their attitude to Jewish immigration, the British permitted the immigration into Britain of more than 200,000 Eastern Europeans, including 150,000 Polish servicemen and their families, 93,000 European Voluntary Workers (mostly taken from DP camps, who were recruited to work in heavy industry where there was a labour shortage), and 15,000 German and 8,000 Ukrainian POWs who allegedly had nowhere else to go.[35] As late as 1949, when some 300,000 people had been admitted to Britain under the EVW scheme, the Royal Commission on Population asserted that large-scale immigration 'could only be welcomed without reserve if the immigrants were of good human stock' and that Britain did not have the ability 'to absorb immigrants of alien race and religion' on anything other than a small scale. This clearly excluded Jewish DPs as well as black immigrants from the British Empire.[36]

These facts help us to appreciate the claim of former JDC worker Ralph Segalman that 'The British point of view is the most difficult for the Jew to understand.' Segalman was referring to Britain's refusal to treat Jewish survivors differently from other victims of Nazism or even their oppressors – a stance he approvingly noted had been called 'pseudo liberalism' by others.[37] Such arguments were first and foremost being made in relation to Britain's Palestine policy. In Föhrenwald, as elsewhere, Jewish DPs regularly protested against this policy; in November 1945 JRU worker Shea Abramovicz recorded in a letter to London that there had been 'a hunger strike here against the National Socialist British Government and its policies in Palestine and decrease of rations in DP camps'.[38] The choice of words, though clearly hyperbolic, was designed to provoke, as was Samuel Gringauz's claim at the Second Congress of She'erit Hapleitah in the US zone in February 1947:

> We must proclaim that keeping the camps going is a slow form of genocide … the selfsame crime which the International Military Tribunal at Nuremberg tried. The camps are destroying our readiness to return to life in the same way as the concentration camps destroyed our lives.[39]

In the DP press, every issue was dominated by tragic stories of lonely survivors desperate to get to Palestine but forced to endure life in the camps in the land of the perpetrators in a continent they no longer trusted. An article in *Undzer Shtime* from July 1946 is typical: the author, Simon Kempler, reported on a visit to the small DP camp in Lübeck where he encountered some 600 Polish Jews who had recently arrived from Soviet exile via Poland. Quartered in the Lübeck synagogue, the image of these 'uprooted, exhausted, starving' people with 'faces white as chalk' reminded Kempler of 1940, when the Jews of the Warthegau, trying to flee the Nazis, lived temporarily in synagogues. Sparing none of readers' emotions, Kempler focused on a six-year-old child from Rovno, 'young in years but rich in sorrows and restless wandering [*ruhelosem Umherirren*]' who had travelled from the Caucasus to Germany via Poland with the sole wish of reaching Palestine. The child asked Kempler how much longer he would have to travel before he would see Tel Aviv or Jerusalem: 'I answered that his dream would soon be realized. But in my heart resides the fear that the child might in the near future bring his path of suffering [*Leidensweg*] to an end . . . The intelligent, black, twinkling little eyes of the children tore my heart and I cried over the annihilation and the tragedy of our people.'[40]

It was clearly the case that, as historian Hagit Lavsky notes, 'Through their actions, the British liberators thus defeated their own purpose. Their anti-Jewish policies created a broad Jewish front inside and outside Germany aimed at the achievement of immediate Jewish national goals. From here, the move to long-range national goals was only a matter of time.'[41] At the same time, and as the DPs' own words indicate, Zionism in the DP camps was not only created by British policies; rather, it was a deeply-held conviction, grasped and sustained by people who were accustomed to suffering and who were likely to become more rather than less attached to it by attempts to prevent its realisation. As the Central Committee of Liberated Jews explained in a letter to the United Nations Special Committee on Palestine: 'the fact that the disaster which befell European Jewry reached such dimensions can only be ascribed to the homelessness of our people . . . We, therefore, firmly believe that for our and our children's safety and peace the establishment of a Jewish State in Palestine is an absolute necessity.'[42] Zionism, for many Jews, followed logically from the fact of liberation.

No wonder then that the Zionist organisations took a dim view of British policies towards the DPs, and held their own actions in encouraging emigration in high regard. The Jewish Agency for Palestine, for example, established in 1921 in response to the terms of the British Mandate for Palestine in order to coordinate the establishment of a Jewish national home with the British authorities, argued in 1947 that 'the remnants of the survivors of the gas chambers are still living victims of the Nazi terror – despairing and with only one desire – to settle in Palestine'.[43] After the establishment of Israel, it reported on its own activities in glowing terms. With the DPs' hopes for swift relocation to Palestine dashed, the JAP put into place its 'long-term program' for preparing DPs for life in Palestine, helping to establish schools, kindergartens, youth organisations, kibbutzim and vocational training centres. By its own estimation, the organisation also 'encouraged transitory migration and succeeded in settling some 7,000 people for further training in France, from whence they eventually reached Palestine'. Without admitting any involvement in the process (it was affiliated to IRO so had to be careful), the JAP noted that: 'Many thousands of the best among youth and the active elements, did not wait for an improvement in their situation. They ventured to cross mountains and seas to reach the shores of their promised land.'[44] The American Jewish Conference shared the JAP's assessment, noting the polls of Jews in DP camps that revealed that 98 per cent wanted to go Palestine where they could 'live as free Jews'. The Conference, a nationwide body that included non-Zionist groups, thus 'directed its efforts to opening the doors of Palestine to European Jewry'.[45]

Yet despite Zionist pressure and the dominant voice of the Zionist majority among the DPs (and, one might add, the Zionist tenor of much historiography),[46] many DPs wanted to go to America. In fact, the waves of infiltrees arriving in the US zone, according to one historian, put pressure not so much on the British – who did their best to resist American tactics to allow immigration into Palestine – as on the Americans themselves.[47] Had they the choice, perhaps as many as half of all Jewish DPs would have gone to the US.[48] Much has been made of the fact that Truman pressured Attlee into allowing 100,000 Jewish DPs to enter Palestine; less has been said about Truman's less than entirely altruistic position, which was designed to appease both the Jewish and anti-immigration vote in the US. At the same time, many American Jews, though moved by the plight of the European Jews and entering into an unprecedented wave of support for Zionism, were worried that admitting Jews to the US in large numbers would provoke anti-Semitism. The JDC too, despite protesting its innocence, was involved in assisting with illegal immigration to Palestine where it could, primarily by using American money to fund the operation.[49] As Crossman noted while the AACI was still hearing representations from interested parties in Washington before leaving for Europe, the American call for a Jewish state was satisfying 'many motives':

> They are attacking the Empire and British imperialism, they are espousing a moral cause, for whose fulfilment they will take no responsibility, and most important of all, they are diverting attention from the fact that their own immigration laws are the basic cause of the problem.[50]

Crossman at this stage was not yet a full-fledged convert to Zionism and his response smacks of the offended Englishman, clearly irritated at having to listen to the criticisms of those who seemed blind to their own shortcomings.

But despite the hyperbole – one can hardly maintain that American immi-gration laws were 'the basic cause of the problem' – Crossman's point was not without merit. The evidence is the way in which the Washington administration stalled on changing its immigration legislation, revising it only once the most pressing need to do so had passed. On 1 July 1948, the American DP Law permitted 250,000 DPs to enter the US, albeit with strong restrictions on Jews. Only with the 1950 DP Act – promoted by the tireless activism of the Citizens' Committee on Displaced Persons – did the door to the US finally open to Jewish immigration from the DP camps to an extent that equitably met demand.

The numbers are hard to ascertain, but by 1952 over 80,000 Jewish DPs had immigrated to the US. Substantial numbers of Jewish DPs also immigrated to Australia (about 17,000), Canada (about 16,000), Belgium (about 8,000), South Africa, Argentina and other countries (about 5,000).[51] Nevertheless, the considerable number of DPs who decided to remain in the camps in Germany when, had they wanted to settle somewhere more stable, they might have crossed the still-fluid borders into the countries of Western Europe (as many native French, Belgian and Dutch Jewish survi-vors had done at the end of the war), points to a determination to reach Palestine that suggests the *she'erit hapleitah*'s Zionism was heartfelt.

It is ultimately impossible to assess with certainty the extent to which the DPs' Zionism was generated by outside forces or by an inner drive. The vocal Yishuv with its underground networks provided one of the few options to leave Germany before 1948, and it is probable that many who availed themselves of this choice saw Palestine as a stepping-stone to further emigration. On the other hand, the statements of the *she'erit hapleitah* mean that they cannot simply be regarded as putty in the hands of stronger forces; even if many chose to go to the US, Australia or else-where, the clarity of the DPs' position from the moment the camps were liberated was impossible to ignore: Palestine was their goal. 'Open the gates of Palestine!' Jewish demonstrators called to Bartley Crum when he visited Zeilsheim DP camp.[52] It was a scene repeated many times. There was a coincidence of wants between the Yishuv, which feared that the Holocaust might destroy the chances of realising statehood now that most of the potential population of the country had been killed, and the survivors (including the 'infiltrees') who, irrespective of where they eventually ended up, were largely in agreement that Jewish life in the Diaspora was no longer viable and thus that Palestine was their only real option. And as Crossman also noted in 1946, America was not prepared to open its doors, and so for the DPs it was logical to reach the Zionist conclusion: 'Better to die fighting as members of a Hebrew nation than to rot away month after month in Assembly Centres in Germany, run by British and Americans who talked of humanity but shut their doors to human suffering.'[53]

The Jewish Agency itself, presciently anticipating future criticism, acknowledged that the DPs 'have never been regarded by us as mere objects for our various activities, but as a community capable of self-administration, to whom we render our advice and assistance. It was mainly because of this attitude of respect on our part towards the people we were servicing, that our advice carried weight and we were successful in establishing a moral authority over the Jewish D.P.s.'[54] The claim echoes that made by an UNRRA official at Zeilsheim who was asked by Frederick Morgan if the Zionists were running the camp. He responded by saying: 'No, sir. The people are Zionists. Without any outside influence they have developed into Zionists.'[55] If that was true, it was also a result of objective circumstances, which meant primarily that the lack of visas for the US and the logic of the situation made pressure on the British to relent on Palestine the most likely outcome.[56] Nevertheless, it is worth bearing in mind that only around half of the approximately 250,000 Jewish DPs finally settled in Israel. Indeed, between July and September 1949, according to an article written for the US army journal *Stars and Stripes*, the trend was for the majority of DPs to favour the US as opposed to 'economically hard-pressed Israel'.[57] America offered many DPs a chance to make a fresh start which was at least as attractive as Israel to those who believed in the impossibility of Jewish life in Europe.

The number of DPs reduced very quickly after the establishment of the State of Israel. Just before May 1948 there were about 165,000 Jewish DPs still in Germany; by September that number had dropped to 30,000 (the total number of DPs at that point was about 648,000, of whom 435,000 were in camps and 203,000 were 'free livers'). In 1951 the IRO formally handed over control of the DP camps to the Federal Republic of Germany; thenceforth they were no longer called DP camps but were referred to formally as Government Transit Camps for Homeless Foreigners. In 1952, the remaining residents of Feldafing, Landsberg and Lechfeld (near Augsburg) were moved to Föhrenwald, which became the last of the Jewish DP camps. Despite its new status, it retained its Jewish character by prior agreement of the IRO and the Bavarian authorities.

After 1948, apart from the German-Jewish communities that were re-establishing themselves, the 30,000 or so DPs still in Germany were known as 'hard core' cases, people who either could not or would not leave Germany or who refused to integrate into German society. They included people who had established businesses in Germany and whose success persuaded them to stay, but who nevertheless wanted to live in the DP camp; people who had married non-Jewish Germans who were living in the camp; and people who were too old or ill – many with tuberculosis – to be moved from the protection afforded by the DP camp. Embarrassingly for the JDC and the Israeli government, the 'hard core' contingent also included some 3,000 returnees from Israel who had found life there too hard or simply too different from what they had expected.[58] In Föhrenwald's final years these returnees constituted 50 per cent of the camp's population.[59] Although the US authorities debated whether the returnees should be permitted back into Germany as DPs, it was decided that not letting them in could dissuade receiving countries, especially those in Latin America, from continuing to accept DPs. 'Ultimate return of relatively few DPs is price which must be paid to effect resettlement large numbers', as one military report of July 1948 put it.[60]

Thus despite their fears about living under German administration, whether because of illness or a reluctance to live elsewhere, or thanks to West Germany's 'economic miracle' which was in full swing by 1950, the last few thousand Holocaust survivors preferred to stay in the land of the perpetrators. The position held by this 'hard core' of remaining DPs thus provides a fascinating window into the nature not just of the Holocaust survivors' long-running trials and tribulations but of the changing West German state.[61] Although they had decided to stay in Germany, the residents of Föhrenwald remained traumatised by the Nazi years and their difficult liberation. They lived in fear of the German authorities and sometimes those fears boiled over into conflict. In the context of the early Cold War, especially, the last DPs found that their special position was increasingly marginalised as, much to their disgust, the rehabilitation of West

Germany as an anti-communist ally proceeded far more quickly than they could tolerate.

Still, despite the desire of the German government and the Jewish relief organisations to see it closed, Föhrenwald did not finally shut its gates until February 1957. By that time its residents had left for the four corners of the globe, from Bolivia to Australia, Argentina to New Zealand, assisted by the Hebrew Immigrant Aid Society (HIAS), the JDC and other organisations.[62] Those who could not leave were re housed in newly-built apartments and, at least according to a survey conducted in 1959, were quite well integrated into German society. They thus contradicted the well-meaning claim made in the *Manchester Guardian* a few years earlier that 'These Jews [in Föhrenwald] provide the single exception to the rule that D.P.s can gradually be "integrated" into the life of the German community'.[63]

It is debatable whether, as the *Jewish Chronicle* hopefully proclaimed, the shutting of the camp 'will bring to a close one of the darkest chapters in Jewish history, an era which began with the advent of Hitlerism'. Paying tribute 'to the Western occupation authorities for their aid to Jewish refugees once the barbed-wire fences were removed from the camps, to the workers of the refugee and welfare agencies in Germany, and to the countries which threw open their gates to the survivors of Hitlerism', the newspaper's deputy editor left a lot about the obstacles to postwar Jewish emigration unsaid.[64] Nevertheless, when Föhrenwald did finally close, the story of the Jewish DPs in Europe also ended, at least in an official sense. The last Föhrenwalders, more than ten years after the war, were obliged to start again in Argentina, Brazil or wherever they now found themselves.

Cold War Effects

On 10 September 1948 a Romanian Jew, Beno Fuchs, was interviewed in Rome by caseworkers from the International Refugee Organization; they were to hear his appeal against their decision in June that he did not meet the criteria for IRO assistance. Fuchs had survived forced labour in a Hungarian labour battalion in occupied Russia and was then deported to Auschwitz. After the war, back in his native Romania, he had been unable to make a living in the fur business and, using a falsified Romanian passport, entered Italy via Hungary. From today's perspective it is striking

PC/SJM Form No. SJM/.....................

PREPARATORY COMMISSION FOR THE INTERNATIONAL
REFUGEE ORGANIZATION
———
DECISION OF THE REVIEW BOARD   No.: Geneva ...2720...
.......P.266/..........

Zone: .....ITALY.......... District: .....ROME......... Case No.: .R/4021

In accordance with the Provisional Constitution of the Review Board,

the undersigned have, on this ...13th......... day of ..September. 1948, sitting at

.........Rome........., reviewed the appeal of ......Beno FUCHS.................................

against the decision taken on ..8.6.48.. Petitioner was interviewed on ..10.9.48.

Having examined the case-file and found it to be reasonably complete,

the Review Board has reached the following decision, which has been placed on

the records of the Board.

Petitioner is declared ~~eligible~~
ineligible

Consulted: Prof. N. Royse   .... Chairman

concurring ....Ms Royse...........   ....D.L. Price....... Member
                                          D.L. Price
dissenting .... Member

                                          .... Member

                                          .... Recorder

Assistant ...F. McAskell............

        Petitioner is a Rumanian Jew, who when his homeland was
occupied by the Hungarians in 1942, was deported to Russia for
forced labour. After 18 months, however, he was allowed to return
home because of illness, then in May 1944 the Hungarians sent him
to the Ausschwitz Concentration Camp, from which he was released
eight months later by the Russians and permitted to go back to
Rumania.

        On 14 March 1948 petitioner left his home illegally for
Hungary where he altered an invalid Rumanian Passport and succeeded
in using it to reach Italy. During his interview before the Review
Board on 10 September 1948 he admitted that conditions in the fur
business were extremely bad and that he had had emigration to
Canada or Paraguay in mind since 1945, but was always refused a
Rumanian passport. Petitioner also admitted that he has never been
persecuted, and that his sole activity was as a member of the Zionist
Party.

        Petitioner is not within the mandate of the Organization.

to read of a survivor of Auschwitz supposedly say that 'he has never been persecuted' – 'at home' is added in pen by the caseworker – 'and that his sole activity was as a member of the Zionist Party'.[65] In rejecting his application for resettlement by the IRO, the caseworkers clearly regarded Fuchs as a migrant (what today would be called an 'economic migrant') and thus felt obliged to dismiss his case. Although one cannot tell from this document what subsequently happened to Fuchs – it is unlikely he was returned to Romania in 1948 – the form reminds us that the IRO was operating at the height of the Cold War. Fuchs' appeal was founded less on his experiences in Russia and Auschwitz (which is misspelt by the caseworker) than on the fact that his livelihood had been deprived in postwar Romania, a country that had fallen under communist control very quickly after the war. Other applicants fared better, especially non-Jewish ones who persuaded their assessors that they had a genuine fear of persecution were they to be returned to the communist east. (And one cannot discount the possibility that IRO workers were influenced by the commonly-held stereotype of the Jewish Bolshevik.)

Many authors have hinted at the links between the emerging Cold War and the liberation and its aftermath.[66] After the experience of the Allied forces working together to defeat Nazism, in the process resisting Himmler's attempts to inveigle them into concluding separate peace treaties, the development of intra-Allied tensions indicated that a possible postwar world of international harmony following the collapse of the Third Reich was unlikely. In reality it was only the war that had held the Allies together; possible conflicts had been brewing for years but were held in check by the necessity of defeating fascism. But the liberated Jews did not have the luxury of hindsight and, seeing their aspirations gradually dissipating, raged against what they saw as a betrayal.

Referring to the trials of Mauthausen guards held in 1946, Evelyn Le Chêne wistfully pondered what might have been if Allied cooperation at Mauthausen had continued:

The culmination of the struggle now achieved over the Nazis could have been the beginning of a new era of understanding between nations. The fault lies with both East and West that it is otherwise. The Americans should have understood the terrible sufferings endured by the Russians at the hands of the Nazis and shown compassion in this respect in the months which followed. The Russians, for their part, should have given the Americans credit for their wonderful devotion to humanity and for the compassion and generosity shown by US forces to all in need.[67]

The way in which the emerging Cold War smoothed the passage for former Nazis to become future allies was in fact well understood at the time. Kurt Grossman noted in a report for the JDC that 'the East–West conflict brings a great advantage to the former Nazis and reactionaries, who willingly jump on the anti-East bandwagon, and are well received by our U.S. Government forces, as long as they think that their anti-Bolshevism is sincere'.[68] And the survivors themselves could hardly believe how things were turning out. They were 'enraged by the fact that America was starting to rebuild the German economy and the German cities while we, the German victims, remained helpless on German soil'.[69]

The clearest statement of this connection was made by Samuel Gringauz, chairman of the Jewish camp committee in Landsberg, in an article of 1948 as the Cold War was reaching its height. The unfortunate fact was that the surviving Jews were now still living, through no desire of their own, 'in the midst of the people who were the source of all their sufferings and humiliations'. Worse, the American zone was 'also becoming the nerve center of American world policy and the front line of American defense'. From the new American perspective, 'Germany is no longer our foe in a war not yet concluded, but a potential ally in a war that has not yet begun'. However explicable this process might have been from a geopolitical standpoint, it was not only galling to the Jewish DPs but left them in even more awkward circumstances because, as Gringauz pointed out: 'The Jewish survivors in the occupied zone of Western Germany are an obstacle to this development. What makes their situation intolerable is that they are still in acute conflict with the nation which Allied occupation policy wants to make into an ally'. The DPs were in danger not only of distrusting the Germans and of falling out with their British liberators, but of breaking with the Americans too.[70] As Gringauz concluded, the new situation demanded a swift resolution to the emigration crisis that had been in place since 1945. Crossman had since 1946 been stating that the DP camps could be closed within a month if the visas to Palestine were issued. Now, over two years later, Gringauz stressed that if that goal could not be achieved out of humanitarian concerns, it could at least be won as a result of hard-nosed *realpolitik*:

> today the emigration of the Jews from Germany would seem an indispensable adjunct to the success of our general European policy, and particularly our German policy . . . What a pro-Jewish policy could not accomplish can be accomplished by the necessities of our present pro-German policy. What a DP policy could not do a broad American policy-need can do. What a Palestine policy could not give us can be obtained from a European policy. What as a humanitarian duty was trampled under foot may be respected as a move in the game of power politics.[71]

Gringauz's argument, however, fell largely on deaf ears.

In practice, as the Allies passed sovereignty to the West Germans so DP claims to self-government and extraterritorial status first came under threat, and then were then eroded altogether. The unity and integrity of a West German state that would act as a good anti-communist ally increasingly claimed the Allies' attention in preference to the irritating and seemingly outdated needs and assertions of the DPs. Allowing the Germans to take charge of their own affairs and to run their own state meant 'limiting the authority of groups that wished to remain outside the German body politic and granting Germans the right to define the parameters of political life'.[72] The result was increased friction and clashes between the Jewish DPs, the German authorities and the German population. Although the Germans maintained Föhrenwald longer than was anticipated when they took charge of it in 1951, nevertheless the DP camps' last vulnerable residents felt keenly the irony of their situation: being governed by Germans and confronted by German regulations and German police, was not what they had anticipated or desired.

After 1948–49 there was a wave of DP dissatisfaction with the West German state which, with American blessing, was becoming increasingly confident in asserting its own interests. The gradual acquisition of state sovereignty meant a change of focus in West German political culture, from re-education to humanism and contrition for anti-Semitism to an emphasis on pro-NATO and anti-communist sentiment, a shift that had negative consequences for the Jewish DPs.[73] Nothing illustrates this claim more clearly than the demonstration on the Möhlstrasse in Munich on 10 August 1949, a response to the *Süddeutsche Zeitung*'s publication of a vehemently anti-Semitic letter. German police violently broke up the demonstration and attacked Jewish DPs whilst American soldiers looked on. Responding to police violence by attacking officers and burning a police car, the Jewish DPs clearly now regarded the West German police 'as merely Nazis in new uniforms'.[74] At the same time there was a reduction in employment opportunities for DPs thanks to the arrival in Germany and Austria of POWs released from Soviet captivity and ethnic Germans expelled from Eastern Europe. These two factors 'stimulated many refugees living in the local economy to seek assistance or to plan for resettlement'.[75] This process was itself responsible for bringing more cases before the IRO, thus increasing its workload and intensifying its involvement in Cold War politics.

Growing anger at and distrust of the German authorities went hand in hand with an increasing lack of confidence in the international refugee organisations. UNRRA was replaced by the IRO in 1947 (initially the Preparatory Commission of the IRO, then the IRO as a functioning legal entity in 1948), and the latter was itself wound up in 1952, to be replaced by the UNHCR. Where UNRRA was devoted to repatriating civilians at war's end, the IRO's mandate was to resettle those who could not or would not be repatriated.[76] For that reason the Soviets would not work with it. Although a great deal of time and effort went into handling the Jewish DPs, who made up a minority of all displaced persons, the issues surrounding their care were more complex than the organisations had initially expected. First, they refused to be classified by nationality; they did not want to be Polish or Romanian, they wanted to be labelled as Jews, which was not on UNRRA's list of nationalities. Second, and relatedly, the bulk of the Jewish DPs now had no home to go to. Once they were firmly ensconced in the German and Austrian DP camps, further problems arose: should the IRO facilitate their 'illegal' departure for Palestine? To do so would be in the spirit of the IRO's mandate, and would reduce its expenses, but at the same time it would obviously be regarded as an unwarranted interference in diplomatic matters. A large proportion of the

IRO staff, many of whom were British, in any case opposed wholesale emigration for Palestine.

All DP-related issues were complex. UNRRA and the IRO had not anticipated the difficulties of distinguishing between Poles who had been forced labourers and 'Poles' who a few years earlier had been *Volksdeutsche* ('ethnic Germans' from outside the borders of the Reich) or who had volunteered for work in Nazi Germany, or indeed Poles who had fought in the Home Army but refused to return to a Poland dominated by communists. They had not anticipated the difficulties of distinguishing between Ukrainian collaborators and Ukrainians who had fought with the Red Army or who had been forced labourers. The anguish of deciding was in some cases a matter of life and death, as returning a DP to the Soviet Union could mean their further incarceration in the Gulag – and some Ukrainian DPs, much to the horror of the US army, committed suicide rather than allow themselves to be forcibly repatriated.[77] UNRRA and the IRO did not initially go against the Soviets' wishes (and the terms of the October 1944 agreement between the USSR, the US and the UK that Soviet citizens would be returned) and by December 1945 some 2,034,000 Soviet citizens had already been repatriated.[78] But the general direction of its decision-making after the onset of the Cold War, so the Jewish DPs felt, was to give the refugees the benefit of the doubt.

The result was that many who made a show of their anti-communism were accepted for resettlement programmes, with few questions asked about their wartime activities – contrary to the stated guidelines in the IRO's own manuals instructing eligibility officers. By contrast, so the Jews felt, they, the genuine victims, were being kept waiting. Indeed, even after the creation of the State of Israel the American authorities were complaining on financial and moral grounds that the IRO was failing to fulfil its mandate by refusing to transfer Jewish DPs with Israeli visas to Israel, saying that 'present IRO policy has the effect of slowing departure of Jews from US occupied areas and thus thwarting achievement of the US occupation mission'. The IRO's position was, officially, held on the basis that it could neither use its funds to transport refugees nor sanction the transfer of 'fighting personnel' to a war zone.[79] But the American delegate to a meeting with the IRO's Director-General and Deputy Director-General 'argued that the IRO offered such assistance to all other categories of DPs, and therefore, in effect, was discriminating against Jewish DPs by refusing such assistance'. He complained too that the IRO was being backed up by the British.[80] Only at the end of 1948 did the IRO implement a compromise position whereby it would reimburse the JAP and the JDC the costs incurred in transporting Jewish DPs to Israel – a job that the IRO should have shouldered.

These sorts of problems that the Jewish DPs faced were caused partly by the Palestine question and partly by emerging Cold War tensions – although in reality the two were connected. When the IRO was established, its remit included taking over DP camps from the military. Many of these were small facilities which were closed and consolidated as people emigrated. The IRO's most important new task, though, was 'determining, in accordance with its constitution, the displaced person or refugee status of persons, whether or not they are now receiving care'. As Harry Messec, the author of this document, also noted, 'it is clear that basic political differences and fear of reprisals or persecution will continue to deter the majority of the remaining displaced persons from being repatriated'.[81] He was not only referring to Jews. Indeed, the growth of mutual mistrust between the US and the Soviets was itself a contributory factor in the rise of DP numbers in Germany and Austria.[82] Coupled with the IRO's basic position, authorised by the US Under Secretary of State Dean Acheson, that 'we will not force them back against their will to the countries from which they were uprooted', the IRO's work of dealing with the remaining DPs after 1948 became more not less complicated, despite the relatively small numbers of people involved.[83] The biggest problem facing the IRO as it began its work in 1947 was deciding the validity of applicants' claims to refugee status and thus their eligibility for IRO assistance. As the Cold War developed, so the IRO's decision-making felt the influence of outside currents. If it is true that 'the right of Jews to international protection was unanimously accepted' after the war, the next few years made it clear that the Jewish DPs would not be allowed to go where they wanted when they wanted.[84] Many Jewish refugees were still having their claims for IRO support heard at the start of the 1950s.

As early as October 1946, Gitta Sereny, later to become famous as the author of studies of Treblinka commandant Franz Stangl and leading Nazi Albert Speer, resigned from her post with UNRRA in protest at the screening process which allowed war criminals to acquire DP status.[85]

By 1947–48 the investigation process was detailed but still not always satis-factory. Despite some knowledge of the Nazi camps the IRO's officers' manual was quite confused on what had transpired in them and did not mention mass murder. As a result there was considerable lack of under-standing of the specific policies to which the Jews had been subjected; this misunderstanding translated into a somewhat harsh approach to Jewish refugees. 'There are a number of factors which must be kept in mind when interviewing Jewish refugees', the IRO officers' manual indicated:

> a) A Jewish refugee as any other must produce some evidence that he is a *bona fide* refugee within the mandate of IRO.
> b) While this evidence may differ in degree because of the knowledge that there is anti-Jewish feeling in some countries, the applicant must make it plausible why he does not wish to return, even though the Organisation may not require him to produce evidence of the exact persecution which he as an individual fears. The mere decision to go to Palestine or elsewhere is not considered acceptable as a valid objection.

Such stipulations, whilst understandable in the abstract, failed to account for the fact that Holocaust survivors did not always have ready paperwork to hand to account for their movements. It is clear that at this stage, despite a widespread knowledge of the Nazi camps, an understanding of the particular persecution that the Jews had suffered under the Nazi regime had not yet coalesced into a narrative of 'the Holocaust'. Indeed, implying a relative downgrading of the consequences of racial persecution, the eligibility handbook went on to say that *political* objections to repatriation – i.e. anti-communism – 'may be regarded as valid'. Paradoxically, and contradicting section (a), the handbook ended by noting that people who had to hand all the paperwork facilitating resettlement somewhere other than their country of origin would be regarded as emigrants rather than *bona fide* refugees and displaced persons (though the latter category would still be permitted if the person could demonstrate reasonable 'fear of religious or racial persecution or compelling family reasons based on previous persecution').[86] So, whereas Jews found in Germany at the end of the war were not subjected to screening but, as racial persecutes, were regarded as genuine DPs, by 1947–48 the problem, as the IRO and the

Allied governments perceived it, of emigrants (unworthy of IRO help) mingling with genuine refugees (deserving of help) meant that Jews were subjected to closer scrutiny. This distinction between 'refugees' and 'migrants' would continue to inform thinking on refugee policy throughout the postwar period.[87]

Although people who tried to claim refugee status were regularly denied it when they did not meet the criteria, in the IRO's so-called 'opposition proceedings' – through which those turned down were given the chance to appeal against the decision – it is nevertheless quite startling to see cases of Eastern Europeans given the benefit of the doubt on the basis of their anti-communism and to find examples of Jews who had been in Auschwitz denied IRO assistance on technical grounds.

These IRO sources, which are held in their tens of thousands at the International Tracing Service in Bad Arolsen, provide a fascinating glimpse into the decision-making process of this fledgling international organisation. More importantly, they allow us to hear the voices of Holocaust survivors in ways that often unexpectedly fail to conform to our standard template of liberation followed by rehabilitation, Allied assistance and a new life. In fact, although the sources document the remarkable extent of postwar sympathy and genuine care for the Jewish survivors of Nazi genocide, they also bring to light a trail of bureaucratic obstacles and delays, petty red tape, and sometimes brutal disregard on the part of those tasked with helping them.

As part of their initial assessment, DPs were required to submit a Care and Maintenance (CM/1) form. Apart from basic information, such as name, place of birth and languages spoken, the forms also asked if the applicant wished to stay in their country of residence and, if not, what their reasons were for leaving. They were asked whether they had relatives in the country in which they wished to resettle and, finally, there was a section on the form which invited details of 'Other preferences for resettlement and reasons'. The answers to such questions condense an array of emotions and experiences into a few words. Although some of the files are quite long, including detailed summaries by the IRO caseworkers, most contain brief statements whose poignancy lies in their brevity.

Take the unremarkable case of Pinkas Knoller: in response to the question 'Do you wish to return to your country of former residence?' the answer is a

CM/I

Addendum to Form CM/I
Administrative Order No. 29

21. Future Plans / Zukunftspläne

(a) Do you wish to return to your country of former residence?   *Nein!*
Wollen Sie nach Ihrer Heimat bzw. Ihrem früheren Aufenthaltsort zurückkehren?

If not, why?   *Meine ganze familie ist ermordet worden.*
Falls nein, warum?

(b) Do you wish to remain in Germany?   *Nein!*
Wollen Sie in Deutschland bleiben?

Have you any relatives, friends or resources in Germany?   *Nein!*
Haben Sie Verwandte, Bekannte oder sonstige Einnahmemöglichkeiten in Deutschland?

(c) Do you wish to emigrate to some other country? If so, complete the following:
Wollen Sie nach anderen Ländern auswandern; falls ja, wohin?

Country of first preference   *Palestine*
Nennen Sie von Ihnen bevorzugte Länder:

Do any factors exist which might facilitate your emigration to this country?
Gibt es irgendwelche Gründe, die Ihre Auswanderung nach dem betreffenden Lande erleichtern?

What close relatives have you in this country? Give addresses, state relationship and whether any such relatives are prepared to help you financially or otherwise.

Welche näheren Verwandten haben Sie in dem betreffenden Land, geben Sie Adresse und Verwandtschaftsgrad an; sind Ihre Verwandten bereit, Sie materiell bzw. anders zu unterstützen?

Ich will nach Palestine fahren damit ut meine arbeit zu helfen anbaue das vaterland

Other preferences as to resettlement and reasons
Ziehen Sie andere Länder zur Auswanderung vor, welche und warum?   *Palestine*

22.   *Lsotte Pinkas*
Signature / Unterschrift

23.   *Zederman*   *21. 5. 48*
Signature of interviewer / Unterschrift des Verhörenden   Date / Datum

24.   *Lederman Salomon.*
Interviewer's name typed / Name des Verhörenden in Schreibmaschinenschrift

firm 'Nein!' The reason? 'My whole family has been murdered.' His only desire was to go to Palestine. In the box asking after relatives in the chosen country of immigration, Knoller wrote simply: 'I want to go to Palestine so that I can help to build the fatherland.'[88] There are endless similar examples; one applicant wrote: 'I have nobody there [Germany] but I have a son in Palestine and I want to go to Palestine to use my study for our land'; another that she wanted to join her brother and sister in the US, saying: 'I want not to remain in Germany, because I was imprisoned and slave worker and I lost my parents, grandmother and many other members of my family in the gas chambers.'[89]

Like the Care and Maintenance applications, the opposition proceedings forms reveal in stark terms the bare facts of the horrors through which those filling them out had lived. The difference here is that the caseworkers tended to take a more sceptical tone towards the stories they were noting down; sometimes, in fact, they were downright sarcastic or summed up an applicant's (supposed) travails with a succinctness which reminds us how great a distance separates us today from an age when Holocaust survivors were not merely regarded as normal people but were even treated with a degree of distaste. Although the strongest opprobrium was reserved for Gentiles who were trying to pass themselves off as refugees or persecutees when in fact they simply wanted (quite understandably) the chance to immigrate to the US or Canada, the caseworkers sometimes used disparaging comments to discuss Jewish applicants whose circumstances did not meet the criteria for IRO assistance. Most often, however, we are reminded of just how complicated most survivors' trajectories were, and we see many cases of people who received treatment by the IRO which does not conform to our expectations of what happened to people after the war. This was especially the case for Jews who had non-Jewish spouses or whose experiences during the war did not include a spell in the Nazi camps. The example of the Austrian Jewish refugee Katharina Freund, for example, is noteworthy not just for the circuitous nature of her travels as a refugee (Tanganyika and Cyprus) but for the fact that she wanted to return to Austria and was thus declared eligible for repatriation only.[90]

Likewise, Ella Freudenheim, interviewed for the opposition proceedings in West Berlin in October 1949, was deemed ineligible by the IRO despite having twice been married to Jewish men and having been persecuted 'as a

INTERNATIONAL REFUGEE ORGANIZATION

DECISION OF THE REVIEW BOARD   No. : Geneva _____ 15044

BA-114/K   K.0194/B

Zone : ____US/G____   District : __B e r l i n__   Case No. : __603467__

In accordance with the Provisional Constitution of the Review Board,

the undersigned have, on this ____26th____ day of ____October____ 1949, sitting at

Bad Kissingen__, reviewed the appeal of __F.R.E.U.D.E.N.H.E.I.M., Ella__

against the decision taken on __23.11.1948__ Petitioner was interviewed on __20.10.49__

Having examined the case-file and found it to be reasonably complete, the

Review Board has reached the following decision, which has been placed on the records

of the Board.

Petitioner is declared ~~within the mandate~~
not within the mandate

Recommendation: Reparations Fund grant.

Consulted : E. C. GRIGG   _____ Chairman

concurring ___F.H.K___   _____ Member
                                                    E. S. KENNEDY

dissenting _____   _____ Member

                                              _____ Member

                                              _____ Recorder

Assistant ____J. M. Dancy____
            J. M. DANCY   Strictly confidential. The contents of this
                                          copy should **NOT** be communicated to
                                          the petitioner nor to any person outside
                                          the Organization.

Petitioner was born in Berlin in 1896 and was twice married to
Jewish husbands. The second husband emigrated to Uruguay in 1946 through
the Inter-Governmental Committee and Petitioner was later unable to join him
owing to the ban on further immigrants to Uruguay. Petitioner stated that
she was persecuted as a Jewish wife and asks recognition as a refugee under
Part I, Section A, para. 3. Her persecution does not warrant recognising
her under the restrictive provisions of this paragraph. She is a German
in Germany who cannot be considered a genuine refugee by IRO definitions.

Petitioner may, however, if her claims are substantiated, be entitled
to reparations as a non-Jewish victim of the Nazi regime from the Reparations
fund.

Petitioner is not within the Mandate of the Organisation.

Recommendation: Reparations Fund grant.

Neither Section A nor B, Part I.

Jewish wife'. The caseworker decided that she was 'a German in Germany who cannot be considered a genuine refugee by IRO definitions' and suggested that, 'as a non-Jewish victim of the Nazi regime', she might apply to the reparations fund instead.[91] The same happened to Hermine Heimbach, even though her Jewish husband had been killed at Auschwitz: 'Petitioner is a German in Germany, is non-Jewish and cannot therefore be considered a refugee by IRO definitions.'[92] One senses here that even if the assessors were sympathetic to the applicants, their inflexible application of IRO definitions resulted in some harsh decisions. Other similar decisions were reached without even receiving a sympathetic hearing.

Mordchaj Rottstein's application to be treated as a refugee – and thus eligible for resettlement – was handled with disdain. The assessors objected to his 'stereotyped appeal', implying that his form had been filled out by some unnamed helper. He was declared ineligible for IRO assistance. At the same time as objecting to this shady Zionist-inspired application, the assessors' response hints at antipathy towards his lack of courage in avoiding military service in Israel. Rottstein was interviewed in Bari in April 1949 – a reminder of how even almost a year after the creation of Israel the IRO did not always facilitate the travel wishes of Holocaust survivors. It reminds us too that people who might today be considered 'Holocaust survivors' were not thought of in that light in the immediate postwar period, especially not if, like Rottstein, they had spent the war years working as painters in the eastern Soviet Union.[93]

It is nevertheless important to recognise how complicated the IRO's job was and to note that open-and-shut cases did get handled as such, even if it sometimes took a while to arrive at that conclusion. Jsacco Rubinsztein, for example, had been rejected by the IRO because he had left Poland to study in Strasbourg before the war. After an initial unsuccessful appeal he managed to make the IRO caseworkers understand that his trajectory had from the start been caused by persecution and that he had not ended up in Italy by choice. It is unclear why this had not been obvious from the outset, but in his review of 25 November 1949 the IRO official noted, in a slight tone of remonstration towards previous assessors, that Rubinsztein 'is outside of his country of origin, was a refugee from racial persecution by the Germans and has expressed valid objections to return'. He concluded that Rubinsztein 'must be accepted within the mandate'.[94]

INTERNATIONAL REFUGEE ORGANIZATION

DECISION OF THE REVIEW BOARD   No. : Geneva _7344_
                                                         LI. 623

Zone : ____ITALY____   District : ____BARI____   Case No. : ____

      In accordance with the Provisional Constitution of the Review Board,
the undersigned have, on this ____13th____ day of ____April____ 1949, sitting at
____Rome____, reviewed the appeal of ____ROTTSTEIN Mordchaj____
against the decision taken on ___29.9.48___ Petitioner was interviewed on __5.4.49__

      Having examined the case-file and found it to be reasonably complete, the
Review Board has reached the following decision, which has been placed on the records
of the Board.

Petitioner is declared ~~eligible~~
ineligible

Consulted :   I. H. D. WHIGHAM   _____ Chairman

    concurring _____   _____ Member

    dissenting _____   _____ Member
                                           _____ Member
                                           _____ Recorder

Assistant _____
      H. Mundy

Petitioner is a Polish Jew who fled to the Russian zone of Poland
at the time of the German occupation and was sent to Eastern
Russia where he worked as a painter throughout the war. He was
repatriated to Cracow in 1946 and entered a Jewish collective farm
there. He remained for a year and then set out with his brother to
emigrate to Palestine.

Petitioner left Poland with an organised group of Palestine emigrants.
In Northern Italy, however, he left the group and went to work for a
year in Milan because, he states, he preferred to work as an
independent worker rather than as a member of an organised group in
Palestine. It is possible that he wished to avoid military service.
The brother has now gone to Palestine, however, and Petitioner wishes
to join him.

In his stereotyped appeal, prepared in the same terms and handwriting
as every other appeal seen by the Board in this camp, Petitioner is
stated to fear anti-semitism in Poland. In his original application,
however, and when closely questioned by the Board he firmly denied
any such fear or any objections to Poland other than his desire to
emigrate. Petitioner has no valid objections against returning to
Poland.

     Not within the mandate of the Organization

INTERNATIONAL REFUGEE ORGANIZATION
—
7506

DECISION OF THE REVIEW BOARD   No. : Geneva __BI.5056__

Zone : __ITALY__   District : __ROME__   Case No. : ____

In accordance with the Provisional Constitution of the Review Board,

the undersigned have, on this __25th__ day of __November__ 1949, sitting at

__Rome__, reviewed the appeal of __RUBINSTEIN Isaaco__

against the decision taken on __09.7.49__. Petitioner was interviewed on __25.11.49__

Having examined the case-file and found it to be reasonably complete, the

Review Board has reached the following decision, which has been placed on the records

of the Board.

Review Board decision   Petitioner is declared within the mandate
of 29.7.49 is hereby   and within the mandate.
cancelled.

Consulted :   _____ Chairman

concurring __R H Gerner__   __E. S. Kennedy__ Member

dissenting _____ Member

        _____ Member

        _____ Recorder

Assistant __M. MUNDY__   Strictly confidential. The contents of this
        copy should NOT be communicated to
        the petitioner nor to any person outside
        the Organisation.

Petitioner addressed a second appeal to the Board and was re-
interviewed. He related that he left Poland in 1939 to study in
France because of the difficulties presented by the University authorities
to Jewish students of medicine. He studied in Strasbourg, but was
evacuated at the outbreak of war. He worked and studied in Southern
France until September 1943, when following the capitulation, he fled
to Italy for greater security, as Southern France was then taken over
entirely by the Germans. He continued his studies under difficulties
in Italy, was arrested in May 1944 and released from detention by the
Allies in June 1944.

Petitioner presented documents, including a yellow Permesso di
Soggiorno No.49,7120-147-G, showing date of entry to Italy as 9
September 1943 and a certificate establishing his detention by the
Italians and release by the Allies. His account related in interview
was consistent throughout and with the information supplied in the
first instance. He claims, however, that certain discrepancies which
appear in his account to the Board on his first appeal, were occasioned
by faulty interpretation. His parents and brother have left Poland
and are now in Germany.

Petitioner is in possession of a passport issued by the Polish
Government in London and his objections to returning to Poland, based
on the recrudescence of anti-semitism and his opposition to Communism
are accepted as being within the provisions of Section C. He is
outside of his country of origin, was a refugee from racial persecution

...../....

by the Germans and has expressed valid objections to return. He
must be accepted within the mandate under Part I, Section A, para 1(a).

WITHIN THE MANDATE OF THE ORGANIZATION

Likewise Leon Frenkel, a sixty-one-year-old Romanian Jew who had
spent the war years in Czernowitz (Cernăuți, today Chernivtsi in Ukraine),
ended up in Vienna first as a result of Nazi persecution and then because
he was unable to find work in communist-dominated Bucharest, which he
fled in 1945. His assessor regarded him as clearly within the scope of the
IRO's mandate.[95]

The same rigour applied to Gentiles trying to persuade the IRO to assist
them. Although much has rightly been made of collaborators quietly being
admitted into the US, Canada or Britain, the IRO did its work in stopping
former Nazis from abusing the system. It also rejected the appeals of
numerous Eastern Europeans who had gone to Germany voluntarily as
forced labourers and had naturalised as Germans; they were considered
to be 'Germans within their country of citizenship' and therefore not
within the IRO's remit. The case of Gustav Freitag is typical: a Polish

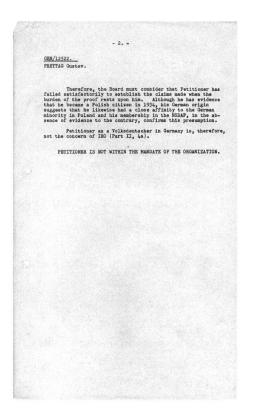

merchant of German origin, he claimed that he joined the Nazi Party in order to try and assist the Polish underground. The IRO, noting that he could not furnish any evidence to support his claims, concluded firmly that 'Petitioner as a Volksdeutscher in Germany is, therefore, not the concern of the IRO.'[96]

That said, many Eastern Europeans did manage to persuade the IRO to take them under its wing. Many were entirely legitimate refugees – mostly forced labourers – but many presented evidence that was far more ambiguous. One Lithuanian, Eugeniusz Vaselis, at first suspected of being a member of the SS, had been resettled in East Prussia in May 1943, 'not to obtain privileges in Germany or to collaborate but to avoid deportation'. He was declared 'a refugee with valid objections' and was eligible for IRO support.[97] Albert Vaart, an Estonian airman who had flown in the Luftwaffe's Estonian squadron, claimed to have served because his year group were called up and he had no choice (which was probably true). Most important, 'As an Estonian he cannot return to his country which is now incorporated in the Soviet Union.' He was accepted as within the mandate.[98] And there were many whose claims to IRO help had nothing at all to do with the war, but who were simply escaping from communist control. Mircea Valescu, for example, left Romania in 1945 'claiming he did not want to join the Communist Party'. Working as a stoker, he ended up unemployed in Genoa when the ship he had been working on was sold. Without a permit to stay in Italy he was arrested and sent by the Italian authorities to the Fraschette collection centre. Valescu was considered 'a Rumanian citizen now outside his country of nationality, whose objections to returning to Rumania are considered as valid'. He was accepted as a refugee and granted IRO care.[99]

In the face of all these decisions, some clearly correct, others more debatable, the best that one can say with regard to the IRO caseworkers, like UNRRA's before them, is that they were inconsistent.[100] With so many cases to handle and with the need to recruit and train so many staff at short notice, that should not come as a surprise. Many of the decisions with respect to the Eastern European refugees were undoubtedly correct, in terms of the appropriate application of the IRO's mandate. But from the point of view of the Jewish DPs it was deeply disturbing to see petitioners who had become refugees at the end of the war but had not suffered during it being granted the same, if not more, assistance than themselves.

These stories of Holocaust survivors and other postwar refugees remind us that their futures lay largely in the hands of others and that those who were making life-and-death decisions about these DPs/migrants were increasingly coming under pressure to adhere to the requirements of Cold War politics. The Palestine question was bound up with American immigration policy as well as Soviet attempts to undermine British imperialism. The DPs' intransigence was intimately tangled with the emergence of Adenauer's new West Germany. It was a toxic brew.

*   *   *

The link between Holocaust survivors and postwar ideological competition was in evidence throughout the Cold War. At the height of the Palestine problem, when Britain had begun interning immigrants on Cyprus, the British attempted to win the Americans round to their point of view by suggesting that the more than 16,000 migrants about to sail from Constanţa aboard the *Pan York* and *Pan Crescent* presented a danger to Western interests. Lord Inverchapel, the British ambassador to Washington, claimed that 'only the Russians would gain from the proposed operation through greatly increased disturbances throughout the Middle East and introduction of large numbers of communist agents'.[101] This recycling of the well-worn stereotype of 'Judeo-Bolshevism' (only very recently employed to powerful effect by the Nazis) might suggest the desperation of the British government with the Zionist policy of 'flooding' the Cyprus camps; but it also indicates the depths to which diplomats and politicians were willing to stoop in order to defend 'national interests'.[102] However, Washington's own recognition of Jewish power convinced the US that criticising Britain's Palestine policy was more likely to win them support than taking the British side on Palestine would help to roll back the Soviets.

Such cynical exploitation of Holocaust survivors for Cold War gains continued throughout the postwar period, and was by no means only a speciality of the Western powers. At the 1981 Washington conference that brought liberators together, one of the Soviet soldiers, General Petrenko, made the connection explicit. He began his speech by recognising that, after thirty-six years, 'the memories have not been erased and the horror of horrible crimes is still there. The bleeding wounds of millions of those who have suffered at the hands of fascist butchers are still open.' Petrenko then went on to argue that the chief reason to remember Auschwitz (or as he preferred to call it, Oświęcim concentration camp) was to prevent nuclear war and the threat to human existence. This noble aim, he claimed, was clear in the Soviet Union's stance: 'There is only one way to resolve this situation. That is immediate, honest, equal, and effective negotiations. This is precisely what our country proposes – concrete measures to curb, reduce, and finally destroy nuclear missiles. Mankind must do and should be able to do it. Participants of this conference', he implored, 'inmates of concentration camps, and the liberators: this is a noble cause that we are pursuing.'[103] At a point in time when détente had collapsed, the Brezhnev Doctrine dominated the politics of the Warsaw Pact, and when Carter and then Reagan were embarking on a new, aggressive phase in US–Soviet relations that came to be known as the 'Second Cold War', Petrenko's words could only be construed as Soviet propaganda.[104] The easy linkage between camp survivors, liberators and the competing ideologies of the postwar world was one that served many purposes. At the same time as Petrenko was recalling Auschwitz in order to defend the Soviet vision of nuclear détente (a cynical policy driven by the cost of the arms race more than by the ethics of non-proliferation), Washington was announcing the establishment of the President's Commission on the Holocaust which would lead to the building of the United States Holocaust Memorial Museum, spelling out in simple language the connection between the survivors' freedom from Nazism and American democracy.

The Cold War in the narrow sense of superpower antagonism was not, however, the sole source of policy-making in the aftermath of the Second World War. The rebuilding of Europe, although it was unavoidably part of the Cold War world, was also driven by other concerns, most notably the European states' national aspirations, at least as their governments understood them. The development of the European Community, based around the EEC or the 'common market', aimed not only to rebuild economic prosperity in a devastated continent but to keep communism at bay in Western Europe and to integrate West Germany into a framework that would eradicate conflict between Germany and other European states, principally France, Belgium and the Netherlands. Long regarded as an idea with roots in the idealism of interwar dreamers such as Count von Coudenhove-Kalergi and the wartime resistance movements, European integration also held some appeal for the DPs. Although they did not welcome German statehood or a German release from Allied tutelage, the DPs did recognise the value of a project that bound Germany to its neighbours under international scrutiny. They might have agreed with the Chatham House analysts who held that the West Germans would follow Adenauer into European integration because 'that policy offers an imaginative political idea and a quick and easy way back to equality of rights'.[105] But in the face of the communist threat, what was the alternative? Integration was an idea whose time had come.

For one former Polish-Jewish industrialist who spent most of the war years in exile in the Soviet Union, mostly in Djambul (Kazakhstan), the notion of pan-Europeanism seemed most appealing when it was most unlikely:

In these critical times the thought never left my head that it was the right moment to create a Pan-Europe. Russia could expect that even if the attack on Moscow was fought off, the danger existed that in the coming spring the Germans would begin again with a new, powerful offensive . . . Pan-Europe, however, could at least partly deal with colonial hunger and bring about freedom for all the peoples of Europe as well as promote the easy exchange of trade [*Produktion*]. I dreamed of the idea that a Pan-European Union would emerge in which every state, even the smallest, would have a representative who, together with all the others, would be able to decide on all European questions.

He realised, however, that there were impediments in the way of this vision. Besides the actual events through which he was living – during in which the Nazis were aiming at European integration of a very different sort – there was the attitude of the British to take into account. Mentioning his dream to his fellow refugee, a Dr Rosner, he received the reply that 'England would be against it and would destroy the Union. Straight away I saw that too and my soap bubble immediately burst.'[106] The integration of Europe was not the most pressing of the Jewish DPs' concerns but this little vignette is a reminder that, as with so many of their aspirations that suddenly seemed possible after liberation, the great powers stood in the way of their realisation.

Conclusion:
The Sorrows of Liberation

As the Nazi regime was collapsing, contemporaries began slowly to understand the extent of its crimes. 'Is this our progress over other more barbarous ages?' asked Judah Leib Magnes, head of the Hebrew University in Jerusalem, in his opening address of the academic year on 1 November 1944. 'What carrion foulness, what a stench of burnt bodies arises from these camps and fills the void of the world – that same world wherein so much of beauty is, light, love and joy. Man created in the Image proves to be the wildest and cruelest of raging beasts – man, who is at times but little lower than the angels.'[1] Only weeks before Magnes wrote these words in freedom in Jerusalem, Zalman Gradowski, one of the members of the Auschwitz *Sonderkommando*, the group of inmates forced to work in the gas chamber and crematorium complex disposing of the corpses, addressed his hoped-for reader in an extraordinary text penned in the heart of the killing machine and buried in the earth next to the gas chamber:

> Tell them that even if your heart turns to stone, your brain to a cold calculator and your eyes to camera lenses, even then, you will never again return to them. They would do better to seek you in the eternal forests, for you will have fled from the world inhabited by men, to seek comfort among the cruel beasts of the field, rather than live among cultured demons. For although even animals have been restrained by civilization – their hooves have been dulled and their cruelty greatly curbed – man has not, but has become a beast. The more

highly developed a culture, the more cruel its murderers, the more civilized a society, the greater its barbarians; as development increases, its
deeds become more terrible.[2]

The extent of the Nazis' crimes could barely be taken in. Communities
across Europe were devastated and the surviving Jews of Eastern Europe
were left bereft.

Liberation did not mean the end of the Holocaust. The survivors – in
the camps, in hiding and in exile – faced years of further struggles to find a
place to call home and to rebuild their lives, to the extent that they ever did.
Those who came to the UK or the US found that their experiences were
subsumed in a general narrative of war suffering and that they were rarely
listened to outside of their own small circles. It would be decades before a
general image of 'the camps', meaning a world of unspecified suffering,
would slowly give way to a differentiated understanding that acknowledged
the ways in which victims were targeted differently depending on which
group the Nazis had assigned them to. In the years after the war, the Jews
were rarely distinguished from the Nazis' other victims. And any mention
of Nazi victims was often countered with the response that during the war
everyone had suffered. Broadcasts, newsreels, exhibitions and trials (such
as the Belsen trial) almost always failed to mention that Jews had been the
Nazis' specific target, not just a randomly selected group among many
others.[3] As the victims were beginning to gather documents, testimonies
and material remains, the wider world preferred to focus on a universal
message of the defeat of fascism and a future-oriented narrative centred on
national rebuilding. Although the resources were at hand for a more
nuanced understanding of Nazi criminality – in Knauth's and Sington's
books, for example – the liberated victims of Nazism would have to wait
many years before 'the Holocaust' began to be comprehended. The appeals
of the DPs were widely regarded as noisy, unwelcome special pleading
rather than the desperate cries of stricken people. Allied policy towards
them only exacerbated the problem of mutual misunderstanding.

The actions of the US, Britain, the Yishuv, the Soviets and their local
communist allies across Eastern Europe all combined to create a situation
whereby Jews could no longer live in most of their old communities. The
Western Allies paradoxically first helped the survivors – not least by

liberating the camps, albeit with 'liberations' that were often unplanned and not prepared for – and then set about effectively re-imprisoning them. The camps in Cyprus were regarded with especial disdain as those in them were so close to reaching their goal. The Yishuv, though it did not create Zionism in the DP camps, encouraged a scenario in which the loudest voice in the camps would be demanding the one thing the survivors could not have: access to Palestine. The Soviets and their satellite governments in Poland, Romania and elsewhere behind the newly-descended 'iron curtain' mischievously upped the ante by encouraging Jewish emigration from their lands towards Germany, under the pseudo-humanitarian guise of acknowledging the survivors' plight and demands. Instead of stamping out local anti-Semitism the communists used it as one of the strategies that enabled them to take power and provide their authority with solid local roots across the region. The DPs themselves thus lived increasingly frustrated lives, engaging in all sorts of 'normal' social, religious, cultural and political activities, but always on the basis of a shaky knowledge that they were waiting for their departure.

The sorrows of liberation therefore forced survivors into 'illegal' immigration, into conflict with local populations and military and civilian authorities, and into psychological turmoil. Non-Jewish DPs were rapidly repatriated or, as with 'unwilling' Soviet citizens (or those now suddenly finding themselves claimed as Soviet citizens after the occupations and border shifts of 1945), were generally resettled within a year or so of the war. By contrast, tens of thousands of Jewish DPs remained in camps for years after the end of hostilities. After 1950 only the 'hard core' cases remained, but these were not properly dealt with until the middle of that decade. By that time there had been conflict between Jewish and non-Jewish DPs, between Jewish DPs and German and Austrian civilians and authorities and, most significantly, between the Jewish survivors and their liberators. This last conflict, whereby the admiration and love between survivors and those who helped them was sullied by bitterness, ingratitude and resentment, is one of the aspects of liberation hardest to bear.

That shift in relations, however, also helps to explain the connection between the liberation of the camps and the wider geopolitics of the Cold War and British imperial decline. The Soviets backed DP Zionism not just to make local anti-Semites in the satellite states accomplices of the new regimes but also to press the British in terms of economic overstretch and moral standing. Increasing tensions in Palestine placed the British in the invidious position of trying to find a balance between maintaining cordial relations with the Arab states and responding satisfactorily to the Jews whom they had just liberated. The British response, in the face of intense pressure from the DP leadership, American recommendations over immigration to Palestine and, not least, an inability to continue funding expensive imperial missions, was to abandon the Mandate. Although people were not killed in the huge numbers seen during the partition of India, when the British rapidly left the country to its fate, the war that followed Israel's declaration of independence saw a new group of displaced persons appear: the Palestinians. The Palestine–Israel conflict is today as far from being resolved satisfactorily as it has ever been. The long-term effects of the geopolitics of liberation are still felt in the Middle East and in the politics of Holocaust memory across the globe. And the Holocaust's after-effects will be with us for some time yet. Liberation was not only not the end of the Holocaust, it was the bridge between the wartime alliance and Cold War tension.

If, as Auden wrote, 'existence is believing / We know for whom we mourn and who is grieving', then the Holocaust, like all genocides, shattered the grounds of existence.[4] The survivors knew neither for whom they should mourn nor who was mourning, and many never found out. What they did know was that everything they had believed to be stable and dependable had been destroyed. Their survival could not alter that basic fact, as is clear in Isabella Leitner's words:

We are . . . we are – what? What are we? We are . . . we are . . . We are liberated!

Barefoot, wearing only a single garment each, we all surge out into the brutal January frost and snow of eastern Germany and run toward the troops. Shrieks of joy. Shrieks of pain. Shrieks of deliverance. All the pent-up hysteria accumulated over years of pain and terror suddenly released.

I have never since heard sounds like those we uttered, sounds released from the very depths of our being. The sheer force of it must have scattered the ashes of Auschwitz to every corner of the universe, for our cries of joy suddenly turned into a bitter wail: 'We are liberated! We are liberated!' But where are they all? They are all dead![5]

Notes

Introduction: Explaining Liberation

1. Wilzig in Chamberlin and Feldman (eds.), *Liberation*, 157. Radnóti, 'Peace, Horror', in *Forced March*, 32.
2. Knoller, *Living with the Enemy*, 209.
3. Rosensaft, *Yesterday*, 51–52. See the slightly different version of these words cited in Menachem Z. Rosensaft, 'Bergen-Belsen: The End and the Beginning', in USHMM, *Children and the Holocaust*, 117–136, here 119 and, slightly different again in German, in Buser, *Überleben von Kindern und Jugendlichen*, 265–266.
4. There are two general surveys, Abzug, *Inside the Vicious Heart*, and Bridgman, *The End of the Holocaust*, both out of date and unsatisfactory in several ways, though still also useful. There is a large specialist literature as the bibliography indicates but it has not yet been incorporated into standard narratives of the Holocaust, which still usually end in May 1945.
5. Sack, *Dawn after Dachau*, 28.
6. Langer, *Holocaust Testimonies*, 67. On the impossibility of 'closure' for Holocaust survivors and their compulsion to tell and retell, write and rewrite, see Eaglestone, *The Holocaust and the Postmodern*, 64–67.
7. W. J. Sachs, written account (n.d), Archive of the VJHC in Cracow, statement no. 114, in Hochberg-Mariańska and Grüss (eds.), *The Children Accuse*, 45.
8. Bernard Warsager, interview with David Boder, 1 September 1946, transcript at: http:// voices.iit.edu/interview?doc=warsagerB&display=warsagerB_en. The original German interview is also on the website. An earlier synthesis of Warsager's comments (without Boder's interjections or Warsager's hesitations) can be found in Niewyk, *Fresh Wounds*, 79.
9. Josephs, *Survivors*, 178.
10. Lanzmann, *Shoah*, 200. Compare his account in Kazik, *Memoirs of a Warsaw Ghetto Fighter*, 50–52. My thanks to Anna Solarska for making me think about loneliness.
11. Rabbi Baruch G. in Greene and Kumar (eds.), *Witness*, 214–215.
12. Leon Bass, USC Visual History Archive: http://vha.usc.edu/viewingPage.aspx?testimon yID=47936&returnIndex=0
13. *The Seventy-First Came . . . to Gunskirchen Lager*, 5.
14. Smith, *Forgotten Voices of the Holocaust*, 280.
15. Hutler cited in Kolinsky, *After the Holocaust*, 79.

16. Karoly cited in Kushner and Knox, *Refugees in an Age of Genocide*, 204.
17. Birkin in Gill, *The Journey Back from Hell*, 429.
18. Swift in Flanagan and Bloxham (eds.), *Remembering Belsen*, 37.
19. Sington, *Belsen Uncovered*, 28.
20. Phillips (ed.), *Belsen Trial*, 716.
21. Ibid., 718.
22. Sington, *Belsen Uncovered*, 25.
23. Le Chêne, *Mauthausen*, 171-174.
24. Ibid., 166.
25. Loidl, *Entweihte Heimat*, cited in Horwitz, *In the Shadow of Death*, 164-165 (translation slightly modified).
26. Horwitz, *In the Shadow of Death*, 170 (quotation), 171 (building plans).
27. Nikolaus Wachsmann, 'The Dynamics of Destruction: The Development of the Concentration Camps, 1933-1945', in Caplan and Wachsmann (eds.), *Concentration Camps in Nazi Germany*, 23; Goeschel and Wachsmann, 'Before Auschwitz.' For a detailed overview of the camp system see Wachsmann, *KL*.
28. Knigge, 'Kultur und Ausgrenzung', 202-203.
29. Wachsmann, 'Dynamics of Destruction', 25; Wünschmann, 'Cementing the Enemy Category'; Wünschmann, 'Konzentrationslagererfahrungen deutsch-jüdische Männer'.
30. Wachsmann, 'Dynamics of Destruction', 27-29.
31. Wachsmann, 'Dynamics of Destruction', 33.
32. Gellately, *Backing Hitler*, 204. 'Concentration Camps in Public Spaces' is the title of the chapter beginning on that page.
33. See for example Leitner, *Fragments of Isabella*, whose testimony stresses the importance of the author being with her three sisters in the camps, or Klüger, *Landscapes of Memory*, which also emphasises the role of the family group.
34. Joop Zwart, 'The Last Days of Bergen-Belsen', WL P.III.h.No.780 (Bergen-Belsen), 10.
35. See Stone, 'Christianstadt.'
36. See Ulrich Herbert, 'Das 'Jahrhundert der Lager': Ursachen, Erscheinungsformen, Auswirkungen', in Reif-Spirek and Ritscher (eds.), *Speziallager in der SBZ*, 17
37. Buggeln, 'Were Concentration Camp Prisoners Slaves?', 125.
38. Distel, 'Die Befreiung des Konzentrationslagers Dachau', in *Dachauer Hefte*, 1 (1993), 3.
39. Lavsky, *New Beginnings*.
40. Bauer, 'Death Marches'.
41. IMT XXXVII, 487, Doc. 053-L. 'Unter allen Umständen muß vermieden werden, das Gefängnisinsassen oder Juden vom Gegner, sei es WB oder Rote Armee, befreit werden bzw. ihnen lebend in die Hände fallen.'
42. Bauer, 'Death Marches'; Bauer, 'The DP Legacy', in Rosensaft (ed.), *Life Reborn*, 25; Broszat, *The SS State*, cited in Marrus, *The Holocaust in History*, 196, 198.
43. Blatman, *Death Marches*, 416.
44. Marc Masurovsky, 'Visualizing the Evacuations from the Auschwitz-Birkenau Camp System: When Does an Evacuation Turn into a Death March?', in Blondel et al. (eds.), *Auf den Spuren der Todesmärche*, 108-121.
45. Grevenrath cited in zur Nieden, 'Kriegsende und Befreiung in Sachsenhausen', 61.
46. Garbarz and Garbarz, *A Survivor*, 223.
47. Amariglio, *From Thessaloniki to Auschwitz and Back*, 121.
48. Daniel Blatman, 'On the Traces of the Death Marches: The Historiographical Challenge', in Blondel et al. (eds.), *Auf den Spuren der Todesmärche*, 85-107.
49. Horwitz, *In the Shadow of Death*, 162.
50. Blatman, 'On the Traces of the Death Marches', 107. And for a fuller analysis see Blatman, *The Death Marches*.
51. Bornstein cited in Albert Knoll, 'Die Todesmärsche des KZ Dachau im Spiegel der Berichte Überlebender', in Blondel et al. (eds.), *Auf den Spuren der Todesmärche*, 208.

52. Knoll, 'Die Todesmärsche des KZ Dachau', 209–210.
53. Lowe, *Savage Continent*, 101.
54. See Litvak, 'Polish-Jewish Refugees'.
55. Perlov, *The Adventure of One Yitzchok*, 256.
56. Grossmann, 'Victims, Villains, and Survivors', 296. See also Grossmann, *Jews, Germans, and Allies*, 131–132 and 316–317 n.11; Jockusch, 'Memorialization through Documentation', 182; Kochavi, 'Liberation and Dispersal', 511; Grossmann, *The Jewish DP Problem*, 10–11. For a fictionalised account of these different groups of people meeting at the end of the war, see Schwarz, *Displaced Persons*.
57. UNRRA Agreement, cited in Reinisch, 'Preparing for a New World Order': UNRRA and the International Management of Refugees', in Stone (ed.), *Post-War Europe*, 3.
58. FO 945/591, 'SHAEF Outline Plan for Displaced Persons and Refugees', cited in Holian, *Between National Socialism and Soviet Communism*, 43.
59. Berger, 'Displaced Persons', 45.
60. See Reinisch, '"Auntie UNRRA" at the Crossroads'.
61. Kochavi, 'British Policy on Non-Repatriable Displaced Persons', 367; 'Agreement Relating to Prisoners of War and Civilians Liberated by Forces Operating under Soviet Command and Forces Operating under United States of America Command', 11 February 1945, online at: http://avalon.law.yale.edu/20th_century/sov007.asp
62. Proudfoot, 'Anglo-American Displaced Persons Program', 47.
63. Reinisch, *The Perils of Peace*, 160.
64. Proudfoot, 'Anglo-American Displaced Persons Program', 51.
65. Janco, 'Unwilling'.
66. Arendt, 'Stateless People', 144.
67. Cohen, *In War's Wake*, 'Introduction'.
68. Kolinsky, 'Jewish Holocaust Survivors'.
69. Granata, 'Political Upheaval and Shifting Identities.'
70. Alexander von Plato, 'Sowjetische Speziallager in Deutschland 1945 bis 1950: Ergebnisse eines deutsch-russischen Kooperationsprojektes', in Reif-Spierek and Ritscher (eds.), *Speziallager in der SBZ*, 125.
71. Reichel, *Politik mit der Erinnerung*, 131.
72. Wierling, 'The War in Postwar Society', 218.
73. Harold Marcuse, 'The Afterlife of the Camps', in Caplan and Wachsmann (eds.), *Concentration Camps in Nazi Germany*, 190–191.
74. Stone, *Underground to Palestine*, 21.
75. Wetzel, 'An Uneasy Existence', 137.
76. Feinstein, *Holocaust Survivors in Postwar Germany*, 6; Moeller, *War Stories*; Niven (ed.), *Germans as Victims*.
77. Jarausch and Geyer, *Shattered Past*, 209: 'Since they were greeted with mutual relief, these departures left little trace in collective recollection [in Germany].' See also Olick, *In the House of the Hangman*, 99–105.
78. Weckel, 'Disappointed Hopes', 52.
79. Jürgen Bassfreund interview with David Boder, 20 September 1946, Munich, online at: http://voices.iit.edu/interview?doc=bassfreundJ&display=bassfreundJ_de ('real Germans' is Boder's phrase, the word Bassfreund used in the original is 'Stockdeutschen').
80. Geve, *Guns and Barbed Wire*, 203.
81. For example, Browning, *Remembering Survival*, 'Introduction'; Gildea, *Marianne in Chains*, 10–13; Portelli, *The Order Has Been Carried Out*.
82. Rosen, *The Wonder of Their Voices*. The interviews are at voices.iit.edu
83. See Waxman, *Writing the Holocaust*.
84. Stone, *Histories of the Holocaust*.
85. Cpl. Jerry Tax, 'And Afterwards . . .', in *The Seventy-First Came . . . to Gunskirchen Lager*, 28.
86. Bornstein cited in Langbein, *People in Auschwitz*, 477.

1 Liberated by the Soviets

1. Shek, 'Ein Theresienstädter Tagebuch', 196, entry for 9 May 1945 [in original: 'Man sieht nur Tod und Elend, das Erste ist besser, denn Leben können wir den Leuten nicht geben, auch wenn sie lebendig bleiben']; Alisa Shek wrote her diary in German but using Hebrew characters. Rebecca C. in Kittel, 'Liberation – Survival – Freedom', 258.
2. Michalczyk, *Filming the End of the Holocaust*, 63. See also Hicks, *First Films of the Holocaust*.
3. David Boder interview with George Kaldore, 31 August 1946, Tradate, online at: http://voices.iit.edu/interview?doc=kaldoreG&display=kaldore_en. See also Niewyk, *Fresh Wounds*, 373–389. In the original German, Kaldore says, with a greater sense of expectation, 'Wir sehen dass es kommt . . . es kommt etwas . . . es kommt die Befreiung für uns.'
4. See also the Introduction and Chapter 2.
5. Klier, 'The Holocaust and the Soviet Union', 287.
6. Grossman, 'The Hell of Treblinka', 129.
7. Ibid., 175–176.
8. Ibid., 178.
9. On the Roma experience of Transnistria see Michelle Kelso's film *Hidden Sorrows*.
10. Arad, *Holocaust in the Soviet Union*, 345.
11. Shapira cited in ibid., 344.
12. Ancel, 'The New Jewish Invasion', 233–236.
13. Rotman, 'Romanian Jewry', 292. For further examples see Ionescu, 'În umbra mortii'.
14. Ioanid, *The Holocaust in Romania*, 223. For an example, see Shachan, *Burning Ice*, Ch. 20.
15. Govrin in Kleiman and Springer-Aharoni (eds.), *Anguish of Liberation*, 40; see also Govrin, *In the Shadow of Destruction*, 72.
16. Aharon Cohen, 'The Jews and Zionism in the New Romania', *Mishmar*, 19 (1947), cited in Ancel, 'The New Jewish Invasion', 251. See also Natalia Lazăr, 'Emigrarea evreilor din România în perioada 1948–1952', in Rotman et al. (eds.), *Noi perspective în istoriografia evreilor din România*, 193–210.
17. Werth, *Russia at War*, 896–897.
18. Kranz, 'Between Planning and Implementation,' 224.
19. Marszałek, *Majdanek*, 183.
20. Ibid., 185–186.
21. Werth, *Russia at War*, 890.
22. Simonov, *The Lublin Extermination Camp*, 3.
23. Ibid., 5.
24. Hicks, '"Too Gruesome to be Fully Taken In"', 242–243.
25. Simonov, *The Lublin Extermination Camp*, 12. See also Simonov, 'Extermination Camp', in Pavlenko (ed.), *Liberation* (no pagination).
26. Cited in Berkhoff, 'Total Annihilation of the Jewish Population', 92–93.
27. Werth, *Russia at War*, 894.
28. Cited in Kondoyanidi, 'The Liberating Experience', 450.
29. Cited in ibid., 452.
30. This paragraph is indebted to Liebman, 'Documenting the Liberation of the Camps.'
31. Hirsh, *The Liberators*, 147–153, 293 (quotation 149).
32. Chomicz cited in Strzelecki, 'L'Evacuation, la liquidation et la libération du camp', 306.
33. Kor at: http://www.pbs.org/auschwitz/40-45/liberation/
34. Kor, *Echoes from Auschwitz*, 140.
35. Durlacher, *Stripes in the Sky*, 75, 99, 100.
36. Levi, *The Truce*, 188–189.
37. Czech, *Auschwitz Chronicle*, 804; Strzelecki, *Evacuation, Dismantling*, 220.
38. Kondoyanidi, 'The Liberating Experience', 443

39. Steinbacher, *Auschwitz*, 128; Andrzej Strzelecki, 'The Plunder of Victims and Their Corpses', in Gutman and Berenbaum (eds.), *Anatomy of the Auschwitz Death Camp*, 260–261.
40. Kondoyanidi, 'The Liberating Experience', 443–444.
41. Gromadsky at: http://www.pbs.org/auschwitz/40–45/liberation/
42. Elisavetskii cited in Kondoyanidi, 'The Liberating Experience', 455.
43. Petrenko cited in ibid. 455.
44. Berkhoff, 'Total Annihilation of the Jewish Population', 95–96.
45. Bridgman, *The End of the Holocaust*, 26.
46. Hartmann, *Operation Barbarossa*, 138.
47. Nikitin cited in Kondoyanidi, 'The Liberating Experience', 456.
48. Strzelecki, 'L'Evacuation, la liquidation', 307–312.
49. Maria Rogoż cited in Strzelecki, *The Evacuation, Dismantling*, 223.
50. Chowaniec cited in Langbein, *People in Auschwitz*, 474.
51. Hyman Yantian, 'First News of Fate of Survivors' (9 June 1945), WL P.IV.a.680.
52. Though see also Shneer, *Through Soviet Jewish Eyes*, 178–181.
53. Adelsberger, *Auschwitz*, 131.
54. Drywa, *The Extermination of Jews*, 326.
55. Schneider in Mahoney (ed.), *1945: The Year of Liberation*, 88.
56. Riva Chirurg, *Bridge of Sorrow, Bridge of Hope* (1994), cited in Drywa, *The Extermination of Jews*, 283.
57. See, for example, the harrowing account of Haim Kuznitsky in Kleiman and Springer-Aharoni (eds.), *Anguish of Liberation*, 20–34.
58. http://www.stiftung-bg.de/below/
59. Antje Zeiger, 'Die Todesmärsche', in Morsch and Reckendrees (eds.), *Befreiung Sachsenhausen*, 68.
60. Alfred Reckendrees, 'Das Leben im befreiten Lager', in Morsch and Reckendrees (eds.), *Befreiung Sachsenhausen*, 108: '*Sie waren zwar aus dem Konzentrationslager und von dem Terror des SS befreit worden, ihre Freiheit hatten sie damit aber noch nicht erhalten.*'
61. Peter Jahn, 'Die Befreiung des Konzentrationslagers Sachsenhausen im Verlauf der Kampfhandlungen zur Eroberung Berlins', in Morsch and Reckendrees (eds.), *Befreiung Sachsenhausen*, 87. On the camp hierarchy, see Suderland, *Inside Concentration Camps*, 161–162.
62. Yisrael Gutman, 'Social Stratification in the Concentration Camp', in Gutman and Saf (eds.), *Nazi Concentration Camps*, 167.
63. Lues cited in zur Nieden, 'Kriegsende und Befreiung in Sachsenhausen', 62–63. Published originally in a 1946 collection of documents dealing with the last 24 hours in the camp.
64. Reckendrees, 'Das Leben im befreiten Lager', in Morsch and Reckendrees (eds.), *Befreiung Sachsenhausen*, 100.
65. Chilczuk in Chamberlin and Feldman (eds.), *Liberation*, 28.
66. Cited in zur Nieden, 'Kriegsende und Befreiung in Sachsenhausen', 67.
67. Rebecca C., interview, 20 January 2000, in Kittel, 'Liberation – Survival – Freedom', 247. On the rescue, see Saidel, *Jewish Women*, Ch. 13.
68. Jacobeit and Erpel, '*Ich grüsse Euch als freier Mensch*', 35. In the German text the word *Kameradinnen* makes it clear these are female comrades.
69. Erma M., interview, 26 February 1999, in Kittel, 'Liberation – Survival – Freedom', 248.
70. Maurel, *Ravensbruck*, 118.
71. Amariglio, *From Thessaloniki to Auschwitz and Back*, 133–134. For another graphic example of rape, see Gabor, *My Destiny*, 142–144.
72. Gertruda P., interview, 19 April 1997, in Kittel, 'Liberation – Survival – Freedom', 252.

73. Hanna H., interview, 22 July 1999, in ibid., 254.

74. Maurel, *Ravensbruck*, 141.

75. Garusik, letter of 20 April 1966, in Jacobeit and Erpel, *'Ich grüsse Euch als freier Mensch'*, 141.

76. Jacobeit and Erpel, *'Ich grüsse Euch als freier Mensch'*, 163.

77. Hauptmann Makarow, oral report, 10 May 1965, in ibid., 149.

78. Morrison, *Ravensbrück*, 305. Thälmann had been shot in Buchenwald in 1944.

79. Bacall-Zwirn and Stark, *No Common Place*, 97.

80. Sprenger, *Groß-Rosen*, 295.

81. Udel Stopnitsky, interview with David Boder, 12 September 1946, Hénonville (original interview in Yiddish), online at: http://voices.iit.edu/interview?doc=stopnitskyU&display=stopnitskyU_en

82. Lubatsch (28 May 1968), testimony held at the Zentrale Stelle für Landesjustizverwaltungen zur Aufklärung von NS-Verbrechen in Ludwigsburg, cited in Sprenger, *Groß-Rosen*, 297.

83. Israel Kühn, cited in Gutterman, *A Narrow Bridge to Life*, 220.

84. Anonymous testimony, cited in ibid., 221.

85. Blodig, *Terezín in the 'Final Solution of the Jewish Question' 1941–1945*, 113.

86. See Ruth Bondy, 'The Theresienstadt Ghetto: Its Characteristics and Perspective', in Gutman and Saf (eds.), *Nazi Concentration Camps*, 303–313.

87. Shek, 'Ein Theresienstädter Tagebuch', 178 (entry for 29 January 1945). Auschwitz had of course been liberated on the 27th. Bauschowitz is the German name for the Czech town Bohušovice nad Ohří, the closest train station to Theresienstadt and the station from which deportees had to walk to the camp. Shek's father did survive Auschwitz, and her non-Jewish mother remained in Prague throughout the war.

88. Ibid., 187 (entry for 20 April 1945) and 202 n. 47.

89. Ibid., 195 (entries for 8 May and 7 May 1945).

90. Cited in Bridgman, *The End of the Holocaust*, 98 (no name given).

91. Stark in Mahoney (ed.), *1945: The Year of Liberation*, 145.

92. David Boder interview with Nechama Epstein-Kozlowski, 31 August 1946, Tradate, online at: http://voices.iit.edu/interview?doc=epsteinN&display=epsteinN_en

93. Krakowski in Kleiman and Springer-Aharoni (eds.), *Anguish of Liberation*, 13–14, 16.

94. Spies, *My Years in Theresienstadt*, 188.

95. Roubíčková, *We're Alive and Life Goes On*, 173–174.

96. David Boder interview with Pinkhus Rosenfeld, 13 September 1946, Hénonville, online at: http://voices.iit.edu/interview?doc=rosenfeldP&display=rosenfeldP_en. According to the ITS files, Rosenfeld was sent from Auschwitz to Hohenstein in September 1944 and was liberated in Karlsbad on 7 May 1945.

97. Braver in Kleiman and Springer-Aharoni (eds.), *Anguish of Liberation*, 19.

98. USC VHA: http://vha.usc.edu/viewingPage.aspx?testimonyID=5769&returnIndex=4

99. Tichauer, *I Was No. 20832 at Auschwitz*, 89.

100. Samson, *Hide*, 140–142.

101. Ibid., 144. It is interesting to compare this 'ending', which rings true, to the more redemptive closure that Samson provides the book as a whole (193–194) where she insists that her survival was a form of revenge against the Nazis.

102. Lengyel, *Five Chimneys*, 207–215.

103. Wells, *The Death Brigade*, 244.

104. Michelson, *I Survived Rumbuli*, 221–224.

105. For example, the case of Raisa in Bendremer, *Women Surviving the Holocaust*, 84.

106. M. Lichtenstein, 'Eighteen Months in the Oswiecim Concentration Camp', *Jewish Survivor's Report. Documents of Nazi Guilt*, 1 (1962), WL 068-WL-1631, 14–15.

107. Arain Rosenfeld, cited in Gutterman, *A Narrow Bridge to Life*, 223.

2 The Western Allies

1. Knauth, *Germany in Defeat*, 33; Gellhorn, 'Dachau', 30.
2. Lang, *Die Namen der Nummern*.
3. Shneer, *Through Soviet Jewish Eyes*, 182.
4. See for example, Stone, *Responses to Nazism in Britain 1933–1939*; Plesch, *America, Hitler and the UN*.
5. Bourke-White, *Dear Fatherland, Rest Quietly*, 76.
6. Mayer Birnbaum, cited in Kolinsky, *After the Holocaust*, 38–39.
7. Lowe, *Savage Continent*, 82.
8. Abzug, *Inside the Vicious Heart*, 30.
9. David Malachowsky, cited in Kolinsky, *After the Holocaust*, 39.
10. Knauth, *Germany in Defeat*, 44. Salaspils was not a death camp so Gewürtz's claim seems to be confused.
11. Cited in Shephard, *The Long Road Home*, 100.
12. 'The Most Terrible Example of Organised Cruelty in the History of Civilisation. Mass Murder by the Germans at the Majdanek "Camp of Annihilation"', *Illustrated London News*, 14 October 1944, 442–443.
13. *Daily Mail*, 4 September 1944. See also *Singleton Argus* (NSW), 6 September 1944, for a similar report. Moser's statement was first published in English in Simonov, *The Lublin Extermination Camp*, 20–24.
14. Werth, *Russia at War*, 890.
15. Kushner and Knox, *Refugees in an Age of Genocide*, 205.
16. Murrow, 'They Died 900 a Day in "the Best" Nazi Death Camp', *PM* (16 April 1945). Murrow's broadcast can be listened to online at various sites including http://archive.org/details/EdwardR.Murrow-BuchenwaldReport
17. Holmila, *Reporting the Holocaust*, 32. On reluctance to believe, see Lowe, *Savage Continent*, 80–81.
18. See Stone, *Responses to Nazism in Britain 1933–1939*, Ch. 3.
19. Abzug, *Inside the Vicious Heart*, 4–9.
20. Hertz cited in Holmila, *Reporting the Holocaust*, 34.
21. Sington, *Belsen Uncovered*, 47. See also Knauth, *Germany in Defeat*, cited below.
22. Blatz in Hirsh, *Liberators*, 79–80.
23. De La Torre in ibid., 81.
24. Herder, 'Liberation of Buchenwald', online at: http://www.remember.org/witness/herder.html
25. Interview with Guy Stern, 1 May 1990. USHMM Archives RG–50.030*0223, 11.
26. Murrow, 'They Died 900 a Day'.
27. See the chronology on the Buchenwald museum's website: http://www.buchenwald.de/en/466/ See also Niven, *The Buchenwald Child*.
28. Heymann in Hackett (ed.), *The Buchenwald Report*, 325. Its role in East German myth-making in other respects aside, Frank Beyer's remarkable 1963 film *Naked Among Wolves* is at least honest about this point.
29. Hackett (ed.), *Buchenwald Report*, 334.
30. Fleck and Tenenbaum, 'Buchenwald: A Preliminary Report', 6. Crossman Papers 154/3/PW1/9–17, online at: http://contentdm.warwick.ac.uk/cdm/compoundobject/collection/tav/id/1348/rec/3
31. Ibid., 10.
32. Ibid., 2.
33. Heymann in Hackett (ed.), *The Buchenwald Report*, 330–331.
34. Fleck and Tenenbaum, 'Buchenwald: A Preliminary Report', 2.
35. Ibid., 14.
36. Rappaport in Hirsh, *Liberators*, 86.
37. *Buchenwald Camp: The Report of a Parliamentary Delegation*, 4.

38. Ibid., 7.
39. Knauth, *Germany in Defeat*, 32. Knauth's original report was 'Buchenwald'. In the book, the text is slightly modified and greatly extended to make a full-length book chapter.
40. Ibid., 32.
41. Ibid., 38.
42. Ibid., 40–41.
43. Ibid., 42, 65. Knauth qualified the latter statement over the next paragraphs.
44. Franklin, 'An Army Nurse at Dachau', *American Journal of Nursing*, 45 (1945), 901–902, in Mahoney (ed.), *1945: Year of Liberation*, 133.
45. Corbett in Dann (ed.), *Dachau 29 April 1945*, 42.
46. Creasman in ibid., 48.
47. Kelling in Chamberlin and Feldman (eds.), *Liberation*, 32.
48. Sparks, 'Tell Us Who Were There That it Never Happened', Speech given at USHMM, 8 May 1995, online at: http://www.remember.org/witness/sparks.html
49. Quinn in Chamberlin and Feldman (eds.), *Liberation*, 33.
50. Seventh US Army, *SS Dachau*, 16. The book has been reprinted as Perry (ed.), *Dachau Liberated*.
51. Cowling, 'Report', 2 May 1945, online at: http://remember.org/witness/cowling.html Also in Dann (ed.), *Dachau 29 April 1945*, 19. The train was the Buchenwald-Dachau 'death train' mentioned above; see also Hirsh, *Liberators*, 194–196.
52. Smith, *Dachau: The Harrowing of Hell*, 80.
53. Nathan Futterman, 8th Infantry Division, interviewed 18 November 1978, in Eliach and Gurewitsch (eds.), *The Liberators*, 51.
54. Joseph Wright, testimony of June 1981, in ibid., 32.
55. Ralph Talanian, 71st Infantry Division, interviewed 22 June 1981, in ibid., 49.
56. Lt. George Moise, 'Concentration Camp at Nordhausen', in Mahoney (ed.), *1945: Year of Liberation*, 136–137.
57. Sidney Aronson, 84th Infantry Division, interviewed 6 November 1974, in Eliach and Gurewitsch (eds.), *The Liberators*, 28–29. See also Mahoney (ed.), *1945: Year of Liberation*, 144; Hart, *Return to Auschwitz*, 200.
58. Lea Fuchs-Chayen cited in Hirsh, *Liberators*, 95.
59. Kosiek, 'Liberation of Mauthausen (and KZ Gusen I, II and III)', online at: www.gusen.org/kosiek1x.htm
60. Sherman in Hirsh, *Liberators*, 261.
61. Mahlen and Petershohn in ibid., 267 and 270.
62. David A. Hackett, 'Introduction', in Hackett (ed.), *Buchenwald Report*, 9.
63. For the fullest account, see Reilly, *Belsen*.
64. Rosensaft, *Yesterday*, 48.
65. 'Richard Dimbleby's Despatch of 17 April 1945', in Flanagan and Bloxham (eds.), *Remembering Belsen*, xiii.
66. Sington, *Belsen Uncovered*, 16.
67. Collis, 'Belsen Camp', 814.
68. Lavsky, 'The Day After', 38.
69. Hardman and Goodman, *The Survivors*, 2–3.
70. Ibid., *The Survivors*, 10.
71. Brigadier H. L. Glyn Hughes, 'Belsen Camp, April 1945', in Irgun Sheerit Hapleita, *Belsen*, 94–95.
72. Mosley, *Report from Germany*, 92.
73. Flanagan and Bloxham, *Remembering Belsen*, 10–11.
74. Gonin in ibid., 15.
75. Walker, *The Lid Lifts*, 43.
76. Levy, *Witness to Evil*, 10.

77. Sington, *Belsen Uncovered*, 23.
78. N.A. Midgley, description of Belsen, 18 April 1945, IWM Documents.4502, 2.
79. Mosley, *Report from Germany*, 95; Gollancz, *In Darkest Germany*.
80. Rosensaft, 'Our Belsen', in Irgun Sheerit Hapleitah, *Belsen*, 27.
81. Kolinsky, *After the Holocaust*, 74–75. See also Schwarz, *The Redeemers*, 17–23.
82. Wilson, *Aftermath*, 41.
83. Charlotte Chaney, 127th Evacuation Hospital, interviewed 30 March 1981, in Eliach and Gurewitsch (eds.), *The Liberators*, 45, 47.
84. Doherty, *Letters from Belsen 1945*, 42–43. As Doherty arrived at Belsen after the huts of Camp One were burnt down, these sentences must have been based on others' descriptions.
85. Levi, *A Cat Called Adolf*, 57.
86. Věra Hájková-Duxová, 'Such Was Life' in Franková et al., *The World Without Human Dimensions: Four Women's Memories*, 122.
87. Stroumsa, *Violinist in Auschwitz*, 66.
88. Braun in Kleiman and Springer-Aharoni (eds.), *Anguish of Liberation*, 45.
89. B.G. Banfill, report of 28 May 1945, in Dann (ed.), *Dachau 29 April 1945*, 28.
90. Bridgman, *The End of the Holocaust*, 67.
91. Rosenfeld in Kleiman and Spinger-Aharoni (eds.), *Anguish of Liberation*, 48.
92. Poremba in ibid., 52.
93. Heymann in Hackett (ed.), *Buchenwald Report*, 330.
94. Keim in ibid., 258–259.
95. Mendel Herskovitz interview with David Boder, Chateau Boucicaut, near Paris, 31 July 1946 (orig. interview language Yiddish), online at: http://voices.iit.edu/interview?doc=herskovitzM&display=herskovitzM_en
96. Henry Sochami, interview with David Boder, Paris, 12 August 1946 (orig. language of interview Spanish); online at: http://voices.iit.edu/interview?doc=sochamiH&display=sochamiH_en
97. Berler, *Journey Through Darkness*, 156.
98. Levy-Hass, *Inside Belsen*, 68–69.
99. See also Lavsky, *New Beginnings*, 37–40 for the idea of 'Belsen as a Death Camp'.
100. USC VHA: http://vha.usc.edu/viewingPage.aspx?testimonyID=21963&returnIndex=20
101. Boder, *I Did Not Interview the Dead*, 159.
102. Brunstein in Reilly et al. (eds.), *Belsen in History and Memory*, 214.
103. Lasker-Wallfisch in ibid., 236.
104. Lasker-Wallfisch, 'A Survivor's Memories of Liberation', in Bardgett and Cesarani (eds.), *Belsen 1945*, 25.
105. Rosensaft, 'Our Belsen', in Irgun Sheerit Hapleitah, *Belsen*, 25.
106. Wollheim, 'Belsen's Place in the Process of "Death-and-Rebirth" of the Jewish People', in Irgun Sheerit Hapleitah, *Belsen*, 52.
107. Dixey cited in Paul Kemp, 'The British Army and the Liberation of Bergen-Belsen, April 1945', in Reilly et al. (eds.), *Belsen in History and Memory*, 143. See also Collis, 'Belsen Camp', 815.
108. Interview with Guy Stern, 1 May 1990. USHMM Archives RG–50.030*0223, 14. See, for example, Levy, *Witness to Evil*, 19, or Doherty, *Letters from Belsen 1945*, 50 on survivors' fear of intravenous feeding.
109. Rosensaft, *Yesterday*, 48 (immunity), 53 (appointment), 54–55.
110. Ernest Landau, 'Men versus Supermen', in Schwarz (ed.), *The Root and the Bough*, 130–32. The whole book is very much in this celebratory and unconvincingly upbeat style.
111. Donat, *Holocaust Kingdom*, 290.
112. Victor, *Buchenwald*, 75–76.
113. Boder, *I Did Not Interview the Dead*, 22, 23, 25. See also Shik, 'Infinite Loneliness', 130.
114. Bridgman, *The End of the Holocaust*, 87.

115. Lisa Scheuer, *Vom Tode, der nicht stattfand. Theresienstadt, Auschwitz, Freiberg, Mauthausen. Eine Frau überlebt* (Aachen, 1998), cited in Mernyi and Wenninger (eds.), *Die Befreiung des KZ Mauthausen*, 71.

116. Max Sprecher, interview with David Boder, Feldafing, 23 September 1946 [orig. Yiddish], online at: http://voices.iit.edu/interview?doc=sprecherM&display=sprecherM_en

117. Lutz Hammer, 'My Illegal Life, Deportation and Liberation' (1960), WL P.III.d.No.1195, 4.

118. Mirchuk, *In the German Mills of Death*, 182.

119. Drahomir Bárta, cited in Freund, *Concentration Camp Ebensee*, 54. See also Venezia, *Inside the Gas Chambers*, 141–142.

120. Cited in Freund, *Concentration Camp Ebensee*, 57–59.

121. Cited in ibid., 60.

122. Persinger cited in Hirsh, *Liberators*, 247.

123. George Hartman in Smith, *Forgotten Voices*, 267; Freddie Knoller in Smith, *Forgotten Voices*, 284, also Knoller, *Living with the Enemy*, 210–211 for the same incident described with slightly different wording.

124. Venezia, *Inside the Gas Chambers*, 144–145.

125. Cited in Clay, 'The Liberators of Dachau', 86.

126. http://www.remember.org/witness/herder.html

127. Fred Mercer, interviewed by Kaethe Solomon, 8 June 1980. Emory University Witness to the Holocaust, online at: http://www.library.gatech.edu/holocaust/mercerframe.htm

128. Benjamin Piskorz, interview with David Boder, 1 September 1946, Tradate, online at: http://voices.iit.edu/interview?doc=piskorzB&display=piskorzB_en (original interview in Yiddish). See also Niewyk, *Fresh Wounds*, 134.

129. Szlama Rosencwaig, 'Permission from the Russian Liberators to Take Revenge on Nazi-Murderers', typescript of testimony given in Melbourne, 3 April 1959, WL P.III.h. No.1102 (Skarzisko Kamienne), 4.

130. And on the rarity of acts of revenge, see Roseman, '. . . but of revenge not a sign'.

131. Alexander Gertner, interview with David Boder, 26 August 1946, Geneva, online at: http://voices.iit.edu/interview?doc=gertnerA&display=gertnerA_en (original interview in Yiddish).

132. Leo Reichl in Mernyi and Wenninger (eds.), *Die Befreiung des KZ Mauthausen*, 83–84.

133. Mosley, *Report from Germany*, 93–94.

134. Collis and Hogerzeil, *Straight On*, 51–52. See also Lowe, *Savage Continent*, 86–87 for more variations on this report, the correct version of which cannot be verified.

135. Sachar, *The Redemption of the Unwanted*, 9.

136. Knauth, *Germany in Defeat*, 65.

137. Cowling in Dann (ed.), *Dachau 29 April 1945*, 24.

138. Ellmann in Hirsh, *Liberators*, 266. For further examples see Ast, *Confronting the Holocaust*, Ch. 5 (n.p.).

139. Levi, *The Drowned and the Saved*, 29–31.

140. Bárta and Lafitte cited in Freund, *Concentration Camp Ebensee*, 55.

141. Maršálek, *Gusen*, 43.

142. Maršálek, *Die Geschichte des Konzentrationslagers Mauthausen*, 338–339.

143. MacDonald, *Inside the Gates*, 40. See also Sington, *Belsen Uncovered*, ch4 for a discussion of 'Gaolers and Overseers'.

144. Tobias and Zinke, *Nakam*, 37–52; Lang, *The Future of the Holocaust*, 146–147.

145. Gavin, interview of 16 July 1981, in Eliach and Gurewitsch (eds.), *The Liberators*, 53.

146. Heymont, *Among the Survivors*, 78 (31 October 1945).

147. Levy, *Witness to Evil*, 24; Doherty, *Letters from Belsen 1945*, 57.

148. Lavsky, 'The Day After', 46.

149. *Undzer Shtime*, 5 (29 November 1945), 7, cited in Schlichting, 'Offnet die Tore von Erez Israel', 16.

3 Out of the Chaos

1. Graham (ed.), *Poetry of the Second World War*, 212.
2. Warhaftig, *Uprooted*, 88.
3. Klüger, *Landscapes of Memory*, 193.
4. Wieviorka, *Déportation et génocide*, 91: 'Car la misère qui règne dans Bergen-Belsen, malgré la disparition des violences dues aux SS, reste semblable à celle des pires jours du camp.' This seems to suggest that it should have been within British powers to end the suffering and misery at Belsen immediately.
5. Zwart, 'The Last Days of Bergen-Belsen', WL P.III.h.No.780 (Bergen-Belsen), 16. See also Lavsky, 'The Day After', 41.
6. McConahey cited in Ast, *Confronting the Holocaust*, n.p. (Ch. 4).
7. Rabbi Irving Greenberg, 'Preface', quoting Menachem Z. Rosensaft, in Rosensaft (ed.), *Life Reborn*, 1.
8. Lasker-Wallfisch, 'A Survivor's Memories of Liberation', in Bardgett and Cesarani (eds.), *Belsen 1945*, 25.
9. Glyn Hughes, evidence for the prosecution, 18 September 1945, in Phillips (ed.), *Belsen Trial*, 33. It is worth noting here that Glyn Hughes rightly refers to starvation as a disease.
10. H. L. Glyn Hughes, 'German Concentration Camps: Early Measures at Belsen' in Tidy (ed.), *Inter-Allied Conferences on War Medicine*, 457.
11. Williams in Reilly et al., *Belsen in History and Memory*, 247. See also Williams, 'The First Day in the Camp', in Bardgett and Cesarani (eds.), *Belsen 1945*, 27–30.
12. Lavsky, 'The Day After', 42–43.
13. Doherty, *Letters from Belsen 1945*, 47 (July 1945).
14. Ibid., 49 (July 1945).
15. 'Report from J. M. Parkinson', in Friends' Relief Service, 'Reports on Team 100 at Belsen Camp' (June 1945), WL HA6A-3/3/21.
16. See Hargrave, *Bergen-Belsen 1945*, 33 (7 May 1945) for a drawing and description of the 'human laundry'.
17. British soldier cited in Shephard, *After Daybreak*, 113; Doherty, *Lessons from Belsen 1945*, 106 (29 August 1945).
18. MacAuslan, 'Some Aspects of the Medical Relief', 61. But note also the comments of Janet Vaughan, 'The Value of Hydrolysates in the Treatment of Severe Starvation at Belsen', in Tidy (ed.), *Inter-Allied Conferences on War Medicine*, 471–474.
19. Hargrave, *Bergen-Belsen 1945*, 73 (22 May 1945).
20. Doherty, *Letters from Belsen 1945*, 55 (July 1945).
21. Collis, 'Belsen Camp', 814.
22. Lewis, 'Medical Problems at Belsen', 123. See also Trepman, 'Rescue of the Remnants', 283.
23. Ben-Sefer, 'Surviving Survival', 103–104; Beardwell, *Aftermath*, 38.
24. Beardwell, *Aftermath*, 40–41.
25. Jane E. Leverson, 'Bergen Belsen Concentration Camp' (6 May 1945), WL HA6A-1/9/9. See also Williams, *A Page of History in Relief*, 36.
26. Vella, 'Belsen: Medical Aspects', 40. See also Lipscomb, 'German Concentration Camps: Diseases Encountered at Belsen', in Tidy (ed.), *Inter-Allied Conferences on War Medicine*, 462–465.
27. Glyn Hughes cited in MacAuslan, *Some Aspects of the Medical Relief*, 91.
28. Here I follow MacAuslan, ibid., 93–96.
29. Lewis, 'Medical Problems at Belsen', 125; see also MacAuslan, *Some Aspects of the Medical Relief*, 128.
30. Trepman, 'Rescue of the Remnants', 285.
31. Collis and Hogerzeil, *Straight On*, 53.
32. L.G.R. Wand in Reilly et al., *Belsen in History and Memory*, 243.
33. Rosensaft, 'Our Belsen', in Irgun Sheerit Hapleitah, *Belsen*, 29.
34. Roy cited in Kolinsky, 'Jews in Germany, 1945–1950', 2.
35. Priest in Hirsh, *Liberators*, 119.

36. Macdonald in ibid., 121–122.
37. Priest in ibid., 124.
38. Boder, *I Did Not Interview the Dead*, 49.
39. Jürgen Bassfreund, interview with David Boder, Munich, 20 September 1946 (orig. German), online at: http://voices.iit.edu/interview?doc=bassfreundJ&display=bass freundJ_en
40. Neuman, *The Narrow Bridge*, 173–180.
41. Sack, *Dawn after Dachau*, 31, 36.
42. Le Chêne, *Mauthausen*, 169.
43. Hirsch, *Liberators*, 274.
44. Le Chêne, *Mauthausen*, 170.
45. Sereny, *The German Trauma*, 22–23.
46. See Plotkin, 'The *Kinderheim* of Bergen-Belsen' and Verolme, *The Children's House of Belsen.*
47. Rudman cited in Ben-Sefer, 'Surviving Survival', 107.
48. Zvi Asaria, cited in Kolinsky, 'Experiences of Survival', 262.
49. Zippy Orlin, 'What it's Really Like in a DP Camp: A South African Girl in Belsen', in Somers and Kok (eds.), *Jewish Displaced Persons in Camp Bergen-Belsen*, 157. Orlin's article was first published in *The Zionist Record* in South Africa, 4 March 1949.
50. Boaz Cohen, ' "And I was only a Child": Children's Testimonies, Bergen-Belsen 1945', in Bardgett and Cesarani (eds.), *Belsen 1945*, 155. See Ch. 4 below for more detail.
51. Andrew Matthews, medical student, in Kemp (ed.), *The Relief of Belsen*, 25.
52. Kaufman in ibid., 26.
53. Collis, *Straight On*, 57.
54. Collis, 'Belsen Camp', 815.
55. Schwarz, *The Redeemers*, 10.
56. Collis, 'Belsen Camp', 815.
57. Hilliard, *Surviving the Americans*, 78–80.
58. Rosensaft, 'Our Belsen', in Irgun Sheerit Hapleitah, *Belsen*, 32.
59. For a very critical appraisal, see Boris Pliskin, Leon Retter and Samuel Shlomowitz, 'An Evaluation of the American Joint Distribution Committee Program in the American Occupied Zone of Germany, from its Inception to January 1947', 28 January 1947, Central Zionist Archive, Jerusalem, C7/1254, papers of Eva Kolinsky.
60. Bauer, *Out of the Ashes*, 55.
61. Heymont, *Among the Survivors*, 27–28 (28 September 1945).
62. Myers, 'Jewish Displaced Persons', 310.
63. See Lavsky, 'The Experience of the Displaced Persons', 233.
64. On the JCRA see Gottlieb, *Men of Vision*, 177–182.
65. Lavsky, 'The Experience of the Displaced Persons', 234.
66. 'Extracts from Letter to the Jewish Committee for Relief Abroad from the Only British Jewish Civilian Relief Workers at Bergen Belsen Concentration Camp', May 1945, WL HA6A-1/9/10.
67. Leverson, 'Bergen Belsen Concentration Camp' (6 May 1945), WL HA6A–1/9/9.
68. Henriques to Mr Henriques, 20 July 1945, WL HA 6A–4/1/15.
69. Henriques, 'Notes on the Present Position of Jewish D.P.s' (2 July 1945), WL HA6A-4/1/33.
70. Henriques to Lt. Col. A.J. Hicks (29 August 1945), WL HA6A-4/1/39.
71. Henriques, 'Further Report on Work at Celle' (2 September 1945), WL HA4A-4/1/55.
72. Henriques, 'Report of the Work of 132 J.R.U. from September 24th to October 12th 1945' (12 October 1945), WLHA4A–4/1/58.
73. Henriques, 'This Freedom' (20 November 1945), WL HA6A-4/1/117.
74. Henriques, 'The Work of the 132 Jewish Relief Unit from November – December 3rd, 1945' (n.d.), WL HA6A-4/1/126.
75. Levy, *Witness to Evil*, 58. For his earlier complaints, see *Witness to Evil*, Ch. 2 and his letter of 11 May 1945 to JCRA, WL HA6A-1/10/2.

76. Rosensaft, *Yesterday*, 82, 83.
77. Hyman Yantian, 'First News of Fate of Survivors' (9 June 1945), WL P.IV.a.No.680.
78. Erik Somers and René Kok, 'The Album and Zippy Orlin', in Somers and Kok (eds.), *Jewish Displaced Persons in Camp Bergen-Belsen*, 23.
79. Hardman and Goodman, *The Survivors*, 86.
80. Rosensaft, *Yesterday*, 82. Here Rosensaft is borrowing the words of Alex L. Easterman, 'They Were Liberated – But Not Free', in Irgun Sheerit Hapleita, *Belsen*, 93. Here see Chapter 5 below for more detail.
81. Kolinsky, 'Experiences of Survival', 263.
82. Robinson, *Uprooted Jews*, 302–303.
83. There were no DP camps in the Soviet Union and most of the Jews who had spent the war years in exile in the USSR left quickly after the war ended. Once the small number of ill survivors of Auschwitz and other camps liberated by the Red Army were nursed to a state in which they could travel, they also left quickly, initially for 'home' and, if that was no longer available, to DP camps in the western occupation zones of Germany and Austria. Some who were Soviet citizens suffered the terrible fate of being sent again to camps, this time part of the Soviet Gulag. See, for example, Herbermann, *The Blessed Abyss*, 250–251. On Jews in the Soviet Occupation Zone of Germany, see Geller, *Jews in Post-Holocaust Germany*, Ch. 3.
84. Grinberg, 'We are Living Corpses . .', *Aufbau*, 11:34 (24 August 1945), 7. See also Mankowitz, *Life Between Memory and Hope*, 30–31 and Hilliard, *Surviving the Americans*, 7–55 for an almost identical speech by Grinberg on 27 May and Hilliard's response to it.
85. Klüger, *Landscapes of Memory*, 181.
86. Warhaftig, *Uprooted*, 86–87.
87. Adelsberger, *Auschwitz*, 132. Feinstein talks of survivors' 'fantasies of liberation' in *Holocaust Survivors in Postwar Germany*, 11.
88. Feinstein, *Holocaust Survivors in Postwar Germany*, 19.
89. Hirschmann, *The Embers Still Burn*, 90 (Funk Caserne); 74 (Zeilsheim); 85–86 (Kloster Indersdorf).
90. See for example Feinstein, *Holocaust Survivors in Postwar Germany*, 257–258.
91. See Ossenberg, *Documentary Holdings of the ITS*, Ch. 2.
92. Bauer, 'DP Legacy', in Rosensaft (ed.), *Life Reborn*, 26–27; Ouzan, 'Rebuilding Jewish Identities', 101–103.
93. *Frankfurter Rundschau*, 1 February 1946, cited in Kolinsky, *After the Holocaust*, 108.
94. Feinstein, *Holocaust Survivors in Postwar Germany*, 17.
95. Richard van Dam, 'As Medical orderly in Auschwitz', interview, January 1958 (Rotterdam), WL P.III.h. No. 781 (Auschwitz), 8.
96. The Harrison Report is reprinted in Dinnerstein, *America and the Survivors*, 291–305, here 291–292, and is available online at: http://www.ushmm.org/museum/exhibit/online/dp/resourc1.htm
97. Dinnerstein, *America and the Survivors*, 293.
98. Ibid., 295 (Jews as special group), 298–299 (Palestine).
99. Ibid., 300–301.
100. Grossmann, 'Victims, Villains, and Survivors', 296–297. Also Bauer, *Out of the Ashes*, 50–51 and Bauer, 'DP Legacy', in Rosensaft (ed.), *Life Reborn*, 27: 'Harrison complained, in a vastly exaggerated way, about the treatment of the Jews by the army.'
101. Nadich, *Eisenhower and the Jews*, 34; Bauer, *Out of the Ashes*, 60–61. The post of Adviser on Jewish Affairs remained in existence until October 1949, with the last incumbent being Harry Greenstein. From start to finish, Abraham Hyman acted as deputy adviser and he was responsible for winding up the office in December 1949.
102. Hilliard, *Surviving the Americans*, 137.
103. Ibid., 192.

104. Nadich, *Eisenhower and the Jews*, 41.
105. Schulze, 'A Continual Source of Trouble: The Displaced Persons Camp Bergen-Belsen (Hohne), 1945–1950', in Stone (ed.), *Post-War Europe*.
106. Nadich, *Eisenhower and the Jews*, 51.
107. On Poland see Cohen, *In War's Wake*, 138–139; on Romania, Natalia Lazăr, 'Emigrarea evreilor din România în perioada 1948–1952' in Rotman et al. (eds.), *Noi perspective în istoriografia evreilor din România*, 193–210. By 1952, a third of Romania's Jews (about 110,000 people) had left for Israel.
108. Warhaftig, *Uprooted*, 80–81.
109. Ibid., 83.
110. Yehuda Bauer, 'The Brichah', in Gutman and Saf (eds.), *She'erit Hapletah*, 58.
111. Henriques, 'Patchwork and Its Effect on British Prestige' (27 December 1945), WL HA6A-4/1/127. Henriques typed 'previous' instead of 'precious'.
112. Jacob Oleiski, interview with David Boder, Paris, 20 August 1946, online at: http://voices.iit.edu/interview?doc=oleiskiJ&display=oleiskiJ_en
113. Paysach Milman, 'Experiences of Polish Jews in Ghettoes and Concentration Camps' (n.d.), WL P.III.h No. 379, 4.
114. Henriques, 'Calico and the Little Men' (31 July 1945), WL HA6A-4/1/19.
115. Leverson, 'Bergen Belsen Concentration Camp' (6 May 1945) WL HA6A-1/9/9.

4 Displaced Persons or Betrayed Persons? Life in the DP Camps

1. Graham (ed.), *Poetry of the Second World War*, 211; Henriques to Mr Henriques, received 20 July 1945, WL HA6A-4/1/15.
2. Heymont, *Among the Survivors*, 5 (19 September 1945).
3. Ibid., 6.
4. My thanks to Simone Gigliotti for this point.
5. 'Human debris' was a term used by American Jewish journalist I. F. Stone in *Underground to Palestine*, cited in Grossmann, *Jews, Germans, and Allies*, 148.
6. Königseder and Wetzel, *Waiting for Hope*, 6.
7. Gill, *Journey Back from Hell*, 321.
8. Ibid., 312–313.
9. Ahubia cited in Kolinsky, 'Experiences of Survival', 260.
10. Hirschmann, *The Embers Still Burn*, 140–141. Hirschmann was New York mayor Fiorello H. La Guardia's representative in Asia and Europe.
11. Boder, 'The Impact of Catastrophe', 41.
12. Henriques to Mr Henriques, received 20 July 1945, WL HA6A-4/1/15.
13. Hirschmann, *The Embers Still Burn*, 65.
14. Segalman, 'The Psychology of Jewish Displaced Persons', 361.
15. Hirschmann, *The Embers Still Burn*, 122.
16. Bernstein, 'Europe's Jews: Summer, 1947', 107.
17. Wilson, *Aftermath*, 117.
18. Schulze, 'A Continual Source of Trouble', 8.
19. See Kolinsky, *After the Holocaust*; Geller, *Jews in Post-Holocaust Germany* for general surveys of German-Jewish life after the war.
20. Kolinsky, *After the Holocaust*, 137 (census), 151 (Dortmund), 152 (Marx).
21. JCRA, 'The Jews of Berlin', 25 August 1945, WL HA6A-3/3/52.
22. Hirschmann, *The Embers Still Burn*, 69.
23. Handlin, *A Continuing Task*, 94.
24. 'Summary of Reports on the Position of the Jews in Germany' (n.d., *c.* mid-July 1945), WL HA 6A-3/3/2.
25. 'What a Jewish G.I. Thinks about Aid to Europe's Needy', a News-Sheet by the 'JOINT', WL P.IV.A.341. According to the Wiener Library index, the letter was written on 15 May 1945 but this is too early and the letter itself is dated 9 August 1945.

26. Vida, *From Doom to Dawn*, 18, 25.
27. Ibid., 76.
28. Abramovicz to JCRU, 22 October 1945, WL HA6A-1/3/9. In another report (WL HA6A-1/3/10) Abramovicz regretted that a colleague, Miriam Warburg, had to leave work because of illness, since she was 'efficient and understanding', 'Two qualities that are not to be found nor even deemed essential among U.N.R.R.A. personnel (not for publication).'
29. Schochet, *Feldafing*, 47.
30. Sington, *Belsen Uncovered*, 206.
31. See letter from JCRA board to volunteers reporting on meeting of 11 October 1950, WL HA5-6/8/81: 'The essential task for which the Committee was established, has happily, in large measure, been achieved.'
32. Königseder and Wetzel, *Waiting for Hope*, 210.
33. Levent cited in Kolinsky, 'Experiences of Survival', 256.
34. Nadich, *Eisenhower and the Jews*, 58. In fact, survivors of the western camps were for the most part simply fortunate that they had arrived there in the camps' last days.
35. See Abraham S. Hyman, 'Introduction', in Grossmann, *The Jewish DP Problem*, 7. '*She'erit hapletah*' is from Ezra 9:14-15: 'O Lord God of Israel, you are righteous; now as before, we are only a remnant that has survived.'
36. Gringauz, 'Jewish Destiny as the DPs See it', 502–503.
37. Henriques to JCRA, 3 August 1945, WL HA6A-4/1/26.
38. Adelsberger, Letter to a Friend (Frau Goldschmidt), 10 January 1946, WL P.III.h.No.126 (Auschwitz).
39. Schochet, *Feldafing*, 40.
40. Rosensaft, *Yesterday*, 94.
41. Dawidowicz, *From That Time and Place*, 278.
42. Abramovicz to JCRA, 7 October 1945. WL HA6A-1/13 (Relief Workers' Reports: Shea Abramovicz, 1945-6). Tfilen = phylacteries; Tzitzit = knotted undergarment worn by orthodox Jewish men; 'chumashen' [chumashim] = prayer books; Sefer Torah = Torah scrolls.
43. Abramovicz to JCRA, 3 May 1946, WL HA6A-1/3/42.
44. M. Karger, 'Juden in Deutschland 1952', *Jüdische Rundschau* (18 September 1952), copy in WL HA6E-10/119.
45. Michael Berkowitz and Suzanne Brown-Fleming, 'Perceptions of Jewish Displaced Persons as Criminal in Early Postwar Germany: Lingering Stereotypes and Self-Fulfilling Prophecies', in Patt and Berkowitz (eds.), '*We are Here*', 167–193.
46. Schochet, *Feldafing*, 82.
47. *Undzer Shtime* (15 December 1946), 3; Harck, *Unzer Sztyme*, 60–61.
48. Schulze, 'A Difficult Interlude', 74–75.
49. Biber, *Risen from the Ashes*, 16–17.
50. Schochet, *Feldafing*, 131–132.
51. Grobman (ed.), *In Defense of the Survivors*, 360 (Legal Aid Report, 30 April 1946).
52. 'The Last Jewish "D.P.s": The Foehrenwald Camp', *Manchester Guardian* (9 September 1952), 6.
53. Berkowitz and Brown-Fleming, 'Perceptions of Jewish Displaced Persons', in Patt and Berkowitz (eds.), *We are Here*, 185.
54. Segalman, 'The Psychology of Jewish Displaced Persons', 362, 363.
55. JCRA, 'Summary of Reports on the Position of Jews in Germany' (n.d., c.mid-July 1945), WL HA6A-3/3/2.
56. 'An Interview with Rabbi E. Munk Who Worked in Celle, near Hanover', in Jewish Central Information Office, *Jews in Europe To-Day: Two Reports by Jewish Relief Workers in Germany* (November 1945), 1. WL HA6A-3/3/76.
57. Grobman (ed.), *In Defense of the Survivors*, 47–48 (letter of 6 November 1945).
58. Heymont, *Among the Survivors*, 75 (29 October 1945).

59. Miriam Warburg, 'Conditions of Jewish Children in a Bavarian Rehabilitation Camp', in Jewish Central Information Office, *Jews in Europe To-Day: Two Reports by Jewish Relief Workers in Germany* (November 1945), 7. WL HA6A-3/3/79.
60. Biber, *Risen from the Ashes*, 8-9.
61. Ibid., 11, 14.
62. Segalman, 'The Psychology of Jewish Displaced Persons', 364.
63. Ibid., 368.
64. Abramovicz to JCRA, 21 January 1946, WL HA6A-1/3/22.
65. Pinson, 'Jewish Life in Liberated Germany', 110.
66. Ibid., 108, 110.
67. Biber, *Risen from the Ashes*, 47.
68. Ibid., 53.
69. It is the perpetrators' perspective that is crucial here since many of those persecuted as Jews were in fact baptised Christians or had little or no engagement with Judaism as a religion or with other varieties of Jewish communal life.
70. Gringauz, 'Jewish Destiny as the DPs See it', 503.
71. Jacobmeyer, 'Jüdische Überlebende als "Displaced Persons"', 451-452 on this paradox.
72. See Tobias, *Vorübergehende Heimat*, on *Undzer Vort*, and Schlichting, '*Öffnet die Tore von Erez Israel*', 31-35, on *Undzer Shtime*.
73. Königseder and Wetzel, 'Displaced Persons 1945-1950': The Social and Cultural Perspective', in Stone (ed.), *Post-War Europe*, 8.
74. Brenner, *After the Holocaust*, 19-22; Feinstein, *Holocaust Survivors*, 224-226; Pinson, 'Jewish Life in Liberated Germany', 123-125.
75. Jacob Pat, cited in Laura Jockusch, 'Chroniclers of Catastrophe: History Writing as a Jewish Response to Persecution Before and After the Holocaust', in Bankier and Michman (eds.), *Holocaust Historiography in Context*, 135.
76. Shmuel Krakowski, 'Memorial Projects and Memorial Institutions Initiated by She'erit Hapletah', in Gutman and Saf (eds.), *She'erit Hapletah*, 388-398; Ada Schein, ' "Everyone Can Hold a Pen": The Documentation Project in the DP Camps in Germany', in Bankier and Michman (eds.), *Holocaust Historiography in Context*, 126.
77. Cited in Laura Jockusch, 'A Folk Monument to Our Destruction and Heroism: Jewish Historical Commissions in the Displaced Persons Camps of Germany, Austria and Italy', in Patt and Berkowitz (eds.), '*We are Here*', 32. See also Jockusch, 'Breaking the Silence: The Centre de Documentation Juive Contemporaine in Paris and the Writing of Holocaust History in Liberated France', in Cesarani and Sundquist (eds.), *After the Holocaust*, 73-74.
78. Cited in Jockusch, 'A Folk Monument', 35. See also Jockusch, 'Historiography in Transit', 79
79. Pinson, 'Jewish Life in Liberated Germany', 125.
80. See Kassow, *Who Will Write Our History?*
81. Auerbach, 'Testimonies: On the Margins of Yad Vashem's Activities' (in Hebrew), cited in Dalia Ofer, 'The Community and the Individual: The Different Narratives of Early and Late Testimonies and Their Significance for Historians', in Bankier and Michman (eds.), *Holocaust Historiography in Context*, 527.
82. Friedman, 'European Jewish Research', 504-505.
83. Ofer, 'The Community and the Individual', in Bankier and Michman (eds.), *Holocaust Historiography in Context*, 523-524.
84. David G. Roskies, 'Dividing the Ruins: Communal Memory in Yiddish and Hebrew', in Cesarani and Sundquist (eds.), *After the Holocaust*, 87-89; Finder, 'Yizkor!', 243. Later commemorative volumes followed a similar format; see, for example, Bloch (ed.), *Holocaust and Rebirth*, a large volume comprised mostly of photographs from Belsen.
85. Warburg, 'Conditions of Jewish Children', 10. WL HA6A-3/3/80.
86. See Zahra, 'Lost Children'; Zahra, 'A Human Treasure'.
87. Holian, 'Displacement and the Post-war Reconstruction of Education.'
88. Andlauer, *Zurück ins Leben*, 107.
89. Abramowicz to JCRA, 14 October 1945. WL HA6A-1/3/5.

90. Papanek, 'They are Not Expendable', 314, 315.
91. Marie Syrkin, 'The D.P. Schools', *Jewish Frontier*, 15:3 (1948), 17, cited in Giere, ' "We're On Our Way, But We're Not in the Wilderness" ', 707.
92. Grobman (ed.), *In Defense of the Survivors*, 40 (letter of 3 November 1945).
93. Giere, 'We're On Our Way, But We're Not in the Wilderness', 707.
94. Brenner, *After the Holocaust*, 22–23.
95. Abramovicz to Leonard Cohen, 12 December 1945, WL HA6A-1/3/17.
96. 'Assignment Germany', *J.D.C. Digest*, 5:2 (February 1946), 14.
97. Warburg, 'Conditions of Jewish Children', in Jewish Central Information Office, *Jews in Europe Today* (November 1945), WL HA6A-3/3/79, 8.
98. Cited in Tobias, *Der Kibbutz auf dem Streicher-Hof*, 24, and (with precise date), Tobias and Schlichting, *Heimat auf Zeit*, 92.
99. *Yidishe Sport Tsaytung*, 21 (1948), cited in Tobias and Schlichting, *Heimat auf Zeit*, 91.
100. Fetthauer, *Musik und Theater im DP-Camp Bergen-Belsen*, 25.
101. Sadie Rurka, report in *JCRA Volunteers' News Letter*, 12 (November 1945), WL HA5-6/8/31.
102. Schlichting, '*Offnet die Tore von Erez Israel*', 19.
103. FO 1049/81, Appendix C: Central Jewish Committee for Germany.
104. Fetthauer, *Musik und Theater im DP-Camp Bergen-Belsen*, 228–229.
105. Feinstein, *Holocaust Survivors*, 231–234.
106. Warburg, 'Conditions of Jewish Children', in Jewish Central Information Office, *Jews in Europe Today* (November 1945), WL HA6A-3/3/79, 8.
107. Biber, *Risen from the Ashes*, 27.
108. Tobias, *Der Kibbutz auf dem Streicher-Hof*, 27.
109. Feinstein, *Holocaust Survivors*, 228–229.
110. Abramovicz to JCRA, 7 October 1945. WL HA6A-1/13 (Relief Workers' Reports: Shea Abramovicz, 1945–6).
111. Feinstein, 'Jewish Observance in Amalek's Shadow: Mourning, Marriage, and Birth Rituals among Displaced Persons in Germany', in Patt and Berkowitz (eds.), *We are Here*, 265.
112. Zippy Orlin, 'What it's Really Like in a DP Camp: A South African Girl in Belsen', in Somers and Kok (eds.), *Jewish Displaced Persons in Camp Bergen-Belsen*, 155–156.
113. Baumel, *Double Jeopardy*, 237–238.
114. Königseder and Wetzel, *Waiting for Hope*, 195-196; Lavsky, 'A Community of Survivors: Bergen-Belsen as a Jewish Centre after 1945', in Reilly et al. (eds.), *Belsen in History and Memory*, 171–172; Thaler, 'History and Memory'.
115. Gringauz, 'Yizker', *Landsberger Lager Tsaytung* (8 October 1945), 3, cited in Finder, 'Yizkor!', 233.
116. Y. Marguliets et al., *A zikorn far Rovne* (1947), cited in Finder, 'Yizkor!', 241.
117. Thomas Rahe, 'Social Life in the Jewish DP Camp at Bergen-Belsen', in Somers and Kok (eds.), *Jewish Displaced Persons in Camp Bergen-Belsen*, 72; Brenner, *After the Holocaust*, 26.
118. Landau, 'The First Days of Freedom', in Brenner, *After the Holocaust*, 85.
119. Vida, *From Doom to Dawn*, 76.
120. Biber, *Risen from the Ashes*, 54.
121. Feinstein, 'Jewish Observance in Amalek's Shadow', in Patt and Berkowitz (eds.), *We are Here*, 275.
122. Max B. Wall, letter of 31 October 1945, in Feldberg, 'The Day is Short and the Task is Great', 621.
123. Werber, *Saving Children*, 122.
124. Melville Marks, Report from Admont Camp, 12 August 1946, in *JCRA Volunteers' News Letter*, 19 (August/September 1946), WL HA5-6/8/58.
125. Tobias and Schlichting, *Heimat auf Zeit*, 33.
126. Abramovicz to JCRA, 14 October 1945. WL HA6A-1/3/5.
127. J. Silbiger, Joint Representative, Föhrenwald, to P.I.R. Hart, JCRA, 20 June 1948, WL HA6B/2-15/8/D (letter of 20 June, population report enclosed from 30 May 1948).
128. Rahe, 'Social Life', in Somers and Kok (eds.), *Jewish Displaced Persons in Camp Bergen-Belsen*, 73.

129. Sadie Sendler, JDC Report, April 1946, cited in Baumel, *Double Jeopardy*, 236.
130. Orlin, 'What it's Really Like in a DP Camp', in Somers and Kok (eds.), *Jewish Displaced Persons in Camp Bergen-Belsen*, 158.
131. Grossmann, 'Victims, Villains, and Survivors', 302–308.
132. See the essays in Pines, *A Woman's Unconscious Use of Her Body*, and Davidson, 'The Transmission of Psychopathology in Families of Concentration Camp Survivors', in Davidson, *Holding on to Humanity*, 88–120.
133. *Three Years of ORT Activities: Report for the Period August 1946–June 1949* (Geneva: ORT Union, 1949), 77, reprinted in Person, *ORT and the Rehabilitation of Holocaust Survivors*, 86.
134. Kavanaugh, 'ORT and the Rehabilitation of Holocaust Survivors', 164.
135. Glassgold (1947) cited ibid., 169–170.
136. Heymont, *Among the Survivors*, 13, cited in Kavanaugh, 'ORT and the Rehabilitation of Holocaust Survivors', 171.
137. Oleiski cited in Kavanaugh, *ORT, the Second World War*, xii. See also David Boder's interview with Oleiski of 20 August 1946 in Paris, online at: http://voices.iit.edu/interv iew?doc=oleiskiJ&display=oleiskiJ_en
138. 'Report by Mr. Leonard Cohen of the Jewish Committee for Relief Abroad on His Visit to the Continent' (6 June 1945), WL HA6A-1/6.
139. Rotman, 'Romanian Jewry', 297.
140. Grossmann, *The Jewish DP Problem*, 22.
141. Abramovicz to JCRA, 15 November 1945, WL HA6A-1/3/12.
142. Abramovicz to JCRA, 3 May 1946, WL HA6A-1/3/42.
143. Major C.C.K. Rickford, 'Report on 'Jewish Congress' at Höhne Camp 25–27 September', in Flanagan and Bloxham (eds.), *Remembering Belsen*, 85.
144. Yablonka, 'Holocaust Survivors in Israel: Time for an Initial Taking of Stock', in Ofer et al. (eds.), *Holocaust Survivors*, 187.
145. Gringauz, 'Jewish Destiny as the DPs See it', 503.
146. Pinson, 'Jewish Life in Liberated Germany', 117.
147. Yablonka, 'Holocaust Survivors in Israel', in Ofer et al. (eds.), *Holocaust Survivors*, 192; Yablonka, *Survivors of the Holocaust*, 9–10. See also Patt, *Finding Home and Homeland*, 253–257, and Patt, 'Stateless Citizens of Israel: Jewish Displaced Persons and Zionism in Post-War Germany', in Reinisch and White (eds.), *The Disentanglement of Populations*, 162–182 for a useful analysis of the *giyus* (conscription) plan in the DP camps.
148. Cited in Zahra, 'Lost Children', 75.
149. Abramovicz to JCRA, 20 December 1945, WL HA6A-1/3/21.
150. Judith Tydor Baumel, 'Kibbutz Buchenwald', in Gutman and Saf (eds.), *She'erit Hapletah*, 440.
151. 'Homecoming in Israel: Journey of Kibbutz Buchenwald', in Schwarz (ed.), *The Root and the Bough*, 319 (17 July 1945); cited (slightly incorrectly) in Mankowitz, *Life Between Memory and Hope*, 29.
152. Crossman, *Palestine Mission*, 90.
153. Mankowitz, *Life Between Memory and Hope*, 147.
154. Baumel, *Kibbutz Buchenwald*, 65.
155. Baumel, 'Kibbutz Buchenwald and Kibbutz Hafetz Hayyim', 237, 242.
156. Baumel, *Kibbutz Buchenwald*, 64.
157. Joint Statistical Office, 20 May 1947, cited in Mankowitz, *Life Between Memory and Hope*, 144.
158. Lewinsky cited in Giere, ' "We're On Our Way, But We're Not in the Wilderness" ', 702, and in Mankowitz, *Life Between Memory and Hope*, 149.
159. Baumel, *Kibbutz Buchenwald*, 66.
160. 'Homecoming in Israel', in Schwarz (ed.), *The Root and the Bough*, 319 (17 July 1945).
161. Hirschmann, *The Embers Still Burn*, 101.
162. Abramovicz, 'Six Months in D.P. Camp Fohrenwald', 3 March 1946, WL HA6A-1/3/26.

163. Schochet, *Feldafing*, 166.
164. Stone, *Underground to Palestine*, 21.
165. Bernd, *Die Situation von heute*, 1: '*Jedoch der krasseste Pessimist hat wohl eine Zeit wie die heutige nicht vorausgesehen*'.
166. Berger, 'Displaced Persons', 50.
167. Gringauz, 'Our New German Policy and the DPs', 508. See Chapter 5 below.
168. Berger, 'Displaced Persons', 50.
169. Abramovicz to JCRU, 6 June 1946, WL HA6B-2-15/6/C.
170. Hirschmann, *The Embers Still Burn*, 72.
171. Shephard, *The Long Road Home*, 347.

5 Transitions: DPs in a Changing World

1. Hannah Arendt to Karl Jaspers, 17 August 1946, in Kohler and Saner (eds.), *Hannah Arendt and Karl Jaspers: Correspondence*, 53–54; Crossman, Palestine Mission, 101.
2. Pinson, 'Jewish Life in Liberated Germany', 109 n8.
3. Ibid., 109.
4. Tobias, *Der Kibbutz auf dem Streicher-Hof*, 43.
5. Cohen, *In War's Wake*, 129.
6. Mankowitz, *Life Between Memory and Hope*, 301. See interview with Nadich USHMM RG-50.470.0017 for explanation of how he diverted American food supplies in Paris originally intended for POWs to Jewish migrants en route to Marseille.
7. Crossman, *Palestine Mission*, 84, 85.
8. Crum, *Behind the Silken Curtain*, 121; also cited in Mankowitz, *Life Between Memory and Hope*, 126.
9. Report of the Anglo-American Committee of Inquiry on Palestine (April 1946), online at: https://www.jewishvirtuallibrary.org/jsource/History/anglotoc.html
10. Sachar, *Redemption of the Unwanted*, 201–206.
11. Attlee cited in Leonard Dinnerstein, 'The United States and the Displaced Persons', in Gutman and Saf (eds.), *She'erit Hapletah*, 354.
12. Bevin cited in Kochavi, 'Britain's Image Campaign against the Zionists', 298.
13. Cohen, 'The Genesis of the Anglo-American Committee on Palestine', 185.
14. *The Times*, 2 January 1947.
15. Königseder and Wetzel, 'DP Camp 1945–1950: The British Section', in Somers and Kok (eds.), *Jewish Displaced Persons*, 51.
16. Stone, *Underground to Palestine*, 147 (Dutch youngsters), 148 ('floating Babel').
17. Ibid., 144 ('slaver'), 169–214 (journey and arrival at Haifa).
18. Königseder and Wetzel, 'DP Camp 1945–1950: The British Section', in Somers and Kok (eds.), *Jewish Displaced Persons*, 51–53. See also Kochavi, *Post-Holocaust Politics*, 266–273.
19. Hirschmann, *The Embers Still Burn*, 34.
20. Laub, *Last Barrier to Freedom*, 58.
21. Ofer, 'Holocaust Survivors as Immigrants', 3. See also Nahum Bogner, 'Holocaust Survivors in the Cyprus Detention Camps', in Gutman and Saf (eds.), *She'erit Hapletah*, 418–426.
22. Kochavi, *Post-Holocaust Politics*, 70.
23. Laub, *Last Barrier to Freedom*, 22.
24. Hadjisavvas, '"The Strangest Episode"', Ch. 3.
25. Shmuel Bogler in Margalit Bejarano and Amija Boasson, 'Slave Labour and Shoah: A View from Israel', in von Plato et al. (eds.), *Hitler's Slaves*, 347.
26. Laub, *Last Barrier to Freedom*, 6–7.
27. Ibid., 98.
28. Kochavi, 'The Struggle against Jewish Immigration to Palestine', 163.

29. TNA: CO 537/1811, 'Reactions to HMG Statement', British Ambassador in Washington Lord Inverchapel to Foreign Office, 14 August 1946, cited in Hadjisavvas, '"The Strangest Episode"', 22.
30. Bauer, 'Impact of the Holocaust', 551.
31. Cesarani, 'Great Britain', 615. See also Kochavi, 'Anglo-American Discord', 534.
32. Grafftey-Smith to FO, 14 October 1945, cited in Kochavi, 'The Struggle against Jewish Immigration to Palestine', 147.
33. Kochavi, 'The Struggle against Jewish Immigration to Palestine', 151.
34. Kushner, 'Anti-Semitism and Austerity.'
35. Cesarani, 'Great Britain', 615-616.
36. Schaffer, Racial Science and British Society, 1930-62, 109.
37. Segalman, 'The Psychology of Jewish Displaced Persons', 366. Segalman anticipates Kushner's arguments in The Holocaust and the Liberal Imagination.
38. Abramovicz to JCRU, 15 November 1945, WL HA6A-1/3/10.
39. Gringauz cited in Mankowitz, Life Between Memory and Hope, 283.
40. Simon Kempler, 'Zu Besuch in Lübeck', Undzer Shtime, 11 (12 July 1946), 19, in Harck (ed.), Unzer Sztyme, 39-40.
41. Lavsky, 'The Experience of the Displaced Persons', 238.
42. Central Committee to UN Special Committee on Palestine, 22 July 1947, cited in Holian, Between National Socialism and Soviet Communism, 173.
43. Jewish Agency for Palestine, The Palestine Issue, 5.
44. Chaim Hoffman, 'Report of Activities 1946-1948', n.d. (1948), 2-3. Institut für Zeitgeschichte, Munich, Dw 379.001, papers of Eva Kolinsky.
45. Sylvia Gilman, 'The American Jewish Conference: Spokesman for a United American Jewry', n.d (1947), Central Zionist Archive, Jerusalem, C7, 313/1, 3, papers of Eva Kolinsky.
46. See especially the works listed in the bibliography by Peck, Patt, Mankowitz, Kochavi, Baumel, Lavsky and Bauer. The opposite strand, which stresses the manipulation of the DPs by the Yishuv (e.g. Zertal, Grodzinsky), has received less of a hearing but is guided by no less presentist concerns.
47. Wetzel, '"Mir szeinen doh"', 349.
48. Yehuda Bauer, 'The Holocaust and the Struggle of the Yishuv as Factors in the Establishment of the State of Israel', in Gutman and Rothkirchen (eds.), The Catastrophe of European Jewry, 620.
49. Kochavi, 'British Response.'
50. Crossman, Palestine Mission, 46 (3 January 1946).
51. See for example, Harold Troper, 'Canada and the Survivors of the Holocaust: The Crisis of the Displaced Persons', in Gutman and Saf (eds.), She'erit Hapletah, 261-285; Tobias, Neue Heimat Down Under and Rutland, 'Resettling the Survivors' for the figure of 17,000 Jewish DPs immigrating to Australia between 1945 and 1954. For statistics, see also Grossmann, Jews, Germans, and Allies, 252, and cf. Hyman, The Undefeated, Ch. 18. See also Stats, 'Characteristically Generous?' for the wider context of Australia's immigration policies.
52. Crum, Behind the Silken Curtain, 85.
53. Crossman, Palestine Mission, 88. On the coincidence of wants between the Yishuv and the DPs, see also Avinoam J. Patt, 'Stateless Citizens of Israel: Jewish Displaced Persons and Zionism in Post-War Germany', in Reinisch and White (eds.), The Disentanglement of Populations, 177-178.
54. Hoffmann, 'Report of Activities 1946-1948', 23.
55. Crum, Behind the Silken Curtain, 86.
56. See Engel, 'Palestine in the Mind of the Remnants of Polish Jewry', 232-234.
57. 'IRO Closes Out Last Center for Jewish DPs', copy of article for Stars and Stripes, 19 September 1949, USNA RG 165/827, papers of Eva Kolinsky.
58. Grossmann, Jews, Germans, and Allies, 260, gives the figure of 2,500-3,000; Königseder and Wetzel, Waiting for Hope, 161, suggest 3,500.

59. Webster, 'American Relief', 294.
60. Confidential State Department letter of 22 July 1948, USNA RG165/831, papers of Eva Kolinsky.
61. Grossmann, *Jews, Germans, and Allies*, 252, 260–262.
62. See comments of James P. Rice, JDC Director in Germany, in 'Erstrebtes und Erreichtes', *Allgemeine Jüdische Wochenzeitung* (15 September 1955), 2.
63. Königseder and Wetzel, *Waiting for Hope*, 165; 'The Last Jewish "D.P.s": The Foehrenwald Camp', *Manchester Guardian* (9 September 1952), 6.
64. David Pela, 'The End of an Unhappy Era: Last D.P. Camp to Close', *Jewish Chronicle* (19 March 1954), 13.
65. Beno Fuchs, IRO Review Board Form, 13 September 1948, 3.2.1.5/81255158_0_1/ITS Digital Archive Wiener Library.
66. E.g. Kochavi, 'Liberation and Dispersal', 510; Diner, 'Elemente der Subjektwerdung'.
67. Le Chêne, *Mauthausen*, 176–177.
68. Kurt R. Grossman, 'Report on Germany', 10 August 1948, JDC NY AR194554/4/32/6/312, 2. See also Ginsburgs, 'The Soviet Union and the Problem of Refugees', 356–357.
69. Biber, *Risen from the Ashes*, 77.
70. Gringauz, 'Our New German Policy and the DPs', 508.
71. Ibid., 514.
72. Holian, *Between National Socialism and Soviet Communism*, 197.
73. Stern, 'Historic Triangle', 221–222; Holian, *Between National Socialism and Soviet Communism*, 208.
74. Holian, *Between National Socialism and Soviet Communism*, 205. See 198–210 for full details of the demonstration.
75. IRO, 'Preliminary Recommendations of the Director General with a View to the Termination of the IRO Program', 8 March 1949, USNA RG 165/850/1, 2, papers of Eva Kolinsky.
76. The Constitution of the IRO, which became effective as of 20 August 1948, can be found online at: http://avalon.law.yale.edu/20th_century/decad053.asp
77. Shephard, *The Long Road Home*, 88–89.
78. Kochavi, *Post-Holocaust Politics*, 19.
79. Cohen, *In War's Wake*, 143.
80. Brigadier General G.L. Eberle, Chief, Civil Affairs Division, 'Memorandum for the Under Secretary of the Army', 6 January 1949 [dated 1948 but must be 1949], USNA RG 165/842/2, papers of Eva Kolinsky.
81. Harry S. Messec, Report to Military Governor, 15 August 1947, USNA RG 260/177/25, papers of Eva Kolinsky.
82. Kochavi, 'Liberation and Dispersal', 511; Kochavi, 'British Policy on Non-Repatriable Displaced Persons.'
83. Acheson, 'Statement of the Honorable Dean Acheson', 3.
84. Cohen, *In War's Wake*, 137.
85. Sereny, *The German Trauma*, 50–51.
86. International Refugee Organization, *Manual for Eligibility Officers*, 102–103.
87. Cohen, *In War's Wake*, 57; Cohen, 'Politics of Recognition'.
88. Pinkas Knoller CM/1 Form, 21 May 1948, 3.2.1.1/79357229_0_3/ITS Digital Archive Wiener Library.
89. Judith Frank CM/1 Form, 29 January 1948, 3.2.1.1/79092004_0_3/ITS Digital Archive Wiener Library; Herta Stein CM/1 Form, 16 December 1949, 3.2.1.1/79809898_0_4/ITS Digital Archive Wiener Library.
90. Katharina Freund, IRO Review Board Form, 4 November 1948, 3.2.1.5/81254489_0_3/ITS Digital Archive Wiener Library. In other words, Freund was ineligible for resettlement in a different country.
91. Ella Freudenheim, IRO Review Board Form, 26 October 1949, 3.2.1.5/81278240_0_1/ITS Digital Archive Wiener Library.

92. Hermine Heimbach, IRO Review Board Form, 1 December 1949, 3.2.1.5/81282819_0_1/ ITS Digital Archive Wiener Library. Ironically, Heimbach's husband, as a German Jew, would have been eligible for refugee status.

93. Mordchaj Rottstein, IRO Review Board Form, 13 April 1949, 3.2.1.5/81263840_0_1/ ITS Digital Archive Wiener Library.

94. Jsacco Rubinsztein, IRO Review Board Form, 25 November 1949, 3.2.1.5/81264158_0_1/ ITS Digital Archive Wiener Library and 3.2.1.5/81264159_0_2/ITS Digital Archive Wiener Library.

95. Leon Frenkel, IRO Review Board Form, 20 March 1950, 3.2.1.5/81288333_0_1/ITS Digital Archive Wiener Library.

96. Gustav Freitag, IRO Review Board Form, 1 March 1950, 3.2.1.5/81273544_0_1/ITS Digital Archive Wiener Library and 3.2.1.5/81273544_0_3/ITS Digital Archive Wiener Library.

97. Eugeniusz Vaselis, IRO Review Board Form, 10 June 1948, 3.2.1.5/81250836_0_1/ITS Digital Archive Wiener Library.

98. Albert Vaart, IRO Review Board Form, 31 July 1950, 3.2.1.5/81287558_0_1/ITS Digital Archive Wiener Library.

99. Mircea Valescu, IRO Review Board Form, 5 April 1950, 3.2.1.5/81282659_0_1/ITS Digital Archive Wiener Library.

100. See Salvatici, '"Help the People to Help Themselves"'.

101. TNA ADM1/20793 FO to Washington, no. 13356, 27 December 1947, cited in Kochavi, 'Britain's Image Campaign against the Zionists', 305.

102. On the 'flooding' of the camps, see Kimche and Kimche, *The Secret Roads*, 205–210. And for a good overview of events surrounding the *Pan* ships, see Kochavi, *Post-Holocaust Politics*, 82–86.

103. Chamberlin and Feldman (eds.), *Liberation*, 181, 183. Also Petrenko, *Avant et après Auschwitz*.

104. See Stone, *Goodbye to All That?*, Ch. 6.

105. Royal Institute of International Affairs, *Defence in the Cold War*, 81.

106. Rabinowicz, 'Autobiography', 148, papers of Eva Kolinsky.

Conclusion: The Sorrows of Liberation

1. Magnes, *Dissenter in Zion*, 410.

2. Gradowski, 'Writings', 175. See also Stone, 'The Harmony of Barbarism'.

3. Kushner, *The Holocaust and the Liberal Imagination*, 205–247.

4. Auden, 'In Memory of Ernst Toller (d. May 1939)' in *Collected Shorter Poems*, 144.

5. Leitner, *Fragments of Isabella*, 85.

Bibliography

Archival Sources

American Jewish Joint Distribution Committee, New York City
    1945–54 Records

Georgia Institute of Technology
    Witness to the Holocaust Project, online at: http://www.library.gatech.edu/holocaust/

Illinois Institute of Technology
    Voices of the Holocaust Project, online at: http://www.voices.iit.edu

Imperial War Museum, London
    Bergen-Belsen Collection

USC Shoah Foundation Institute
    Visual History Archive

United States Holocaust Memorial Museum, Washington, DC
    Oral History Collection
    Paul Seres Papers

University of Warwick, Modern Records Centre
    Crossman Papers

Wiener Library, London
    International Tracing Service Collections
    Joseph Sheldon, Account of Liberation of Esterwege
    Rose Henriques Archive
    Testaments to the Holocaust

Papers of Eva Kolinsky

Jakow Rabinowicz, 'Autobiography' (typescript, possession of Ilana Ben-Sasson)

Printed Primary Sources

Acheson, Dean, 'Statement of the Honorable Dean Acheson, Under Secretary of State' (24 February 1947), in *Hearing before the Committee on Foreign Relations, United States Senate* (Washington, DC: United States Government Printing Office, 1947).

Adelsberger, Lucie, *Auschwitz: A Doctor's Story* (London: Robson Books, 1996).

Amariglio, Erika Kounio, *From Thessaloniki to Auschwitz and Back: Memories of a Survivor from Thessaloniki* (London: Vallentine Mitchell, 2000).

Arendt, Hannah, 'The Stateless People', *Contemporary Jewish Record*, 8:2 (1945), 137–153.

Arnold–Forster, W., 'UNRRA's Prospects', *Political Quarterly* (1944), 57–65.

—— 'U.N.R.R.A.'s Work for Displaced Persons in Germany', *International Affairs*, 22:1 (1946), 1–13.

Arnothy, Christine, *I am Fifteen and I Do Not Want to Die* (London: Collins, 1956).

Bacall-Zwirn, Alina, and Jared Stark, *No Common Place: The Holocaust Testimony of Alina Bacall-Zwirn* (Lincoln: University of Nebraska Press, 2000).

Barkow, Ben (ed.), *Testaments to the Holocaust: Documents from the Wiener Library, London* (Reading: Thomson Gale, 2005) [online resource].

Bauer, Yehuda, 'The Death Marches, January–May 1945', *Modern Judaism*, 3:1 (1983), 1–21.

Beardwell, M. F., *Aftermath* (Ilfracombe: Arthur H. Stockwell Limited, n.d. [1953]).

Béon, Yves, *Planet Dora: A Memoir of the Holocaust and the Birth of the Space Age* (Boulder, CO: Westview Press, 1997).

Berger, Joseph A., 'Displaced Persons: A Human Tragedy of World War II', *Social Research*, 14:1 (1947), 45–58.

Berler, Willy, *Journey through Darkness: Monowitz, Auschwitz, Gross-Rosen, Buchenwald* (London: Vallentine Mitchell, 2004).

Bernd, Addi, *Die Situation von heute* (Koblenz: Landesverband der jüdischen Gemeinden von Rheinland-Pfalz, 1946).

Bernstein, David, 'Europe's Jews, Summer 1947', *Commentary* (1947), 101–109.

Biber, Jacob, *Risen from the Ashes: A Survivor's Continuing Story of the Holocaust*, 2nd edn (Asheville, NC: Star, 2005).

Bitton-Jackson, Livia, *I Have Lived a Thousand Years: Growing Up in the Holocaust* (New York: Simon and Schuster, 1997).

Bloch, Sam E. (ed.), *Holocaust and Rebirth: Bergen-Belsen 1945–1965* (New York/Tel-Aviv: Bergen-Belsen Memorial Press of the World Federation of Bergen-Belsen Associations, 1965).

Blumstein, Rita Blattberg, *Like Leaves in the Wind* (London: Vallentine Mitchell, 2003).

Boder, David P., 'The Displaced People of Europe', *Illinois Tech Engineer*, 13:2 (1947), 18–21, 32–34.

—— *I Did Not Interview the Dead* (Urbana, IL: University of Illinois Press, 1949).

—— 'The Impact of Catastrophe: I. Assessment and Evaluation', *Journal of Psychology*, 38 (1954), 3–50.

Bourke-White, Margaret, *Dear Fatherland, Rest Quietly: A Report on the Collapse of Hitler's 'Thousand Years'* (New York: Simon and Schuster, 1946).

Brailsford, H.N., *Our Settlement with Germany* (Harmondsworth: Penguin, 1944).

Buchenwald Camp: The Report of a Parliamentary Delegation (London: His Majesty's Stationery Office, 1945).

Chamberlin, Brewster, and Marcia Feldman (eds.), *The Liberation of the Nazi Concentration Camps: Eyewitness Accounts of the Liberators* (Washington, DC: United States Holocaust Memorial Council, 1987).

Christophe, Francine, *From a World Apart: A Little Girl in the Concentration Camps*, trans. Christine Burls (Lincoln, NE: University of Nebraska Press, 2000).

Cohen, Elie, *Human Behaviour in the Concentration Camp* (London: Free Association Books, 1988).

Cole, G.D.H., *The Intelligent Man's Guide to the Post-War World* (London: Victor Gollancz, 1947).

Collis, W.R.F., 'Belsen Camp: A Preliminary Report', *British Medical Journal* (9 June 1945), 814–816.

Collis, Robert, and Han Hogerzeil, *Straight On* (London: Methuen & Co., 1947).

Crossman, Richard, *Palestine Mission: A Personal Record* (London: Hamish Hamilton, 1946).

Crum, Bartley C., *Behind the Silken Curtain: A Personal Account of Anglo-American Diplomacy in Palestine and the Middle East* (New York: Simon and Schuster, 1947).

Czech, Danuta, *Auschwitz Chronicle 1939–1945* (New York: Henry Holt and Company, 1990).

Dagerman, Stig, *German Autumn*, trans. Robin Fulton (London: Quartet Books, 1988 [1947]).

Dann, Sam (ed.), *Dachau 29 April 1945: The Rainbow Liberation Memoirs* (Lubbock, TX: Texas Tech University Press, 1998).

Dawidowicz, Lucy S., *From That Time and Place: A Memoir, 1938–1947* (New York: W. W. Norton & Co. 1989).

Doherty, Muriel Knox, *Letters from Belsen: An Australian Nurse's Experiences with the Survivors of War*, (eds.) Judith Cornell and R. Lynette Russell (St Leonards, NSW: Allen & Unwin, 2000).

Donat, Alexander, *The Holocaust Kingdom* (New York: Secker & Warburg, 1965).

Durlacher, Gerhard, *Stripes in the Sky: A Wartime Memoir* (London: Serpent's Tail, 1991).

Eliach, Yaffa, and Brana Gurewitsch (eds.), *The Liberators: Eyewitness Accounts of the Liberation of Concentration Camps. Volume I: Liberation Day* (Brooklyn, NY: Center for Holocaust Studies Documentation & Research, 1981).

Feldberg, Michael, '"The Day is Short and the Task is Great": Reports from Jewish Military Chaplains in Europe, 1945–1947', *American Jewish History*, 91:3–4 (2003), 607–625.

Flanagan, Ben, and Donald Bloxham (eds.), *Remembering Belsen: Eyewitnesses Record the Liberation* (London: Vallentine Mitchell, 2005).

Fox, Grace, 'The Origins of UNRRA', *Political Science Quarterly*, 65:4 (1950), 561–584.

Frankova, Anita, Anna Hyndrakova, Vera Hajkova and Frantiska Faktorova, *The World Without Human Dimensions: Four Women's Memories* (Prague: State Jewish Museum, 1991).

Friedman, Hildegard Taussig, *Meine Lebensgeschichte* (1967), online at: http://access.cjh.org/home.php?type=extid&term=807257#1

Friedman, Philip, 'European Jewish Research on the Holocaust', in Ada June Friedman (ed.), *Roads to Extinction: Essays on the Holocaust* (New York: Jewish Publication Society of America, 1980), 500–524.

Gabor, Georgia M., *My Destiny: Survivor of the Holocaust* (Arcadia, CA: Amen Publishing, 1981).

Garbarz, Moshé, and Elie Garbarz, *A Survivor* (Detroit, MI: Wayne State University Press, 1992).

Garcia, Max R., *As Long As I Remain Alive* (Tuscaloosa, AL: Portals, 1979).

—— *Auschwitz Auschwitz I Cannot Forget You as Long as I Remain Alive* (San Jose, CA: Think Social, 2008).

Gellately, Robert, *Backing Hitler: Consent and Coercion in Nazi Germany* (New York: Oxford University Press, 2001).

Gellhorn, Martha, 'Dachau: Experimental Murder', *Collier's* (23 June 1945), 16, 28, 30.

Geve, Thomas, *Guns and Barbed Wire: A Child Survives the Holocaust* (Chicago, IL: Academy Chicago, 1987).

Giere, Jacqueline, and Rachel Salamander (eds.), *Ein Leben aufs Neu: Das Robinson-Album. DP-Lager: Juden auf deutschem Boden 1945–1948* (Vienna: Verlag Christian Brandstätter, 1995).

Ginsburgs, George, 'The Soviet Union and the Problem of Refugees and Displaced Persons 1917–1956', *American Journal of International Law*, 51:2 (1957), 325–361.

Gödecke, Monika (ed.), *Konzentrationslager Bergen-Belsen: Berichte und Dokumente* (Hannover: Niedersächsische Landeszentrale für politische Bildung, 1995).

Gollancz, Victor, *In Darkest Germany* (London: Victor Gollancz, 1947).

—— *Our Threatened Values* (London: Victor Gollancz, 1946).

—— *Political Diaries 1932–1971*, ed Robert Pearce (London: The Historians' Press, 1991).

—— *What Buchenwald Really Means* (London: Victor Gollancz, 1945).

Govrin, Yosef, *In the Shadow of Destruction: Recollections of Transnistria and Illegal Immigration to Eretz Israel, 1941–1947* (London: Vallentine Mitchell, 2007).

Gradowski, Zalman, 'Writings', in Ber Mark (ed.), *The Scrolls of Auschwitz* (Tel Aviv: Am Oved, 1985), 173–205.

Graham, Desmond (ed.), *Poetry of the Second World War: An International Anthology* (London: Pimlico, 1998).

Greene, Joshua M., and Shiva Kumar (eds.), *Witness: Voices from the Holocaust* (New York: The Free Press, 2000).

Grinberg, Zalman, 'We are Living Corpses . . .', *Aufbau*, 11:34 (24 August 1945), 7.

Gringauz, Samuel, 'Jewish Destiny as the DPs See It: The Ideology of the Surviving Remnant', *Commentary* (1947), 501–509.

—— 'Our New German Policy and the DPs: Why Immediate Resettlement is Imperative', *Commentary*, 5 (1948), 508–514.

Grobman, Alex (ed.), *In Defense of the Survivors: The Letters and Documents of Oscar A. Mintzer, AJDC Legal Advisor, Germany, 1945–46* (Berkeley, CA: Judah L. Magnes Museum, 1999).

Gros, Louis, with Flint Whitlock, *Survivor of Buchenwald: My Personal Odyssey Through Hell* (Brule, WI: Cable Publishing, 2012).

Grossman, Vasily, 'The Hell of Treblinka', in *The Road: Short Fiction and Articles* (London: Maclehose Press, 2011), 126–179.

Grossmann, Kurt R., *The Jewish DP Problem: Its Origin, Scope, and Liquidation* (New York: Institute of Jewish Affairs, 1951).

Gruenbaum, Thelma, *Nešarim: Child Survivors of Terezín* (London: Vallentine Mitchell, 2004).

Hackett, David A. (ed.), *The Buchenwald Report* (Boulder, CO: Westview Press, 1995).

Halévy, Elie, 'The Age of Tyrannies', *Econometrica*, n.s. 8 (1941), 77–93.

Harck, Hildegard (ed.), *Unzer Szytme: Jiddische Quellen zur Geschichte der jüdischen Gemeinden in der britischen Zone 1945–1947* (Kiel: Landeszentrale für Politische Bildung Schleswig-Holstein, 2004).

Hardman, Leslie H., and Cecily Goodman, *The Survivors: The Story of the Belsen Remnant* (London: Vallentine Mitchell, 2009 [1958]).

Hargrave, Michael John, *Bergen-Belsen 1945: A Medical Student's Journal* (London: Imperial College Press, 2013).

Hart, Kitty, *Return to Auschwitz: The Remarkable Story of a Girl Who Survived the Holocaust* (London: Panther Books, 1983).

Haulot, Arthur, 'Lagertagebuch Januar 1943–Juni 1945', *Dachauer Hefte*, 1 (1993), 129–203.

Hemmendinger, Judith, and Robert Krell, *The Children of Buchenwald: Child Survivors of the Holocaust and Their Post-War Lives* (Jerusalem: Gefen, 2000).

Herbermann, Nanda, *The Blessed Abyss: Inmate #6582 in Ravensbrück Concentration Camp for Women* (Detroit: Wayne State University Press, 2000).

Heyman, Éva, *The Diary of Éva Heyman: Child of the Holocaust*, trans. Moshe M. Kohn (New York: Shapolsky Publishers, 1988).

Heymont, Irving, 'After the Deluge: The Landsberg Jewish DP Camp 1945' (unpublished ms, 1960).

—— *Among the Survivors of the Holocaust – 1945: The Landsberg DP Camp Letters of Major Irving Heymont, United States Army* (Cincinnati, OH: American Jewish Archives, 1982).

Hilliard, Robert L., *Surviving the Americans: The Continued Struggle of the Jews after Liberation* (New York: Seven Stories Press, 1997).

Hirschmann, Ira A., *The Embers Still Burn: An Eye-Witness View of the Postwar Ferment in Europe and the Middle East and Our Disastrous Get-Soft-with-Germany Policy* (New York: Simon and Schuster, 1949).

Hoffman, Chaim, 'Report of Activities 1946–1948', n.d. (1948).

Hyman, Abraham S., 'Displaced Persons', *American Jewish Year Book*, 50 (1948–1949), 455–473.

International Refugee Organization, *Manual for Eligibility Officers* (Geneva: IRO, 1950).

Irgun Sheerit Hapleita, *Belsen* (Tel Aviv: Irgun Sheerit Hapleita Me'Haezor Habriti, 1957).

Jacobeit, Sigrid, and Simone Erpel (eds.), 'Ich grüsse Euch als freier Mensch': Quellenedition zur Befreiung des Frauen-Konzentrationslagers Ravensbrück im April 1945 (Berlin: Hentrich, 1995).

JDC Israel, Camp Fohrenwald: Growth of a DP Community (Jerusalem: JDC Israel, n.d.)

Jewish Agency for Palestine, The Palestine Issue: A Factual Analysis. Submitted to the Members of the United Nations by the Jewish Agency for Palestine 1947 (n.p.: Jewish Agency for Palestine, 1947).

Johnston, Denis, 'Buchenwald' (1945), in John Horgan (ed.), Great Irish Reportage (London: Penguin, 2013).

Kazik (Simha Rotem), Memoirs of a Warsaw Ghetto Fighter (New Haven, CT: Yale University Press, 1994).

Kemp, Paul (ed.), The Relief of Belsen: April 1945 Eyewitness Accounts (London: Imperial War Museum, 1991).

Kertész, Imre, Roman eines Schicksallosen (Reinbek: Rowohlt, 1998).

Kielar, Wieslaw, Anus Mundi: Five Years in Auschwitz. A Personal Record (Rickmansworth: Allen Lane, 1981).

Kimche, Jon, and David Kimche, The Secret Roads: The 'Illegal' Migration of a People 1938–1948 (London: Secker and Warburg, 1954).

Kleiman, Yehudit, and Nina Springer-Aharoni (eds.), The Anguish of Liberation: Testimonies from 1945 (Jerusalem: Yad Vashem, 1995).

Klüger, Ruth, Landscapes of Memory: A Holocaust Girlhood Recalled (London: Bloomsbury, 2003).

Knauth, Percy, 'Buchenwald', Time, 45:18 (30 April 1945), 42–43.

—— Germany in Defeat (New York: Alfred A. Knopf, 1946).

Knoller, Freddie, with John Landaw, Living with the Enemy: My Secret Life on the Run from the Nazis (London: Metro Publishing, 2005).

Kogon, Eugen, The Theory and Practice of Hell: The German Concentration Camps and the System Behind Them (London: World Distributors, 1958).

Kohler, Lotte and Hans Saner (eds.), Hannah Arendt and Karl Jaspers: Correspondence 1926–1969 (San Diego: Harcourt Brace & Company, 1992).

Konieczny, Alfred, KL Gross-Rosen (Wałbrzych: Państwowe Muzeum Gross-Rosen, 1997).

Kor, Eva Mozes, as told to Mary Wright, Echoes from Auschwitz. Dr Mengele's Twins: The Story of Eva and Miriam Mozes (Terre Haute, IN: Candles, Inc., 1995).

Kovner, Abba, 'The Mission of the Survivors', in Yisrael Gutman and Livia Rothkirchen (eds.), The Catastrophe of European Jewry: Antecedents – History – Reflections (New York: Ktav/Jerusalem: Yad Vashem, 1976), 671–683.

Krall, Hanna, The Subtenant / To Outwit God (Evanston, IL: Northwestern University Press, 1992).

Lasker-Wallfisch, Anita, Inherit the Truth, 1939–1945 (London: Giles de la Mare, 1996).

Laub, Morris, Last Barrier to Freedom: Internment of Jewish Holocaust Survivors on Cyprus 1946–1949 (Berkeley, CA: Judah L. Magnes Museum, 1985).

Leitner, Isabella, Fragments of Isabella: A Memoir of Auschwitz (New York: Thomas Y. Crowell, 1978).

Lengyel, Olga, Five Chimneys (London: Granada, 1972).

Levi, Primo, If This Is a Man / The Truce (London: Abacus, 1987).

Levi, Trude, A Cat Called Adolf (London: Vallentine Mitchell, 1995).

Levy, Isaac, Witness to Evil: Bergen-Belsen 1945 (London: Peter Halban, 1995).

Levy-Hass, Hanna, Inside Belsen (Brighton: Harvester Press, 1982).

Lewin, Rhoda G. (ed.), Witness to the Holocaust: An Oral History (Boston, MA: Twayne Publishers, 1990).

Lewis, J. T., 'Medical Problems at Belsen Concentration Camp (1945)', Ulster Medical Journal, 54:2 (1985), 122–126.

Loidl, Franz, Entweihte Heimat: K.Z. Ebensee (Linz: Verlag H. Muck, 1946).

McClelland, Grigor, Embers of War: Letters from a Quaker Relief Worker in War-torn Germany (London: British Academic Press, 1997).

McNeill, Margaret, *By the Rivers of Babylon: A Story of Relief Work among the Displaced Persons of Europe* (London: The Nannisdale Press, 1950).

Magnes, Judah L., *Dissenter in Zion: From the Writings of Judah L. Magnes*, (ed.) Arthur A. Goren (Cambridge, MA: Harvard University Press, 1982).

Malin, Patrick Murphy, 'The Refugee: A Problem for International Organization', *International Organization*, 1:3 (1947), 443–459.

Maurel, Micheline, *Ravensbruck* (London: Anthony Blond, 1959).

Mernyi, Willi, and Florian Wenninger (eds.), *Die Befreiung des KZ Mauthausen: Berichte und Dokumente* (Vienna: Verlag des ÖGB, 2006).

Michelson, Frida, *I Survived Rumbuli* (New York: Holocaust Library, 1979).

Millu, Liana, *Smoke over Birkenau* (Philadelphia, PA: Jewish Publication Society, 1991).

Mirchuk, Petro, *In the German Mills of Death 1941–1945*, 2nd edn (New York: Vantage Press, 1985).

Moorehead, Alan, *Eclipse* (London: Hamish Hamilton, 1945).

Mosley, Leonard O., *Report from Germany* (London: Victor Gollancz, 1945).

Murphy, H.B.M., 'The Resettlement of Jewish Refugees in Israel, with Special Reference to Those Known as Displaced Persons', *Population Studies*, 5:2 (1951), 153–174.

Murray, C. de B., *Rebuilding Europe* (London: Grafton & Co., 1944).

Nadich, Judah, *Eisenhower and the Jews* (New York: Twayne Publishers, 1953).

National Museum of American Jewish Military History (ed.), *GIs remember: Liberating the Concentration Camps* (Washington, DC: National Museum of American Jewish Military History, 1993).

Neuman, Isaac, with Michael Palencia-Roth, *The Narrow Bridge: Beyond the Holocaust* (Urbana, IL: University of Illinois Press, 2000).

Neurath, Paul Martin, *The Society of Terror: Inside the Dachau and Buchenwald Concentration Camps* (Boulder, CO: Paradigm Publishers, 2005).

Niewyk, Donald L., *Fresh Wounds: Early Narratives of Holocaust Survival* (Chapel Hill, NC: University of North Carolina Press, 1998).

Nyiszli, Miklos, *Auschwitz: A Doctor's Eye-Witness Account* (St Albans: Mayflower Books, 1973).

Padover, Saul K., *Psychologist in Germany: The Story of an American Intelligence Officer* (London: Phoenix House, 1946).

Papanek, Ernst, 'They are Not Expendable: The Homeless and Refugee Children in Germany', *Social Service Review*, 20:3 (1946), 312–319.

Pavlenko, N.G. (ed.), *Liberation* (Moscow: Progress Publishers, 1974).

Pawlak, Zacheusz, *'Ich habe überlebt . . .' Ein Häftling berichtet über Majdanek* (Hamburg: Hoffmann und Campe, 1979).

Peck, Abraham J. (ed.), *The Papers of the World Jewish Congress 1945–1950: Liberation and the Saving Remnant*. Archives of the Holocaust, Vol. 9 (New York: Garland, 1990).

Pelz-Bergt, Jutta, *Die ersten Jahre nach dem Holocaust: Odyssee einer Gezeichneten*, in Sigrid Jacobeit (ed.) (Berlin: Hentrich, 1997).

Perlov, Yitzchok, *The Adventure of One Yitzchok* (New York: Award Books, 1967).

Perry, Michael W. (ed.), *Dachau Liberated: The Official Report* (Inkling Books, 2000).

Petrenko, Vassili, *Avant et après Auschwitz* (Paris: Flammarion, 2002).

Phillips, Raymond (ed.), *Trial of Josef Kramer and Forty-four Others (The Belsen Trial)* (London: William Hodge and Company, 1949).

Pinson, Koppel S., 'Jewish Life in Liberated Germany: A Study of the Jewish DPs', *Jewish Social Studies*, 9:2 (1947), 101–126.

Pivnik, Sam, *Survivor: Auschwitz, the Death March and My Fight for Freedom* (London: Hodder and Stoughton, 2012).

Polevoi, Boris, *The Final Reckoning: Nuremberg Diaries*, trans. Janet Butler and Doris Bradbury (Moscow: Progress Publishers, 1978).

'Potiphar', *They Must Not Starve* (London: Victor Gollancz, 1945).

Proudfoot, Malcolm J., 'The Anglo-American Displaced Persons Program for Germany and Austria', *American Journal of Economics and Sociology*, 6:1 (1946), 33–54.

Radnóti, Miklós, *Forced March: Selected Poems*, trans. George Gömöri and Clive Wilmer (London: Enitharmon Press, 2010).

Rajchman, Chil, *Treblinka: A Survivor's Memory, 1942–43* (London: Maclehose Press, 2012).

Robinson, Jacob, *Uprooted Jews in the Immediate Postwar Period* (New York: The Institute of Jewish Affairs of the American Jewish Congress and World Jewish Congress, 1943).

Rosensaft, Hadassah, *Yesterday: My Story*, 2nd edn (New York: Yad Vashem, 2005).

Rothchild, Sylvia (ed.), *Voices from the Holocaust* (New York: New American Library, 1981).

Roubíčková, Eva, *We're Alive and Life Goes On: A Theresienstadt Diary*, trans. Zaia Alexander (New York: Henry Holt & Company, 1998).

Rousset, David, *L'Univers concentrationnaire* (Paris: Éditions de Minuit, 1965).

Royal Institute of International Affairs, *Defence in the Cold War: A Report by a Chatham House Study Group* (London: Royal Institute of International Affairs, 1950).

Sachar, Abram L., *The Redemption of the Unwanted: From the Liberation of the Death Camps to the Founding of Israel* (New York: St Martin's/Marek, 1983).

Sack, Joel, *Dawn after Dachau* (New York: Shengold Publishers, 1990).

Samson, Naomi, *Hide: A Child's View of the Holocaust* (Lincoln, NE: University of Nebraska Press, 2000).

Schochet, Simon, *Feldafing* (Vancouver: November House, 1983).

Schwartz, Abba P., 'International Refugee Organization', *American Jewish Year Book*, 50 (1948–1949), 473–483.

Schwarz, Leo W., *The Redeemers: A Saga of the Years 1945–1952* (New York: Farrar, Straus and Young, 1953).

—— *The Root and the Bough: The Epic of an Enduring People* (New York: Rinehart & Company, 1949).

Segalman, Ralph, 'The Psychology of Jewish Displaced Persons', *Jewish Social Service Quarterly* (1947), 361–369.

Seventh US Army, *Dachau* (n.p., 1945).

Shachan, Avigdor, *Burning Ice: The Ghettos of Transnistria* (Boulder, CO: East European Monographs, 1996).

Shek, Alisah, 'Ein Theresienstädter Tagebuch 18 Oktober 1944–19 Mai 1945', *Theresienstädter Studien und Dokumente* (1994), 169–205.

Shuster, Zachariah, 'Must the Jews Quit Europe? An Appraisal of the Propaganda for Exodus', *Commentary*, 1:1 (1945), 9–16.

Simonov, Constantine, *The Lublin Extermination Camp* (Moscow: Foreign Languages Publishing House, 1944).

Sington, Derrick, *Belsen Uncovered* (London: Duckworth, 1946).

Smith, Lyn (ed.), *Forgotten Voices of the Holocaust: True Stories of Survival – From Men, Women and Children Who Were There* (London: Ebury Press, 2006).

Smith, Marcus J., *Dachau: The Harrowing of Hell* (Albany, NY: State University of New York Press, 1995).

Spender, Stephen, *European Witness* (London: Hamish Hamilton, 1946).

—— 'The Intellectuals and Europe's Future: Reopening the Lines of Communication in Western Culture', *Commentary*, 3 (1947), 7–12.

Spies, Gerty, *My Years in Theresienstadt: How One Woman Survived the Holocaust*, trans. Jutta R. Tragnitz (New York: Prometheus Books, 1997).

Srole, Leo, 'Why the DPs Can't Wait: Proposing an International Plan of Rescue', *Commentary*, 3 (1947), 13–24.

Stadulis, Elizabeth, 'The Resettlement of Displaced Persons in the United Kingdom', *Population Studies*, 5:3 (1952), 207–237.

Steinberg, Paul, *Chronik aus einer dunklen Welt* (Munich: Carl Hanser Verlag, 1998).

Stone, Dan (ed.), *Post-War Europe Series I: Refugees, Exile and Resettlement, 1945–50* (Reading: Thomson Gale, 2007) [online resource].

Stone, I. F., *Underground to Palestine and Reflections Thirty Years Later* (London: Hutchinson, 1979).

Stroumsa, Jacques, *Violinist in Auschwitz: From Salonica to Jerusalem 1913–1967* (Konstanz: Hartung-Gorre Verlag, 1996).

Tartakower, Arieh, and Kurt R. Grossmann, *The Jewish Refugee* (New York: Institute of Jewish Affairs of the American Jewish Congress and World Jewish Congress, 1944).

Tedeschi, Giuliana, *There is a Place on Earth: A Woman in Birkenau* (London: Lime Tree, 1993).

Thaler, Franz, *Unvergessen: Option, Konzentrationslager, Kriegsgefangenschaft, Heimkehr. Ein Sarner Erzählt* (Munich: Piper, 1991).

The Seventy-First Came . . . to Gunskirchen Lager (n.p., 1945).

Tichauer, Eva, *I Was No. 20832 at Auschwitz* (London: Vallentine Mitchell, 2000).

Tidy, Henry Letheby (ed.), *Inter-Allied Conferences on War Medicine 1942–1945* (London: Staples Press, 1947).

Toivi Blatt, Thomas, *From the Ashes of Sobibor: A Story of Survival* (Evanston, IL: Northwestern University Press, 1997).

Tolstoy, Alexei, *The Making of Russia* (London: Hutchinson, 1945).

Trial of the Major War Criminals before the International Military Tribunal, Nuremberg 14 November 1945–1 October 1946 (Nuremberg: International Military Tribunal, 1946–49), 42 vols.

Venezia, Shlomo, *Inside the Gas Chambers: Eight Months in the Sonderkommando of Auschwitz* (Cambridge: Polity Press, 2009).

Verolme, Hetty E., *The Children's House of Belsen* (London: Politico's, 2005).

Victor, Paul, *Buchenwald: A Survivor's Memories* (Tucson, AZ: Wheatmore, 2006).

Vida, George, *From Doom to Dawn: A Jewish Chaplain's Story of Jewish Displaced Persons* (New York: Jonathan David, 1967).

Vogler, Henryk, *Lessons in Fear* (London: Vallentine Mitchell, 2002).

Walker, Patrick Gordon, *The Lid Lifts* (London: Victor Gollancz, 1945).

Warhaftig, Zorach, *Uprooted: Jewish Refugees and Displaced Persons after Liberation* (New York: American Jewish Congress and World Jewish Congress, 1946).

Wells, Leon Weliczker, *The Death Brigade (The Janowska Road)* (New York: Holocaust Library, 1978).

Werber, Jack, with William B. Helmreich, *Saving Children: Diary of a Buchenwald Survivor and Rescuer* (New Brunswick: Transaction, 1996).

Werth, Alexander, *Russia at War 1941–45* (London: Barrie and Rockliff, 1964).

When Hostilities Cease: Papers on Relief and Reconstruction Prepared for the Fabian Society (London: Victor Gollancz, 1943).

Williams, Eryl Hall, *A Page of History in Relief: London – Antwerp – Belsen – Brunswick. Quaker Relief: 1944–1946* (York: Sessions Book Trust, 1993).

Wilson, Francesca M., *Aftermath: France, Germany, Austria, Yugoslavia 1945 and 1946* (West Drayton: Penguin, 1947).

Newspapers

Fun Letstn Khurbn
JDC Digest
Jewish Chronicle
Landsberger Lager Tsaytung
Manchester Guardian
The Times
Undzer Shtime

Secondary Sources

Abzug, Robert H., *Inside the Vicious Heart: Americans and the Liberation of Nazi Concentration Camps* (New York: Oxford University Press, 1985).

Ahonen, Pertti, et al., *People on the Move: Forced Population Movements in Europe in the Second World War and Its Aftermath* (Oxford: Berg, 2008).

Allen, Michael Thad, *The Business of Genocide: The SS, Slave Labor, and the Concentration Camps* (Chapel Hill, NC: University of North Carolina Press, 2002).

Amiel, Irit, *Scorched: A Collection of Short Stories on Survivors* (London: Vallentine Mitchell, 2006).

Ancel, Jean, '"The New Jewish Invasion': The Return of the Survivors from Transnistria', in David Bankier (ed.), *The Jews are Coming Back: The Return of the Jews to their Countries of Origin after WWII* (New York: Berghahn Books, 2005), 231–256.

Andlauer, Anna, *Zurück ins Leben: Das internationale Kinderzentrum Kloster Indersdorf 1945–46* (Nuremberg: Antogo Verlag, 2011).

Arad, Yitzhak, *The Holocaust in the Soviet Union* (Lincoln, NE: University of Nebraska Press, 2009).

Ast, Theresa, *Confronting the Holocaust: American Soldiers Enter Concentration Camps* (n.p.: Nomenklature Publications, 2013).

Auden, W.H., *Collected Shorter Poems, 1927–1957* (London: Faber & Faber, 1969).

Auerbach, Karen, *The House at Ujazdowskie 16: Jewish Families in Warsaw after the Holocaust* (Bloomington, IN: Indiana University Press, 2013).

Balint, Ruth, 'The Use and Abuse of History: Displaced Persons in the ITS Archive', *International Tracing Service Yearbook*, 4 (2015).

Ballinger, Pamela, 'Entangled or "Extruded" Histories? Displacement, National Refugees, and Repatriation after the Second World War', *Journal of Refugee Studies*, 25:3 (2012), 366–386.

Bankier, David, and Dan Michman (eds.), *Holocaust Historiography in Context: Emergence, Challenges, Polemics and Achievements* (Jerusalem: Yad Vashem, 2008).

Bardgett, Suzanne, David Cesarani, Jessica Reinisch and Johannes-Dieter Steinert (eds.), *Survivors of Nazi Persecution in Europe after the Second World War: Landscapes after Battle Volume 1* (London: Vallentine Mitchell, 2010).

Bardgett, Suzanne, and David Cesarani (eds.), *Belsen 1945: New Historical Perspectives* (London: Vallentine Mitchell, 2006).

Baron, Lawrence, 'The Holocaust and American Public Memory, 1945–1960', *Holocaust and Genocide Studies*, 17:1 (2003), 62–88.

Bauer, Yehuda, 'The Impact of the Holocaust on the Establishment of the State of Israel', in Yisrael Gutman and Avital Saf (eds.), *Major Changes within the Jewish People in the Wake of the Holocaust: Proceedings of the Ninth Yad Vashem International Historical Conference* (Jerusalem: Yad Vashem, 1996), 545–552.

—— *Out of the Ashes: The Impact of American Jews on Post-Holocaust European Jewry* (Oxford: Pergamon Press, 1989).

Baumel, Judith Tydor, *Double Jeopardy: Gender and the Holocaust* (London: Vallentine Mitchell, 1998).

—— 'Kibbutz Buchenwald and Kibbutz Hafetz Hayyim: Two Experiments in the Rehabilitation of Jewish Survivors in Germany', *Holocaust and Genocide Studies*, 9:2 (1995), 231–249.

—— *Kibbutz Buchenwald: Survivors and Pioneers* (New Brunswick, NJ: Rutgers University Press, 1997).

—— 'The Politics of Spiritual Rehabilitation in the DP Camps', *Simon Wiesenthal Center Annual*, 6 (1989), 58–79.

Bendremer, Jutta T., *Women Surviving the Holocaust: In Spite of the Horror* (Lewiston, ME: Edwin Mellen Press, 1997).

Bennett, Gill (ed.), *The End of the War in Europe 1945* (London: HMSO, 1996).

Ben-Sefer, Ellen, 'Surviving Survival: Nursing Care at Bergen-Belsen 1945', *Australian Journal of Advanced Nursing*, 26:3 (2009), 101–110.

Benz, Wolfgang and Barbara Distel (eds.), *Der Ort des Terrors: Geschichte der nationalsozialistischen Konzentrationslager*, 8 vols. (Munich: C.H. Beck, 2005–).

Berenbaum, Michael, and Abraham J. Peck (eds.), *The Holocaust and History: The Known, the Unknown, the Disputed, and the Reexamined* (Bloomington, IN: Indiana University Press, 1998).

Berkhoff, Karel C., *Motherland in Danger: Soviet Propaganda during World War II* (Cambridge, MA: Harvard University Press, 2012).

—— '"Total Annihilation of the Jewish Population": The Holocaust in the Soviet Media, 1941–45', *Kritika: Explorations in Russian and Eurasian History*, 10:1 (2009), 61–105.

Bessel, Richard, *Germany 1945: From War to Peace* (London: Pocket Books, 2010).

Bessel, Richard, and Claudia B. Haake (eds.), *Removing Peoples: Forced Removal in the Modern World* (Oxford: Oxford University Press, 2009).

Blatman, Daniel, *The Death Marches: The Final Phase of Nazi Genocide* (Cambridge, MA: The Belknap Press of Harvard University Press, 2011).

—— '"Why Didn't They Mow Us Down Right Away?" The Death-March Experience in Survivors' Testimonies and Memoirs', in Norman J. W. Goda (ed.), *Jewish Histories of the Holocaust: New Transnational Approaches* (New York: Berghahn Books, 2014), 152–169.

Blodig, Vojtěch, *Terezín in the 'Final Solution of the Jewish Question' 1941–1945* (Prague: Oswald, 2006).

Blondel, Jean-Luc, Susanne Urban and Sebastian Schönemann (eds.), *Auf den Spuren der Todesmärsche*. Freilegungen: Jahrbuch des International Tracing Service, 1 (Göttingen: Wallstein Verlag, 2012).

Brenner, Michael, *After the Holocaust: Rebuilding Jewish Lives in Postwar Germany* (Princeton: Princeton University Press, 1997).

Bridgman, Jon, *The End of the Holocaust: The Liberation of the Camps* (Portland, OR: Areopagitica Press, 1990).

Brooks, Jane, '"Uninterested in Anything Except Food": The Work of Nurses Feeding the Liberated Inmates of Bergen-Belsen', *Journal of Clinical Nursing*, 21 (2012), 2958–2965.

Brown, Adam, *Judging 'Privileged' Jews: Holocaust Ethics, Representation and the 'Grey Zone'* (New York: Berghahn Books, 2013).

Browning, Christopher R., *Remembering Survival: Inside a Nazi Slave-Labor Camp* (New York: W. W. Norton, 2010).

Buggeln, Marc, 'Were Concentration Camp Prisoners Slaves? The Possibilities and Limits of Comparative History and Global Historical Perspectives', *International Review of Social History*, 53 (2008), 101–129.

Buser, Verena, *Überleben von Kindern und Jugendlichen in den Konzentrationslagern Sachsenhausen, Auschwitz und Bergen-Belsen* (Berlin: Metropol, 2011).

Caplan, Jane, and Nikolaus Wachsmann (eds.), *Concentration Camps in Nazi Germany: The New Histories* (London: Routledge, 2010).

Carruthers, Susan L., 'Between Camps: Eastern Bloc "Escapees" and Cold War Borderlands', *American Quarterly*, 57:3 (2005), 911–942.

—— 'Compulsory Viewing: Concentration Camp Film and German Re-education', *Millennium – Journal of International Studies*, 30:3 (2001), 733–759.

Cesarani, David, 'Great Britain', in David S. Wyman (ed.), *The World Reacts to the Holocaust* (Baltimore, MD: Johns Hopkins University Press, 1996), 599–641.

—— 'How Post-War Britain Reflected on the Nazi Persecution and Mass Murder of Europe's Jews: A Reassessment of Early Responses', *Jewish Culture and History*, 12:1&2 (2010), 95–130.

—— 'A New Look at Some Old Memoirs: Early Narratives of Nazi Persecution and Genocide', in Suzanne Bardgett, David Cesarani, Jessica Reinisch, and Johannes-Dieter Steinert (eds.), *Landscapes after Battle, Vol. 2: Justice, Politics and Memory in Europe after the Second World War* (London: Vallentine Mitchell, 2011), 121–168.

Cesarani, David, and Eric J. Sundquist (eds.), *After the Holocaust: Challenging the Myth of Silence* (London: Routledge, 2012).

Chare, Nicholas, and Dominic Paul Williams (eds.), *Representing Auschwitz: At the Margins of Testimony* (Houndmills: Palgrave Macmillan, 2013).

Clay, Theresa Ast, 'The Liberators of Dachau', in Carolyn W. White (ed.), *Essays in European History: Selected from the Annual Meetings of the Southern Historical Association, 1990–1991* (Lanham: University Press of America, 1996), vol. 3, 79–117.

Cohen, Boaz, 'The Children's Voice: Postwar Collection of Testimonies from Child Survivors of the Holocaust', *Holocaust and Genocide Studies*, 21:1 (2007), 73–95.

Cohen, Gerard Daniel, 'Between Relief and Politics: Refugee Humanitarianism in Occupied Germany 1945–1946', *Journal of Contemporary History*, 43:3 (2008), 437–449.

—— *In War's Wake: Europe's Displaced Persons in the Postwar Order* (New York: Oxford University Press, 2012).

—— 'The Politics of Recognition: Jewish Refugees in Relief Policies and Human Rights Debates, 1945–1950', *Immigrants and Minorities*, 24:2 (2006), 125–143.

Cohen, Michael J., 'The Genesis of the Anglo-American Committee on Palestine, November 1945: A Case Study in the Assertion of American Hegemony', *Historical Journal*, 22:1 (1979), 185–207.

Comet, Theodore, 'Life Reborn in the Displaced Persons Camps (1945–51): An Untold Story of Courage', *Journal of Jewish Communal Service* (2000), 299–303.

Crago-Schneider, Kierra Mikaila, 'Jewish 'Shtetls' in Postwar Germany: An Analysis of Interactions among Jewish Displaced Persons, Germans, and Americans between 1945 and 1957 in Bavaria' (unpublished PhD thesis, University of California, Los Angeles, 2013).

Czech, Danuta, Stanisław Kłodziński, Aleksander Lasik and Andrzej Strzelecki, *Auschwitz 1940–1945: Central Issues in the History of the Camp, vol. 5: Epilogue* (Oświęcim: Auschwitz-Birkenau State Museum, 2000).

Dachauer Hefte, 1: Die Befreiung (Munich: dtv, 1993).

Dachauer Hefte, 5: Die vergessenen Lager (Munich: dtv, 1994).

Davidson, Shamai, *Holding on to Humanity – The Message of Holocaust Survivors: The Shamai Davidson Papers*, in Israel W. Charny (ed.) (New York: New York University Press, 1992).

Diner, Dan, 'Elemente der Subjektwerdung: Jüdische DPs in historischem Kontext', in Fritz Bauer Institut (ed.), *Überlebt und Unterwegs: Jüdische Displaced Persons im Nachkriegsdeutschland* (Frankfurt am Main: Campus Verlag, 1997), 229–249.

Diner, Hasia, 'Post-World-War-II American Jewry and the Confrontation with Catastrophe', *American Jewish History*, 91:3–4 (2003), 439–467.

Dinnerstein, Leonard, *America and the Survivors of the Holocaust* (New York: Columbia University Press, 1982).

—— 'The U.S. Army and the Jews: Policies Toward the Displaced Persons after World War II', *American Jewish History*, 68:3 (1979), 353–366.

Distel, Barbara, '29 April 1945: The Liberation of the Concentration Camp at Dachau', in Wolfgang Benz and Barbara Distel (eds.), *Dachau and the Nazi Terror 1933–1945, vol. 2: Studies and Reports* (Dachau: Verlag Dachauer Hefte, 2002), 9–17.

Dorland, Michael, *Cadaverland: Inventing a Pathology of Catastrophe for Holocaust Survival. The Limits of Medical Knowledge and Memory in France* (Waltham, MA: Brandeis University Press, 2009).

Douglas, Lawrence, *The Memory of Judgment: Making Law and History in the Trials of the Holocaust* (New Haven, CT: Yale University Press, 2001).

Drea, Edward J., 'Recognizing the Liberators: U.S. Army Divisions Enter the Concentration Camps', *Army History*, 24 (1992–93), 1–5.

Drywa, Danuta, *The Extermination of Jews in Stutthof Concentration Camp, 1939–1945*, trans. Tomasz S. Gałązka (Gdańsk: Stutthof Museum in Sztutowo, 2004).

Dublon-Knebel, Irith (ed.), *A Holocaust Crossroads: Jewish Women and Children in Ravensbrück* (London: Vallentine Mitchell, 2010).

Ducey, Corinne, 'The Representation of the Holocaust in the Soviet Press, 1941–1945', *Slavonica*, 14:2 (2008), 119–138.

Dwork, Debórah, and Robert Jan van Pelt, *Flight from the Reich: Refugee Jews, 1933–1946* (New York: W.W. Norton, 2009).

Eaglestone, Robert, *The Holocaust and the Postmodern* (Oxford: Oxford University Press, 2004).

Eley, Geoff, 'Europe after 1945', *History Workshop Journal*, 65 (2008), 195–212.

Engel, David, 'Palestine in the Mind of the Remnants of Polish Jewry', *Journal of Israeli History*, 16:3 (1995), 221–234.

Fassl, Peter, Markwart Herzog, and Jim G. Tobias (eds.), *Nach der Shoa: Jüdische Displaced Persons in Bayerisch-Schwaben 1945–1951* (Konstanz: UVK Verlagsgesellschaft, 2012).

Favez, Jean-Claude, *The Red Cross and the Holocaust* (Cambridge: Cambridge University Press, 1999).

Feinstein, Margarete Myers, 'Absent Fathers, Present Mothers: Images of Parenthood in Holocaust Survivor Narratives', *Nashim: A Journal of Jewish Women's Studies and Gender Issues*, 13 (2007), 155–182.

—— *Holocaust Survivors in Postwar Germany, 1945–1957* (Cambridge: Cambridge University Press, 2010).

—— 'Jewish Women Survivors in the Displaced Persons Camps of Occupied Germany: Transmitters of the Past, Caretakers of the Present, and Builders of the Future', *Shofar: An Interdisciplinary Journal of Jewish Studies*, 24:4 (2006), 67–89.

Fetthauer, Sophie, *Musik und Theater im DP-Camp Bergen-Belsen: Zum Kulturleben der jüdischen Displaced Persons 1945–1950* (Neumünster: von Bockel Verlag, 2012).

Finder, Gabriel N., 'Yizkor! Commemoration of the Dead by Jewish Displaced Persons in Postwar Germany', in Alon Confino, Paul Betts and Dirk Schumann (eds.), *Between Mass Death and Individual Loss: The Place of the Dead in Twentieth-Century Germany* (New York: Berghahn Books, 2008), 232–257.

Freund, Florian, *Concentration Camp Ebensee: Subcamp of Mauthausen*, 2nd edn (Vienna: Austrian Resistance Archives, 1998).

Fritz Bauer Institut (ed.), *Überlebt und Unterwegs: Jüdische Displaced Persons in Nachkriegsdeutschland* (Frankfurt am Main: Campus, 1997) [=Jahrbuch 1997 zur Geschichte und Wirkung des Holocaust].

Frunchak, Svetlana, 'Commemorating the Future in Post-War Chernivtsi', *East European Politics and Societies*, 24:3 (2010), 435–463.

Garbarini, Alexandra, *Numbered Days: Diaries and the Holocaust* (New Haven, CT: Yale University Press, 2006).

Gardiner, Juliet, *Wartime Britain 1939–1945* (London: Review, 2005).

Gatrell, Peter, 'Introduction: World Wars and Population Displacement in Europe in the Twentieth Century', *Contemporary European History*, 16:4 (2007), 415–426

Gay, Ruth, *Safe Among the Germans: Liberated Jews after World War II* (New Haven, CT: Yale University Press, 2002).

Geller, Jay Howard, *Jews in Post-Holocaust Germany, 1945–1953* (Cambridge: Cambridge University Press, 2005).

Gemie, Sharif, Fiona Reid and Laure Humbert, with Louise Ingram, *Outcast Europe: Refugees and Relief Workers in an Era of Total War 1936–48* (London: Continuum, 2012).

Giaccaria, Paolo and Claudio Minca (eds.), *Hitler's Geographies* (Chicago, IL: University of Chicago Press, 2015).

Giere, Jacqueline, '"We're On Our Way, But We're Not in the Wilderness"', in Michael Berenbaum and Abraham J. Peck (eds.), *The Holocaust and History: The Known, the Unknown, the Disputed, and the Reexamined* (Washington, DC: United States Holocaust Memorial Museum and Bloomington: Indiana University Press, 1998), 699–715.

Gigliotti, Simone, *The Train Journey: Transit, Captivity and Witnessing in the Holocaust* (New York: Berghahn Books, 2009).

Gilbert, Shirli, 'Buried Monuments: Yiddish Songs and Holocaust Memory', *History Workshop Journal*, 66 (2008), 107–128.

Gildea, Robert, *Marianne in Chains: Daily Life in the Heart of France During the German Occupation* (New York: Metropolitan Books, 2002).

Gill, Anton, *The Journey Back from Hell: Conversations with Concentration Camp Survivors* (London: HarperCollins, 1994).

Goeschel, Christian, and Nikolaus Wachsmann, 'Before Auschwitz: The Formation of the Nazi Concentration Camps, 1933–9', *Journal of Contemporary History*, 45:3 (2010), 515–534.

Gottlieb, Amy Zahl, *Men of Vision: Anglo-Jewry's Aid to Victims of the Nazi Regime 1933–1945* (London: Weidenfeld & Nicolson, 1998).

Gow, James, Milena Michalski and Rachel Kerr, 'Pictures of Peace and Justice from Nuremberg to the Holocaust: *Nuremberg: Its Lesson for Today, Memory of the Camps*, and *Majdanek:*

Cemetery of Europe – Missing Films, Memory Gaps and the Impact beyond the Courtroom of Visual Material in War Crimes Prosecutions', *History*, 98 (2013), 549–566.

Granata, Cora, 'Political Upheaval and Shifting Identities: Holocaust Survivors in the Soviet Occupied Zone of Germany, 1945–1949', in Sara R. Horowitz (ed.), *Lessons and Legacies, vol. 10: Back to the Sources: Reexamining Perpetrators, Victims, and Bystanders* (Evanston, IL: Northwestern University Press, 2012), 123–140.

Greiner, Bettina, and Alan Kramer (eds.), *Die Welt der Lager: Zur 'Erfolgsgeschichte' einer Institution* (Hamburg: Hamburger Edition, 2013).

Grobman, Alex, *Rekindling the Flame: American Jewish Chaplains and the Survivors of European Jewry, 1944–1948* (Detroit, MI: Wayne State University Press, 1993).

Grodzinsky, Yosef, *In the Shadow of the Holocaust: The Struggle between Jews and Zionists in the Aftermath of World War II* (Monroe, ME: Common Courage Press, 2004).

Grossmann, Atina, *Jews, Germans, and Allies: Close Encounters in Occupied Germany* (Princeton, NJ: Princeton University Press, 2007).

—— 'Victims, Villains, and Survivors: Gendered Perceptions and Self-Perceptions of Jewish Displaced Persons in Occupied Postwar Germany', in Dagmar Herzog (ed.), *Sexuality and German Fascism* (New York: Berghahn Books, 2005).

Gutman, Yisrael, and Michael Berenbaum (eds.), *Anatomy of the Auschwitz Death Camp* (Bloomington, IN: Indiana University Press, 1994).

Gutman, Yisrael, and Livia Rothkirchen (eds.), *The Catastrophe of European Jewry: Antecedents – History – Reflections* (New York: Ktav/Jerusalem: Yad Vashem, 1976).

Gutman, Yisrael, and Avital Saf (eds.), *The Nazi Concentration Camps: Structure and Aims, The Image of the Prisoner, The Jews in the Camps. Proceedings of the Fourth Yad Vashem International Historical Conference, Jerusalem, January 1980* (Jerusalem: Yad Vashem, 1984).

—— *She'erit Hapletah, 1944–1948: Rehabilitation and Struggle. Proceedings of the Sixth Yad Vashem International Historical Conference, Jerusalem, October 1985* (Jerusalem: Yad Vashem, 1990).

Gutterman, Bella, *A Narrow Bridge to Life: Jewish Forced Labor and Survival in the Gross-Rosen Camp System, 1940–1945* (New York: Berghahn Books, 2008).

Hadjisavvas, Eliana, '"The Strangest Episode in the Long History of This Island"': British Policy and the Cypriot Internment Camps, 1946–49' (unpublished MA thesis, University of Birmingham, 2013).

Handlin, Oscar, *A Continuing Task: The American Jewish Joint Distribution Committee 1914–1964* (New York: Random House, 1964).

Hartmann, Christian, *Operation Barbarossa: Nazi Germany's War in the East, 1941–1945* (Oxford: Oxford University Press, 2013).

Hayes, Peter 'Auschwitz: Capital of the Holocaust', *Holocaust and Genocide Studies*, 17:2 (2003), 330–350.

Herbert, Ulrich, Karin Orth and Christoph Dieckmann (eds.), *Die nationalsozialistischen Konzentrationslager: Entwicklung und Struktur*, 2 vols. (Frankfurt am Main: Fischer Taschenbuch Verlag, 2002).

Heß, Christiane et al. (eds.), *Kontinuitäten und Brüche: Neue Perspektiven auf die Geschichte der NS-Konzentrationslager* (Berlin: Metropol, 2011).

Hicks, Jeremy, *First Films of the Holocaust: Soviet Cinema and the Genocide of the Jews, 1938–1946* (Pittsburgh, PA: University of Pittsburgh Press, 2012).

—— '"Soul Destroyers": Soviet Reporting of Nazi Genocide and its Perpetrators at the Krasnodar and Khar'kov Trials', *History*, 98 (2013), 530–547.

—— '"Too Gruesome to be Fully Taken In": Konstantin Simonov's "The Extermination Camp" as Holocaust Literature', *Russian Review*, 72:2 (2013), 242–259.

Hilton, Laura J., 'The Experiences and Impact of the Stateless in the Postwar Period', *International Tracing Service Yearbook*, 4 (2015).

Hirsh, Michael, *The Liberators: America's Witnesses to the Holocaust* (New York: Bantam Books, 2010).

Hitchcock, William I., *Liberation: The Bitter Road to Freedom, Europe 1944–1945* (London: Faber & Faber, 2009).

Hochberg-Mariańska, Maria, and Noe Grüss (eds.), *The Children Accuse*, trans. Bill Johnston (London: Vallentine Mitchell, 1996).

Holian, Anna, 'The Ambivalent Exception: American Occupation Policy in Postwar Germany and the Formation of Jewish Refugee Spaces', *Journal of Refugee Studies*, 25:3 (2012), 452–473.

—— 'Anticommunism in the Streets: Refugee Politics in Cold War Germany', *Journal of Contemporary History*, 45:1 (2010), 134–161.

—— *Between National Socialism and Soviet Communism: Displaced Persons in Postwar Germany* (Ann Arbor, MI: University of Michigan Press, 2011).

—— 'Displacement and the Post-war Reconstruction of Education: Displaced Persons at the UNRRA University in Munich', *Contemporary European History*, 17:2 (2008), 167–195.

Holmila, Antero, *Reporting the Holocaust in the British, Swedish and Finnish Press, 1945–50* (Houndmills: Palgrave Macmillan, 2011).

Hördler, Stefan, 'Die Rationalisierung des KZ-Systems 1943–1945: Arbeitsfähigkeit und Arbeitsunfähigkeit als ordnende Selektionskriterien', in Marc Buggeln and Michael Wildt (eds.), *Arbeit im Nationalsozialismus* (Oldenbourg: De Gruyter, 2014), 349–370.

Horwitz, Gordon J., *In the Shadow of Death: Living Outside the Gates of Mauthausen* (New York: Free Press, 1990).

Hyman, Abraham S., *The Undefeated* (Jerusalem: Gefen, 1993).

Ioanid, Radu, *The Holocaust in Romania: The Destruction of Jews and Gypsies under the Antonescu Regime, 1940–1944* (Chicago, IL: Ivan R. Dee, 2000).

Ionescu, Ştefan, 'În umbra morţii: memoria supravieţuitorilor Holocaustului din România', *Studia Hebraica*, 4 (2004), 362–390.

Jacobmeyer, Wolfgang, 'Jüdische Überlebende als "Displaced Persons": Untersuchungen zur Besatzungspolitik in den deutschen Westzonen und zur Zuwanderung osteuropäischer Juden 1945–1947', *Geschichte und Gesellschaft*, 9 (1983), 421–452.

—— 'Die Lager der jüdischen Displaced Persons in den deutschen Westzonen 1946/47 als Ort jüdischen Gemeinden im Kalten Krieg', in Micha Brumlik, Doron Kiesel, Cilly Kugelmann, and Julius H. Schoeps (eds.), *Jüdisches Leben in Deutschland seit 1945* (Frankfurt am Main: Athenäum, 1986), 31–48.

Jahr, Christoph, and Jens Thiel (eds.), *Lager vor Auschwitz: Gewalt und Integration im 20. Jahrhundert* (Berlin: Metropol, 2013).

Janco, Andrew Paul, ' "Unwilling": The One-Word Revolution in Refugee Status, 1940–1951', *Contemporary European History*, 23:3 (2014), 429–446.

Jarausch, Konrad H., and Michael Geyer, *Shattered Past: Reconstructing German Histories* (Princeton: Princeton University Press, 2003).

Jockusch, Laura, *Collect and Record: Jewish Holocaust Documentation in Early Postwar Europe* (New York: Oxford University Press, 2012).

—— 'Historiography in Transit: Survivor Historians and the Writing of Holocaust History in the Late 1940s', *Leo Baeck Institute Yearbook*, 58 (2013), 75–94.

—— 'Memorialization through Documentation: Holocaust Commemoration among Jewish Displaced Persons in Allied-Occupied Germany', in Bill Niven, and Chloe Paver (eds.), *Memorialization in Germany since 1945* (Houndmills: Palgrave Macmillan, 2010), 181–191.

Jockusch, Laura, and Tamar Lewinsky, 'Paradise Lost? Postwar Memory of Polish Jewish Survival in the Soviet Union', *Holocaust and Genocide Studies*, 24:3 (2010), 373–399.

Josephs, Zoe, *Survivors: Jewish Refugees in Birmingham 1933–1945* (Warley: Meridian Books, 1988)

Judt, Tony, *Postwar: A History of Europe since 1945* (London: William Heinemann, 2005).

—— *Reappraisals: Reflections on the Forgotten Twentieth Century* (London: Vintage Books, 2009).

Kassow, Samuel D., *Who Will Write Our History? Rediscovering a Hidden Archive from the Warsaw Ghetto* (London: Penguin, 2009).

Kavanaugh, Sarah, *ORT and the Rehabilitation of Holocaust Survivors* (London: Vallentine Mitchell, 2008).

—— 'ORT and the Rehabilitation of Holocaust Survivors: From the DP Camps to Israel', in Rachel Bracha, Adi Drori-Avraham and Geoffrey Yantian (eds.), *Educating for Life: New Chapters in the History of ORT* (London: World ORT, 2010), 164–180.

Kellenbach, Katharina von, *The Mark of Cain: Guilt and Denial in the Post-War Lives of Nazi Perpetrators* (New York: Oxford University Press, 2013).

Kemp, Paul, 'The Liberation of Bergen-Belsen Concentration Camp in April 1945: The Testimony of Those Involved', *Imperial War Museum Review*, 5 (1990), 28–41.

Kilby, Jane, and Antony Rowland (eds.), *The Future of Testimony* (London: Routledge, 2014).

Kittel, Sabine, 'Liberation – Survival – Freedom: Jewish Prisoners of Ravensbrück Concentration Camp Recall Their Liberation', in Irith Dublon-Knebel (ed.), *A Holocaust Crossroads: Jewish Women and Children in Ravensbrück* (London: Vallentine Mitchell, 2010).

Klier, John, 'The Holocaust and the Soviet Union', in Dan Stone (ed.), *The Historiography of the Holocaust* (Houndmills: Palgrave Macmillan, 2004), 276–295.

Knigge, Volkhard, 'Kultur und Ausgrenzung: Zur Geschichte des KZ Buchenwald auf dem Ettersberg bei Weimar', in Getrud Koch (ed.), *Bruchlinien: Tendenzen der Holocaustforschung* (Cologne: Böhlau Verlag, 1999), 201–229.

Kochavi, Arieh J., Anglo-American Discord: Jewish Refugees and United Nations Relief and Rehabilitation Administration Policy, 1945–1947', *Diplomatic History*, 14:4 (1990), 529–552.

—— 'Britain and the Illegal Immigration to Palestine from France following World War II', *Holocaust and Genocide Studies*, 6:4 (1991), 383–396.

—— 'Britain's Image Campaign against the Zionists', *Journal of Contemporary History*, 36:2 (2001), 293–307.

—— 'British Diplomats and the Jews in Poland, Romania and Hungary during the Communist Takeovers', *East European Quarterly*, 29:4 (1995), 449–464.

—— 'British Policy on Non–Repatriable Displaced Persons in Germany and Austria, 1945-7', *European History Quarterly*, 21 (1991), 365–382.

—— 'British Response to the Involvement of the American Jewish Joint Distribution Committee in Illegal Jewish Immigration to Palestine', *Immigrants and Minorities*, 8:3 (1989), 223–234.

—— 'The Displaced Persons Problem and the Formulation of British Policy in Palestine', *Studies in Zionism: Politics, Society, Culture*, 10:1 (1989), 31–48.

—— 'Indirect Pressure: Moscow and the End of the British Mandate in Palestine', *Israel Affairs*, 10:1–2 (2004), 60–76.

—— 'Liberation and Dispersal', in Peter Hayes and John K. Roth (eds.), *The Oxford Handbook of Holocaust Studies* (Oxford: Oxford University Press, 2010), 509–523.

—— *Post-Holocaust Politics: Britain, the United States, and Jewish Refugees, 1945–1948* (Chapel Hill, NC: University of North Carolina Press, 2001).

—— 'The Struggle against Jewish Immigration to Palestine', *Middle Eastern Studies*, 34:3 (1998), 146–167.

Kolinsky, Eva, 'Jewish Holocaust Survivors between Liberation and Resettlement', in Johannes-Dieter Steinert and Inge Weber-Newth (eds.), *European Immigrants in Britain 1933–1950* (Munich: K.G. Saur, 2003), 121–136.

—— 'Jews in Germany, 1945–1950' (unpublished ms).

—— *After the Holocaust: Jewish Survivors in Germany after 1945* (London: Pimlico, 2004).

—— Experiences of Survival', *Leo Baeck Institute Yearbook*, 44 (1999), 245–270.

Kondoyanidi, Anita, 'The Liberating Experience: War Correspondents, Red Army Soldiers, and the Nazi Extermination Camps', *Russian Review*, 69:3 (2010), 438–462.

Konieczny, Alfred, *Frauen im Konzentrationslager Groß-Rosen in den Jahren 1944–1945* (Wałbrzych: Państwowe Muzeum Gross-Rosen, 1994).

Königseder, Angelika, *Flucht nach Berlin: Jüdische Displaced Persons 1945–1948* (Berlin: Metropol, 1998).

Königseder, Angelika, and Juliane Wetzel, *Waiting for Hope: Jewish Displaced Persons in Post-World War II Germany* (Evanston: Northwestern University Press, 2001).

Kotek, Joël and Pierre Rigoulot, *Le siècle des camps: Détention, concentration, extermination. Cent ans de mal radical* (Paris: J. C. Lattès, 2000).

Kranz, Tomasz, 'Between Planning and Implementation: The Lublin District and Majdanek Camp in Nazi Policy', in Larry V. Thompson (ed.), *Lessons and Legacies, vol. 4: Reflections on Religion, Justice, Sexuality, and Genocide* (Evanston, IL: Northwestern University Press, 2003), 215–235.

Kushner, Tony, 'Anti-Semitism and Austerity: The August 1947 Riots in Britain', in Panikos Panayi (ed.), *Racial Violence in Britain in the Nineteenth and Twentieth Centuries*, rev. edn. (London: Leicester University Press, 1996), 150–170.

—— *The Holocaust and the Liberal Imagination: A Social and Cultural History* (Oxford: Blackwell, 1994).

Kushner, Tony, and Katherine Knox, *Refugees in an Age of Genocide: Global, National and Local Perspectives during the Twentieth Century* (London: Frank Cass, 1999).

Laczó, Ferenc, 'Articulating the Unprecedented: Hungarian Jewish Witness Accounts from 1945–46 on Key Features of the Holocaust', *Dapim: Studies on the Shoah* (forthcoming).

—— 'Documenting Responsibility: Jenő Lévai and the Birth of Holocaust Historiography in Hungary during the 1940s', *Holocaust Studies* (forthcoming).

—— ' "I could hardly wait to get out of this camp, even though I knew it would only get worse until liberation came": On Hungarian Jewish Accounts of the Buchenwald Concentration Camp from 1945–46', *Hungarian Historical Review*, 2:3 (2013), 605–638.

Lagrou, Pieter, *The Legacy of Nazi Occupation: Patriotic Memory and National Recovery in Western Europe, 1945–1965* (Cambridge: Cambridge University Press, 2000).

—— 'Victims of Genocide and National Memory: Belgium, France and The Netherlands 1945–1965', *Past and Present*, 154 (1997), 181–222.

Lang, Berel, *The Future of the Holocaust: Between History and Memory* (Ithaca, NY: Cornell University Press, 1999).

Lang, Hans-Joachim, *Die namen der Nummern: Wie es gelang, die 86 Opfer eines NS-Verbrechen zu identifizieren* (Hamburg: Hoffmann und Campe, 2004).

Langbein, Hermann, *People in Auschwitz* (Chapel Hill, NC: University of North Carolina Press, 2004).

Langer, Lawrence L., *Holocaust Testimonies: The Ruins of Memory* (New Haven, CT: Yale University Press, 1991).

Lanzmann, Claude, *Shoah: The Complete Text of the Film* (New York: Pantheon Books, 1985).

Lavsky, Hagit, 'The Day After: Bergen-Belsen from Concentration Camp to the Centre of the Jewish Survivors in Germany', *German History*, 11:1 (1993), 36–59.

—— 'The Experience of the Displaced Persons in Bergen-Belsen: Unique or Typical Case?', in Avinoam J. Patt, and Michael Berkowitz (eds.), *'We are Here': New Approaches to Jewish Displaced Persons in Postwar Germany* (Detroit, MI: Wayne State University Press, 2010), 227–256.

—— *New Beginnings: Holocaust Survivors in Bergen-Belsen and the British Zone in Germany, 1945–1950* (Detroit, MI: Wayne State University Press, 2002).

Le Chêne, Evelyn, *Mauthausen: The History of a Death Camp* (London: Methuen & Co., 1971).

Leff, Laurel, ' "Liberated by the Yanks": The Holocaust as an American Story in Postwar News Articles', *Journal of Ecumenical Studies*, 40:4 (2003), 407–430.

—— 'When the Facts Didn't Speak for Themselves: The Holocaust in the *New York Times*, 1939–1945', *Harvard International Journal of Press Politics*, 5:2 (2000), 52–72.

Levi, Primo, *The Drowned and the Saved* (London: Abacus, 1989).

Liebman, Stuart, 'Documenting the Liberation of the Camps: The Case of Aleksander Ford's *Vernichtungslager Majdanek – Cmentarzysko Europy* (1944)', in Dagmar Herzog (ed.), *Lessons and Legacies, vol. 7: The Holocaust in International Perspective* (Evanston: Northwestern University Press, 2006), 333–351.

Litvak, Yosef, 'Polish-Jewish Refugees Repatriated from the Soviet Union at the End of the Second World War and Afterwards', in Norman Davies and Antony Polonsky (eds.), *Jews in Eastern Poland and the USSR, 1939–46* (London: Macmillan, 1991), 227–239.

Longerich, Peter, 'Davon haben wir nichts gewusst!' Die Deutschen und die Judenverfolgung 1933-1945 (Munich: Siedler, 2006).

Losson, Nicolas, and Annette Michelson, 'Notes on the Images of the Camps', October, 90 (1999), 25-35.

Lowe, Keith, Savage Continent: Europe in the Aftermath of World War II (London: Viking, 2012).

MacAuslan, Olivia Gemei Rowan, 'Some Aspects of the Medical Relief of Belsen Concentration Camp April–May 1945' (unpublished MPhil thesis, Birkbeck College, University of London, 2012).

MacDonald, Richard, Inside the Gates: The Nazi Concentration Camp at Ebensee, Austria (Bloomington, IN: XLibris, 2010).

MacDonogh, Giles, After the Reich: From the Liberation of Vienna to the Berlin Airlift (London: John Murray, 2007).

Mahoney, Kevin (ed.), 1945: The Year of Liberation (Washington, DC: United States Holocaust Memorial Museum, 1995).

Mankowitz, Ze'ev W., 'The Affirmation of Life in She'erith Hapleita', Holocaust and Genocide Studies, 5, 1 (1990), 13-21.

—— Life Between Memory and Hope: The Survivors of the Holocaust in Occupied Germany (Cambridge: Cambridge University Press, 2002).

Marrus, Michael R., The Holocaust in History (Rickmansworth: Penguin, 1989).

—— The Unwanted: European Refugees in the Twentieth Century (New York: Oxford University Press, 1985).

Maršálek, Hans, Die Geschichte des Konzentrationslagers Mauthausen, 3rd edn (Vienna: Österreichischen Lagergemeinschaft Mauthausen, 1995).

—— Gusen: Vorraum zur Hölle. Ein Nebenlager des Konzentrationslagers Mauthausen, 2nd edn (Vienna: Österreichischen Lagergemeinschaft Mauthausen, 1987).

Marszałek, Józef, Majdanek: The Concentration Camp in Lublin (Warsaw: Interpress, 1986).

Michalczyk, John J., Filming the End of the Holocaust: Allied Documentaries, Nuremberg and the Liberation of the Concentration Camps (London: Bloomsbury, 2014).

Michman, Dan, Holocaust Historiography: A Jewish Perspective. Conceptualizations, Terminology, Approaches and Fundamental Issues (London: Vallentine Mitchell, 2003).

—— 'She'erit Hapletah, 1944-1948: Rehabilitation and Political Struggle', Holocaust and Genocide Studies, 7:1 (1993), 107-116.

Moeller, Robert G., War Stories: The Search for a Usable Past in the Federal Republic of Germany (Berkeley, CA: University of California Press, 2001).

Morrison, Jack G., Ravensbrück: Everyday Life in a Women's Concentration Camp 1939-45 (Princeton, NJ: Markus Wiener, 2000).

Morsch, Günter, and Alfred Reckendrees (eds.), Befreiung Sachsenhausen 1945 (Berlin: Hentrich, 1996).

Moyn, Samuel, 'In the Aftermath of Camps', in Frank Biess and Robert G. Moeller (eds.), Histories of the Aftermath: The Legacies of the Second World War in Europe (New York: Berghahn Books, 2010), 49-64.

Myers, Margarete L., 'Jewish Displaced Persons: Reconstructing Individual and Community in the US Zone of Occupied Germany', Leo Baeck Institute Yearbook, 42 (1997), 303-324.

Netz, Reviel, Barbed Wire: An Ecology of Modernity (Middletown, CT: Wesleyan University Press, 2004).

Niven, Bill, The Buchenwald Child: Truth, Fiction, and Propaganda (Rochester, NY: Camden House, 2007).

Niven, Bill (ed.), Germans as Victims: Remembering the Past in Contemporary Germany (Houndmills: Palgrave Macmillan, 2006).

Ofer, Dalia, 'Holocaust Survivors as Immigrants: The Case of Israel and the Cyprus Detainees', Modern Judaism, 16:1 (1996), 1-23.

Ofer, Dalia, Françoise S. Ouzan, and Judith Tydor Baumel-Schwartz (eds.), Holocaust Survivors: Resettlement, Memories, Identities (New York: Berghahn Books, 2012).

Olick, Jeffrey K., In the House of the Hangman: The Agonies of German Defeat, 1943-1949 (Chicago, IL: University of Chicago Press, 2005).

Orgeron, Marsha, 'Liberating Images? Samuel Fuller's Film of Falkenau Concentration Camp', *Film Quarterly*, 60:2 (2006), 38–47.

Orth, Karin, *Das System der nationalsozialistischen Konzentrationslager: Eine politische Organisationsgeschichte* (Zürich: Pendo, 2002).

Ossenberg, Uwe, *The Document Holdings of the International Tracing Service* (Bad Arolsen: ITS, 2009).

Ouzan, Françoise, 'Rebuilding Jewish Identities in Displaced Persons Camps in Germany, 1945–1957', *Bulletin du Centre de recherche français à Jérusalem*, 14 (2004), 98–111.

Overy, Richard 'The Concentration Camp: An International Perspective', *Eurozine* (2011).

Patt, Avinoam J., *Finding Home and Homeland: Jewish Youth and Zionism in the Aftermath of the Holocaust* (Detroit, MI: Wayne State University Press, 2009).

Patt, Avinoam J., and Michael Berkowitz (eds.), *'We are Here': New Approaches to Jewish Displaced Persons in Postwar Germany* (Detroit, MI: Wayne State University Press, 2010).

Peck, Abraham J., 'Jewish Survivors of the Holocaust in Germany: Revolutionary Vanguard or Remnants of a Destroyed People?', *Tel Aviver Jahrbuch für deutsche Geschichte*, 19 (1990), 33–45.

—— 'Liberated But Not Free: Jewish Displaced Persons in Germany after 1945', in Walter H. Pehle (ed.), *November 1938: From 'Kristallnacht' to Genocide* (New York: Berg, 1991), 222–235.

—— '"Our Eyes Have Seen Eternity": Memory and Self-Identity among the She'erith Hapletah', *Modern Judaism*, 17:1 (1997), 57–74.

Person, Katarzyna, *ORT and the Rehabilitation of Holocaust Survivors: ORT Activities 1945–1956* (London: World ORT, 2012).

Pines, Dinora, *A Woman's Unconscious Use of Her Body: A Psychoanalytical Perspective* (London: Virago, 1993).

Plesch, Dan, *America, Hitler and the UN: How the Allies Won World War II and Forged a Peace* (London: I.B. Tauris, 2010).

Plotkin, Diane, 'The *Kinderheim* of Bergen-Belsen', in Michael A. Grodin (ed.), *Jewish Medical Resistance in the Holocaust* (New York: Berghahn Books, 2014), 206–218.

Polian, Pavel, 'The Internment of Returning Soviet Prisoners of War after 1945', in Bob Moore and Barbara Hately-Broad (eds.), *Prisoners of War, Prisoners of Peace: Captivity, Homecoming and Memory in World War II* (Oxford: Berg, 2005), 123–139.

Portelli, Alessandro, *The Order Has Been Carried Out: History, Memory, and Meaning of a Nazi Massacre in Rome* (New York: Palgrave Macmillan, 2003).

Potter, Lou, with William Miles and Nina Rosenblum, *Liberators: Fighting on Two Fronts in World War II* (New York: Harcourt Brace Jovanovich, 1992).

Reichel, Peter, *Politik mit der Erinnerung: Gedächtnisorte im Streit um die nationalsozialistische Vergangenheit* (Munich: Carl Hanser Verlag, 1995).

Reif-Spirek, Peter, and Bodo Ritscher (eds.), *Speziallager in der SBZ: Gedenkstätten mit 'doppelter Vergangenheit'* (Berlin: Christoph Links Verlag, 1999).

Reilly, Joanne, *Belsen: The Liberation of a Concentration Camp* (London: Routledge, 1998).

Reilly, Jo, David Cesarani, Tony Kushner and Colin Richmond (eds.), *Belsen in History and Memory* (London: Frank Cass, 1997).

Reinisch, Jessica, '"Auntie UNRRA" at the Crossroads', *Past and Present*, Supplement 8 (2013), 70–97.

—— 'Internationalism in Relief: The Birth (and Death) of UNRRA', *Past and Present*, Supplement 6 (2011), 258–89.

—— *The Perils of Peace: The Public Health Crisis in Occupied Germany* (Oxford: Oxford University Press, 2013).

Reinisch, Jessica, and Elizabeth White (eds.), *The Disentanglement of Populations: Migration, Expulsion and Displacement in Post-War Europe, 1944–9* (Houndmills: Palgrave Macmillan, 2011).

Riera, Monica, and Gavin Schaffer (eds.), *The Lasting War: Society and Identity in Britain, France and Germany after 1945* (Houndmills: Palgrave Macmillan, 2008).

Roseman, Mark, '". . . but of revenge not a sign": Germans' Fear of Jewish Revenge after World War II', *Jahrbuch für Antisemitismusforschung*, 22 (2013), 79–95.

Rosen, Alan *The Wonder of Their Voices: The 1946 Holocaust Interviews of David Boder* (New York: Oxford University Press, 2010).

Rosensaft, Menachem Z. (ed.), *Life Reborn: Jewish Displaced Persons 1945–1951* (Washington, DC: United States Holocaust Memorial Museum, 2001).

Rotman, Liviu, 'Romanian Jewry: The First Decade after the Holocaust', in Randolph L. Braham (ed.), *The Tragedy of Romanian Jewry* (New York: Columbia University Press, 1994), 287–331.

Rotman, Liviu, Camelia Crăciun and Ana-Gabriela Vasiliu (eds.), *Noi perspective în istoriografia evreilor din România* (Bucharest: Hasefer, 2010).

Rudorff, Andrea, *Frauen in den Außenlagern des Konzentrationslagers Groß-Rosen* (Berlin: Metropol, 2014).

Rutland, Suzanne, 'Postwar Anti-Jewish Refugee Hysteria: A Case of Racial or Religious Bigotry?', *Journal of Australian Studies*, 27:1 (2003), 69–79.

—— 'Resettling the Survivors of the Holocaust in Australia', *Holocaust Studies*, 16:3 (2011), 33–56.

—— 'Subtle Exclusions: Postwar Jewish Emigration to Australia and the Impact of the IRO Scheme', *Journal of Holocaust Education*, 10:1 (2001), 50–66.

—— '"The Unwanted": Pre- and Post-World War II Migration to Australia', *Yalkut Moreshet*, 4 (2006), 9–27.

Rutland, Suzanne D., and Sol Encel, 'No Room at the Inn: American Responses to Australian Immigration Policies, 1946–54', *Patterns of Prejudice*, 43:5 (2009), 497–518.

Sachar, Abram L., *The Redemption of the Unwanted: From the Liberation of the Death Camps to the Founding of Israel* (New York: St Martin's/Marek, 1983).

Saidel, Rochelle G. (ed.), *The Jewish Women of Ravensbrück Concentration Camp* (Madison, WI: University of Wisconsin Press, 2004).

Salvatici, Silvia, '"Help the People to Help Themselves": UNRRA Relief Workers and European Displaced Persons', *Journal of Refugee Studies*, 25:3 (2012), 428–451.

Schaffer, Gavin, *Racial Science and British Society, 1930–62* (Houndmills: Palgrave Macmillan, 2008).

Schlichting, Nicola, *'Öffnet die Tore von Erez Israel': Das jüdische DP-Camp Belsen 1945–1948* (Nuremberg: Antogo Verlag, 2005).

Schulze, Rainer, 'A Difficult Interlude: Relations between British Military Government and the German Population and Their Effects for the Constitution of a Democratic Society', in Alan Bance (ed.), *The Cultural Legacy of the British Occupation in Germany: The London Symposium* (Stuttgart: Verlag Hans-Dieter Heinz/Akademischer Verlag, 1997), 67–109.

Schwarz, Ghita, *Displaced Persons: A Novel* (New York: William Morrow, 2010).

Selzer, Michael, *Deliverance Day: The Last Hours at Dachau* (Philadelphia, PA: J.B. Lippincott Company, 1978).

Sereny, Gitta, *The German Trauma: Experiences and Reflections 1938–2000* (London: Allen Lane, 2000).

Shandler, Jeffrey, 'The Testimony of Images: The Allied Liberation of Nazi Concentration Camps in American Newsreels', in Robert Moses Shapiro (ed.), *Why Didn't the Press Shout? American and International Journalism during the Holocaust* (New York: Ktav, 2003), 109–125.

Shapiro, Paul A., 'Vapniarka: The Archive of the International Tracing Service and the Holocaust in the East', *Holocaust and Genocide Studies*, 27:1 (2013), 114–137.

Shephard, Ben, *After Daybreak: The Liberation of Belsen, 1945* (London: Jonathan Cape, 2005).

—— *The Long Road Home: The Aftermath of the Second World War* (London: Vintage, 2011).

Shik, Na'ama, 'Infinite Loneliness: Some Aspects of the Lives of Jewish Women in the Auschwitz Camps According to Testimonies and Autobiographies Written between 1945 and 1948', in Doris L. Bergen (ed.), *Lessons and Legacies, vol. 8: From Generation to Generation* (Evanston, IL: Northwestern University Press, 2008), 125–156.

Shneer, David, 'Ghostly Landscapes: Soviet Liberators Photograph the Holocaust', *Humanity: An International Journal of Human Rights, Humanitarianism, and Development*, 5:2 (2014), 235–246.

—— *Through Soviet Jewish Eyes: Photography, War, and the Holocaust* (New Brunswick: Rutgers University Press, 2011).

Sofsky, Wolfgang, *The Order of Terror: The Concentration Camp* (Princeton, NJ: Princeton University Press, 1997).

Somers, Erik, and René Kok (eds.), *Jewish Displaced Persons in Camp Bergen-Belsen 1945–1950: The Unique Photo Album of Zippy Orlin* (Seattle, WA: University of Washington Press, 2004).

Sprenger, Isabell, *Groß-Rosen: Ein Konzentrationslager in Schlesien* (Cologne: Böhlau Verlag, 1996).

Stafford, David, *Endgame 1945: Victory, Retribution, Liberation* (London: Abacus, 2008).

Stats, Katrina, ' "Characteristically Generous?": Australian Responses to Refugees Prior to 1951', *Australian Journal of Politics and History*, 60:2 (2014), 177–193.

Steimatsky, Noa, 'The Cinecittà Refugee Camp (1944–1950)', *October*, 128 (2009), 23–50.

Steinbacher, Sybille, *Auschwitz: A History* (London: Penguin, 2005).

Steinert, Johannes-Dieter, 'British Humanitarian Assistance: Wartime Planning and Postwar Realities', *Journal of Contemporary History*, 43:3 (2008), 421–435.

Stern Frank, 'The Historic Triangle: Occupiers, Germans and Jews in Postwar Germany', in Robert G. Moeller (ed.), *West Germany under Construction: Politics, Society, and Culture in the Adenauer Era* (Ann Arbor: University of Michigan Press, 1997), 199–229.

—— *The Whitewashing of the Yellow Badge: Antisemitism and Philosemitism in Postwar Germany* (Oxford: Pergamon Press, 1992).

Stone, Dan, 'Christianstadt: Slave Labor and the Holocaust in the ITS Collections', *Yearbook of the International Tracing Service*, 4 (2015).

—— 'Cold War Ideas', *Contemporary European History*, 22:4 (2013), 675–686.

—— *The Concentration Camp: A Very Short Introduction* (Oxford: Oxford University Press, forthcoming 2016).

—— *Constructing the Holocaust: A Study in Historiography* (London: Vallentine Mitchell, 2003).

—— *Goodbye to All That? The Story of Europe since 1945* (Oxford: Oxford University Press, 2014).

—— 'The Harmony of Barbarism: Locating the Scrolls of Auschwitz in Holocaust Historiography', in Nicholas Chare, and Dominic Williams (eds.), *Representing Auschwitz: At the Margins of Testimony* (Houndmills: Palgrave Macmillan, 2013), 11–32.

—— *Histories of the Holocaust* (Oxford: Oxford University Press, 2010).

—— *History, Memory and Mass Atrocity: Essays on the Holocaust and Genocide* (London: Vallentine Mitchell, 2006).

—— *The Holocaust, Fascism and Memory: Essays in the History of Ideas* (Houndmills: Palgrave Macmillan, 2013).

—— *Responses to Nazism in Britain 1933–1939: Before War and Holocaust*, 2nd edn (Houndmills: Palgrave Macmillan, 2012).

Stone, Dan (ed.), *The Historiography of Genocide* (Houndmills: Palgrave Macmillan, 2008).

—— *The Historiography of the Holocaust* (Houndmills: Palgrave Macmillan, 2004).

—— *The Holocaust and Historical Methodology* (New York: Berghahn Books, 2012).

—— *The Oxford Handbook of Postwar European History* (Oxford: Oxford University Press, 2012).

Struk, Janina, *Photographing the Holocaust: Interpretations of the Evidence* (London: I.B. Tauris, 2004).

Strzelecki, Andrzej, 'L'Evacuation, la liquidation et la liberation du camp', in Franciszek Piper, and Teresa Świebocka (eds.), *Auschwitz: Camp de concentration et d'extermination* (Oświęcim: Le Musée d'Auschwitz-Birkenau, 1994), 294–316.

—— *The Evacuation, Dismantling and Liberation of KL Auschwitz* (Oświęcim: Auschwitz-Birkenau State Museum, 2001).

Suderland, Maja, *Inside Concentration Camps: Social Life at the Extremes* (Cambridge: Polity Press, 2013).

Taylor, Frederick, *Exorcising Hitler: The Occupation and Denazification of Germany* (London: Bloomsbury, 2012).

Tec, Nechama, *Defiance: The Bielski Partisans* (New York: Oxford University Press, 1993).

—— *Resilience and Courage: Women, Men, and the Holocaust* (New Haven, CT: Yale University Press, 2003).

Thaler, Henri Lustiger, 'History and Memory: The Orthodox Experience in the Bergen-Belsen Displaced Persons Camp', *Holocaust and Genocide Studies*, 27:1 (2013), 30–56.

Tobias, Jim G., *Der Kibbutz auf dem Streicher-Hof: Die vergessene Geschichte der jüdischen Kollektivfarmen 1945–48* (Nuremberg: n.p., 1997).

—— *Neue Heimat Down Under: Die Migration jüdischer Displaced Persons nach Australien* (Nuremberg: Antogo Verlag, 2013).

—— *Vorübergehende Heimat im Land der Täter: Jüdische DP-Camps in Franken 1945–1949* (Nuremberg: Antogo Verlag, 2002).

Tobias, Jim G., and Nicola Schlichting, *Heimat auf Zeit: Jüdische Kinder in Rosenheim 1946–47* (Nuremberg: Antogo Verlag, 2006).

Tobias, Jim G., and Peter Zinke, *Nakam: Jüdische Rache am NS-Tätern* (Hamburg: Konkret Literatur Verlag, 2000).

Trepman, E., 'Rescue of the Remnants: The British Emergency Medical Relief Operation in Belsen Camp 1945', *Journal of the Royal Army Medical Corps*, 21:3 (2001), 281–293.

Tzahor, Zeev, 'Holocaust Survivors as a Political Factor', *Middle Eastern Studies*, 24:4 (1988), 432–444.

United States Holocaust Memorial Museum, *Children and the Holocaust* (Washington, DC: United States Holocaust Memorial Museum, 2004).

Van Pelt, Robert Jan, and Debórah Dwork, *Auschwitz 1270 to the Present* (New Haven, CT: Yale University Press, 1996).

Vella, E.E., 'Belsen: Medical Aspects of a World War II Concentration Camp', *Journal of the Royal Army Medical Corps*, 130:1 (1984), 34–59.

Vernant, Jacques, *The Refugee in the Post-War World* (London: George Allen & Unwin, 1953).

Von Plato, Alexander, Almut Leh and Christoph Thonfeld (eds.), *Hitler's Slaves: Life Stories of Forced Labourers in Nazi-Occupied Europe* (New York: Berghahn Books, 2010).

Wachsmann, Nikolaus, *KL: A History of the Nazi Concentration Camps* (London: Little, Brown, 2015).

Waxman, Zoe Vania, *Writing the Holocaust: Identity, Testimony, Representation* (Oxford: Oxford University Press, 2006).

Webster, Ronald, 'American Relief and Jews in Germany, 1945–1960: Diverging Perspectives', *Leo Baeck Institute Yearbook*, 38 (1993), 293–321.

Weckel, Ulrike, 'Disappointed Hopes for Spontaneous Mass Conversions: German Responses to Allied Atrocity Film Screenings, 1945–46', *Bulletin of the German Historical Institute, Washington DC*, 51 (2012), 39–53.

Wetzel, Juliane, ' "Displaced Persons": Ein vergessenes Kapitel der deutschen Nachkriegsgeschichte', *Aus Politik und Zeitgeschichte* (10 February 1995), 34–39.

—— ' "Mir szeinen doh": München und Umgebung als Zuflucht von Überlebenden des Holocaust 1945–1948', in Martin Broszat, Klaus-Dietmar Henke and Hans Woller (eds.), *Von Stalingrad zur Währungsreform: Zur Sozialgeschichte des Umbruchs in Deutschland* (Munich: Oldenbourg, 1988), 327–364.

—— 'An Uneasy Existence: Jewish Survivors in Germany after 1945', in Hanna Schissler (ed.), *The Miracle Years: A Cultural History of West Germany, 1949–1968* (Princeton, NJ: Princeton University Press, 2001), 131–144.

Weinrib, Laura M. (ed.), *Nitzotz: The Spark of Resistance in Kovno Ghetto and Dachau-Kaufering Concentration Camp* (Syracuse, NY: Syracuse University Press, 2009).

Wierling, Dorothee, 'The War in Postwar Society: The Role of the Second World War in Public and Private Spheres in the Soviet Occupation Zone and Early GDR', in Jörg

Echternkamp, and Stefan Martens (eds.), *Experience and Memory: The Second World War in Europe* (New York: Berghahn Books, 2010), 214–228.

Wieviorka, Annette, *Déportation et génocide: Entre la mémoire et l'oubli* (Paris: Plon, 1992).

Wünschmann, Kim, 'Cementing the Enemy Category: Arrest and Imprisonment of German Jews in Nazi Concentration Camps, 1933–1938/9', *Journal of Contemporary History*, 45:3 (2010), 576–600.

—— 'Die Konzentrationslagererfahrungen deutsch-jüdischer Männer nach dem Novemberpogrom 1938: Geschlechtergeschichtliche Überlegungen zu männlichem Selbstverständnis und Rollenbild', in Susanne Heim, Beate Meyer and Francis R. Nicosia (eds.), *'Wer bleibt, opfert seine Jahre, vielleicht sein Leben': Deutsche Juden 1938–1941* (Göttingen: Wallstein Verlag, 2010), 39–58.

Wyman, David, *DPs: Europe's Displaced Persons, 1945–1951* (Ithaca, NY: Cornell University Press, 1998).

Yablonka, Hanna, *Survivors of the Holocaust: Israel after the War* (Houndmills: Macmillan Press, 1999).

Zahra, Tara, '"A Human Treasure": Europe's Displaced Children between Nationalism and Internationalism', *Past and Present*, Supplement 6 (2011), 332–350.

—— 'Lost Children: Displacement, Family, and Nation in Postwar Europe', *Journal of Modern History*, 81:1 (2009), 45–86.

—— *The Lost Children: Reconstructing Europe's Families after World War II* (Cambridge, MA: Harvard University Press, 2011).

—— '"Prisoners of the Postwar": Expellees, Displaced Persons, and Jews in Austria after World War II', *Austrian History Yearbook*, 41 (2010), 191–215.

Zelizer, Barbie, *Remembering to Forget: Holocaust Memory through the Camera's Eye* (Chicago, IL: University of Chicago Press, 1998).

Zertal, Idith, *From Catastrophe to Power: Holocaust Survivors and the Emergence of Israel* (Berkeley, CA: University of California Press, 1998).

zur Nieden, Susanne, 'Kriegsende und Befreiung in Sachsenausen', in Günter Morsch (ed.), *Von der Erinnerung zum Monument: Die Entstehungsgeschichte der Nationalen Mahn-und Gedenkstätte Sachsenhausen* (Berlin: Edition Hentrich, 1996), 59–67.

Illustrations

14 Zvi Silberman holds his newborn son in a DP camp in Austria, 1945–49 (United States Holocaust Memorial Museum, courtesy of Yocheved Fryd Flumenker)

15 Clothing produced at an ORT-UNRRA school, probably at Landsberg DP camp, 1946 (United States Holocaust Memorial Museum, courtesy of Samuel B. Zisman)

16 Kibbutz Nocham, Bergen-Belsen DP camp, 1947 (United States Holocaust Memorial Museum, courtesy of Alex Knobler)

17 Jewish New Year greeting card depicting *Exodus 1947* (Yad Vashem)

18 Protest in Belsen against treatment of *Exodus 1947* passengers, 1947 (akg-images)

19 'British Floating Dachau' protest sticker, 1947

20 Detention Camp no. 55, Cyprus, *c.* 1948 (IDEA–ALM)

21 Wedding portrait in a Cyprus internment camp, 1947 (United States Holocaust Memorial Museum, courtesy of Benny Hershkowitz)

The documents pictured in Chapter 5 are courtesy of the International Tracing Service, Bad Arolsen.

Acknowledgements

My first debt is to Heather McCallum at Yale University Press in London, who suggested that I write this book. Heather and her associate editor Rachael Lonsdale read the manuscript carefully and I have benefitted greatly from the encouragement and constructive criticism that they provided.

Martin Kolinsky, whom I have known since childhood, generously gave me some of his late wife Eva's papers. Her book *After the Holocaust* was an inspiration for my own research and I am very grateful to Martin for the material he passed on to me. I would also like to thank Ilana Ben-Sasson for granting me permission to cite from her grandfather Yakow Rabinowicz's unpublished memoir, and Yad Vashem (Jerusalem), the United States Holocaust Memorial Museum (Washington, DC), the International Tracing Service (Bad Arolsen) and the Jewish Historical Society of Greater Washington for permission to reproduce photographs and documents.

Once again, this book could not have been written without the resources of the Wiener Library, London. My heartfelt thanks go to all the staff there and, in particular, to director Ben Barkow, head librarian Kat Hübschmann, archivist Howard Falksohn and, for her assistance with the ITS collections, Christine Schmidt.

Many people discussed this book with me, offered tips and suggestions, or shared their own research. My thanks to: Ruth Balint, Daniel Beer, Paul Betts, Suzanne Brown-Fleming, Marc Buggeln, David Cesarani, Greg Claeys, Alon Confino, Martin Dean, Bob Eaglestone, Geoff Eley, Lara

Feigel, Matthew Feldman, Yoav Galai, Amos Goldberg, Helen Graham, Eliana Hadjisavvas, Ştefania Hirtopanu, Becky Jinks, Rafael Kropiunigg, Tony Kushner, David Kustow, Ferenc Laczó, Christine Lattek, Bernard Levy, Florin Lobonţ, Edward Madigan, Jens Meierhenrich, Dirk Moses, Rudolf Muhs, Jessica Reinisch, Suzanne Rutland, Paul Salmons, Adam Seipp, Paul Shapiro, Simon Sparks, Jonathan Webber, Helen Whatmore, Daniel Wildmann, and my colleagues in the History Department at Royal Holloway. I'm especially grateful to Mark Donnelly, Margarete Myers Feinstein, Simone Gigliotti, Jeremy Hicks, Rowan MacAuslan, Ewa Ochman, Barbara Rosenbaum, Christine Schmidt, Anna Solarska, Nikolaus Wachsmann, and Yale University Press's anonymous readers who read some or all of the text, made many improvements and picked up a number of errors. Any that remain are of course my own.

The biggest thank you is for my wonderful family, Libby, Greta and Clem, and of course Hilary.

Index